J. Ashdown.

The Caterer's Companion

Julian Morel, FHCIMA

Pitman Publishing

First published 1973

SIR ISAAC PITMAN AND SONS LTD
Pitman House, Parker Street, Kingsway, London WC2B 5PB
P.O. Box 46038, Portal Street, Nairobi, Kenya

SIR ISAAC PITMAN (AUST.) PTY LTD
Pitman House, 158 Bouverie Street, Carlton, Victoria 3053,
Australia

PITMAN PUBLISHING CORPORATION
6 East 43rd Street, New York, N.Y. 10017, U.S.A.

SIR ISAAC PITMAN (CANADA) LTD
495 Wellington Street West, Toronto 135, Canada

THE COPP CLARK PUBLISHING COMPANY
517 Wellington Street West, Toronto 135, Canada

ISBN: 0 273 36121 X

Printed in Great Britain by
Western Printing Services Ltd,
Bristol

G. 4599:16

To
Joan, Jackie and Linda

By the same author:

Progressive Catering (Caxton)
Scientific Catering and Hotel Operating (Pitman)
Contemporary Catering (Barrie & Jenkins)
At Your Service (Educational Explorers)

Julian Morel spent seventeen years as Catering Superintendent of the Pullman Car Company and four years as
Catering Manager of the Pullman Division of the British
Transport Hotels. He is currently with the Hotel and Catering Industry Training Board. He has also published many
articles for the hotel and catering press.

Author's Acknowledgements

I wish to record my thanks to A E Simms, FHCIMA, Maitrise Culinaire, FRSH, for reading through the typescript and for his very helpful comments, and to E B Page, MCFA, author of 'The Great Chefs' (Arnold) for certain information supplied.
Last, and by no means least, to my wife, Joan, for typing a major part of the manuscript.

Metrication

All weights and measures are given in Metric and Imperial quantities, though not necessarily in straight conversions. Where required, suitable adjustments are made in order that the specimen recipes may be read in Metric or in Imperial measurements.

Contents

Introduction

This work is intended as a practical reference book for the catering student and an *aide-mémoire* for the chef, the head waiter and the catering executive. It will also be informative to all others interested in food service, in food preparation and cookery and in catering management.

It has been written to meet the need for an up-to-date work of reference, listing dishes both old and new. It includes time-honoured, classified and standard dishes, as well as new and more recent additions to the culinary repertoire. It equally takes count of the many new developments which have occurred in the practice of professional catering. The work has been designed as a dictionary for ready access and easy reference and not as a cookery book. Dishes are described as clearly and succinctly as possible, but if a description would be inadequate or a dish difficult to describe, then an abridged recipe is given.

Most dishes have their individual history. Some are well known and their legend lives on; others have been lost or forgotten with the passing of time. Often, by the sheer process of evolution, the ingredients, accompaniments, or the make-up of a dish are apt to change. It is also a fact that no two chefs really produce any particular dish identically. Each may impart to it his own interpretation or individuality.

Cookery is nothing if not creative. Creativity and innovation, particularly in display work, are encouraged. But standard dishes should not be radically altered out of all recognition. It should always be possible to recognize a dish by the name listed on the menu. If a chef wishes to alter a standard dish or invent a new one, he is perfectly at liberty to do so, providing that he gives it a new name—his own, for example, or that of the hotel or restaurant where he officiates.

Menu terminology should not mislead, for in certain situations this could have legal implications. For this reason a brief description of dishes is often given on the menu.

A great many dishes and culinary terms are of French origin. France is the cradle of gastronomy and French the language of the kitchen. But British fare is well represented in this book, as is American cookery, Italian and other national fare, since, with the growth of tourism and travel, the culinary art has taken on an international character.

The expansion of the hotel and catering industry and the development throughout the world of catering education and training are the most significant factors in recent times. What was once the privilege of a few is now available to a far wider population. More people than ever before are displaying an intelligent interest in, and a greater appreciation of, good food.

Catering is very much a market-orientated industry where price is, or should be, commensurate with value in terms of the quality of the food and the standards of craftmanship, presentation and appointments of service. There is no substitute for quality and, though different standards of catering are needed to meet the different requirements of the various markets (conventional or popular, commercial, industrial and institutional), it is the degree of professionalism by which all standards are measured.

This book will provide invaluable assistance to all whose job entails menu composing. Novelty is a major factor in function catering. In many of the great hotels and famous restaurants, the widest possible menu selection is featured. But the trend in quite large sections of the industry favours shorter menus offering an adequacy of choice. Variety is essential and this is introduced through periodic menu change. Innovation in eating out is epitomized by the speciality restaurants and the theme houses of the extensive licensed trade. Menu composing, however, is increasingly demanding. Fortunately, as this book serves to illustrate, there is ample inspiration and no lack of ideas; for cookery, like most other arts and technologies, is virtually an inexhaustible subject.

Hors-d'œuvre, Starters and Salads

HORS-D'ŒUVRE

The conventional classification of hors-d'œuvre is hot or cold. The cold are again sub-divided as de-luxe and simple.

But with so many variables, hard and fast classifications can be deceptive. Hors-d'œuvre overlap into salads—simple and compound—and the hot variety into savouries and even on to snacks.

Therefore, we list the de-luxe as Starters and the simple under Salads, while a further section is devoted to the hot varieties and related savoury fare.

Speculation varies over the term, said to derive from *hors de l'œuvre*, meaning outside our work. Having paused from our work, set aside our *œuvre* or job for the table, we are now ready to eat. Hence, incidentally, no 'S' in hors-d'œuvre. Thus the apt term of starter. In this context the fare is of a savoury nature to stimulate the appetite in preparation for the heavier dishes to follow.

Hors-d'œuvre also refers to a selection of side dishes offered from a trolley or cart. It also could mean an hors-d'œuvre salad—perhaps a contradiction of terms! The individual components found in the straight hors-d'œuvre are listed under Salads.

STARTERS

Avocado Pear
Exotic, sub-tropical pear-shaped fruit with a shiny green skin. The pulp should be soft and buttery. Unripe it is woody and tasteless.

One avocado cut in half, with the large centre seed removed, goes to the portion. Has a nutty flavour but inclined to be bland, so it is served dressed or combined with other food of a savoury or sweet flavour. Dressings include French, lemon, cream, egg, mayonnaise, sweet, thousand island or tomato. The avocado is presented on lettuce leaves garnished with lemon wedges and tomato quarters to make it look colourful.

Avocado Américaine. Equal amounts of diced avocado and flaked crabmeat, chopped tomato and green pepper, and a sprinkling of chopped chives. Dress in mayonnaise flavoured with tarragon vinegar and a dash of Worcester sauce. Pile in half shells and top with sliced peeled tomatoes, pimento stuffed olives and pickled black olives.

Avocado Cocktail. Avocado combined with honeydew or cantaloup melon balls macerated in lemon juice and ginger sugar. Served in stem glassware topped with a cocktail cherry, red (maraschino), green (crème de menthe), or orange (curaçao).

Avocado Cocktail Maison. Avocado and melon balls macerated in ginger sugar and lemon juice, with shrimps and mandarin segments, dressed with lemon dressing. Served in stem glassware topped with green or orange cocktail cherries.

Avocado Pear and Honeydew Melon Delmonico. Equal amounts of diced avocado, honeydew melon, eating apple and celeriac, dressed with mayonnaise thinned out with cream, touched with lemon juice and checked with salt and cayenne. The filling is piled in the half shells which are then arranged on lettuce leaves and garnished with lemon wedges and tomato quarters.

Avocado Pear with Seafood. Popular presentation: combination of diced avocado mingled with seafood—crabmeat, lobster, shrimps and scampi—dressed and replaced in half shells.

Avocado à la Reine. Equal amounts of diced avocado and white chicken meat dressed in mayonnaise. Pile in half shells and garnish with bouquet of asparagus tips held with strip of red pimento and a truffle blade.

Avocado au Saumon Fumé. Avocado balls rolled in smoked salmon. Three balls to the roll and three rolls to the portion. Dress on lettuce, serve with lemon wedges and pepper mill and brown bread and butter.

Avocado Seafood Cocktail. Equal amounts of diced avocado, lobster, white crabmeat and small peeled shrimps dressed in cocktail sauce and served in half shells.

Avocado Waldorf. Equal amounts of diced avocado, apple, celeriac, cooked new potatoes and peeled shrimps. Sauce with lemon juice, sugar and dash of ground clove and nutmeg. Dress with half-whipped cream and add peeled walnuts. Serve in the half shells.

Avocado West Coast. Equal amounts of diced avocado, grapefruit segments and plumped prunes, with shrimps and pitted red cherries, dressed in lemon dressing with chopped anchovy fillets. Served in half shells with lemon and tomato quarters.

Avocado Woodman Style. Diced avocado mixed with chopped celery, diced pineapple and banana dressed in lemon mayonnaise. Served in half shells with lemon wedges.

Hollywood. Diced avocado, peach, pineapple, celery, red and green pimento in lemon dressing piled in half shells, arranged on lettuce leaves and garnished with tomato and lemon wedges.

Pasadena. Diced avocado mixed with equal amount of flaked crabmeat. Dressed with the following dressing: mayonnaise loaded with chopped tomato, minced green pepper, chopped chives, flavoured with tarragon vinegar, chili and Worcester sauce. Piled into half shells and topped with tomato rondels and stuffed olives.

Bird Eggs
Birds' eggs are served hard-boiled.

Plover's Eggs are olive brown with black blotches. They are placed in cold water, brought to the boil, simmered for 5 minutes and cooled. The eggs are presented dressed in a basket, or a bird's nest, accompanied by celery salt and brown bread and butter.

When plover's eggs are unobtainable or prohibited, others are featured as an alternative.

Gull's Eggs are green in colour with white speckles.

Partridge Eggs are greenish brown and speckled.

Quail's Eggs are small and tasty and need simmering for only 30 seconds and cooled in their cooking water.

Canapés
Small savoury fare for cocktail and sherry parties or hors-d'œuvre consisting of smoked salmon, parma ham, sardines, rollmop, cheese, savoury butters and the like, dressed upon rondels, squares, diamonds or oblongs of buttered toast or fried bread, decorated with piped savoury butter and glazed in aspic.

Caviar (Caviare)
The most coveted and expensive of all delicacies.

It is the female roe of a group of fish of the *Acipenserides* species which frequents the Volga delta and the Caspian Sea. Russia and Persia are the main suppliers. There are five members of the species: the sturgeon, sterlet, sevruga, ocientrova and the beluga, which gives the rarest and finest caviar. The roe is cleared of its membrane, passed through a special sieve to separate and grade the grain, salted, packed in tins and refrigerated.

Quality is told by colour and grain size, ranging in order of quality from large grey to small black grains.

Caviar is kept refrigerated, spooned out in small quantities and escorted with lemon and hot toast. Other garniture consists of sieved, separated, hard-cooked egg white and yolk and minced onion.

There are several imitation caviars on the market and a red coloured type, keta, made from salmon roe. Also produced in Russia is chibis, a synthetic protein caviar.

Caviare au Blinis. Served sandwiched between two small thick pancakes. Sour cream and beet juice are passed separately.
To make blinis: Make equal amounts of wheat and buckwheat flour and a pinch of salt into a batter, the consistency of cream, with milk Whip in one egg per 250g (8 oz) of flour and stand for an hour. Make pancakes in lightly oiled blinis pans 6mm deep by 6cm diameter ($\frac{1}{4}$ in by $2\frac{1}{2}$ in).

Foie Gras
Famous culinary delicacy from Alsace. Rich goose liver pâté encrusted with truffle and cooked with spices and wine. Available in several

3

forms: large croûte, foie gras encased in pastry; terrines; pots and canned medaillons; tunnel shaped parfait; roulade; timbale; the bloc and the individual portion. There are also mousses and spreading pâtés. All are variations in shape and pack of truffled foie gras. Also available au naturel without truffles.

Served in small portions accompanied by thick slices of hot toast.

Fruit Juices

Fruit juices as starters made their appearance on the culinary scene in the early 1930s. The fore-runner was tomato. Orange, grapefruit and pineapple followed. The full range now includes apricot, apple, carrot, clam, grape, guava, papaya, peach, pear, prune, sauerkraut, various vegetable juices and others. Fruit juice cocktails and cups are devised by mixing juices together in divers combinations.

Most juices are marketed bottled or canned; some are sold frozen and in instant form.

Fruit juices should always be served well chilled.

Tomato Juice. Served plain with Worcester sauce, offer celery salt separately.

Tomato Juice Cocktail. Tomato juice shaken with a dash of Worcester sauce and a pinch of celery salt.

Grapefruit (Pamplemousse)

Served in and out of its skin, in the half or suprême, and in segments as a cocktail.

For the suprême the fruit is halved, the segments detached and the centre pith removed with the point of a sharp knife. To serve, the suprême is topped with a maraschino cocktail cherry. Flavour may be enhanced with kirsch or maraschino.

For the cocktail, the grapefruit is peeled and the fruit sliced out in segments. They are dressed well juiced in a stem glass topped with a cherry. Added colour is given with a small sprig of fresh mint.

Grapefruit cans well and canned segments have a good flavour.

California Grapefruit Cocktail. Mix and macerate the grapefruit segments and several plumped California prunes in their juices. Serve in stem glassware topped with maraschino cherries.

Grapefruit and Mandarin Caprice. Mix and macerate equal amounts of grapefruit and orange segments and pitted red cherries with their juices and sauce with curaçao. Serve in stem glassware.

Grapefruit and Orange Cocktail Cerisette. Equal quantities of grapefruit and orange segments well juiced and served with a few pitted red cherries.

Grilled Grapefruit. Prepare half a grapefruit as for suprême, sprinkle with demerara sugar and flash under a grill to caramelize the topping. Dress with a cherry and serve hot.

4

Minted Grapefruit Petals. Allow a few sprigs of fresh green mint to macerate with grapefruit segments and sweeten suitably with sugar. Serve in glasses with mint leaves and a crème de menthe cocktail cherry.

Melon

Various types of melon appear with the seasons, thereby ensuring an almost year-round continuity of supply.

There are two main types, the cantaloup and the honeydew. Cantaloups are recognized by their rough and ridged light yellow to greenish skin and their soft, fragrant and mellow pulp. Honeydews have a firm, shiny and wrinkled skin, bright green or yellow, with a sweet and refreshing pulp.

Other types include the tiger melon of the cantaloup family which is smaller, the famous charantais with its delicious perfumed flavour, and the large water melon with a green skin and pink and white watery pulp.

To serve, the larger melons are cut into ample portions and the seeds removed. The seeds of the water melon, embedded in the pulp, are cut away with the tip of a sharp knife. A slice is taken from the curved base to enable the piece to stand on a plate. The fruit should be ice cold, eaten with a spoon and fork with sugar and ground ginger offered separately. Smaller fruits are cut through the middle as two portion melons, while the charantais is the individual portion. In this case the top is sliced off to serve as a lid and the seeds removed with a spoon.

Honeydew melon may be garnished with glacé cherries and sometimes lemon is passed separately. The practice of pre-cutting the melon pulp into bite-size portions is not recommended.

It has become fashionable to offer ginger sugar with melon. This consists of a mixture of ground ginger and castor sugar.

Delmonico. Use a two portion fruit. Halve, seed, remove pulp, dice and combine with diced eating apple and celeriac. Dress in a mayonnaise enriched with half-whipped cream. Check seasoning, pile in the half shells and top with a maraschino cocktail cherry.

Exotique (Cocktail). Avocado pear and melon scooped into balls, prawns, diced apple, pear and pineapple, dressed in mayonnaise spiced with a little curry powder and touched with brandy. Topped with glacé cherry.

Honeydew and Avocado Caprice. Similar presentation to the en surprise. Mix melon with an equal quantity of avocado pear balls cut to even size. Add a few candied red cocktail cherries and macerate in suger, lemon juice and pernod. Serve in the half melon shells.

Melon Ball Cocktail. Scoop the pulp into balls with a parisienne cutter, working over a bowl to catch the juices. Sprinkle with sugar

5

and a dash of ground ginger and allow to macerate under cold. Serve in stem glassware topped with a glacé cherry.

This method is applicable to all melons; cantaloup and honeydew melons can be combined in this way.

Melon Cocktail Suprême. Equal amounts of honeydew and cantaloup melon and avocado pear balls cut to equal size, macerated in ginger sugar, lemon juice and maraschino. Dressed in stem glassware with green, red or orange cocktail cherries.

Melon Cocktail en Surprise. Cut round a medium-sized honeydew in a zig-zag pattern and separate the two halves. Scoop out the pulp into balls and macerate with ginger sugar. Replace the fruit in the half shells, top with a cocktail cherry and a sprig of mint.

Menthe (Honeydew à la). Cut into portions, separate the melon into segments, arrange a fresh mint leaf between each. Garnish with one or two crème de menthe cocktail cherries and serve with ginger sugar.

Notre Façon (Melon Cup Cocktail). Cantaloup, honeydew and water melon and avocado pear scooped into even-sized balls. Dressed with olive oil, lemon juice, sugar and a touch of paprika, and left to macerate under cold. Served in stem glassware, topped with a curaçao cherry and lemon wedges.

Mousse

A light and delicate pâté type preparation made from foie gras, chicken, duck, turkey, ham, salmon or other main ingredient. Served in small portions as for any pâté or with other fare.

Cornets of York Ham Mogador. Cornets of thinly cut lean ham filled with ham mousse mixed with a purée of plumped prunes and touched with grated horse-radish. Masked and piped with sherry-flavoured aspic.

Ham Mousse. Chop lean ham, rub through a sieve and combine purée with half-whipped cream. Season with cayenne, lemon juice and dry sherry. Check colour with carmine. Strengthen with gelatine and whip well. Pour into glass dish to set. Decorate and top with thin layer of aspic.

Mousse de Foie Gras. Press foie gras through a wire sieve and combine purée with half-whipped cream into a light mousse. Season with salt, cayenne, lemon juice and dry sherry or brandy. Add very small quantity of gelatine melted in hot consommé and whisk to blend. Pour into glass dish or mould to set. Decorate as desired and top with a layer of aspic.

Chicken and turkey mousses are prepared in a similar manner, so is duckling but the preparation is coloured with carmine as required.

Salmon Mousse. As for ham, but flavour with dry sherry or white wine, and pink with carmine.

Orange Suprême Cerisette

Select large and juicy oranges and prepare and serve as for grapefruit suprême. Sweeten to taste with honey. Serve topped with maraschino cherry. May also be flavoured and sweetened with curaçao, grand marnier or cointreau.

Oysters (Huîtres)

Oysters are considered in season when there is an R in the month. The fisheries are sited in the estuaries of rivers. The best natives are those from Colchester, Whitstable and Helford. They are also imported from France, Holland, Portugal and Norway. Oysters are graded by size, i.e. royals, banquets, buttons.

To serve, the oysters are carefully opened with the aid of an oyster knife, detached and dressed in the deep shell. Lemon and brown bread and butter are the accompaniments. Sometimes the pepper mill, spiced vinegar and tabasco are also offered. Oysters in restaurants sell in units of six. They should be handled with care, complete freshness is essential, they should come from a reputable source and should be alive (the shells will be tightly closed).

Huîtres au Caviare. Open the required number of oysters and set on a dish upon cracked ice. Place a small serving of iced caviar into each shell. Serve with lemon and brown bread and butter.

Papaya

Papaya or pawpaw is a large sub-tropical fruit resembling a melon. Fresh and ripe, it is handled and eaten as for melon. Is also available in canned dices when it is presented as a cocktail, topped with a cherry and served with lemon wedges.

Pâté Maison

Pâté or Terrine Maison is the name given to various kitchen-prepared rich liver pâtés. It is served spooned out or cut into thick slices, dressed upon lettuce, garnished with aspic squares, tomato and lemon wedges. Hot toast is always offered separately.

There is no standard recipe for Pâté Maison since many variations exist; the following is representative procedure.

Trim and cube calves or pigs liver and combine with raw veal or chicken, a little bacon fat and baked whole onion. Pass through a coarse and then a fine mincer. Season with salt, pepper and mixed herbs. Press into a terrine, cover, place a weight on top and cook bain-marie style in an oven for 2 hours. When cooked and cooled the pâté should be firm. Seal with layer of clarified butter or lard.

Other pâté ingredients include foie gras, the liver of poultry and game, but the bulk is usually made up with other liver, such as calves and pigs, and with bacon fat. Richer pâtés are lined with cubed lean ham, chicken, tongue and whole truffle and are also flavoured with brandy.

7

Pâté de foie truffle, terrine du chef liver pâté, truffled chicken liver, and pork liver, together with hare and other game pâtés, are all variations upon the pâté theme. It is now the custom to serve Cumberland sauce to accompany game pâtés.

Commercial Pâtés. Term denoting 'bought in' pâtés sold in terrines, foil wrapped slabs or blocks and also in canned form.

A wide range of pâtés are now made on premises, or 'bought in', including smoked haddock, smoked salmon, crab, smoked trout, smoked mackerel, smoked cod's roe and varieties of wild game.

Polish Hors-d'œuvre (Hors-d'œuvre Polonaise)

Type of open sandwich, smaller than the Scandinavian type, featured as an hors-d'œuvre. Slices of buttered brown, granary bread or pumpernickle on which various ingredients are arranged and decorated. They are presented in variety on a large tray.

Ingredients include: anchovy fillets; breast of chicken, duck or game dusted with cayenne or paprika; roast beef with grated horseradish; composite savoury butters; cheeses; caviar, ham; pastes and pâtés; sardines; tongue; foie gras; smoked fare and scrambled egg.

Decorations include: capers; gherkins; sieved or shredded egg; truffle; coloured butters and various juliennes.

Each piece is seasoned or accompanied as required and dusted with chopped parsley.

Potted Game

Traditional preparation applicable to all game. Prepared from cooked meat minced and pounded into a smooth paste with a pestle and mortar or rubbed through a wire sieve. To the paste is added a third of its weight of butter. The preparation is seasoned with salt, cayenne and ground mace, mixed well, pressed into pots and covered with a thick layer of clarified bacon fat or pure lard.

Potted Shrimps

Usually purchased ready made and served with lemon, pepper mill and hot toast. To prepare, season peeled shimps with salt, cayenne, a touch of ground clove, nutmeg and mace. Toss in hot butter, pack into a pot, cover with clarified butter and allow to set.

Seafood Cocktails

All these cocktails are prepared in a similar manner and presented in stem glassware, scollop shell or a special glass which fits into a metal (EPNS or stainless steel) container for shaved ice. Line the cocktail receptacle with salt-dusted shredded lettuce. Arrange the seafood on the lettuce and mask with the cocktail sauce. Sprinkle with chopped parsley and garnish as required with lemon and tomato.

The best known seafood cocktails are prawn, scampi, lobster, crab and oyster. A standard seafood cocktail would indicate a mixture of assorted seafoods. The term 'prawn cocktail' is loosely applied to large shimps termed prawns.

Lido Prawn Cocktail. As for standard prawn cocktail with minced celery and anchovy fillets incorporated in the masking sauce. Topped with a red pimento stuffed Spanish olive and anchovy fillet coil.

Lobster Cocktail Florida. Diced lobster with grapefruit and orange segments and pineapple. Dressed on shredded lettuce. Masked with mayonnaise pinked with tomato ketchup, creamed and touched with tabasco.

Prawn Cocktail Madras. As for a standard prawn cocktail, but masked with a sauce lightly coloured and flavoured with curry powder and topped with a piece of mango chutney.

Shrimp and Grapefruit Cocktail. Grapefruit segments and peeled shrimps dressed with lemon dressing, arranged in a cocktail glass and topped with a glacé cherry.

Smoked Fare

Cornucopia of Smoked Salmon. Cut required slices of york ham in squares and cover with smoked salmon. Arrange portion of potted shrimps on each square and roll up in cornets. Secure with cocktail stick. Serve with lemon and brown bread and butter.

Smoked Buckling. Norwegian speciality served as for smoked trout.

Smoked Cod's Roe. Purchased ready prepared. Served with brown bread and butter or toast and lemon wedges.

Smoked Eel (Anguille Fumé). Served thinly cut in fillets with horse-radish sauce, lemon and brown bread and butter.

Smoked Ham. The best known is the Italian Parma (Jambon de Parme), the French equivalent is Jambon de Bayonne and the German Westphalian. There are other varieties but the most usual is parma ham. Smoked ham is sliced wafer thin and served with lemon, pepper mill and brown bread and butter.

Jambon de Parme is the subject of several speciality features and is served with fresh figs, fresh pineapple, or melon, usually honeydew. (The melon is rinded.)

Smoked Salmon (Saumon Fumé). Famous British Fare delicacy, purchased by the side. For plate service the salmon, cleared of its outer surface and of all bones, is sliced wafer thin and offered with lemon, pepper mill and brown bread and butter.

May accompany other fare, i.e. potted shimps and melon, and be used as a wrapping for dressed crab or ham mousse.

Smoked Trout (Truite Fumé). Served whole and skinned with horse-radish sauce, lemon and brown bread and butter.

Other Smoked Fish. Other smokings include sturgeon and swordfish. Presented as for smoked salmon. May also be dressed with tomato, lemon and cucumber slices.

9

Zakouski

The zakouski, a Russian hors-d'œuvre, is an elaborate affair ranging from small dishes to such delicacies as smoked salmon and caviar. The service à la Russe consists of arranging the dishes on a side table for the guests to serve themselves. The service is accompanied by neat vodka served iced in small glasses.

The side table of hors-d'œuvre, a derivative of the zakouski, is practised in Scandinavian countries where a range of smoked fish and salads is displayed, accompanied by schnapps in the form of aquavitae.

SALADS

Salads are graded as *simple*—one main component—and *compound* —made up with several ingredients.

Under simple salads are included simple hors-d'œuvre. Speciality salads and mayonnaises are listed under the compound salad heading.

Simple Salads and Hors-d'œuvre

The term simple salad in this context indicates one main salad ingredient suitably prepared and presented cold. Others listed are component preparations for hors-d'œuvre.

Anchovy.   Best known is the fillet, flat or rolled, olive oil canned.

Asparagus Tips.   Canned, fresh or frozen. Arranged in bouquets. Vinaigrette dressed.

Baked Beans.   Canned beans in sauce, usually tomato, but also curry or a brown sauce. Sprinkled with chopped parsley.

Bean Shoots.   Chinese canned bean shoots. Attractive addition to the hors-d'oeuvre trolleys.

Beetroot.   Whole or sliced, small or large, cooked beets, well drained and vinaigrette dressed.

Butter Beans.   Previously soaked, cooked in stock or water with onion, carrot and seasoning. Drained, dressed, finished with chopped parsley.

Celeriac.   Julienne-cut celeriac with cream and seasoning.

Celery.   Whole hearts, fresh cooked or canned. Drained and vinaigrette and chopped parsley dressed.

Cole-Slaw.   Finely shred crisp white heart of raw cabbage, wash well and drain. Add shredded raw carrot and beetroot, few plumped currants or raisins, French dressing with touch of mustard powder and ground clove as required. Serve well mixed and chilled. May also be dressed in creamed mayonnaise. *Pine-Slaw* is cole-slaw with shredded pineapple dressed in creamed mayonnaise and lemon juice.

Cucumber.   Sliced, peeled or unpeeled, or cut in crescents with seeds removed. Vinaigrette and chopped parsley dressing.

Delicatessen. All pork charcuterie slicing sausages: salami, mortadella and liver sausage most popular features.

Egg Mayonnaise. Sliced, halved or quartered hard-boiled eggs, masked with mayonnaise and sprinkled with cayenne or chopped parsley.

Fonds d'Artichauts. Canned and ready prepared. Whole or quartered in vinaigrette or tomato sauce.

French Beans. Left whole and dressed. All vegetables may be featured cold and suitably dressed, including peas and the various green and white beans.

Fruit. Lemon-dressed orange segments, or fruit salad with orange, grapefruit, apple, pear, grapes and dried fruits. Citrus fruits are most acceptable in salads and for hors-d'œuvre. Many fruits are also savoury-dressed for the hors-d'œuvre selection.

Herring. Appears as an hors-d'œuvre in many guises, best known being the Bismark or soused herring which is pickled in vinegar. Herring fillets are also smoked; 'saur' in olive oil; à la Russe in sour cream and chives; in white or red wine and dressed with spices. A whole range of canned herring from Norway makes for much variety on the cold table. Another member is the Gaffelbitar, dressed with spice and wine.

Lettuce. Represents greenery indispensable to most if not all salads. There is the savoy lettuce, cos or romaine, curley, frissé or chicory and escarolle. Other greenery is supplied by lamb's lettuce or mâche, watercress and mustard and cress.

Mushrooms. Sliced in sauce, whole in dressing or pickled. Thin sliced raw mushrooms are used in salads.

Olives. Two basic types: the large Spanish and the small French. There are also black pickled olives. Olives are stuffed with red pimento, capers, anchovy and crabmeat.

Pasta. Dressed and baked in one of the sauces associated with pasta i.e. bolonaise, napolitaine, as well as curry and brown savoury sauces. Spaghetti, noodles and other shapes have many possibilities as hors-d'oeuvre.

Peppers. Red and green, seeded, shredded and vinaigrette dressed, they add colour as well as flavour.

Pickles. All varieties may be used in hors-d'œuvre—mixed, vinegar, mustard or sweet; pickled button mushrooms, onions, cherries, gherkins, agourcis, walnuts, olives and various kinds of chutney.

Potato. Best made with new potatoes. Boiled in jackets, peeled, cut in rondels, mayonnaise dressed and sprinkled with chopped parsley.

Radishes and Spring Onions. Indispensable with salads, hors-d'œuvre and with the cheese tray.

11

Rice. Boiled and risotto of rice, dressed with oil, vinegar, seasoned and garnished with diced pimento, sliced mushrooms, peas, plumped raisins or currants. Curried fried rice in various sauces is acceptable for hors-d'œuvre and salads.

Sardines. No hors-d'œuvre is complete without sardines canned in olive oil. They improve with keeping, therefore there are vintage sardines. Store with care and turn cans periodically so oil moves evenly through the contents. Also canned with truffles, or in tomato and ravigote sauces. Smoked sardines are also available.

Seafood. Peeled whole shrimps au naturel are the most popular; cooked mussels dressed in vinaigrette or mayonnaise; oysters smoked in oil; smoked octopus; whelks; winkles; clams and other shellfish.

Sweetcorn. Cooked whole kernels cream dressed, or canned creamed corn, drained, cream dressed and paprika dusted.

Tomato. Cored, blanched, skinned, sliced or quartered, dressed in vinaigrette and dusted with chopped parsley.

Tunny Fish. The French thon canned in olive oil.

Vegetable Macédoine. Mixed vegetable salad. Best results from fresh ingredients. Cooked diced carrot, turnip, French beans, sweetcorn kernels, peas and small broad beans. Mayonnaise dressed.

Compound Salads

Alexis. Julienne of celery, chopped nuts, French dressed and arranged on cos lettuce.

Alice. Diced pineapple, grapefruit segments, chopped nuts, lemon dressed and served on lettuce.

Alsacienne. Rondels of potato, sliced truffle, chopped nuts and beetroot. Mayonnaise dressing.

Astoria. Grapefruit and orange segments, sliced pear and red and green peppers served on cos lettuce with French dressing.

Beaucaire. Julienne of celeriac, celery, endive, chicken and mushroom. Dressed in mayonnaise and chopped fines herbes.

Bon Ton. Shredded lettuce, sliced red pimento and tomato, asparagus tips with French dressing.

California. Diced pineapple, orange segments, cooked cauliflower sprigs, French and lima beans and pitted cherries on quartered lettuce with French dressing.

Caprice. Lettuce and fonds d'artichauts, julienne of ham, chicken, tongue and truffle. French dressing.

Chiffonade. Shredded lettuce, thick julienne of beetroot, cubed hard-boiled eggs and tomato. Served with chopped parsley and French dressing.

Chrysanthemum. Peeled shrimps and diced potatoes, bound with mayonnaise flavoured with soy sauce. Sprinkled generously with chrysanthemum petals, which have been blanched in boiling water, cooled in ice water, drained and lemon dressed. Salad garnished with strips of red pimento, diced tomato and chopped chervil.

Congress. Celery hearts, grapefruit and orange segments, pitted grapes and cherries. Mayonnaise dressing.

Coronado. Sliced pear, orange segments, pitted black cherries and cos lettuce. Cream dressing.

County Club. Cos lettuce, sliced tomato and asparagus tips. Thousand island dressing.

Delmonico. Diced celeriac and eating apple in a cream dressing served on lettuce.

Demi-Deuil (half mourning). Arrange rondels of cooked new potato and truffle alternately in a salad bowl. Dust with chopped parsley. Dress with mustard and cream dressing.

Diatz. Layer of cos lettuce, sliced tomato, lettuce, rondels of green and red peppers and onion, julienne of beetroot. French dressing.

Diplomate. Julienne of pineapple, celery, apple and cherries. Cream mayonnaise dressing.

Doctor's Salad. Cottage cheese with chives on lettuce, decorated with watercress and tomato.

Don Juan. Lettuce, fonds d'artichauts à la grecque, pimento and asparagus tips. French dressing.

Everglades. Grapefruit segments, sliced beetroot, red and green peppers served on lettuce with French dressing.

Fantasia. Diced pineapple, apple, tomato and celery. Minted French dressing.

Florida. Grapefruit segments, pineapple, julienne of celery, banana rondels and diced apple. Mayonnaise dressing.

French. Lettuce, beetroot, egg and tomato. French dressing with fines herbes.

Garde Manger. Lettuce, sliced tomato, asparagus tips, hard-boiled egg and green peppers. French dressing.

Garden. Cos and escarolle, sliced tomato, cucumber, radishes and watercress. Thousand island dressing.

Garibaldi. Orange rondels, julienne of celery, pitted grapes, shelled nuts and lettuce. Mayonnaise dressing.

Hollywood. Sliced peaches and avocado, red and green peppers and lettuce. French dressing.

Hors-d'œuvre Salad. Composite salad of sardine, egg mayonnaise; tomato, potato and Russian salad; celery in cream dressing; salami, gherkin, olive; all dressed on lettuce.

13

Imperial. Diced cooked new potatoes and fonds d'artichauts with a julienne of cooked celeriac and truffle. Dress with French dressing with a touch of English mustard and arrange on lettuce.

Isabella. Sliced cucumber, radishes, julienne of celery, green and red peppers and lettuce. Thousand island dressing.

Italian. Name given to Russian salad in Scandinavia. A mixed vegetable salad or macédoine of vegetables, rather than the elaborate orthodox Russian salad.

Japonnaise. Banana rondels, sliced tomato and orange segments on lettuce. Masked with a well chilled sauce made up with equal amounts of cream and tomato ketchup, lemon juice, salt, cayenne, a little sugar and a touch of freshly grated horse-radish.

Jockey Club. Julienne of truffle and asparagus tips. French dressing with mayonnaise, mustard seasoned.

Ladies Delight. Grapefruit and orange segments, pineapple, cream cheese, maraschino and crème de menthe cherries.

Lorette. Salad of mâche (corn or lamb's lettuce) with julienne of celery and beetroot. Chopped parsley and lemon dressing.

Magnolia. Grapefruit segments, green figs and cottage cheese. Cream dressing.

Maison d'Or. Sliced orange and tomato, grapefruit segments, shredded red and green pepers, walnuts, hearts of lettuce. Thousand island dressing.

Mascotte. Quartered fonds d'artichauts, rondels cooked new potato and sliced truffle. Arrange in a salad bowl, add chopped fines herbes and French dressing.

Merry Widow. Lettuce, avocado, red and green peppers and tomato. French dressing.

Miami. Mandarin and grapefruit segments, sliced tomato and lettuce. French dressing.

Mimosa. Plain lettuce or a salad of beetroot, tomato, egg and lettuce. Well sprinkled with sieved egg yolk. Lemon dressing.

My Fancy. Sliced orange and green pepper. Lettuce. Mayonnaise dressing.

Niçoise. Lettuce foundation, tomato rondels, shredded cucumber and sliced egg. Mustard dressing.

Olivier. Sliced cooked new potato, cucumber, pitted olives, sliced gherkin and truffle arranged in a salad bowl. Mayonnaise dressed at table.

Orange. Orange segments sprinkled with kirsch and arranged on lettuce. Salad may consist of just orange segments touched with lemon juice.

Panaché. Culinary term for a mixed salad. Made with two or more salad components and dressed as required.

Rachel. Quartered fonds d'artichauts, asparagus tips, julienne of cooked new potatoes, truffle and celery. Arrange in bowl, sprinkle well chopped parsley, dress with equal parts of mayonnaise and vinaigrette.

Russian Salad. A massive compound salad of which there are several variations. A simple one is diced vegetable salad: cooked carrot, turnip, potato, French beans, peas and sweetcorn dressed in mayonnaise.

This is the original method of preparation of a true Russian salad:

1. Julienne of anchovy fillet, white of chicken, ham, pickled cucumber or large gherkins, lobster meat, mushroom, white of egg and truffle.

2. Dried cooked carrot, turnip, potato and French beans.

3. Cooked peas, capers and pitted olives.

Arrange the three sets of ingredients on lettuce leaves in a glass bowl. Top with a portion of caviar. Dress with mayonnaise at table.

Sarah Bernhardt. Sliced fonds d'artichauts, asparagus tips, chopped egg, shredded lettuce. Mayonnaise dressing.

Savoy. Cos lettuce quarters, red pimento strips, orange and grapefruit segments. Chopped parsley. Dress as required.

Truffle. Wafer thin raw truffle arranged in glass dish. Dust with chopped parsley. Lemon dressing.

Victoria. Asparagus tips, sliced fonds d'artichauts, tomato, chopped egg and shredded lettuce. Lemon dressing.

Waldorf. There are two versions of this classic salad:

1. Select large eating apple, slice off top in a lid, remove pulp and dice. Mix with equal amount diced celeriac and add roughly chopped skinned walnuts. Bind in cream dressing. Fill apple shell and replace lid. Set filled apple on lettuce. Garnish with lemon and tomato wedges.

2. Same as method one, but instead of filling apple shell, arrange on lettuce leaves.

Winter. Sliced salsify; potato, carrot and beet rondels; diced anchovy fillets; sliced gherkins; few capers; dressed in mayonnaise vinaigrette. Sprinkled with chopped parsley and sieved egg.

Woodman's. Variation on the waldorf: fill scooped-out apple with diced apple, celery, pineapple and banana. Cream mayonnaise dressing.

Yam Yam. Whole French beans, sliced seeded cucumber, julienne of celery and quartered lettuce. French dressing.

Note: In compiling this list of salads, the author acknowledges a number of preparations to the La Salle Hotel, Chicago, Illinois, U.S.A.

Mayonnaise and Speciality Salads

Most mayonnaise dishes are prepared identically. There is also a similarity between the preparation and presentation of speciality salads.

American Chicken Salad. Equal quantities diced chicken, new potato, egg and tomato arranged on shredded lettuce and masked with cream dressing. Decorated with pineapple wedges, orange and grapefruit segments and banana rondels.

Dressing is prepared with equal amounts of olive oil and whipped cream, lemon juice, salt and touch of vinegar.

Chicken Mayonnaise—Chicken Salad. Chicken version of salmon mayonnaise; prepared identically.

Chicken Salad California. Arrange sliced chicken meat on lettuce. Whip required amount of cream, beat in small amount of olive oil, flavour with lemon juice, sugar, dash of ground clove and little salt and mask the chicken. Decorate with orange and grapefruit segments, sliced peaches and banana rondels sauced with lemon juice. Sprinkle with julienne of ham.

Crab Mayonnaise—Crab Salad. As for lobster mayonnaise. Ensure flaked crabmeat is well cleared of bone and fibre splinters.

Dressed Crab. Remove the dead man's fingers from a large cooked crab. Strip out all the meat from the body and claws and place in a bowl. Season with salt and cayenne and dress with mayonnaise and a dash of Worcester sauce. Mix well. Pile in the crab shell, smooth over and decorate with chopped parsley, sieved egg and chopped lobster coral in a fancy pattern. Decoration may also include rondels of tomato, cucumber and egg.

Hawaiian Chicken Salad. Equal quantities of cubed chicken and pineapple. Combine with cooked peas, diced carrot and turnip. Dress in cream dressing and pile on shredded lettuce. Decorate with sliced peaches, banana rondels and shredded sweetened coconut.

Lobster Mayonnaise. Similar preparation as for salmon. Arrange sliced lobster meat around a bed of lettuce and top with the sliced claw meat. Garnish includes crabmeat-stuffed olives. If red coral is found in the lobster, chop and mix with the chopped parsley for the final top sprinkling.

Lobster Salad. As above, but without the mayonnaise masking. Dress with vinaigrette.

Mayonnaise of Chicken Parisienne. Cubed chicken meat, fonds d'artichauts, new potato, tomato and cooked peas. Mix and pile on shredded lettuce. Mask with a preparation of mayonnaise mounted with half-whipped cream. Decorate with rondels of new potato, egg, tomato, asparagus tips and pitted olives. Dust with chopped fines herbes.

Mayonnaise of Chicken Savoy. Equal quantities of diced chicken, new potato, tomato and egg. Bind with guérèbich dressing. Pile on lettuce and top with bouquet of asparagus tips.

16

Mayonnaise of Lobster Savoy. Proceed as above, replacing chicken with diced lobster meat.

Salade de Boeuf Mère Marie. Combine diced lean boiled beef with new potatoes, tomato, and julienne of celery. Dress with French dressing to which is added a well beaten egg, chopped parsley and a very little minced raw onion. Arrange on bed of lettuce.

(Featured by M. Virlogeux when at the Savoy Grill, London.)

Salade de Scampi du Lido. Poach scampi in court bouillon, cool and slice in long collops. Prepare a julienne of raw celery and bind with lemon juice. Line salad bowl with lettuce, add celery and scampi and garnish with concassed tomato and anchovy fillets. Sprinkle with chopped parsley. Dress with vinaigrette loaded with chopped anchovy fillet and fines herbes.

(Created by M. Virlogeux when chef des cuisines, Savoy Grill, London.)

Salade de Volaille à la Russe. Prepare a Russian salad by combining equal quantities of cooked diced carrot, turnip, French beans, peas and sweetcorn. Pile on lettuce leaves. Arrange sliced chicken around the preparation. Surround with a composite julienne of chicken, gherkin (dill pickled cucumber), anchovy fillets, ham, tongue, mushroom, white of egg and truffle. Top with a serviing of caviar. At the table, dress with half mayonnaise and vinaigrette.

Salmon Mayonnaise. The salmon for cold dishes is poached and cooled in a court bouillon. The fish is cleared of all skin and bone and arranged on shredded lettuce, masked with mayonnaise, decorated with julienne of anchovy fillet and dotted with capers to complete a criss-cross pattern. Border garnished with rondels of egg, tomato and cucumber in an overlapping sequence, gherkin fans and stuffed olives and dusted with chopped parsley. Variations are introduced with sauce verte and pink mayonnaise.

Salmon Salad. As above, but without the mayonnaise masking. Dress with vinaigrette at table.

Turbot Mayonnaise—Turbot Salad. As for salmon.

Savoury Jelly

Meat and vegetable extracts i.e. Bovril, Marmite and brown colouring, are used in place of sugar and other sweet agents for savoury jellies. They are garnished with strips of or diced cooked vegetables and julienne of poultry, game and meat.

Aspic is made by adding clear stock or consommé to gelatine. Gelatine may be used to give body to consommé, especially the jellied types, thick soups, sauces and made up fare i.e. hamburgers, cromeskis, rissoles and so on.

Taramasalata
Creamed pâté of smoked cod's roe, onion, garlic, olive oil and cream, served with hot toast.

Tartare Steak
Chop required amount of lean raw fillet of beef and add small quantity of minced onion, white of egg, capers and bone marrow. Shape preparation as a round steak, make indentation on top and set into it a raw egg yolk. Dress on a doily and garnish with rondels of raw onion, sieved white of egg, anchovy fillets, pitted olives, caper, pickled cucumber or gherkin and chopped parsley. At the table the ingredients are chopped on a plate with a knife and fork and blended into the raw meat preparation. Mix well, season with salt, pepper and dash Worcester sauce, reshape and serve.

The whole preparation may, to facilitate service, be performed in the kitchen when all the raw ingredients are passed through a fine mincer. The preparation is seasoned, bound with raw egg yolk and shaped for serving.

Hot Hors-d'œuvre, Savouries and Snacks

The hot equivalent to the cold side dishes and starters is a cold weather feature of the great hotels and restaurants of the world. In a culinary classification the savoury is associated with hot hors-d'œuvre. The modern snack is similar and a derivative outcome of this particular hot fare.

HOT HORS-D'ŒUVRE

The fare employed consists of croquettes and beignets; chicken livers; roes; chipolatas; olives; rice; tomato and pasta in various sauced preparations. A large number of the preparations listed were created by M. Virlogeux who, when at the Savoy Grill, made a speciality feature of Hors-d'œuvre Chaud.

Chicken Livers and Hearts

Liver and heart of chicken picked over and trimmed, seasoned, sauté en beurre and sauced as indicated.

Pilaff aux Foies de Volaille (livers) **Pilaff aux Coeurs de Volaille** (hearts). Sauté of livers or hearts on bed of risotto of rice dressed with madeira sauce and sprinkled with chopped parsley.

Pilaff aux Foies de Volaille Hindu or **Pilaff aux Coeurs de Volaille à l'Indienne.** As above, but the livers or hearts are masked with a curry sauce.

Foies de Volaille à l'Espagnole. Chicken livers braised in concassed tomato, well seasoned and sprinkled with chopped parsley.

Note: All the chicken offal preparations are 'mini' features of larger dishes. Other preparations in this range may feature cocks combs and kidneys.

Foies de Volaille Braisés au Madère. Livers braised in madeira sauce and sprinkled with chopped parsley.

Chipolata Sausages

The long sausages are divided into three baby-sized chipolatas, blanched, sauté in butter and combined with a sauce.

Boudins de Paris en Frito. Pané and deep fried chipolatas. Either whole or baby sized sausages.

Chipolatas Braisés au Madère. With madeira sauce.

Chipolatas Charcutière. With tomato sauce and sliced gherkins—a charcutière sauce.

Chipolatas Diablé. With sauce diable.

Chipolatas à l'Espagnole. Similar to portugaise in tomato sauce.

Chipolatas Indienne. With curry sauce.

Chipolatas aux Petits Oignons. With button onions in madeira sauce.

Chipolatas Piquante. With piquante sauce.

Chipolatas Portugaise. With tomato sauce.

Chipolatas Sautés Chasseur. With chasseur sauce.

Pétits Saucisses au Chablis. With suprême sauce flavoured with dry white wine.

Croquettes and Beignets

Small deep fried goods. Croquettes are ball shaped, beignets are oblong. The main ingredient—meat, fish or cheese—is bound either with reduced fish or veal velouté or, in the case of cheese, it is usual to incorporate choux paste. Alternatively, mashed potato can be used as a binding agent for meat and fish.

If the principal ingredient is cooked meat or poultry, it is usually diced small or passed through a coarse plate of the mincer. Cheese is diced or grated. The preparation is shaped and either passed through beaten egg and white breadcrumbs or a frying batter, deep fried and dressed with bouquets of fried parsley.

Beignets de Fromage. Grated parmesan and gruyère combined with potato or choux paste.

Beignets de Fromage Bercy. Cheese beignets, pané with almond splinters mixed with breadcrumbs.

Beignets de Parmesan aux Piments. Grated parmesan and cooked diced red pimento combined in mashed potato or choux paste.

Beignets de Saumon. Fish beignets prepared with fresh or canned salmon flavoured with anchovy essence.

Cromesquis du Pêcheur. Alternative name for fish croquettes made up with various types of fish.

Croquettes Bombay and Croquettes du Rajah. Curried fish croquettes.

Croquettes d'Oeufs Mère Marie. Chopped or sieved hard-boiled egg preparation.

Croquettes du Pêcheur. Fish croquettes using flaked cooked cod, whiting or turbot. Flavoured with anchovy essence.

Croquettes du Pêcheur d'Islande. Fish croquettes.

Croquettes à la Reine. Minced chicken added to mashed potato, or bound with reduced velouté.

Frites Dubarry Chouron. Sprigs of cauliflower, pané and deep fried.

Fritures d'Okra Farcie. Okra emptied and stuffed with savoury rice, pané and deep fried. (Okra is available fresh or canned.)

Eggs
Sliced, halved or quartered hard-boiled egg, arranged in buttered dish and sauce masked as indicated.

Gratin d'Oeufs à l'Italienne. Egg on bed of spaghetti or noodles, masked with a mornay sauce with concassed tomato added, sprinkled with grated parmesan and glazed in hot oven.

Gratin d'Oeufs Mornay. Sauce mornay masked and gratiné in hot oven.

Oeufs à la Ciboulette. Masked with suprême sauce loaded with chopped chives.

Oeufs au Curry Madras. Curried eggs.

Olives
Large Spanish olives are the best type to use.

Compote d'Olives. Pitted olives with glazed button onions and mushrooms braised in tomato or madeira sauce.

Olives Bonne Bouche. Pitted Spanish olives filled with chopped red pimento, rolled in bacon and grilled.

Olives Braisées à l'Indienne. Pitted olives in curry sauce.

Olives Braisées au Madère. Pitted Spanish or French olives braised in madeira sauce.

Olives Farcies en Fritto—Olives Farcies Gourmande. Pitted olives, filled with crabmeat and pimento preparation, pané and deep fried.

Puff Paste Straws
Hot puff paste straws, similar to cheese straws, but made with anchovy. The anchovy fillets are left whole or chopped and incorporated into the puff paste with cayenne prior to baking.

This line is listed as Les Allumettes d'Anchois; Les Cigarettes du Marinier; Les Banquettes d'Anchois and also Les Paillettes au Parmesan, au Chester or d'Orées. La Galette Maintenon is another feature, being a round puff paste filled with a cheese, fish or poultry savoury preparation. Galette is a type of traditional French pastry cake.

Quenelles
Large sized fish or poultry quenelles, sauce masked as indicated. From this basic preparation come a large number of dishes.

Quenelles de Brochet Chambord. Pike quenelles in a sauce chambord (brown fish sauce).

Quenelles de Brochet Sauce Bisque. Pike quenelles in lobster bisque sauce.

Quenelles Financière. Mushrooms, cocks combs and kidneys, and onions in madeira sauce.

21

Quenelles de Veau à la Crème. Veal quenelles in cream or sauce suprême.

Quenelles de Volaille Suprême. Chicken quenelles in suprême sauce.

Rice

Savoury rice dishes usually cooked as for risotto and dressed with parmesan, butter, seasoning and a cordon of madeira sauce.

Ris d'Agneau en Pilaff à la Grecque. Sweetbreads in cream sauce on pilaff à la grecque—rice garnished with peas and red pimento.

Risotto à la Grecque. Dressed savoury rice with parmesan and butter, loaded with diced pimento, peas and a cordon of madeira sauce.

Risotto Illinois. Dressed rice loaded with peas, sweetcorn and diced red and green peppers.

Roes

Hard and soft herring roes are featured extensively in savoury roles.

Belles Laitances à la Meunière. Dipped in milk, seasoned, floured and pan fried in butter. Finished meunière style with noisette butter and lemon juice.

Laitances Bercy. Poached and masked with bercy sauce.

Laitances Mornay. Poached, drained, mornay sauce masked, sprinkled with grated cheese and gratiné in the oven.

Laitances Pochées Espagnole. Poached in a court bouillon and served with concassed tomato or tomato sauce.

Laitances au Vin Blanc. Poached in white wine, fish sauce masked, garnished with fleurons.

Tomatoes

Tomates Braisées au Madère. Grilled whole in madeira sauce.

Tomates Farcies Bourgeoise. Similar to madère, but in red wine sauce.

Tomates Farcies au Madère. Forcemeat or rice stuffed tomatoes, baked and braised in madeira sauce.

Tripe aux Onions à l'Anglaise

Tripe (cut small) and onions, sprinkled with chopped parsley.

Sundry Hot Hors-d'oeuvre Dishes

Anguilles de Raie au Gratin (also Portugaise). Fillets of cooked skate served gratiné mornay with tomato sauce.

Compote de Panais à la Serbe (also à la Grecque). Small turned parsnips poached and served with concassed tomato, peas and pimento.

Les Friands Charcutière. Breaded and deep fried chipolatas or rondels of slicing sausages.

Julienne Moscovite—Julienne de Légumes à la Russe. Julienne of assorted cooked vegetables in smitane sauce.

Julienne de Tête de Veau Financière—Museau de Veau Ravigote. Shredded calves head with mushrooms, cocks combs and kidneys, and onions in brown sauce or with a hot vinaigrette.

Médaillons de Carpe Chambord. Small médaillons or fish cakes made with carp masked with chambord sauce.

Petits Pâtés Paulin. Spaghetti or noodles, mornay sauced and gratiné.

Pilaff de Crevettes à l'Hongroise. Shrimps in paprika sauce with rice pilaff.

Pilaff de Moules Américaine. Mussels dressed in a ring of rice, masked with Américaine sauce.

Ragoût du Pêcheur. Fish stew with tomatoes and onions. Any type of sea or shell fish. A type of bouillabaise.

SAVOURIES

The savoury is a British Fare institution. It consists of a well seasoned and savoury morsel upon toast or fried bread, served at the end of a meal. The savoury is not to be confused with the toasted snack; each are dealt with separately, though the basic ideas are interchangeable. A savoury could be defined as a small snack.

Unless specified, the savoury is served upon a croûton of bread (square, round or diamond shaped) fried in butter. The ingredients are dressed upon the croûton and the preparation, as required, is finished with noisette butter, a sprinkling and a sprig of parsley.

Anchovies on Toast. Fillets of anchovy neatly arranged upon a croûton, brushed with melted butter and flashed under a grill.

Angels on Horseback—Anges au Cheval. Three or four oysters rolled in bacon and grilled. Noisette butter and chopped parsley garnish.

Caerphilly Rarebit. Welsh rarebit made with caerphilly cheese.

California Croques Monsieur. Sandwich a layer of cheddar in between two slices of bread. Remove crusts, trim to size and fry to a golden brown in butter. Top with bacon rolls and pitted, plumped California prunes, brush with olive oil and grill.

Canapé Bayonne. Chopped smoked ham lié in cream and butter with a touch of cayenne and lemon juice. Piled on a croûton, sauce mornay masked and glazed.

Canapé Bressane. Grilled bacon, mushrooms and sauté chicken livers on toast, finished with noisette butter.

Canapé au Caviare. Portion of caviar on a canapé of fried bread. Heat and serve with lemon wedge.

23

Canapé Cecil. Chopped ham in curry sauce dressed in a dome on a croûton, lightly gratiné under a grill and decorated with a criss-cross of smoked salmon strips.

(Speciality of the one-time Hotel Cecil, London. Dishes termed Cecil and Cecelia originate from this famous hotel.)

Canapé aux Cerises. Pitted pickled cherries rolled in bacon, grilled and served on a croûton.

Canapé Charlemagne. Shrimps in curry sauce on a croûton.

Canapé Chaudes Coquettes. Poached oysters, seasoned with mustard and cayenne, pané and deep fried. Dressed en croûton, 4 or 5 to a portion.

Canapé Diana. Well seasoned chicken livers, rolled in bacon, grilled and dressed 3 or 4 to a portion on a croûton.

The original recipe prescribed a sauté of chopped game with mushroom and truffle in madeira sauce as a canapé. Also featured as a sauté of chicken livers with shallots in a brown sauce.

Canapé Duxelle. Term employed for mushrooms on toast or mushrooms and bacon on toast.

Canapé Exotique. As for ménèlique, but the pitted and plumped prunes are filled with scooped balls of avocado sauced in a lemon dressing.

Canapé des Gourmets. Same as savoy, with the addition of soft roes cooked meunière style.

Canapé Ivanhoe. Diced smoked haddock, touched with cayenne and poached in cream with a little butter added. Dress on a croûton, top with a pickled walnut and glaze quickly.

Canapé Ménèlique. Pitted and plumped California prunes filled with chopped chutney, rolled in bacon, grilled, arranged 3 on a croûton and topped with a pickled walnut. Beurre noisette finishing.

Canapé Mephisto. Butter-fried soft roes on toast in a sauce piquante.

Canapé à la Moelle. Thickish sliced rondels of bone marrow poached in consommé, drained, dressed on a croûton, salt dusted and sprinkled with chopped parsley.

Canapé Nina. Grilled half tomato, mushroom head and pickled walnut on a croûton.

Canapé Quo Vadis. Grilled soft roes and small mushrooms on a croûton.

Canapé Ritchie. Creamed flaked smoked haddock, sliced hard-boiled eggs, on a croûton and glazed.

Canapé Savoy. On a croûton dress one large grilled mushroom, 3 rondels of consommé-poached bone marrow and 2 grilled bacon rashers criss-crossed. Finish with noisette butter.

Crayfish and Bacon Savoury. Cut up 6 bacon rashers and fry gently in a dry pan. Dice 4 cooked écrevisse tails. Combine and toss together for a few minutes. Serve piled on a thick slice of buttered toast.

Devils on Horseback – Diables Noir. Chicken livers well seasoned with ground and cayenne peppers, rolled in bacon and grilled. Finished with noisette butter and chopped parsley.

Mushrooms on Toast. Three large grilled mushrooms arranged on toast or a croûton. Season with ground pepper and finish with a dash of noisette butter.

Rarebit à la Soyer. Dice and melt 250g (8 oz) of matured cheddar, add butter, blend, season with salt, pepper and English mustard reconstituted in vinegar. Flavour with dry sherry. Mix well, spread on a thick slice of buttered toast and glaze in a hot oven. (For special guests, Alexis Soyer used to replace the sherry with champagne.)

Sardines on Toast. Split sardines in half remove backbones and reconstitute fish to original shape. Dress, 3 at a time, on toast, touch with lemon juice and cayenne and finish with dash of noisette butter.

Savoury Toast. Anchovy fillets pounded to a pulp in a mortar and worked to a smooth paste with finely minced shallot, chopped chive and sufficient olive oil, seasoned with lemon juice and a touch of salt. Spread thickly on toast and served very hot.

Scotch Woodcock. Scrambled egg on toast or croûton decorated with criss-crossed julienne of anchovy and dotted with capers. (Also known as Canapé Ecossaise.)

Soft Roes on Toast. Well washed roes, floured, seasoned and sauté in butter. Dressed on toast and finished with squeeze of lemon, noisette butter and chopped parsley.

Welsh Rarebit. Most famous of all savouries. This is claimed as the original recipe. It is the simplest and therefore has much to commend itself.

Grate 120g (4 oz) cheddar cheese and set to melt on 25g (1 oz) butter. Season with a touch of salt, pepper and dash of Worcester sauce. Spread on a square of trimmed toast and glaze under a grill.

This is an alternative method.

Prepare a béchamel sauce and load with grated parmesan, gruyère or cheddar cheese. Season with salt, cayenne and a dash of Worcester sauce. Enrich with one or two beaten egg yolks. Heat without boiling. Spread on a slice of buttered toast or on a croûton. Flash under a grill to glaze.

As a further variation, this may be converted to a raised paste with the addition of a yeast ferment.

Buck Rarebit. Welsh rarebit topped with a poached egg.

Yorkshire Rarebit. Buck rarebit with the addition of two rashers of grilled bacon.

Wiltshire (Canapé). Welsh rarebit preparation loaded with chopped crispy bacon or lean raw ham, checked with cayenne, salt and Worcester sauce, spread on a fried croûton and glazed in the oven or under the grill.

SNACKS

A snack is defined as a quick meal to appease hunger. It is a light refreshment which may be served at any time. The type of fare featured in snack bars, refreshment rooms and call order units.

The original meaning of a snack was something on toast—what caterers know as toasted lines. Toast is a deeply ingrained favourite in Britain originating from the tea and toast habit, and toast at breakfast time. Not for nothing are the British known as a nation of snack eaters!

The toast itself is important; it should be freshly made and the crusts shaved. The toasted snack is a large edition of the savoury. All savouries suitably enlarged are ideal snacks, as are all hot hors-d'oeuvre. The snack has gone beyond the toasted line stage into many other creative areas of the culinary art.

Baked Beans on Toast. Canned beans in tomato sauce, heated and piled on toast. Finished with a chopped parsley dusting.

Beans are also packed in curry, savoury and other sauces and as pork and beans. May be topped with a poached or fried egg.

Cheese Fondue. The fondue de fromage is a savoury which, in recent times, has developed into a cocktail dip. There are hot and cold dips and the original is the fondue.

Remove crusts from a slice of bread, fry in butter without undue crisping and browning. Set in a serving dish. Grate 150g (5 oz) gruyère and melt it in a pan. Season with salt, cayenne, lemon juice and a dash of Worcester sauce. Add a small quantity of dry white wine. Mix well and mask the fried bread with the fondue preparation, heat and serve.

For a dip, the cheese preparation, made in sufficient quantity, is presented in a dish on a hotplate or over a lamp and the guests dip croûtons in it. Many varieties of dip now exist, some with cheese, others without, most people having their own special recipe.

Chili Con Carne. Highly spiced Mexican dish of many varieties. This is a representative recipe.

Soak 500g (1 lb) brown kidney beans for 6 hours. Mince and cook a chopped onion in 25g (1 oz) pork dripping and add a tiny crushed garlic clove. Stir in 500g (1 lb) minced lean beef, then add the beans. Add 500g (1 lb) chopped tomatoes and season with salt and a little desiccated chili powder. Moisten the preparation with stock, cover the pan and bake at 300°F. (150°C.) for 2 hours. Replace liquid as required, check seasoning and serve.

Eggs on Toast. Fried, poached or scrambled eggs, garnished with grilled bacon if liked.

The Frankfurter or Hot Dog. Smoked pork sausage which is either poached in boiling water or grilled. The 'Frank' is placed in a warmed soft finger roll with Continental mustard or a lettuce leaf and slice of dill pickled cucumber.

Spaghetti on Toast. Canned and handled as baked beans. May also be kitchen prepared. Tomato sauce is the most popular canning, also bolonaise, napolitaine and other sauces.

Tomatoes on Toast. Cut in half or left whole, seasoned, grilled and served on toast.

Other Toasted Lines. Mushrooms, roes, sardines, various savoury spreads, and the popular Welsh, Buck and Yorkshire Rarebits.

The Computation Snack Idiom

Consists of a variety of basic items which can be assembled into various compo-dishes. Items include eggs, bacon, sausages, tomatoes, mushrooms, baked beans, pasta, hamburgers, fried bread, deep fried and sauté potatoes.

Hamburger

It was the early Germanic immigrants who introduced the Hamburg Steak to the U.S.A., where it became popularized and glamourized as the Hamburger on an unprecedented scale.

Made with minced lean beef, cereal filler, i.e. rusk or breadcrumbs, and seasonings, it is griddle cooked and served with or without fried onions in a soft toasted roll. A slice of cheese and it becomes a Cheeseburger; top with a fried egg and we have a Brunchburger. Hamburgers are also featured with pineapple and as other exotic and unusual presentations, i.e. double, treble and King-size Hamburgers. Tomato ketchup, relishes, mustards and even tartare sauce are offered as accompaniments. There are variations upon the 'burger theme: beefburger, lamb, bacon, chicken, turkey and others.

Hamburgers are marketed under many names, some registered brands and as franchise operations. One such—the Wimpy—is the pioneer of them all, introduced and sponsored in Europe in 1954 by J. Lyons and Company and now featured world-wide.

Hamburgers should always be freshly cooked to order. This is a basic recipe.

175g (6 oz) milk, 250g (8 oz) breadcrumbs, 120g (4 oz) minced blanched onion, salt, pepper, ground spice, 1½ kilo (3 lb) minced lean beef.

Add milk to the breadcrumbs, onion and seasoning. Add minced beef and mix well. Scale off into 50g (2 oz) burgers. Roll into balls on a floured board, flatten and shape to size. Bake, fry or grill as required.

Hamburger Hawaiian. Sauté in butter, dressed on a flapjack,

27

surmounted with a butter-fried pineapple round with a pitted red cherry in the centre.

Vulcan (Griddled Hamburger). Griddled flapjack, hamburger spread with concassed tomato flavoured with tabasco, fried egg, grilled bacon rasher and chopped parsley sprinkling.

Pizza Pie

Italian speciality fare, eaten hot or cold. Shallow flan usually made with a raised dough, but also with plain flour and water or milk or a short paste. Fillings consist of savoury materials—anchovy, tomato, cheese, olives and minced veal or chicken. A good pizza should have plenty of anchovies.

For a raised dough: warm and sift 250g (8 oz) flour with 5g ($\frac{1}{4}$ oz) salt. Beat 2 eggs in a little warmed milk, add a little sugar, and 8g ($\frac{3}{4}$ oz) fresh yeast to make a ferment. Mix and stand 5 minutes. Add flour and 1 tablespoon olive oil to the ferment, mix, cover and stand to prove for 45 minutes. When proved, knead well with palm of hand and shape into a soup plate.

Note: if short paste is used, shape it into a 20cm (8 in) lightly oiled and floured flan case.

For the filling: mince half an onion or equivalent in shallots and a tiny garlic clove and melt in butter. Add 500g (1 lb) peeled, chopped tomatoes, about 8 chopped anchovies, parsley, little olive oil and seasoning and reduce slowly over heat for 3 minutes. Spread filling over case, decorate with julienne of anchovies, stud with pitted black olives, sprinkle liberally with grated parmesan. If raised dough, stand to prove for 10 minutes. Bake in oven at 200°C. (400°F.) for 20 minutes.

Best cheese for pizzas is the Italian Mozzarella, made from buffalo milk.

'Bought-in' pizzas are marketed frozen for on-premises end-cooking, as required, in a special high temperature pizza oven.

Quiche Lorraine

The French Quiche is similar to the Italian Pizza. Both are savoury preparations eaten hot or cold and with each the fillings are many and various.

Line a greased and floured 20cm (8 in) flan case with 250g (8 oz) short pastry. Slice and blanch a medium sized onion, melt in butter and spread over pastry. Place 120g (4 oz) grated parmesan cheese, 2 to 3 well beaten eggs and 250g (8 oz) cream in a bowl, season with salt, pepper and pinch of mustard powder, beat and pour into pastry case. Top with 6 to 8 whole button onions, previously cooked in salted water, butter and lemon juice. Cook in oven at 200°C. (400°F.) for 30 minutes.

Other ingredients for fillings are bacon, ham or charcuterie; all are added and cooked in the savoury custard preparation.

Savoury Pancakes

The batter is similar to that used for sweet pancakes, but the sugar and vanilla essence are replaced by salt, cayenne and ground pepper.

The cakes are filled with a savoury filling of fish, meat, poultry, game or vegetables, or served with a savoury sauce. Some preparations indicate glazed à la mornay. For added eye appeal, the batter mix may be loaded with chopped parsley.

American Pancake. Load batter with chopped parsley and small amount minced cooked onion, make up pancake and fill with diced ham, cooked sweetcorn kernels, peas and lima beans.

Bolonaise Pancake. Served hot and masked with bolonaise sauce.

Crabe (Crêpe de). Filled with flaked crab in white sauce flavoured with brandy and garnished with cooked sliced mushrooms.

Epicurean (Crêpe des Epicures). Savoury pancake well flecked with chopped fines herbes. Lay flat when cold, line with smoked salmon and potted shrimps down the centre. Roll up and serve with lemon wedges and brown bread and butter.

Fisherman's Pancake. Filled with any cooked flaked fish, either singly or mixed, lié in a well seasoned sauce and glazed mornay. The fillings may be lié in cream or butter and flavoured with anchovy or other savoury essence or sauce.

There are several derivatives of the Fishermen's Pancake: Joinville, indicating shrimps or prawns; Cancalaise, shrimps, mussels, oysters and other shell fish; Casino, a medley of white and shellfish in cream, flavoured and coloured with pounded anchovies or a concentrated essence.

Ivanhoe (Crêpe). Filled with diced smoked haddock cooked in milk and glazed mornay.

Mushroom Pancake. Filled with sliced mushrooms stewed in butter and bound with cream, garnished with a line of sliced cooked or raw mushrooms and dusted with chopped parsley.

Pancake Snack. Pancake on a round of toast, built up with lean ham, another pancake, topped with a fried egg and glazed mornay. Unglazed grilled bacon can replace the ham and the egg can be decorated with criss-crossed anchovy, capers and pimento stuffed olives. Served with noisette butter and chopped parsley.

Reine (Crêpe à la)—Chicken Pancake. Filled with minced creamed chicken and glazed with mornay sauce.

Reine Pedauque (Crêpe). As for à la reine with sparing addition of chopped truffle. Top with truffle blade, mask with mornay sauce, sprinkle with grated parmesan and glaze. Preparation may be flavoured with brandy.

Salmon Pancake. Filled with flaked cooked salmon in butter coloured and seasoned with anchovy essence and glazed mornay.

Savoyarde (Crêpe). As for reine pedauque with added topping of asparagus tips and concassed tomato. In view of the heavy garnishing a larger sized cake is made.

Sandwich Snacks

Legend has it that the Fourth Earl of Sandwich (1718–92) invented the preparation which now carries his name throughout the world. The Earl, an inveterate gambler, created the sandwich so that he and his guests could eat while they played without leaving the gaming table.

This section is devoted to the speciality sandwiches served as hot snacks and for other occasions.

All sandwiches should be freshly cut to order and the ingredients seasoned as required.

American Toasted Sandwich. Sandwich a square shaped grilled hamburger spread with concassed tomato and red pimento between two slices of toast. Trim, top with fried egg and serve with fried potatoes and cole-slaw.

Bacon Sandwich. Grilled bacon between buttered toast, seasoned with mustard, cut diagonally into four. Garnish with tomato wedge and serve with sweet pickles or chutney. (One-time speciality of the 'Brighton Belle' Pullman train.)

Bookmaker. Minute steak, seasoned, grilled to underdone, sandwiched between two slices of toast. Meat smeared with mustard as required, crusts shaved and served hot. Better known now as the Minute Steak Sandwich.

Broadway Sandwich. Toasted sandwich made up of shredded lettuce, smoked salmon, hard-boiled egg rondels and finished with second layer of shredded lettuce. Trimmed and served hot.

Chicken Liver Toasted Sandwich. Minced shallot, sliced mushrooms and chicken livers, seasoned and sauté in butter, bound with brown sauce and chopped parsley added. Used as a filling.

Chicken Suprême Toasted Sandwich. Minced onion and chopped mushrooms stewed in butter, chopped chicken added, seasoned and lié in cream sauce. Used as filling.

Club Sandwich. Two slices of thick toast spread with mayonnaise, built up with shredded lettuce, grilled bacon, sliced chicken, sliced tomato, rondels of hard-boiled egg and finished with shredded lettuce. Fillings seasoned as required, crusts shaved, heated in oven and served.

Club House Sandwich. Same as club sandwich, using turkey in place of chicken.

Croque-Monsieur. Fried sandwich with cheese, ham and other fillings. Similar to the sandwich idéale, but usually cut into bite-size pieces.

Curried Shrimp Sandwich. Peeled shrimps lié in a thickish hot curry sauce and used for toasted sandwich filling.

Double Decker Egg and Bacon Sandwich. On a round of buttered toast arrange some grilled bacon. Place a second round, buttered both sides, on top, add a fried egg and finish with a third piece of toast.

Exotic Toasted Sandwich. Stew minced shallot in butter, add minced cooked lamb, chopped California plumped prunes and small amount of seedless raisins. Moisten with stock, season, reduce and add chopped parsley. Use as filling.

Scrambled Sandwich. Toasted sandwich filled with scrambled egg. May be garnished with grilled bacon, sliced sauté mushrooms and chicken livers.

Super Gammon Sandwich. Toasted sandwich of grilled gammon. Trim, top with fried egg and dust with chopped parsley.

Toasted Hamburger Sandwich. Hamburger filling is shaped to the size of the toast, grilled and sandwiched between two slices of buttered toast. Served with or without onions.

For cheeseburger add ribbon of processed cheese; for brunch-burger top with fried egg.

Fried Sandwiches
The sandwich is prepared in the usual manner with thickish white bread and the selected filling. It is trimmed, breadcrumbed and deep fried to a golden brown. During the frying process, the sandwich must be submerged in the fat. Drain well and serve.

Fried Sandwich Idéale
The sandwich Idéale is a Savoy Hotel speciality. Prepared with two slices of thick white bread with the main filling sandwiched between thinly sliced cheese. Trimmed, sauté to a golden brown on both sides in butter and flashed in a hot oven immediately prior to service. Filling can be bacon, ham, salami, chicken, turkey, smoked salmon and smoked ham.

Hot Sandwiches
Made to order, served with pickles and relishes and eaten with knife and fork. Prepared with thick cut white and brown bread and butter and made up with salt beef; hot bacon or gammon; grilled bacon and fried egg; roast beef; roast lamb, turkey and chicken; grilled minute steaks; hamburgers and frankfurters.

Flapjacks
Made in a variety of flavours and garnishings, both sweet and savoury. Feature of the call order snack trade. A griddle line especially acceptable for breakfast.

Basic recipe for 8 servings: Sift 360g (12 oz) plain flour with 4 tablespoons fine semolina and 2 teaspoons baking powder. Season with salt, pepper and dry mustard. Make a well in the centre and break in 2 eggs. Stir slowly and gradually add sufficient milk to form a soft dropping consistency. It is at this stage that garnishing is added, i.e. grated cheese, diced bacon, sliced sausage, chopped parsley and herbs, or the preparation left as it is. Drop a tablespoon of the batter onto a pre-heated and greased griddle. Cook slowly until bubbles appear and burst, turn over and brown the other side.

Sweet Flapjack. Proceed as above, replacing the seasonings with sugar. Sweet Flapjacks are served hot with maple syrup or fresh cream. May be studded with diced apple, pineapple, prunes, dates and so on as fancy dictates.

Soups

In the kitchen soups are classified as 'thick' or 'clear'. The clear soups are the consommés; the thick soups or 'potages épais' may be subdivided into the crèmes; veloutés; purées; bisques and chowders.

For ease in reference we conform to the basic classification of soup being clear or thick, and since many—particularly consommés carry standard garnishings—these will be listed separately.

CONSOMMÉS—CLEAR SOUPS

The French for clear soup is consommé. But the terms are synonymous, as the basis of practically all clear soup is in fact consommé. Consommé is prepared from clarified chicken stock, beef or from stock of other basic ingredients.

Africaine. Chicken consommé lightly flavoured with curry powder and garnished with cooked rice and chicken quenelles flavoured with curry powder.

Alphabet. Consommé garnished with alphabet pasta.

Alsacienne. Consommé garnished with rondels of frankfurter sausage and shredded cooked sauerkraut.

Andalouse. Garnished with diced royale, tomato, cooked rice, julienne of ham and threaded egg.

Bêche de Mer (Consommé au). A sea slug from the Pacific imported dried from which a soup is made, similar to turtle. It contains a mucilaginous substance with a characteristic flavour and requires prolonged soaking. It is then cooked in consommé with an infusion of herbs.

Belle Fermière. Consommé garnished with julienne of cabbage, diced French beans and small pasta.

Belle Gabrielle. Chicken consommé garnished with prawns and chicken quenelles shaped as small olives.

Bortsch. Famous Russian soup. A massive preparation, almost a meal in itself. There are two main versions, one prepared with meat and poultry and the other with fish. Both are heavily garnished soups and each one has an ungarnished clear consommé version.

Meat and poultry Bortsch is prepared with beef, chicken or duck and cabbage, carrots, leeks, turnips, celery, and beetroot—which gives the soup its characteristic rich red colour. The beef and the poultry are cooked in the piece in the soup with the prepared vegetables. For service they are boned and cut into portions.

33

The soup is served from a tureen garnished with rondels of sliced frankfurter or similar smoked sausage. Bortsch is accompanied by sour cream (smetana), beetroot juice and small, hot, forcemeat-stuffed, puff-paste bouchées.

Fish Bortsch is prepared in a similar manner, with vegetables and such fish as salmon, sturgeon and herring, care being taken to suppress any large bones.

Clear Bortsch is prepared by straining and clarifying the parent version. It may be served clear and ungarnished, or garnished with a julienne of chicken, duck and diced beef. This is also accompanied by sour cream, beetroot juice and forcemeat bouchées (meat or fish fillings as appropriate).

Bouquetière. Garnished with cooked peas, stars of carrot and turnip, shredded cabbage, asparagus tips and chervil pluches.

Caroline. Chicken consommé garnished with a julienne of chicken and cooked rice.

Celestine. Garnished with shredded fines herbs savoury pancake. Pancake may also be stamped out in stars or rondels.

Chasseur. Consommé made from game stock. Garnished with a julienne of the meat of any feathered game and sliced mushrooms.

Cheveux d'Ange. Consommé garnished with fine vermicelli known as 'angel's hair'. Grated parmesan cheese is passed separately.

Cockie Leekie or **Cock-a-Leekie.** Chicken consommé garnished with cooked rice, diced chicken meat and shredded leek.

Colbert. Garnished with poached eggs, one per serving.

Crécy. Julienne of carrot and cubes of royale garnish.

Croûte-au-pot. Chicken and beef consommé garnished with stars or rondels of carrot, turnip, shredded leek and julienne of celery. Rondels of bâton roll are passed separately.

Cultivateur. Peas, diced or stars of carrot and turnip.

Cyrano. Consommé prepared from duck. Accompanied by duck quenelles, well seasoned and with added parmesan cheese, set in a dish, gratiné and offered à part.

Diablotins. Chicken consommé topped with sliced rondels of buttered bâton roll or French bread, coated with a reduced béchamel with the addition of grated parmesan, then gratiné.

Diana. Game consommé. Garnished with the meat of any feathered game cut en julienne or diced.

Dolores. Chicken or beef consommé garnished with poached rice, chicken julienne and touched with saffron.

Doria. Chicken consommé garnished with chicken quenelles and cooked cucumber pellets.

Double. Consommé Double indicates double strength. It is allowed to reduce and is then thickened with arrowroot. It should be slightly opaque and oily in consistency.

Dubarry. Consommé garnished with cooked rice and miniature sprigs of cauliflower.

Fermière. Diced carrot, turnips, parsnip and potato, peas and pluches of chervil.

French Onion (Soupe à l'Oignon). Finely shred the required number of large onions, season with salt and pepper and stew without coloration in butter. Moisten with consommé and finish cooking slowly. Serve in individual stone crocks. Top with rondels of long roll or bâton bread, sprinkle with grated cheese and brown quickly under a grill. Offer grated parmesan separately.

French Onion (Flambé). As for French onion soup. Float some whisky over the browned topping (which must be dry) and flame .

Girondine. Consommé garnished with diamonds of royale, chopped ham and julienne of carrot.

Imperial. Chicken consommé garnished with a julienne of chicken, tongue, mushrooms and truffle.

Indienne. Consommé flavoured with curry powder. Garnished with chicken quenelles and rice. Care must be taken to ensure the curry powder is cooked and well blended into the consommé.

Italienne. Chicken consommé garnished with rice and any shape, size or coloured pasta.

Judic. Consommé garnished with poached whole heart of lettuce.

Julienne. Garnished with a julienne of vegetables.

Juliet. Garnished with chicken quenelles, diamonds of hard-boiled egg and diced green coloured royale.

Leopold. Consommé garnished with shredded lettuce, sorrel and chervil previously cooked in consommé with butter added.

Madrilène. Italian consommé coloured with tomato and flavoured with celery.

Madrilène Fin Tasse. Consommé madrilène garnished with a chiffonade of sorrel, vermicelli and a julienne of tomato.

Mille-Fanti. Chicken consommé garnished with scrambled egg mingled with chopped parsley or fines herbs.

Minestrone. Well known Italian soup. Prepared with cubed (à paysanne) turnip, carrot, parsnip, celery, cabbage and leek, peas, haricot beans, short-cut spaghetti, tomato, bacon lardons, rice, onion, garlic, chopped parsley and seasoning, all cooked in stock and served together. Minestrone is accompanied by grated parmesan and toasted flûtes.

35

Minestrone Milanaise. Minestrone with the addition of a generous quantity of short-cut spaghetti and sliced mushrooms, served in crocks with grated parmesan passed separately.

Moelle (à la). Consommé garnished with rondels of bone marrow previously poached in stock.

Monte-Carlo. Chicken consommé thickened with arrowroot or fecula and garnished with asparagus tips and chicken quenelles.

Napolitaine. Consommé garnished with diced tomato and a julienne of ham and celery.

Niçoise. Beef or chicken consommé garnished with vermicelli, concassed tomato and diced French beans.

Nids d'Hirondelles (Consommé aux)—Birds Nest Soup. The basis of this far Eastern speciality soup is the tiny nests of a species of sea swallow found in Malaysia and Indonesia. The nests are made with the saliva secreted by the birds which has gelatinous properties and a special flavour which it imparts to the soup. The nests are cleaned and dried. They are very light and sold by the gram as whole nests and pieces. They are soaked in water, then poached in a light stock and used to garnish the rich consommé produced.

This soup is now usually purchased in cans ready made. Serve in consommé cups.

Oyster Stew. Sophisticated American soup usually prepared to order at the table in a pan over a lamp.

Lightly poach the required number of oysters (6 per portion) in milk. In another pan, warm some milk, add a piece of butter and season with salt, cayenne, grated nutmeg and lemon juice. Add the oysters and their cooking liquor. Heat and serve in soup plates. Pass sieved or crushed breakfast biscuit separately.

Pâtés (Consommé aux), Pasta Consommé. Garnished with any type of small pasta i.e. shells, stars, bows or rings. Grated parmesan should always accompany all consommés garnished with pasta.

Petite Marmite. French speciality and a complete soup. Place a large piece of boiling beef, a boiling chicken and a marrow bone in a pot, season, add a bouquet garni, cover with water, bring to the boil, cook and skim as required. Add thickly sliced celery and leek, prepared carrot and turnip, and a whole onion stuck with a clove. Finish cooking. Remove the bone, beef and chicken, strip off the meat, cut into large dice and replace in the soup. Serve in large soup plates from the marmite at the table. Pass separately rondels of bone marrow, toasted rondels of bâton roll and grated parmesan. (Shredded cabbage may also be added to the vegetables.)

Poule-au-Pot. Literally 'chicken in the pot'. Similar to petite marmite but prepared with a whole chicken cooked in the pot with root vegetables. Served in a similar way to the marmite. (Originated by

36

Henry IV of France (1553–1610) who decreed all his people should have a Poule-au-Pot for their Sunday dinner.)

Prince de Galles. Chicken consommé thickened with tapioca and garnished with shredded, devilled and grilled almonds.

Princesse. Chicken consommé garnished with asparagus tips and white chicken meat cut en julienne.

Printanière. Peas, carrots and turnips cut in stars, diamonds of French beans, asparagus tips and chervil pluches.

Profiteroles (Consommé aux). Chicken consommé garnished with small 'boulets' of dry choux paste. If larger sized profiteroles are featured with this consommé, they are filled with a light purée of foie gras, chicken or game.

Quail (Consommé aux Cailles). Double chicken consommé garnished with hard-boiled quail eggs, sliced or whole.

Ravioli (aux Raviolis). Consommé garnished with small poached ravioli. Grated parmesan is offered separately.

Réjane. Chicken consommé garnished with diced royale and threaded eggs.

Riche. Chicken consommé double flavoured with dry sherry or madeira. Garnished with a julienne of white chicken meat and truffles.

Risi Bisi. Chicken consommé garnished with rice, peas and diced red pimento.

Riz (Consommé au). Poached rice and chervil pluches.

Rossolnick. Clear duck consommé with a julienne of vegetables and served with sour cream. Russian speciality.

Royale. Consommé garnished with cubes or diamonds of royale. It may be left plain, or be coloured or flecked with various ingredients.

Sarah Bernhardt. Chicken consommé thickened with tapioca, garnished with asparagus tips, poached rondels of bone marrow, julienne of truffles and quenelles of chicken, spinach and crayfish.
Another version: Consommé flavoured with a light infusion of turtle herbs and madeira, thickened with tapioca, and garnished with chicken quenelles just flavoured and coloured with tomato, and poached rondels of bone marrow.

Scotch Broth. Popular British soup, prepared with mutton stock and garnished with diced vegetables, mutton and pearl barley.
    Prepare the mutton stock and strain. Add the pearl barley and diced equal amounts of carrot, celery, turnip, leek, onion and peas. When the ingredients are cooked, check seasoning, garnish with diced cooked lean mutton, chopped parsley and chervil pluches.
    There is a thick version—Cream of Scotch Broth.

Solférino. Garnished with small balls of carrot and turnip, diamonds of French beans, julienne of mushroom and chervil pluches.

Talma. Chicken consommé garnished with cooked rice and diamonds or oblongs of royale.

Trianon. Chicken consommé lié with tapioca and garnished with red, green and white rondels of royale.

Trois Couleurs (Consommé aux Trois Couleurs, Consommé aux Allies). Chicken consommé garnished with red, white and blue chicken quenelles in equal quantities.

Trois Fillets (aux). Chicken consommé garnished with a julienne of tongue, chicken and truffle in about equal quantities.

Turtle Soup (Tortue Clair). British Fare speciality. Clear soup prepared from turtle infusion of herbs and stock, flavoured with dry sherry or madeira. Usually garnished with cubes of turtle meat. Served in consommé cups, accompanied with brown bread and butter, lemon wedges and, at special functions, milk punch.

Usually 'bought in' ready prepared in cans, but may be prepared as follows: infuse a packet of turtle herbs in consommé. Strain and thicken into a consommé double with arrowroot. Garnish with cubes of turtle meat and allow the preparation to stand over a low heat prior to service.

Dried turtle meat is purchased for the garnish. It requires prolonged soaking in lightly salted water and when soft is poached in the prepared consommé.

There is also a Thick Turtle Soup.

Tzarine. Double chicken consommé, garnished with diced cooked visega. The stock in which the visega is poached is reduced to an essence and strained into the consommé.

Vatel. Garnished with fish quenelles, peeled whole shrimps and a julienne of truffle.

Vermicelli. Garnished liberally with vermicelli cooked in the consommé. Grated parmesan is offered separately.

Vin (au). Consommé flavoured with port, sherry, madeira, marsala, moselle, hock or a dry white wine of the Burgundy type. These consommés, which are served hot, iced or jellied in consommé cups for special occasions, take on the name of the wine concerned, i.e. Consommé au Porto, Consommé à l'Amontillado, Consommé au Vin du Rhin.

Viveurs. Duck consommé flavoured and coloured with beetroot and celery. Garnished with julienne of celery and paprika diablotins.

Volaille (Consommé de). Chicken consommé garnished with a julienne of white chicken meat.

Xavier. Chicken consommé garnished with threaded egg.

COLD SOUPS

Both Consommé and Madrilène may be featured iced or jellied in consommé cups with lemon wedges passed separately.

While most thick soups may be featured iced, there are some which are specially prepared for cold service, such as Vichyssoise, Crème à la Ritz, Gaspacho, and Cucumber.

THICK SOUPS – POTAGES

Agnès Sorel. Velouté of chicken thickened with a liaison of cream and egg yolks and garnished with diced chicken meat, tongue and mushrooms. The garnish may also be cut en julienne.

Ambassadeur. Purée of peas and rice mixed, garnished with shredded lettuce and sorrel.

Américaine (Crème). Purée of tomatoes with infusion of turtle herbs, thickened with arrowroot.

Andalouse (Crème). Tomato soup garnished with peas and rice.

Argenteuil (Potage). Cream of asparagus garnished with small asparagus tips.

Artichauts (Crème dé). Velouté of fonds d'artichauts thickened with a cream and egg yolk liaison. Garnished with fonds d'artichauts cut en julienne.

Avocado. A cream soup made from avocado pear. A West Indian speciality.

Bagration (Velouté). Velouté of veal, lié with cream and egg yolk, garnished with pieces of macaroni and served with grated parmesan.

Bercy (Crème). Purée of potatoes and turnips lié with cream.

Bisque. Name given to soup prepared from crustacea, i.e. lobster, scampi, crab, shrimp, crayfish and crawfish. The bisque takes the name of the basic ingredient from which it is prepared, i.e. Bisque d'Homard.

The basis of a bisque is the purée of the crustacea concerned, made up with consommé, purée of rice and thickened with cream. Bisques are accompanied by crushed breakfast bisuit passed separately.

Bonne Femme (Potage). White of leek and potatoes in equal amounts à paysanne, seasoned, sweated in butter, moistened with stock and cooked. Check seasoning and consistency, finish with a little cream, garnish with chervil pluches and serve with toasted flûtes.

Bretonne (Crème). Purée of haricot beans and onion thickened with cream.

Brunoise (Crème). Oxtail soup. Chopped parsley topping.

Campbell. Fish velouté lié with cream. Garnished with fish quenelles.

Cardinal (Crème). Cream of fish mixed with crawfish purée. Garnished with diced cooked crawfish meat.

Carmen (Crème). Tomato soup garnished with poached rice.

Céleri (Crème de). Purée of celery with the addition of potato purée and lié with cream.

Celestine (Crème). Cream of chicken with the addition of a purée of fonds d'artichauts. Served with croûtons.

Champenoise. Purée of potato combined with celery soup in about equal amounts. Season, bind with cream, let the preparation blend, sprinkle with chopped parsley and serve with croûtons.

Champignons (Crème de). Cream of mushrooms. Chopped parsley topping.

Chantilly (Crème). Purée of lentils lié with cream. Served with croûtons.

Chowder. American seafood soup prepared with any shellfish or crustacea. Clam Chowder is the best known example.

Wash the live clams, place in cold water and bring to the boil. The shells will open and the clams can be picked out. Prepare a preparation of chopped onion, diced bacon and potato in equal quantities and toss in butter. Add tomato purée, clams and seasoning. Moisten with fish stock, add the well reduced clam cooking liquor and simmer until all the ingredients are cooked. Serve with crushed breakfast biscuit.

Clamart (Crème). Green pea soup garnished with whole peas. Croûtons are passed separately.

Clementine (Crème). Cream of tomato garnished with diced rondels or diamonds of royale.

Conti (Crème). Purée of lentils lié with cream. Garnished with lentils and served with croûtons.

Corn Soup. Simmer 500g (1 lb) corn kernels in clear stock with a little onion, seasoning, a bayleaf and a piece of bacon for about an hour. Sieve and check purée consistency with cream. Serve dusted with chopped chives, pass croûtons separately.

Crécy (Crème). Purée of carrots and rice mixed lié with cream. Garnished with carrot pellets and served with croûtons.

Cucumber, Iced. Special soup for cold service. The cucumber is peeled, diced and cooked in chicken stock. It is blended with half-whipped cream, seasoned and flavoured with grated lemon rind. Served iced in consommé cups sprinkled with chopped chives.

Dartois (Crème). Green pea soup thickened with arrowroot. Croûtons are passed separately.

Doria. Velouté of cucumber with cream and egg yolk liaison. Garnished with pellets of cucumber.

Dubarry (Crème). Cream of cauliflower. Chopped parsley topping.

Espagnole (Crème). Cream of tomato. Chopped parsley topping.

Garbure. Purée of root vegetables and cabbage cooked in stock. Consistency corrected with milk. Served with croûtons.

Gasconne (Potage). Equal quantities of tomato and cream soup enriched with a little cream and seasoning as required. Garnished with a julienne of ham and cooked mushrooms.

Gaspacho. Spanish soup made from uncooked ingredients and served iced. Prepared from tomatoes, onions, green peppers, garlic, oil and vinegar placed in a liquidizer. Seasoned with salt, pepper and lemon juice and served garnished with diced cucumber, croûtons and chopped parsley.

Gentilhomme (Purée). Purée of game and ham with madeira flavoured cream. Garnished with a julienne of ham, mushrooms and rondels of game sausage. Accompanied by sippets.

Germiny (Crème). Light velouté of sorrel thickened with a liaison of egg yolks and cream. Served in consommé cups with cheese straws.

To prepare: chop 120g (4 oz) sorrel and set to melt in butter. Season with salt and pepper and add $\frac{3}{4}$ litre (1$\frac{1}{2}$ pints) consommé. Bring to the boil and add 6 egg yolks beaten in $\frac{1}{8}$ litre ($\frac{1}{4}$ pint) cream. Whisk briskly over heat but do not boil—remove from heat as preparation comes up to boiling point. Finish at the side of the cooker until the soup thickens. Add a small piece of butter and serve topped with chervil pluches.

Gosford. Equal quantities of chicken velouté and purée of white asparagus, checked with chicken stock, thickened with tapioca, lié with a liaison.

Grenada (Crème). Tomato soup lié à la crème.

Ground Nut. Cream soup, prepared with peanut butter and cream of chicken. Accompanied by toasted peanuts and croûtons.

Homard (Bisque d'). Cream of lobster soup. Chopped parsley and crushed breakfast biscuit topping.

Hôtelière (Crème). Purée of potatoes, lentils and haricot beans mixed and lié with cream. Garnished with chervil pluches. Served with croûtons.

Jackson (Potage). Purée of potato and white of leek lié with a cream and egg yolk liaison. Garnished with diced potato.

Juanita (Crème). Tomato soup garnished with chicken or veal quenelles.

Kangaroo Tail. A speciality Australasian soup similar to oxtail. Served flavoured with sherry. Usually 'bought in' ready prepared.

Kidney (Crème aux Rognons). Kidney soup with chopped parsley topping.

Krapivnie Shchi. Russian soup made with young nettle leaves. They are blanched, combined with an equal amount of leaf spinach and cooked together in stock for 35 minutes. Garnished with sliced sausage. Sour cream passed separately.

Lamballe (Crème). Green pea soup garnished with vermicelli. Croûtons passed separately.

La Vallière (Crème). A preparation of equal quantities of cream of chicken and celery soup.

Leek (Cream of). Chopped parsley and chervil pluches topping.

Légumes (Potage)—Vegetable Soup. Paysanne of vegetables: onion, spinach, carrot, leek, turnip, parsnip and potatoes, season, toss in butter, cover with water and cook quickly. Pass preparation through a sieve and lié the purée with an egg yolk and cream liaison. Correct seasoning, add a piece of butter, reheat but do not boil, garnish with chervil pluches and serve with sippets.

Lilly (Potage). Chicken soup garnished with julienne of chicken and chopped sorrel.

Longchamps (Crème). Green pea soup garnished with chervil pluches. Croûtons passed separately.

Longueville (Crème). Green pea soup garnished with sliced or tronçons of macaroni. Croûtons passed separately.

Madelon (Potage). Well creamed tomato soup garnished with vermicelli.

Madrilène (Potage). Tomato soup garnished with vermicelli and chervil pluches.

Marcilly (Crème). Equal amounts of chicken and green pea soups well blended and garnished with cooked long grain rice.

Marrons (Crème). Chestnut soup. The chestnuts are stewed in butter with onions, carrot, celery and seasoning, then cooked in stock and sieved into a purée which is thickened with cream.

Médicis (Potage). Equal quantities of purée of peas and purée of carrots lié with cream.

Minted Cream of Green Peas. Green pea soup, enriched with cream and garnished with chopped fresh mint. Served iced in consommé cups.

Mongole (Crème). A preparation of equal quantities of green pea and tomato soup.

Montespan (Velouté). Velouté of asparagus, bound with a liaison, thickened with tapioca and garnished with asparagus tips and peas.

Mulligatawny. One of the many Indian preparations incorporated into British national cookery. Cream of chicken and rice flavoured with curry and garnished with rice.

As with most fare of national origin there are several versions of the mulligatawny, but the smooth purée type appears to be the most favoured.

Dissect a boiling fowl and sauté in a deep pan in a good dripping with shredded onions, carrots, leeks and celery, and cubed potatoes. Shake in a little flour and flavour with curry powder and a pinch of saffron. Add rice. Cover with stock and simmer with the lid on until the chicken meat clears the carcass. Take out the bones and pass the whole preparation through a strainer. Check the purée for seasoning and correct consistency with cream to a smooth, thick and well spiced soup. Garnish with cooked rice and cubed chicken meat as required.

May also be prepared without using the whole chicken by cooking all the ingredients in chicken stock.

Palestine. Velouté of Jerusalem artichokes lié with cream and egg yolk. Served with croûtons.

Parmentier (Potage). Purée of potatoes and white of leek with added consommé and milk. Served with sippets.

Pauvre Homme (Potage). Potatoes and leeks in equal quantities, cut à paysanne, season, toss in butter, cover with water and boil rapidly. Rub through a sieve and bind the purée with a liaison of egg yolk and cream. Heat, correct seasoning and add a piece of butter. Serve with sippets.

Paysanne (Crème). Purée of potatoes and several mixed root vegetables, i.e. carrot, turnip, parsnip, with consommé and cream.

Pierre-le-Grand (Potage). Equal quantities of cream of chicken and celery soup. Blend well, check seasoning and consistency with cream.

Pompadour (Crème). A preparation of equal quantities of cream of chicken and purée of cauliflower.

Portugaise (Crème). Tomato soup garnished with poached rice.

Potiron. Mixture of purée of pumpkin and potatoes lié with cream. Garnished with rice and served with croûtons.

Princess-Royale (Crème). A preparation of equal quantities of asparagus and chicken soup.

Reine (Crème). Julienne of white of chicken meat garnish.

Reine Margot (Crème). Cream of chicken flavoured with infusion of almonds. Garnished with chicken quenelles.

Reine-Pedauque (Crème). Chicken and asparagus soup garnished with chopped truffle.

Rich Oxtail (Soup). A preparation of equal quantities of oxtail and tomato soup. Chopped parsley topping.

Ritz (Crème Glacée à la). Vichyssoise with the addition of tomato juice. Served iced, garnished with chopped chives. (Louis Diat creation.)

Rossini. Cream of chicken garnished with julienne of truffle and foie gras quenelles.

Saint-Argenteuil (Potage). A preparation of equal quantities of white asparagus and green pea soup.

Saint-Cloud (Crème). Green pea soup garnished with green coloured diced, diamonds or rondels of royale. Croûtons passed separately.

Saint-Germain. Purée of green peas. Chopped parsley topping. Croûtons passed separately.

Saint-Hubert. Game soup with the addition of a purée of lentils. Served with croûtons.

Santé (Crème). Purée of potato, white of leek and sorrel mixed. Lié with cream and egg yolk. Garnished with shredded sorrel and chervil tossed in butter. Served with toasted rondels of bâton roll or fluted bread.

Scotch Broth. Thick version of the clear broth. Prepared as for the clear broth and passed through a sieve. Checked for seasoning and thickened with cream. Garnished with chopped parsley and chervil pluches.

Sharks Fin. Noted Chinese rich cream soup prepared from diced sharks fin. Usually 'bought in' ready made.

Soissonnaise. Purée of haricot beans with onion, lié with cream and served with croûtons.

Solférino (Potage). Purée of tomato and potato. Garnished with small nuts of cooked carrots and potatoes. Cream of Tomato often passes under this name.

Soubise (Crème). Thick onion soup. Chervil pluches topping. Check flavour, which should not be overpowering.

Sultana (Crème). Chicken and green pea soup mixed and garnished with stars and half moons in truffle.

Sultane (Crème de Volaille). Chicken velouté flavoured with an essence of almond milk.

Suzette. Cream of celery soup checked with celery salt and cayenne with the addition of fresh cream.

Sylvestra (Potage). A preparation of equal quantities of cream of chicken and cream of asparagus lié with cream and tinted green with colour compound.

Turtle Soup (thick). Prepared as for clear turtle, then thickened with a brown roux, flavoured with madeira, seasoned with salt, cayenne and lemon juice.

Vichy (Crème). Velouté of carrots lié with cream and egg yolks.

Vichyssoise (Crème). Well creamed leek and potato soup created in 1917 by Louis Diat. Originally served iced as Crème Vichyssoise Glacé. May also be featured hot. Served sprinkled with chopped chives.

Voisin (Crème). Cream of chicken garnished with peas, diced carrots, French beans, chicken meat and chervil pluches.

Waldeze (Potage). Purée of tomato lié with tapioca or fecula, grated parmesan and cream.

Washington (Crème). Purée of sweetcorn combined with a chicken velouté and finished with cream. Garnished with whole sweetcorn kernels.

Windsor (Potage). Thick brown soup. Prepared from a purée of rice enriched with calves foot jelly, thickened with cream and egg yolk and flavoured with an infusion of turtle herbs and madeira. Garnished with cubes or shredded calves foot and quenelles. For a variation, the Windsor may also be flavoured with curry powder.

There are two versions of the Windsor, one a consommé, the other the potage. Both were created by a royal chef. Charles Elmé Francatelli, while in the service of Queen Victoria. There is a basic similarity between the Turtle and the Windsor soups, both the products of Victoriana with two versions of each.

For the jelly, the calves foot is boned, blanched, infused with aromates and simmered in stock for two hours. The rice is made either from a cream of rice powder or cooked and sieved rice made up with consommé. The calves foot liquor is strained onto the rice preparation, corrected for seasoning, thickened with cream and egg yolk and heated without boiling. The calves foot itself is used for the garnish.

CONVENIENCE SOUPS

Soup in convenience form—mixes and canned products—is an expanding market. The quality of the original product is important, as is efficient handling, preparation and correct service.

Most soup mixes are reconstituted with a prescribed amount of water, which must not be exceeded. Canned soups are either in standard or concentrated form. Detailed handling instructions of convenience products are usually found on the packet or can and should be carefully followed.

Sauces

Sauces are integral to the culinary art. They represent the foundations upon which cookery is constructed. In the conventional kitchen, the sauce is the star partie or corner, and the 'Saucier' regarded as the senior Chef de Partie. Sauce work is specialized, for sauces are a vast and complex subject. Their preparation demands knowledge and skill, care and time.

Sauces are classified as basic and derivatives, butter and spiced, gravies and independent, which includes cold sauces. A close relationship exists between soups and sauces; both are liquids and the basis of most soups and a number of sauces is the stock pot.

Sweet sauces are listed in Chapter Eleven. Compound butters are included under the Sauce heading.

Allemande. Chicken velouté reduced and lié with cream and egg yolk.

Anchois (Anchovy Sauce). A dual sauce since it may be prepared from a béchamel or a velouté base.

1. Prepare an adjusted béchamel, colour and flavour with anchovy essence, check seasoning with salt, cayenne and lemon juice.

2. Prepare a fish velouté, add tomato purée to tint and flavour with a purée of anchovy fillets. Check with butter and carmine as required. (The anchovy is either rubbed through a sieve or pounded in a mortar.)

Apple Sauce. Select large, green cooking apples. Peel, halve, quarter and core. Slice finely and place in a pan with a small amount of water and a squeeze of lemon. Bring to the boil, lower heat, cover with a lid and simmer the preparation to a purée.

Aurora. Sauce suprême tinted with paprika. May also be prepared from an adjusted béchamel coloured with tomato purée, corrected for consistency and strained.

Barbecue Sauce. American spiced sauce made by adding vinegar, Worcester sauce, minced onion and brown sugar to tomato ketchup. Season with salt, paprika, cayenne, cinnamon, clove and nutmeg. Apply heat and bring slowly to boiling point. Use hot or cold.

Béarnaise. Yellow coloured and tarragon flavoured butter sauce prepared from an aromatic foundation.

Reduce chopped tarragon, shallot, a few crushed peppercorns and a little salt in vinegar. When well reduced, strain and cool. Place in another pan, add required number of egg yolks and small amount of warm water. Set pan in a bain-marie and mount with a thin trickle of melted butter. Continue whisking until the sauce attains consistency

46

of mayonnaise. Season with salt, cayenne and a touch of lemon juice. Strain through a tammy cloth, reheat, load with chopped tarragon and chervil and re-whisk. At the point of service, top the sauce with a line of meat glaze. To prevent curdling, do not overheat the sauce. The aromatic foundation may be performed with tarragon vinegar.

Béchamel. Basic white sauce prepared from a white roux and milk. Usual proportions are 500g (1 lb) flour and 500g (1 lb) fat to 4 litres (8 pints) milk. Onion is sometimes added, a whole onion stuck with cloves or sliced onion, and heated with the milk.

(Sauce named after the Marquis de Béchamel in 1700, Maître d'Hotel to King Louis XIV of France.)

Bercy. Minced shallot and onion stewed in butter and white wine and bulk made up with fish velouté, Strained, corrected for consistency and loaded with chopped chervil and parsley.

Bigarade. Sauce for duck and game preparations 'à la Bigarade', the name of a type of orange.

Reduce some mixed orange and lemon juice sweetened with sugar. Make up the sauce with demi-glace (half glaze sauce) and the pan gravy in which the parent dish, i.e. duck or game, has roasted. This entails swilling out the roasting tray with stock. Correct sauce for seasoning and consistency. Colour with carmine and finish with butter. Strain and load with blanched julienne or orange peel.

Blanquette. Basic sauce: Mix 120g (4 oz) flour with 250g (8 oz) butter and cook pale for 5 minutes. Slowly add 2¼ litres (4 pints) boiling veal stock to the roux, make up the sauce and cook for 15 minutes. Strain, add ½ litre (1 pint) cream, season with salt, cayenne, lemon juice and thicken, away from heat, with 3 well beaten egg yolks.

Bolonaise. Sauce dressing pasta.

Basic recipe: 175g (6 oz) each fillet of beef, raw liver, lean ham, 250g (8 oz) each onion and butter, 2¼ litres (4 pints) tomato purée, seasoning and veal stock.

Mince onion and stew in butter. Mince the beef, liver and ham and add to the onion. Add tomato purée, season with salt, pepper, nutmeg, clove and a bayleaf. Moisten with sufficient veal stock and braise in a covered pan in the oven until well thickened. Remove bayleaf and use as required.

A crushed garlic clove may be added to the onion. Shallot may replace the onion and sauce may also be enriched with a little dry white wine.

Bordelaise. A brown red wine sauce.

Mince several shallots, mushroom trimmings and a garlic clove and melt without coloration in butter. Add tomato purée, bone marrow, moisten with red wine, season and reduce. Make up bulk with demi-glace, check seasoning and consistency, finish with butter, strain and check for colour with carmine.

Bread Sauce. Warm some milk with a small onion stuck with cloves. Add fresh white breadcrumbs and season with salt and cayenne. Simmer very slowly and carefully until the sauce is thick and white. Remove the onion. Bread sauce may be enhanced with the addition of a small quantity of fresh cream.

Butter Sauce (Beurre Fondue). Melt required amount of butter in a pan over heat and let it clarify but *not* discolour. Skim off any foam forming on top. Season gently with salt and touch of lemon. For service with corn-on-the-cob, add a dash of mixed ground spice i.e. clove, nutmeg and cinnamon.

Câpres (Caper Sauce). Prepared with a foundation of melted butter and flour and made up with the cooking liquor from the fare the sauce will accompany, i.e. leg of mutton, fish. Check seasoning with salt, cayenne, caper juice and load with whole capers.

Chambord. Brown fish sauce. Similar to demi-glace, but prepared from a fish stock and red wine.

Chantilly (Sauce). Mayonnaise combined with half-whipped cream. Lemon juice may be used instead of vinegar in the mayonnaise.

Chasseur. Mince shallots and tiny garlic clove. Melt in butter, add sliced mushrooms, season, cover pan and stew slowly. Moisten with dry white wine, reduce and make up the bulk with demi-glace tomatée (tomato half glaze). Finish with chopped parsley and tarragon, correct seasoning and consistency.

Chaudfroid (brown). This sauce, used for cold buffet work, is prepared by combining demi-glace (flavoured with madeira and truffle essence) and aspic jelly.

Chaudfroid (white). Made by combining sauce suprême and chicken jelly. Used for cold buffet work.

Cocktail Sauces. Mayonnaise pinked with tomato ketchup, sufficient half-whipped cream for smoothness, and checked for piquancy with salt, cayenne, lemon juice, Worcester sauce or tabasco.

Flavour contrasts and derivative sauces are introduced with other agents, such as soy, anchovy and other bottled sauce condiments, mushroom ketchup, angostura bitters, onion juice, minced onion, celery or grated horse-radish, flavoured vinegars and table salts, curry, paprika or ground spices, chopped anchovy and brandy, which imparts richness.

Cranberry Sauces (Sauce aux Airelles). There are several variations of this American sauce, usually a 'bought in' preserve. A cranberry jelly is also available.

To prepare a sauce: cook together 500 g (1 lb) cranberries with 360g (12 oz) sugar in $\frac{1}{4}$ litre ($\frac{1}{2}$ pint) water for 10 minutes until the skins pop open. Cool and use as required.

Spiced Cranberry Sauce. Spice up the sauce with cloves and a cinnamon stick in a muslin bag during cooking.

Tangy Cranberry Sauce. Add 2 teaspoons of finely grated lemon peel to the spiced sauce.

These sauces are used to accompany roast turkey and roast goose.

Crème. Cream sauce prepared with béchamel adjusted with boiling milk or cream and the addition of lemon juice, and checked for seasoning. Should be very white and creamy.

Cumberland. British Fare sauce served hot or cold with game.

Reduce chopped shallot and peppercorns in vinegar. Strain into redcurrant jelly. Heat and add orange and lemon juice. Season with salt, cayenne, ground ginger, nutmeg and English mustard reconstituted in vinegar. Flavour with port.

Curry Sauce. Set minced onion, shallot and garlic clove in butter and olive oil, add curry powder and small quantity of flour and cook for 5 minutes. Add chopped apple, celery, chutney, currants, sultanas, almonds, mushrooms and grated coconut or coconut milk. Stir, heat and add tomato purée. Let preparation stew and cook. Add bouquet garni and bayleaf, and make up bulk with boiling water or stock. Bring to the boil and simmer in a closed pan for an hour or so to thicken. Strain and use as required.

Demi-glace (Half Glaze). Derivative of espagnole. Rich brown sauce prepared by reducing espagnole and estouffade in equal quantities. Reduce to a smooth consistency, correct seasoning and colour as required.

Devine. Hollandaise sauce mounted with double whipped cream.

Diable. Hot spicy sauce for grills.

Set chopped shallot, garlic clove, peppercorns, bayleaf and parsley stalks to reduce in dry white wine. When reduction has taken place, make up with demi-glace tomatée (tomato half-glaze). Reduce again and then strain. Correct with salt, cayenne and lemon juice. Check colour with carmine and brilliancy with butter. Serve very hot.

Egg Sauce. Béchamel sauce adjusted with boiling milk loaded with cubed or sieved hard-boiled eggs. Season with salt and cayenne. Chopped parsley optional.

May also be prepared from a velouté base.

Espagnole. Basic brown sauce prepared from a brown roux and brown stock or estouffade.

Estouffade. A clear brown stock.

Génévoise. Red wine sauce for salmon. Prepared with a mirepoix, bouquet garni, and the chopped head and bones of the fish. Sweat in butter, add red wine, fish stock and espagnole and reduce. Pass through a sieve and correct with butter, seasoning and anchovy essence.

Grand Veneur. Brown game sauce made up with poivrade and demi-glace sauces with the addition of the marinade in which the meat concerned was marinated, redcurrant jelly, cream and pitted raisins.

Gravy (Jus de Rôti. Pan Gravy). Short gravy prepared from the natural juices which escape from roasts during the cooking process. Surplus fat is removed and the roasting tray swilled out (déglacer) with stock to dissolve the juices which adhere to the pan, allowing some reduction over heat. Gravy should be well cleared of fat. Colour may be checked with gravy browning (Black Jack).

Guérèbich Dressing. Load mayonnaise with sieved egg, chopped fines herbes, minced capers and gherkins and thin with tarragon vinegar.

Hollandaise. Basic butter sauce prepared from an aromatic foundation.

Reduce chopped chervil and shallot, peppercorns, parsley stalks, bayleaf and a little salt in vinegar. When well reduced, strain and cool. Place in another pan, add required number of egg yolks and small amount of warm water. Set pan in a bain-marie, whisk thoroughly until the egg yolks have doubled in quantity but do not overheat. Mount the sauce by adding a thin trickle of melted butter, whisking briskly until the sauce attains the consistency of mayonnaise. Season with salt, cayenne and lemon juice. Strain through a tammy cloth, whisk well and reheat in the bain-marie.

Horse-radish Sauce (Sauce Raifort). Select firm roots, wash, scrape, shave or grate finely. Load horse-radish into whipped double cream. Season with salt, cayenne, sugar, lemon juice and English mustard reconstituted in vinegar.
Another method: make up some English mustard with vinegar, work to a smooth paste and load with grated horse-radish. Season and combine with half-whipped double cream.

This sauce is featured hot or cold.

Italienne. Demi-glace with the addition of white wine, ham and tomato purée, chopped mushrooms and fines herbes. Or demi-glace with tomato purée added and loaded with chopped ham, mushrooms and fines herbes.

Ivoire (Ivory Sauce). A sauce suprême or cream sauce touched with meat glaze—glace de viande—to acquire the hue of ivory. Flavour with a little sherry.

Joinville. Fish velouté, corrected with cream and loaded with diced shrimps. Check colour with anchovy essence.

Jus Lié. Pan gravy or veal stock thickened with arrowroot or fecula. Colour and seasoning checked as required. Much use is now made of the jus lié in the kitchen.

Languipière. Sauce vin blanc with addition of fish glaze (prepared similarly to meat glaze).

Lobster. Fish velouté with the addition of lobster butter garnished with a dice of cooked lobster.

Lyonnaise. Demi-glace loaded with shredded onion stewed in butter and a reduction of vinegar, and flavoured with white wine.

Madère (Madeira Sauce). Derivative of espagnole. A demi-glace flavoured with madeira.

Maryland. Ivory sauce flavoured with brandy. Accompanies dishes 'à la maryland'.

Mayonnaise. Proportions are 2 egg yolks per ½ litre (1 pint) olive oil and 70ml (¼ gill) vinegar. Beat yolks in a clean bowl and mount with thin trickle of olive oil. As the sauce thickens so it is broken down with a little vinegar. Finish with the rest of the oil and the vinegar. The sauce should be fairly thick. Season with salt, cayenne and dash of English mustard powder.

Mint Sauce. Select fresh mint and remove stalks. Place leaves on a wooden board and sprinkle with brown sugar. Chop and place in a bowl. Add vinegar, mix and stand for 30 minutes before use. (French chefs favour the use of boiling vinegar.)
Lemon Mint Sauce. Replace vinegar with lemon juice.
   Mint jelly is available ready prepared.

Mornay. Popular white sauce, derivative of béchamel. Béchamel sauce loaded with grated cheese and checked for seasoning with salt, cayenne, lemon juice and a dash of Worcester sauce.

   Parmesan, the culinary cheese, is always indicated. May be used in conjunction and in equal quantities with gruyère.

Mousseline. Butter sauce resembling hot version of a light mayonnaise.

   Whisk the required number of egg yolks with a small amount of hot water in a pan resting in a bain-marie. Mount the sauce, over heat, with a thin trickle of melted butter, whisking briskly until the sauce thickens and resembles a mayonnaise. Season with salt, cayenne and a touch of lemon juice, and add a small quantity of stiffly whipped cream. Should be light, soft, creamy and golden yellow.

Mushroom Sauce. Sliced mushrooms, salted and stewed in butter in closed pan, or button mushrooms cooked in butter, lemon juice, salt and a minimal amount of water. Load cooked mushrooms and their reduced cooking liquor into a béchamel or velouté sauce. Check with salt, cayenne and lemon juice.

Mustard Sauce. Thinned béchamel to which English mustard reconstituted with vinegar, or French mustard, is added. Check with salt and cayenne.

51

Also prepared with a mousseline or hollandaise sauce to which vinegar-reconstituted English mustard or French mustard is added to taste. Heat, whisk and check for flavour.

Normande. Fish sauce prepared from an adjusted fish velouté with butter, lemon juice, mushroom reduction, cream and egg yolk.

Onion Sauce. Finely slice Spanish onions, blanch and set to melt without coloration in butter. Add to an adjusted béchamel, finish with butter, salt and cayenne.

Orange. Madeira sauce with orange juice and zest. Garnished with a julienne of blanched orange peel. Flavoured as required with curaçao.

Orly. Tomato sauce with the addition of melted butter.

Paprika Sauce. Stew minced onion and shallot in butter and olive oil. Stir in paprika and cook. Moisten with stock and thicken with velouté. Strain and correct with cream, lemon juice, salt and cayenne.

Parsley Sauce. Adjusted béchamel loaded with chopped parsley. After chopping, squeeze the parsley in a cloth and hold under running cold water to extract excess green colouring so that it won't tint the sauce.

Peach. Sweet sauce for service with baked ham. Blanch and skin 6 peaches, remove stones and set to stew with a little water, the juice of 2 lemons and oranges, sugar, ground ginger and a glass of port. Stew till tender.
Madeira Peach Sauce. Prepared as above with the addition of madeira.

Périgourdine. There are two versions of this richest of all sauces, a white and a brown.
White périgourdine is prepared from a velouté broken down with cream. It is reduced, strained and loaded with a fine purée of foie gras. When cooked, chopped truffle is added. The sauce is corrected with salt, cayenne and lemon juice and flavoured with brandy or dry sherry.
The brown périgourdine is a sauce madère loaded with purée of foie gras and chopped truffles.

Périgueux. Demi-glace flavoured with madeira and truffle essence and garnished with chopped truffles.

Pickled Peach Sauce. Peel, halve and stone peaches. Place in a pan and sprinkle with mixed spice and sugar. Cover with vinegar. Bring to boil and simmer for 5 minutes. Pick out peaches, place in another pan, strain cooking liquor onto them and reheat.

Piquante. Spiced, hot sauce. Reduce chopped shallot, gherkin, capers, garlic clove, bayleaf, parsley stalks and crushed peppercorns in vinegar. Continue until strong reduction is obtained. Flavour with lemon juice and dry white wine. Reduce again and then make up bulk with demi-glace tomatée. Strain and check for flavour, consistency and colour.

Poivrade. Similar to piquante, but with plenty of peppercorns and with red wine added to the spiced vinegar reduction.

Princière. Shrimp sauce with a salpicon of truffle and diced shrimps. May be applied to crayfish or scampi.

Provençale. Stewed chopped onions in olive oil. Add tomato concassé, crushed garlic clove and seasoning and stew together. Add white wine and reduce. Finish with chopped fines herbes.

Ravigotte. Mayonnaise seasoned with English mustard and loaded with chopped chive, onion, gherkin, capers and fines herbes.

A hot version consists of a chicken velouté prepared with an aromatical reduction of white wine and vinegar with tarragon, shallots and fines herbes. The sauce is then mounted and smoothed with butter.

Réforme. Add redcurrant jelly to sauce diable. Season with salt, cayenne, nutmeg and lemon juice. Heat and strain. Load with a julienne of gherkins, hard-boiled egg white, ham, tongue, mushroom and truffle in equal quantities.

(Famous Alexis Soyer creation for Côtelettes à la Réforme.)

Rémoulade. Mayonnaise well seasoned with cayenne, mustard and anchovy essence and loaded with chopped gherkins, capers and fines herbes.

Riche. Red tinted sauce made from fish velouté, lobster butter, cream and a salpicon of lobster meat and truffle cut in small dice.

Robert. Spiced sauce. Melt chopped onion and shallot in butter. Make up with demi-glace. Check seasoning with salt, cayenne, vinegar and sugar. Flavour with white wine. Reduce, strain, check again with mustard.

Rouennaise. Bordelaise sauce with the addition of a fine purée of duck's livers.

Rouge. Mayonnaise tinted with beet juice or carmine.

Salmis. Game sauce. Prepared with a mirepoix of carrot, onion and chopped cooked game trimmings (carcasses) sauté together in fat and coloured. Preparation is moistened with white wine and reduced, bulk is made up with demi-glace and game stock, cooked for an hour or so, strained and corrected for seasoning, consistency and appearance.

Smitane. Noted Russian sauce. Stewed minced shallot and mushroom parings in butter. Make up with fresh cream and reduce. Sour with lemon juice, correct with salt and cayenne and strain.

May also be prepared with velouté base.

For certain dishes, the smitane is loaded with sliced mushrooms previously salted and stewed slowly in butter in a closed pan.

Soubise. Béchamel sauce with onion purée added, strained and corrected with butter and cream.

Suprême. Well known white sauce, derivative of velouté.

Break down velouté with cream and reduce. Strain and correct seasoning with salt, cayenne and lemon juice, butter for gloss and lightly flavour with dry sherry or brandy. Should be rich, white and glossy.

Tartare. Mayonnaise loaded with chopped gherkins, capers and fines herbes.

Thousand Island Dressing. Mince 1 red pimento, 1 green pepper, 1 celery and add small amount of chili sauce. Blend together with mayonnaise. Check seasoning with salt, cayenne, lemon juice, Worcester sauce or tabasco.

Tomato (Sauce Tomate). Basic sauce prepared from a mirepoix, butter, flour, tomatoes, seasoning and brown stock. The mirepoix is fried in butter, dredged with flour, and worked for 5 minutes. Fresh chopped tomatoes or tomato purée is added and the preparation moistened with brown stock. It is cooked slowly and then strained and corrected for seasoning with salt, cayenne and sugar, for consistency with butter and for colour with compound.

Tomato Béarnaise. Béarnaise sauce coloured and flavoured with the addition of reduced purée.

Tortue. Brown sauce prepared with demi-glace tomatée and an infusion of turtle herbs, madeira and truffle essence. The preparation is strained and corrected with salt, cayenne and lemon juice.

Velouté. Basic white sauce prepared from a blonde roux and white veal stock. The standard white velouté is prepared from veal stock; a fish velouté is prepared from a fish stock.

Vénitienne. Green coloured sauce made with a fresh velouté, white wine and a reduction of chopped fines herbes and spinach leaves in tarragon vinegar.

Verte (Sauce). Mayonnaise coloured green with fresh spinach, parsley juice or vegetable colour compound.

Vin Blanc. White wine sauce for fish preparations. Made from a velouté prepared from a blonde roux made up into a sauce with clear fish stock. It is corrected, strained, flavoured with dry white wine and finished with butter.

For a richer Vin Blanc, and one for glazing, beaten egg yolks are added and the sauce heated without being allowed to boil. Seasoning is checked with salt, cayenne and lemon juice.

Vin Rouge. Same as bordelaise without the bone marrow.

Vinaigrette—French Dressing. Basic salad dressing. Usual proportions of oil and vinegar are three to one.

Mix 3 tablespoons olive oil with 1 tablespoon vinegar. Season with salt, freshly ground peppercorns and a small amount of English mustard made up with vinegar. Chopped parsley, tarragon and chervil may be added if wished.

The best oil is olive oil which comes from France and Italy in bottle and metal containers, though the many nut oils may be used. Malt is the standard vinegar, but there are also red and white wine vinegars and others flavoured with herbs.

To the standard Vinaigrette there are a number of derivatives:

Lemon Dressing. Substitute the vinegar for lemon juice.

Cream Dressing. Half-whipped cream with added olive oil and lemon juice. Season with salt, cayenne and a dash of sugar.

Tomato Dressing. Dilute vinaigrette with tomato ketchup.

Blue Cheese Dressing. Mash a portion of gorgonzola, roquefort, stilton or other blue cheese with a fork and add sufficient vinaigrette to form a smooth sauce.

Parmesan Dressing. Vinaigrette with addition of grated parmesan.

Egg Dressing. Beat raw egg into vinaigrette. Or load vinaigrette with sieved hard-boiled egg white and yolk.

Minted Dressing. Chopped fresh mint added to vinaigrette.

Other ingredients may be added to French dressings, such as Worcester sauce, minced onion, chopped capers and gherkins, various Continental mustards, spices, tabasco, angostura bitters and spices.

Worcester Sauce. Traditional highly flavoured British Fare sauce. Usually purchased manufactured under a proprietary label.

Made by boiling mushroom, shallot and garlic in vinegar spiced with capsicum, cardamon, clove, cinnamon and nutmeg for 30 minutes. The preparation is strained, checked and matured for 30 days.

Zingara. Madeira sauce with tomato purée and loaded with a julienne of ham, tongue, mushroom and truffle.

CONVENIENCE SAUCES

The key points with all these types of supplies are the quality of the original product and the correction of the made-up commodity for service. Much progress is apparent in stocks and aspics in mix and granular form reconstituted with the addition of the prescribed quantity of water. Such sauce mixes as parsley, mushroom, onion, cheese (mornay), béchamel and bread are made up with milk. Sauces may also be made from canned soup and soup mixes. Canned and otherwise packed espagnole, demi-glace, chasseur, curry and others are often in concentrated form and are made up with stock or water as indicated and then corrected.

COMPOUND BUTTERS

Anchovy. Butter worked to a smooth paste, coloured and flavoured with a purée of anchovy fillets or with anchovy essence. Check with salt, pepper and lemon juice as required. Load with chopped parsley.

Colbert. Anchovy butter with glace de viande.

Curry. Butter worked to a smooth paste and coloured and flavoured with curry powder. Check with lemon juice.

Horse-radish. Softened butter with the addition of freshly grated horse-radish. Check with salt and lemon juice.

Lobster. Pound the shell, coral, eggs and intestines in a mortar. Combine with an equal quantity of butter. Pass through a tammy cloth.

Great care must be taken to pound the shell finely, which has been well and slowly dried in the oven.

Similar preparation is made with crayfish.

Maître d'Hotel. Butter worked to a pomade, seasoned with salt, pepper and lemon juice and loaded with chopped parsley. Shape in individual servings or arrange in a sauceboat and harden on ice. Also known as parsley and steakhouse butter.

Manié. More of a kitchen term than a compound butter, but a preparation of butter mixed with flour used to thicken sauces.

Noir (Black butter). Heat until dark brown, blacken with vinegar and season with salt and pepper. Load with capers.

Noisette. Butter cooked until brown then seasoned with salt, pepper and lemon juice. Employed in the finishing of dishes.

Tarragon. Butter with the addition of a purée of tarragon leaves.

Tomato. Butter worked to a smooth paste and coloured and flavoured with concassed or purée of tomato. Check seasoning and load with chopped parsley.

Fish

Bream (Brème)
Round fish, from both sea and fresh water or river. The sea bream, pink in colour, is considered better than its fresh water relative. Can be cooked à la meunière, deep fried or poached with sauces.

Brill (Barbue)
Flat sea fish similar to a small turbot, can be prepared in any of the same ways.

Dugléré. The fillets are baked in the oven with white wine, chopped shallot, tomatoes, butter, fines herbes, seasoning and moistened with fish stock. Served masked with the cooking preparation thickened with beurre manié.

Saint-Germain. Same method as Sole.

Carp (Carpe)
Flat dull coloured fresh water fish. Early recipes indicated the stuffing and baking of carp in much the same way as mutton.

Bleu (au). Poached in a court bouillon for 40 minutes, served with boiled potatoes and accompanied by hollandaise sauce or melted butter. If served cold, escorted by horse-radish or tartare sauce.

Choucroute (à la). Braised whole carp dressed on a bed of sauerkraut and masked with its cooking liquor, well reduced.

Juive (à la). Poached whole in a court bouillon with added white wine, removed and placed to cool on the serving dish. The cooking liquor is well reduced, strained, loaded with glazed button onions and masked over the fish in the manner of aspic. Served cold with horse-radish sauce.

Clams
American bi-valve shellfish with an interesting flavour. Used in chowders, eaten raw like oysters and made into various preparations. Imported live in shell, shelled and canned, or frozen.

Clam Cakes. Prepare a stiff batter with 3 or 4 eggs beaten in $\frac{1}{2}$ litre (1 pint) of milk, thickened with flour and seasoned with salt, cayenne and a pinch of ground nutmeg. Load the preparation with shelled cooked clams, shape into small cakes and shallow fry in butter. Serve with tomato sauce and lemon wedges.

Fried (Frites). The clams are poached in a light court bouillon for about 3 minutes, shelled, dipped in batter or breaded, and deep fried in olive oil. They are then drained, seasoned, replaced in the warmed half shells and served with tartare sauce.

Steamed. Steam the clams in a double pan over a court bouillon until cooked. Serve with lemon wedges and brown bread and butter.

Clams are featured à la meunière, curried, with rice in a sauce suprême and in other ways.

Cockles (Coques)
Ridger bi-valve shellfish treated as for clams or mussels. Cockles and winkles are popular seaside fare sold from carts and stalls.

Cod (Cabillaud)
Baked (à l'Anglaise). Fillet of cod painted with melted butter, coated in breadcrumbs and baked in the oven. Served with caper sauce.

Florentine. As for au gratin but with the flaked cod resting on a bed of cooked leaf spinach, seasoned and tossed in butter.

Fried. Cod fillet breadcrumbed or battered and deep fat fried. Serve with tartare, tomato or béarnaise sauce.

Gratin (au). Arrange flaked poached cod in a buttered dish and pipe with a border of duchesse potato. Mask with mornay sauce, sprinkle with grated cheese and glaze to a golden brown in a hot oven or under a grill.

Orly. Cod fillet coated in batter, deep fried and served with tomato or orly sauce.

Poached. Cod steak or fillet poached for 15 to 20 minutes in a court bouillon. Serve masked with egg or parsley sauce accompanied by whipped potatoes.

Salt Cod. The French Morue, widely known before the advent of the freezer. To prepare: remove the salt by prolonged soaking in water. The fish may then be used for any of the dishes for fresh cod.

Crab
Crabs, like lobsters, are purchased by weight rather than size. The smaller the crab the sweeter the meat. They are bought ready cooked or live and poached at 20 minutes to the ½ kilo (1 lb) in a light court bouillon. The whole contents are edible once the poisonous gills, or dead man's fingers, are removed.

Crab and Corn Fritters. Blend the soft crab meat with that from the claws and combine with an equal quantity of creamed sweetcorn. Mix well, season with salt, cayenne and a touch of Worcester sauce. Bind with cream and beaten egg yolk. Roll in flour to shape into balls or cylinders. Fry in deep fat to a golden brown, drain, dress with fried parsley and serve with tomato sauce.

Crabmeat à la King. White meat from the claws, separated, cleared of bone splinters, heated in cream and seasoned with salt and cayenne. It is then combined with egg yolk beaten in cream and brandy, sliced or diced green or red pimento, and heated without boiling. It is served piled upon thick buttered toast or with a pilaff of rice.

Crawfish (Langouste)

Large spidery type of lobster. Its flesh is sweetish in flavour. It is mainly used in exhibition work for the cold table.

The fish is poached and the body meat removed in one piece. It is sliced in thick rondels, masked in chaudfroid, decorated, aspic glazed and arranged on the back of the shell, which has been painted and glazed with a concentrated aspic solution. The whole piece is set on a socle or a large croûton and lavishly garnished with egg, tomato, cucumber, mushroom and divers salad materials.

The glazing of shell fish for cold is performed with an écarlate, made by colouring a well concentrated aspic solution with red compound. This preparation is also used as a gum to fix the rondels of decorated meat and other garnishings onto the shell.

Crawfish is also used in salads and mayonnaise.

By way of hot dishes, diced or collops of cooked crawfish are lié with various fish sauces, i.e. américaine, nantua, vin blanc, and served with rice pilaff.

Crawfish Tails. Small tails imported frozen from the Carribbean are thawed, the under shell removed, the meat scored into chunks, seasoned, painted with butter and grilled in the shell. Served with grilled mushrooms, bacon, tomato and maître d'hôtel butter or sauce diable.

Crayfish (Écrevisses)

A small fresh water lobster highly prized for its exquisite flavour. Crayfish, rare in Britain, should not be confused with the large spiny type of lobster known as crawfish or with the scampi which is a sea water prawn. They must always be handled alive and are kept, like trout, in a tank to be cooked as and when required. They require skilful handling at all times.

Crayfish are usually served whole at 4 or 6 to the portion. They may be shelled, in which case 8–12 will be served. The former method is preferred since it conserves to the last the tasty part at the top of the tail which adheres to the main body. The fish are boiled from their live state immediately after they have been eviscerated—the gut or intestine, which runs through the body, removed. This is done by seeking out the centre tail fin and, with the aid of a cloth or the point of a knife and thumb, giving a gentle tug. The gut should come away whole. Like the lobster, the écrevisse turns from black to red when cooked.

Américaine (à la). For four covers, toss 16 écrevisses in a deep pan with 175g (6 oz) clarified butter for 3 minutes. Add 4 shallots, a carrot and half a leek, all well chopped. Cook for another 3 minutes. Add half a glass of brandy, one of white wine, 500g (1 lb) chopped fresh tomatoes, a teaspoon chopped tarragon, a bouquet garni and season with salt and pepper. Cook slowly with the lid on for 8 minutes. Take out the écrevisses, remove tail shells, dress in a serving dish and strain the prepared sauce over them. Serve with a pilaff of rice.

Crème (à la). For four covers set 16 écrevisses in a deep pan and cook for 5 minutes in 175g (6 oz) clarified butter until the shells turn red. Remove from the pan and keep hot. Swill out the pan with half a glass of brandy, add a glass of dry white wine and 0·45 litre (¾ pint) cream. Simmer sauce for 6 minutes and season with salt and cayenne. Replace écrevisses, with their tail shells removed, heat and serve.

Nage (à la). Preparation which is served hot with melted butter or cold with a light mayonnaise.

The écrevisses are plunged into a boiling court bouillon and simmered for 12 minutes with the lid on. When cooked, and to facilitate eating, carefully crack and remove the shell covering the tails, but keep the cooked meat retained in the body of the fish. Serve with brown bread and butter.

Note: Let the écrevisses cool in their cooking liquor for cold service.

Nantua. Cook the required number of prepared écrevisses in a court bouillon, cool slightly in their liquor, then remove tails and keep hot. Dry the shells slowly in an oven and pound to a fine powder in a mortar. Mix this powder with twice the quantity of butter and cook slowly together. Moisten with equal amounts of dry white wine and the well reduced and strained cooking liquor. Simmer and strain through a tammy cloth. Reheat the sauce and bind with cream. Add the écrevisses' tails to the sauce, heat carefully and dish up. Serve with a pilaff of rice.

Pilaff for Écrevisses Preparations. Chop a small to medium sized onion and set to stew in butter. Season with salt and pepper mill. Stir in the rice, strain in some court bouillon to the proportion of three times the quantity of rice (3 of liquid to 1 of rice), cover with greaseproof paper and cook in the oven for about 20 minutes.

Parisienne (à la). A cold preparation. Cook and cool the fish in a court bouillon. Remove tail shells, dress on a foundation of Russian salad and decorate with fonds d'artichauts and hard-boiled egg quarters set and masked in aspic. Serve with mayonnaise and a lemon dressed plain lettuce salad.

Dog Fish. See Rock Salmon.

Eel (Anguille)

Fried (Frites). Fillets of eel breadcrumbed, deep fried and served with lemon wedges and tomato sauce.

Eel Pie. Cleaned, cut into 5cm (2 in) lengths, placed in a pie dish with seasoning, mixed herbs, butter, a few currants, suitably moistened with fish stock, covered with suet pastry and baked for about 40 minutes.

Traditional British Fare—one-time speciality of Eel Pie Island on the Thames.)

Jellied. Well known preparation. The fish is skinned and cleaned, the head removed and the body cut into 5cm (2 in) pieces. The eel is simmered in a court bouillon to which a little white wine is added. When cooked, pick out and remove the centre bone. Set the pieces in a bowl and mask with the well reduced and strained cooking liquor loaded with cooked button onions, fancy cut carrot and chopped parsley. The preparation should set in a clear and limpid jelly.

Fish Roe

During the spawning season two kinds of roe are found, according to the sex of the fish: the eggs of the female, hard roe or oeuf de poisson; the sperm of the male, soft roe or laitance.

All roe is prized for eating: caviar from the *Acipenserides* family, of which the sturgeon is a member; keta, a red caviar from salmon; boutarque from the mullet; and others, including cod's roe, which is smoked.

As a garniture to fish dishes the soft roe of the herring is usually selected. It is sold fresh, frozen or canned and must be well washed prior to use and checked for freshness as it is very perishable.

Roe, i.e. laitance, is either shallow fried, meunière or poached.

Matelot (en). Small tronçons of eel cooked in red wine, fish stock and aromates. The sauce is thickened with beurre danié, lemon juice added, and the preparation garnished with button onions and mushrooms and heart-shaped croûtons. One per serving.

Meunière. Wash, pass in milk, season, flour and sauté in butter. Finish with noisette butter, lemon juice and chopped parsley.

Mornay. Wash, poach in milk with butter, lemon juice and seasoning, drain, line in a buttered dish, mask with mornay sauce and glaze.

Frogs (Grenouilles)

As with escargots, a special type is reared for the table. This is the green frog taken from safe waters. Frogs are eaten in France and enjoyed by French communities everywhere. They are also known in the Southern States of America where frogs are plentiful and where they were originally introduced as food by the early French settlers.

Only the back legs are eaten. They are detached from the body, skinned, the flippers removed, dressed on sticks or skewers and well soaked in fresh cold water.

Frogs legs are featured meunière, or poached and masked in delicate sauces of cream, white wine and other ingredients. The usual service consists of 6 legs to the portion.

Prepared frogs legs are also imported in cans from France.

Crème (Cuisses de Grenouilles à la). The legs are seasoned and stewed in butter, placed in a fireproof dish and masked with cream to which is added a little dry white wine. The preparation is covered and heated.

Fines Herbes. The legs are seasoned, sauté in butter and finished with chopped parsley and lemon juice.

Fried (Frites). The legs are seasoned, floured, breaded or battered, deep fried in olive oil and served with lemon.

Meunière (Cuisses de Grenouilles à la). Season, flour, sauté in butter and finish with noisette butter, lemon juice and chopped parsley.

Nymphes à l'Aurore. Escoffier creation which consists of poaching the legs in white wine and serving them cold masked with a chaudfroid sauce tinged with paprika. Another preparation by this great chef featured the cooked legs caught in a light aspic jelly flavoured with Champagne or Moselle wine.

There is a cream soup Velouté des Nymphes which François Latry once featured at the Savoy Hotel for a Réunion des Gastronomes banquet in the thirties. The culinary term 'nymphes' is adopted to indicate frogs legs like escargots for snails; the terms help to make this unusual fare more acceptable.

Poulette. Poached in white wine and mushroom parings, dressed in a sauce poulette and sprinkled with chopped parsley.

The sauce consists of a béchamel incorporating the strained liquor in which the legs are cooked.

Gurnet (Grondin)

Deep sea fish with a long body, small feet like fins and off red in colour. May be poached or fried and is also used in bouillabaisse.

Haddock (Aiglefin)

Sea water fish best known smoked. Fresh haddock with its white and flaky texture and clean taste is very acceptable and may be prepared as for all dishes, i.e. deep or shallow fried, or poached with sauces.

Haddock is distinguished by a fingerprint on each side of the neck just below the head. Culinary lore tells that Jesus Christ, the companion of fisherfolk, on one occasion picked a haddock out of the sea, leaving upon it His imprint. These tell-tale prints are found only on one other fish, the John Dory (Saint Pierre). The dabs on this species are said to be those of St Peter.

Smoked Haddock. Traditional breakfast dish, but also popular as a supper dish. One whole or half a large fish goes to the portion. Also sold in smoked fillets. Smoked haddock is poached in water with milk and a piece of butter added.

Crème (à la). Poach haddock for 5 minutes with few slices of onion in a fireproof dish. Drain, remove onion, pour in fresh cream and a piece of butter. Season with a few turns of pepper mill. Bake for up to 6 minutes in a hot oven.

Colbert. Poached haddock topped with a poached egg. Proceed as for à la crème, adding poached egg.

Haddock and Bacon. Poached haddock garnished with crispy grilled streaky bacon rashers. (Duke of Windsor's favourite breakfast dish.)

Monte Carlo. Poach haddock for 5 minutes then place in fireproof dish on a bed of concassed tomato. Add cream or milk butter and season with freshly ground pepper. Bake in hot oven for 5 or 6 minutes until brown topping forms. (Escoffier creation.)

Scotch Haddock. Set a few slices of well blanched onion in a fireproof dish with some thin rondels of potato. Season with salt and pepper. Place portion smoked haddock on top. Cover with half milk and half water and simmer in slow oven until cooked.

Soufflé. Purée of cooked smoked haddock combined with butter, flour and milk to form a thick soufflé preparation. Egg yolk is added and stiffly whipped egg whites then folded in. Preparation is half filled into a buttered soufflé dish, baked in a hot oven for 20 to 30 minutes and served immediately.

Hake (Merluche)
Sea fish with delicate flavour and texture. Superior variety of cod, prepared in the same ways.

Halibut (Flétan)
Large flat fish similar in most respects to turbot. All preparations as for turbot apply to halibut.

Clamart (Medallion of Halibut). Poach 250g (8 oz) fillet in court bouillon, arrange on a foundation of well creamed and seasoned purée of peas in a dish piped with duchesse potato. Mask with mornay sauce, sprinkle with grated cheese and glaze to a golden brown in the oven.

Herring (Hareng)
Fine flavoured sea fish landed in great numbers and subjected to many processes. It can be smoked when it becomes a *bloater*, or salt cured and smoked when it is known as a *kipper*. Bloaters and kippers are best grilled after a light brushing with olive oil or melted butter.

Herrings are canned and bottled in sauce, pickled and brined in a multiude of ways.

Grilled Herring. Scale, clean, remove gills and wash. Make some incisions on the body, dip in milk, roll in flour, season and grill on both sides. Serve with mustard sauce.

Meunière. Prepare fish, coat in flour, season and shallow fry in half butter and half olive oil. Finish with noisette butter, lemon juice and chopped parsley. Garnish with wafer thin lemon rondels.

Scotch Style. Clean, split and open out. Season, pass in flour, beaten egg and olive oil and coat well with oatmeal or rolled oats. French fry to a crisp golden brown and serve with lemon wedges and tomato sauce.

John Dory (Poisson de Saint-Pierre)
Ugly looking flat sea fish with a large head, but the flesh is white, firm and excellent—comparable to sole or turbot. The fillets may be prepared in any of the ways indicated for these prime fish.

Lamprey (Lamproie)
Similar type of fish to the eel and prepared identically.

Lobster (Homard)
Lobster is judged for quality by weight rather than size. The smaller and heavier are better than the large crustacean which, in relation to size, is light. The ¾ kilo (1½ lb) lobster is considered the ideal weight.

Lobster is cooked by simmering in a light court bouillon for 15 to 20 minutes to the ½ kilo (1 lb) and cooled in the cooking liquor. When cooked the black shell turns a bright red. The hen, with its broader tail, is considered better in flavour to the cock.

Américaine (à l'). This dish should be prepared from a live hen lobster, complete with eggs or spawn carried on the under belly. It is illegal in British waters to land lobster in spawn, a point which must be mentioned though the genuine recipe is given.

Remove the eggs from the live hen, quickly amputate the claws and limbs, sever the body from the tail and split each portion in half. Keep the two head tips for decorating.

Place the eggs in a bowl with the intestines and coral—a black substance—of the lobster. Place all the pieces of the cut lobster to sauté in hot olive oil and season with salt and pepper. As the flesh begins to stiffen, add 4 chopped tomatoes and 2 or 3 minced shallots, toss together, add dry white wine, moisten with fish stock and check seasoning. When the meat is cooked and the shell pieces have turned red, pick out. Keep the claws whole, but discard all the shells. Arrange the meat on a serving dish and keep hot as the sauce is prepared.

Set the contents of the pan in which the meat is cooked to reduce, strain if required, add the masked eggs, intestines and coral which will colour the preparation. Let the sauce form, check seasoning and consistency as required with butter. Just flavour with brandy. Sauce over the lobster meat, garnish with the head tips and serve with a pilaff of rice.

Note: some recipes prescribe flaming the stiffened meat with brandy prior to adding the white wine and stock. Heart-shaped croûtons of fried bread, to indicate the number of portions, are also prescribed.

This classic dish may be prepared from cooked lobster served masked with a sauce américaine, but it is in no way as effective as the dish prepared in the traditional manner.

Cardinal. The lobster is cooked, halved, the meat removed, sliced in collops and arranged back in the lightly buttered half shell with a salpicon of lobster, mushroom and truffle. The preparation is masked with a mornay sauce pinked with tomato purée and glazed. In recent times the salpicon is often omitted and the preparation just glazed with the mornay sauce with the addition of tomato purée. The original recipe suggested colouring the sauce with lobster butter.

Cold Lobster. Half a lobster and one claw is the average portion. The lobster is split through by placing the point of a knife in the centre portion where the tail joins the main body and by cutting down in each direction. The bag in the head and the gut which runs through the length of the body are removed. The head is filled with a few capers and the lobster dressed with lettuce and tomato and hard-boiled egg halves. The claws are cracked so the meat inside may be removed. Mayonnaise is served separately.

Croquettes of Lobster. Similar preparation as for cutlets, but barrel (croquette) shaped, breaded and deep fried.

Curry. Cooked lobster meat cut in large dice or sliced collops in curry sauce, served with boiled rice and mango chutney.

Cutlets of Lobster (Côtelettes d'Homard). Chopped lobster meat with mushrooms and truffle lié in a reduced fish velouté bound with egg yolks, pinked with lobster butter (or tomato purée), shaped in cutlets, breaded and deep fried. Dressed with fried bouquet of parsley and served with mayonnaise.

Delmonico. The lobster is cooked, halved, the meat removed, sliced in collops and arranged back in the lightly buttered half shell with alternating truffle blades and salpicon of shrimps, truffle and mushrooms. The preparation is masked with américaine sauce, glazed and served with rice pilaff and grilled tomatoes.

Grilled (Grillé). Live lobster cut down through the centre, seasoned, oiled and grilled. Served with melted butter or sauce diable.

Mornay. The lobster is cooked, halved, the meat removed, sliced in collops and arranged back in the lightly buttered half shell. It is masked with mornay sauce, sprinkled with grated cheese and glazed to a golden brown in a hot oven.

The original recipes prescribed the addition of a salpicon of lobster, mushroom and truffle.

Newburg. Similar to the américaine and first featured at Delmonico's in New York from the recipe of a regular client, a certain **Dr Newburg.**

Proceed as for américaine from a live loster; if a hen, the eggs and coral are used with the intestines, if a cock, just the intestines are used.

Amputate the claws and limbs, split the body in half then quarter and set to sauté in olive oil. Season. Flame in brandy, add 4 quartered tomatoes and chopped shallots, some dry white wine and moisten with fish stock.

When cooked, pick out the meat and place in a dish, throw away the shells. Strain the cooking liquor, set it to reduce and colour and thicken with the eggs, coral and intestines. Correct with butter if required, season with salt, cayenne and lemon juice, and flavour with brandy. Prepare a pilaff of rice and line a buttered savarin mould with the preparation. Turn out, arrange the lobster meat in the centre of the mould and top with the whole claws. Mask the meat with the américaine sauce and indicate the number of portions with truffle blades.

Note: the original preparation indicated diced truffle with the sauced lobster. This preparation can also be prepared from cooked lobster meat, masked with the sauce américaine and served with a pilaff of rice.

Soufflé. The raw flesh is worked with the white of an egg, seasoned and combined with half-whipped cream. The colour is checked and the preparation topped with truffle blades, baked in the oven in a soufflé dish. It is usually garnished with lobster claws and masked with sauce américaine.

Thermidor. One or two halves go to the portion. The lobster is cooked, split in half and the meat removed from the body and claws. The half shells are brushed with melted butter, the body meat sliced in collops, arranged back in the shells and topped with a whole shelled lobster claw. The preparation is masked with a mornay sauce which incorporates English mustard reconstituted in vinegar, cayenne and lemon juice. The preparation is sprinkled with grated cheese and glazed to a golden brown in a hot oven. It is usual to place a truffle blade upon each half shell prior to glazing.

The term thermidor indicates a sauce which is hot and piquante.

Mackerel (Maquereau)

Sea water fish almost as well known as herring. Usually grilled or shallow fried à la meunière. Care must always be taken with mackerel to ensure fish is perfectly fresh.

Mullet (Rouget)

There are two species of mullet, the grey and the red. Red mullet is better known and highly prized. It comes from the Mediterranean and is known as the quail of the sea. One of the very few fish which are not emptied; the entrails are left intact and only the gills removed.

Baked. Remove gills, carefully scale and place in buttered fireproof dish. Season with salt, pepper and lemon juice. Dot with butter and bake in a slow oven. Finish with noisette butter and chopped parsley.

Baron Brisse. Grilled and garnished with noisette potatoes and beurre maître d'hôtel.

Beurre Fondu (au). Grilled and served with a melted butter sauce touched with fresh lemon juice.

Bordelaise. Baked and masked with bordelaise sauce.

Caisses (en). Mullets are grilled or shallow fried and dressed in paper cases the size of the fish. The fish is then masked with a sauce, i.e. bordelaise, portugaise, or garnished as indicated.

Grenobloise. Floured and sauté in butter, finished with noisette butter, capers, lemon juice, chopped parsley and garnished with lemon wedges.

Grilled. Gill, scale, pass in milk, season and flour. Sprinkle with olive oil and grill on both sides. Serve with maître d'hôtel butter.

Niçoise. Prepared as for meunière: floured and sauté in butter, and garnished with concassed tomato and wafer slice of peeled lemon surmounted with an anchovy fillet curled around a stuffed olive. Beurre noisette, lemon juice and chopped parsley finishing.

Papillots (en). Prepare and sauté the mullet in butter. Place on a piece of oiled greaseproof paper upon a slice of lean ham spread with a preparation of duxelle and concassed tomato. Season and fold the paper over, sealing the edges with a double fold. Place in a hot oven to inflate the paper and thoroughly heat the contents. Serve the whole preparation as it comes out of the oven on a plate.

Portugaise. Poached in a court bouillon with white wine, garnished with a preparation of shallot, tomatoes and chopped mushrooms.

Provençale. Poached and garnished with black olives, anchovy fillet curls, capers and a preparation of chopped shallot and tomatoes sauté in olive oil.

Theodora (Théodore). Stuffed with a duxelle preparation, poached in white wine fumet and served masked with vin blanc sauce.

Vénitienne. Baked and garnished with olives stuffed with a fish quenelle preparation and button mushrooms. Vénitienne sauce offered separately.

Mussels (Moules)

Mussels in the shell are always handled from their live state. As with oysters the shells should be tightly shut. An open shell denotes a dead, hence dangerous, shell fish.

Béchamel. Poached shelled mussels masked with a béchamel sauce, sprinkled with cheese and gratiné. This is usually presented in scollop shells previously piped with duchesse potato.

Beurre (au). The mussels are cooked as for marinière and then removed from their shells. They are lié in a reduction of their cooking liquor checked with dry white wine and thickened with beurre manié.

Bouchées (de Moules). Small bouchée cases filled with cooked mussels with their beards removed and lié in a fish velouté.

Marinière. The mussels are washed and the ligaments by which the shellfish adhere to the rocks are removed. Melt chopped shallot and onion in butter in a deep pan. Add a glass of dry white wine and moisten with fish stock. Add the cleaned mussels and cover the pan. In 5 to 8 minutes the shells will open and their contents be cooked. Pick out, remove the top shell and arrange the mussels in layers in a serving dish or soup plate. Reduce the cooking liquor, correct with beurre-manié, lemon juice and chopped parsley and sauce the mussels with this preparation.

Pilaff (en). Prepare the mussels as for poulette and dress in a moulded ring of rice pilaff. Sprinkle with chopped parsley. (Sometimes described as 'au Riz'.)

Poulette. Prepare and cook as for marinière. Remove the mussels from their shells and lié them in a fish velouté or a béchamel checked with dry white wine and a reduction of the liquor in which the mussels were cooked. Sprinkle with chopped parsley.

Octopus

Small octopus make tender and flavoursome eating. The piece may be poached in a court bouillon, sauté meunière, or breaded or battered and served with lemon wedges and tartare sauce.

Canned, cooked or smoked in oil, octopus is imported from Japan and makes an exotic hors-d'oeuvre.

Oysters (Huîtres)

There are many ways with cooked oysters. In all cases the oyster is dressed in the half deep shell. There are usually 6 to the portion.

Baltimore. Oysters wrapped in bacon, grilled, dressed back in their shells and served with maître d'hôtel butter or sauce diable.

Béchamel (à la). Detached and in their shells, masked with adjusted béchamel sauce, sprinkled with grated cheese and glazed in a hot oven.

Fried (Frites). The oysters are breadcrumbed or battered and deep fried to a golden brown in olive oil. Then dressed in their shells, previously warmed, and served with lemon wedges and brown bread and butter.

Gratin (au). Detached in their shells, sprinkled with white bread-crumbs, chopped parsley, lemon juice and butter and gratiné in a hot oven.

Mornay. The oysters are poached in fish stock with lemon juice and butter. The shells are warmed, painted with melted butter and the oysters set in each, masked with mornay sauce, sprinkled with grated cheese and glazed under a grill.

Roast. The oysters are detached, seasoned with salt, cayenne, touched with lemon and roasted with butter in their shells in a hot oven.

Patelles
Name given to conical shaped shell fish which cling to the rocks in their thousands around all rocky coastlines. They may be eaten raw with lemon juice or the larger ones detached from the shells and poached in a court bouillon.

Periwinkles
The common and popular winkle with a distinctive sweet taste. Cooked by boiling in salted water and served with lemon juice and brown bread and butter.

Pike (Brochet)
Carnivorous river fish. Cookery books of old gave recipes for stuffed and baked pike similar to carp preparation. Pike was also featured au bleu, deep fried, meunière and grilled. It is a very bony fish and its flesh nowadays is better appreciated as quenelles in various rich sauces. Pike quenelles are usually made quite large in size and served 2 or 3 to the portion.

Plaice (Plie)
Flat sea fish principally sold deep frozen, filleted or criss-cross cut and size graded. Plaice has its own distinctive flavour. It is a light and easily digested fish. Can be fried, baked in milk and butter, meunière, or as any of the ways for Dover Sole.

Prawns and Shrimps (Crevettes)
The name prawn is usually given to a large shrimp. Both are cooked by poaching. It is usual to purchase these crustacea ready cooked, frozen or free flowing. Apart from seafood cocktails, both prawns and shrimps are featured curried with rice in suprême sauce or deep fried. For all the following preparations the prawns or shrimps are pre-cooked.

Creole. Sauté in butter, season and add a small quantity of dry white wine or sherry. In a second pan cook some sliced mushrooms in butter, add a sliced green pepper and a red pimento and make up the bulk with tomato purée. Season and check for smoothness with butter and cream. Combine both preparations, let them cohere and serve with a pilaff of rice.

Devilled. Seasoned, passed in milk, floured, deep fried and well seasoned with salt and cayenne pepper. Served with brown bread and butter.

Fried (Frites). Seasoned, passed in milk and flour and deep fried to golden brown. Dressed with fried parsley and lemon wedges. Served with brown bread and butter.

Marinière (Timbale de Crevettes à la). Cooked in a white wine court bouillon, lié in an adjusted fish velouté, checked with butter and served in a puff paste timbale or in the centre of a ring of rice pilaff.

Rock Salmon

Also known as Rock Eel and Dog Fish. Long, thick, sausage shaped sea fish with a pink coloured, soft textured, delicate and sweetish flavoured flesh. Very popular 'Fish and Chips' shop line featured cut on the slant in tronçons, dipped in batter and deep fried 'bone up'.

'Dogs' are usually purchased headed, gutted, film packed and deep frozen. Once defrosted they should be used without delay.

Salmon (Saumon)

Of all fish used in the kitchen salmon is possibly the most esteemed. Salmon breeds in the rivers of northern climes where it swims in from the sea to spawn. The best salmon is fresh, untouched by the freezer, but this can only be enjoyed during the season. Chilled or frozen, it is available all year, imported from Norway, Holland, Ireland, Canada, Alaska or the Pacific, plus, of course, Scottish and English salmon. Quality varies considerably and frozen salmon should be selected with great care. No processed salmon equals the delicate rose pink colour and succulence of the fresh fish. Salmon cans well; canning alters the flavour and appearance, but it is often preferable to inferior frozen fish.

Salmon can be smoked and it then becomes an hors-d'oeuvre de luxe. It has many ways for cold, right up to the realm of exhibition standard where at culinary competitions the whole dressed fish is a speciality feature.

A salmon steak cut across the bone to the thickness of up to 5cm (2 in) is termed a 'darne'; this is the usual cut though it may be prepared as a fillet. With all salmon preparations, hot and cold, cucumber is a traditional accompaniment. The cucumber is sliced wafer thin, lightly dressed in vinaigrette and dusted with chopped parsley.

Dieppoise. Poached salmon, trimmed of all bone and skin, garnished with poached mussels and prawns and masked with sauce vin blanc.

Grilled. Darne of salmon, seasoned, floured, sprinkled with olive oil and grilled on both sides. Serve with sauce diable or maître d'hôtel or anchovy butter.

Maître d'Hôtel. Grilled darne of salmon served with maître d'hôtel butter.

Medicis (Medaillon de Saumon). Poach a 250g (8 oz) fillet in court bouillon and let it cool in the cooking liquor. Remove, drain, breadcrumb and deep fry to a golden brown. Dust with salt, dress with fried parsley and serve with a béarnaise sauce with tomato purée added.

Meunière. The salmon is cut in a darne or a fillet. It is seasoned, floured and sauté in half butter and half olive oil. It is served dressed on a dish, garnished with a rondel of peeled lemon and finished with noisette butter and chopped parsley. The term Belle Meunière is applied to the standard preparation, but it is garnished with whole grilled tomatoes and mushrooms.

Meunière aux Laitances. Indicates a garnish of sauté soft roes.

Mousse of Salmon. Rub the required quantity of cooked salmon through a wire sieve and correct the purée with salt, cayenne, lemon juice and a touch of anchovy essence. Add sufficient half-whipped cream to form a smooth preparation and check colour with carmine. Add sufficient melted fish jelly for setting purposes and run mix into a glass dish. Decorate and top with aspic. The mousse may also be moulded for turning out and decoration and given a final aspic masking.

Niçoise. Darne of salmon meunière, garnished with concassed tomato, capers, peeled lemon rondels, black olives and anchovy curls. Finish with noisette butter and chopped parsley.

Poached. The darne, cut to the required size, is plunged and simmered in a court bouillon (to which white wine may be added) until cooked. This is calculated at 20 minutes to the ½ kilo (1 lb) and is told when the centre bone comes free. The operation is usually performed in a special receptacle. When cooked, the bone and skin are removed and the salmon served with a mousseline sauce, new potatoes (pommes vapeur) and sliced cucumber, vinaigrette dressed.

Salmon for Cold. For cold the salmon is cut and cooked in sections or whole. The ideal size is considered to be 4–5½ kilo (8–12 lb) net weight (eviscerated). The fish is cleaned and the entrails and gills removed, but not the head. The piece is simmered in a court bouillon and allowed to cool in its cooking liquor. For a straight cold service the cooked fish is dressed with lettuce and garnished with hard-boiled egg, tomato and cucumber. It is served with mayonnaise or sauce verte. Cold salmon is also dressed in aspic or chaudfroid and decorated.

Salmon Meunière escorted by Scampis. Cut salmon in darnes. Season, flour and sauté in butter and olive oil on both sides. Remove centre bone and outside skin and set in serving dish. Sauté some whole scampi, seasoned and floured, in butter in another pan, allowing 4 to 6 to the darne. Dress scampi on the salmon and surmount with peeled wafer thin slices of lemon. Finish with noisette butter and chopped parsley.

Vernet (Delice de Saumon). Poached fillet of salmon masked with white wine sauce tinged with anchovy butter and loaded with a julienne of mushrooms, gherkins, hard-boiled egg white and truffle. Pipe the dish with duchesse potato.

Salmon Trout (Truite Saumonée)

A delicate fish described as a cross between salmon and trout with the combined qualities of each. All preparations as for salmon and for trout apply. Also a good medium for cold table work, decorated and aspic or chaudfroid masked. The best hot preparations are those of the meunière range for which the fish is cut and trimmed into fillets or used as a whole long fillet.

Belle Meunière. Prepare fillet to desired size. Season, flour and sauté in half butter and half olive oil. When cooked, set in a serving dish and finish the meunière way, each serving garnished with whole grilled tomato, 2 or 3 mushrooms, thin slices of peeled lemon, noisette butter and chopped parsley.

Cléopâtre. Large sized fillet, seasoned, floured and sauté in butter, served garnished with olives of cucumber étuvé in stock, prawns and soft roes cooked in butter. Finish with noisette butter and chopped parsley.

Laitances (aux). With soft roes cooked as for meunière and the whole preparation finished accordingly, i.e. sliced peeled lemon, noisette butter and chopped parsley.

Niçoise. Meunière and garnished with concassed tomato, lemon rondels, anchovy fillets and black or pimento stuffed olives.

Sardine

Small canning fish. Fresh sardines are good for deep frying. The fish are cleaned and emptied, breadcrumbed and deep fried, garnished with a bouquet of fried parsley and served with lemon wedges and tartare sauce.

Sardines can also be grilled: passed in milk and flour, seasoned, cooked either on a grill, resting on a wire grid, or under a salamander, and served with sauce diable.

Petite Friture. Combination of sardines, sprats and smelts, breaded, deep fried, and dressed en buisson with fried parsley. Served with tartare sauce.

Scampi

Scampi, or *Nephros Norvegicus*, is the large Dublin Bay prawn. Scampi is the Italian name as the original culinary species came from the Adriatic. At one time they came whole and raw and the tails were crushed to remove and clean the meat. Now they are purchased ready cleaned, size graded, deep frozen and free flowing. Scampi is a status food consumed in large quantities.

When scampi are poached and served in a sauce, i.e. newburg, mornay, curry, the sauce is prepared using the reduced liquor in which the fish is cooked.

Brochette (en). In a bowl place the required amount of scampi, medium sized prepared mushrooms, bacon strips and sliced small onion. Moisten with olive oil and season with salt, crushed peppercorns, dash of spice and a bayleaf or so. Let the preparation macerate. Thread the ingredients on a stainless steel brochette (skewer) alternating the scampi, bacon mushrooms and onion. Paint with olive oil and grill quickly. Impale a whole grilled tomato on the end and dress the brochette complete on a bed of pilaff rice plain, à la grecque, à la turque, or à l'orientale.

Côte d'Azur. Sauté in butter with mushrooms, asparagus tips and truffle blade.

Curried. Poached in court bouillon and dressed in curry sauce. Served with boiled rice, mango chutney and curry accompaniments.

Dugléré. French fried scampi served with tartare sauce with chopped tomato and fines herbes added.

Flamed. Prepared at the table. Stew some minced onion in butter in a pre-heated pan, add the scampi (seasoned and floured) and sauté the preparation. When almost cooked, add a glass of marsala and finish cooking. Flame in brandy and serve with a pilaff of saffron rice.

Florentine. As for mornay but with the addition of a bed of cooked leaf spinach seasoned and tossed in butter.

Fried (Frites). The scampi are seasoned, breadcrumbed or battered, deep fried to a golden brown, drained, salt dusted and dressed with a bouquet of fried parsley. Served with lemon wedges and tartare sauce. Battered scampi are now preferred to breadcrumbed.

King (à la). Poached, drained, heated in a cream sauce flavoured with brandy, garnished with shredded green or red peppers, served with pilaff of rice.

Maison. Battered, deep fried and garnished with pieces of crispy grilled bacon, bouquet of fried parsley, lemon wedges and tartare sauce pinked with tomato ketchup and touched with Worcester sauce.

Meunière. Season, flour, sauté in half butter and half olive oil. Finish with noisette butter, lemon juice and chopped parsley.

73

Belle Meunière. Garnished with one whole grilled tomato per serving.

Mornay. Poached in court bouillon with added white wine. Arranged in a buttered fireproof dish piped with duchesse potato, masked with mornay sauce, sprinkled with grated cheese and glazed.

Murat. As for sole murat using scampi in place of the sole fillets. Cut in large julienne and sauté meunière with equal amounts of potato and fonds d'artichauts cut in the same manner. Finish with noisette butter, lemon juice and chopped parsley.

Newburg. Poached in court bouillon, dressed in an adjusted fish velouté pinked with tomato purée, checked with butter, cream and flavoured with brandy. Dressed in the centre of a ring of rice pilaff and topped with truffle blades.

Niçoise. As for meunière with the addition of pimento stuffed olives and anchovy fillet curls.

Provençale. Sauté au beurre with fine herbs, white wine and tomato sauce. Usually prepared at table.

Scampi Platter. Battered and deep fried scampi with slim cut French fried potatoes, lemon wedge and tartare sauce, accompanied by lemon or blue cheese mixed salad and brown bread and butter. The main dish is dressed on an oval platter, the salad in an individual bowl.

(Berni Inn speciality.)

Suprême. Poached in court bouillon, dressed in an adjusted fish velouté checked for seasoning with salt, cayenne and lemon juice and enriched with butter and cream. Dressed in the centre of a ring of rice pilaff and topped with truffle blades.

Scollop (Coquille St Jacques)

Large bi-valve shellfish sold raw, cooked, frozen or canned. Scollop is featured meunière and curried with rice.

Friture St Jacques. Battered deep fried scollops dressed with fried parsley and served with lemon wedges and tartare sauce.

Mornay. The flesh is removed from the shell and poached in a court bouillon. The deep shell is buttered and piped with duchesse potato. The large meat is sliced, arranged in the shell and the orange tongue left whole on the top. The preparation is mornay sauce masked, sprinkled with grated cheese and glazed.

Opéra. The meat is breaded and deep fried, dressed in the deep shell, garnished with grilled bacon and asparagus tips and finished with a touch of noisette butter and chopped parsley.

Vin blanc. The scollop is poached, sliced and arranged in the buttered deep shell piped with duchesse potato. The orange tongue of meat is left whole. The preparation is masked with a white wine sauce prepared from the reduced cooking liquor and glazed.

Sea Urchin (Oursin)

A black coloured round and spiky mollusc which resembles the outer covering of a horse chestnut. It contains a pink coloured shellfish. Raw, the sea urchin is split open and the contents eaten with a touch of lemon juice and brown bread and butter. Urchins are also cooked by poaching in a court bouillon, or deep fried.

Skate (Raie)

An unusual fish in several ways: only the wings are used; whereas all fish should be quite fresh, this one is an exception—it actually improves in flavour with keeping; it is found in the most humble of fish and chip shops and in the most exclusive London restaurants.

Skate is grilled, deep and shallow fried or poached.

Béchamel. The skate is poached in a court bouillon, divided into pieces, dressed in a fireproof dish, masked with béchamel sauce, sprinkled with grated parmesan and browned under a grill or in a hot oven.

Beurre Noir (Raie au). Famous preparation. A thick cut of steak is poached in a court bouillon and set in a serving dish. In a separate pan, burn the required amount of noisette butter with vinegar, throw in some capers and when the preparation blackens, sauce it over the fish. Finish with lemon juice and chopped parsley.

There is a variation: some chefs prefer to shallow fry the skate in butter as for meunière and then give it the black butter treatment.

Fried. The skate is portioned, coated in batter, deep fried to a golden brown and served with lemon wedges and tartare sauce.

Grilled. The skate is portioned and first poached in a court bouillon and allowed to cool. It is then floured, sprinkled with olive oil, coated in breadcrumbs, placed in an oiled dish, grilled and served with tartare sauce.

Smelt (Éperlan)

Small fish much prized for its distinctive flavour. Usually best deep fried.

Anglais (à l'). The smelts are cleaned, split open and the backbones suppressed. The fish are seasoned, passed in flour, dipped in olive oil, coated with breadcrumbs, arranged in an oiled dish and baked in the oven with maître d'hôtel butter.

Bercy. Split open, suppress backbones, cook in a dish in the oven with butter, minced shallot, fish stock, white wine and lemon juice. Mask with a reduction of the cooking liquor.

Buisson. Clean, breadcrumb and deep fry. Dress in buisson with a bouquet of fried parsley in the centre. Serve with lemon wedges.

Colbert. The smelts are opened and the backbones removed. The fish is breaded, deep fried and served with maître d'hôtel butter in a similar manner as the Dover sole dish of this name.

Meunière. Clean, split open and remove backbones. Season, flour and sauté in butter. Dress in a serving dish and finish with noisette butter, lemon juice and chopped parsley.

Orly. The whole fish are breadcrumbed, deep fried and served with tomato or orly sauce.

Richelieu. Same preparation as à l'anglaise, but with added truffle blade garnish on each fish.

Tartare. Whole smelts breadcrumbed, deep fried and served with tartare sauce.

Snails (Escargots)

The appreciation of snails as a table delicacy dates back to Roman times. All snails are edible, but since the common garden ones may feed on certain vegetation poisonous to man, one must be selective in choosing them. The culinary snail is a special type bred for the table. Snails are usually associated with France and the best are the escargots de Bourgoyne, which feed on vine leaves. They are imported live and processed packed in cans with the shells separate and film wrapped. They are ready cooked and just require dressing in their shells.

Snails are appreciated in certain parts of Britain, notably in Northumberland and Somerset. They are known among country folk as wall fish.

Since the name snail may have negative associations, the culinary term escargot is used.

There are many escargot preparations in and out of the shell. *À la Bourguignonne* and *à la Chablisienne,* is a special butter, herbs and wine preparation, are the best known and more usual.

Live or raw snails have to be prepared and are usually handled while in a state of hibernation, protected in the shell by a coating of solidified calcium secreted by the mollusc. They are handled as follows.

With the aid of a knife, scrape away the aperture covering and check the mollusc is alive. A bad odour indicates a dead occupant. Plunge the shells in boiling water and blanch for 3 minutes. Remove snails from their shells and clean by rubbing them in the palms of the hands under running cold water. Place the cleaned snails in a pan with a tiny garlic clove, an onion stuck with cloves, a bouquet garni, a few peppercorns, and a little salt and cover with red wine (Burgundy) or half water and wine. Bring to the boil, simmer for 45 minutes and cool in the liquor.

Clean the empty shells and prepare a garlic butter. Work required quantity of butter with minced shallot and garlic. Season with salt and pepper, load with finely chopped parsley and blend well. Insert a small quantity of the butter in each shell, set in the cooked snail and finish with a packing of more butter.

The prepared snails are now placed in a special grooved dish, heated in the oven and served hot, 6 or 12 per portion. The escargots are handled with tongs and the contents eaten with a pick.

The English way with snails is more straightforward and they are usually eaten out of their shells. The prepared shelled snails are baked in a fireproof dish in butter with a little garlic, salt, pepper and chopped parsley and served hot with lemon and brown bread and butter.

Snoek

Type of barracouta, a large sea fish, usually available canned in olive oil or tomato sauce like the tuna.

To those who remember the post Second World War 'austerity forties' snoek has unfortunate connotations, for the then Minister of Food, John Strachey, made an abortive (and expensive) effort to popularize it.

Sole

This is the Dover sole. There are other 'soles' such as the Torbay witch, the lemon and the grey, plebeian relations of the one and only Dover which, in the kitchen, is almost synonymous with the word fish.

Dover sole is basically prepared in one of two ways: on or off the bone, the whole fish or the fillet. The ideal fish is 300g, 360g or 420g (10, 12 or 14 oz) eviscerated, and 50g (2 oz) trimmed, 2 fillets to the portion. Soles are marketed fresh or frozen. They freeze well and are available at all times.

Whether the whole fish be beheaded or not for service is always a controversial point among chefs and maîtres d'hôtel—it seems to be a matter of opinion. However, the head is usually left on for grilled and fried sole and removed for sauced entrées. The maître d'hôtel is frequently requested by the guest to take the fillets off the bone at the table when the whole fish is presented. The operation is deftly performed with the aid of two table forks. The trend in the service of fish, especially sole, is for fillets, since people no longer want to be bothered with the bones. Convenience eating may outweigh with them the flavour advantages claimed when fish is cooked on the bone.

To cook, both fillets and whole fish are skinned. The whole fish is also trimmed with scissors, the fillets with a knife.

Except where specifically indicated the following recipes apply both to the whole fish and to the fillets.

Ambassadrice. Fillets of sole au vin blanc with poached soft roes, mussels, oysters, shrimps and sliced or button mushrooms in the sauce as a garniture.

Américaine. Poached fillets garnished with collops of lobster and masked with sauce américaine, prepared from the well reduced liquor in which the lobster was cooked, lobster butter, and tomato purée strained and corrected with butter and cream.

Ancienne (à l'). Poached fillets garnished with button onions and mushrooms and masked with a fish velouté to which the reduced cuisson has been added.

Anglaise (à l'). Fillets seasoned, passed in flour, painted with melted butter, coated with breadcrumbs and baked in the oven in a fireproof dish. Finished with lemon juice and chopped parsley.

Argenteuil. Similar to princesse but masked with white wine sauce and not glazed.

Belle Meunière. Indicates the whole fish or its fillets cooked as for meunière and garnished with whole grilled tomato and mushrooms.

Belle Otéro. Fillets spread (filled) with a fish forcemeat (quenelle preparation), rolled and poached. Each fillet is placed in a large hollowed cut baked potato, masked with mornay sauce, topped with a truffle blade and glazed.

Bercy. Whole fish or its fillets poached in fish stock with white wine, mushroom parings, chopped shallot and parsley and butter. The fish is served masked with its cooking liquor well reduced, buttered and glazed.

Betty Lou. Fillets as for meunière, garnished with a whole split banana tossed in butter, sweetcorn kernels and pitted cherries. Finished with noisette butter, lemon juice and chopped parsley.

Beurre Noir. Fillets floured, seasoned and sauté in butter, arranged in a serving dish and sauced with butter burnt with vinegar and garnished with capers. Finish with touch of lemon and chopped parsley. Serve sizzling hot.

Bonne Femme. Famous preparation in which the whole fish or its fillets may be featured. The fish is first poached in a court bouillon and set in a serving dish. Sweat chopped shallot and sliced mushrooms in butter, add required amount of fish velouté and check seasoning with salt, cayenne and lemon juice. Add dry white wine, blend and reduce. Add chopped fines herbes and mask fish with the preparation. Flash under a salamander, or in a hot oven, to glaze topping and serve. Sauce may be wholly made up from the shallot and mushroom preparation with butter, fish stock and white wine, well reduced, checked with cream and glazed.

Bordelaise. Fillets poached in red wine with sliced shallot. Served masked with a bordelaise which incorporates a reduction of the cooking liquor.

Bourguignonne. Whole fish or fillets poached in a reduction of minced shallots, sliced mushrooms and Burgundy. The sauce is reduced, corrected with butter, checked for seasoning and then loaded with small glazed onions and mushrooms and masked over the fish.

Bréval. Similar preparation as for bonne femme, but with the addition of chopped tomatoes.

Cancalaise. Rolled fillets poached in a court bouillon and dressed as a crown in a round dish. The centre is filled with shrimps and mussels and the whole preparation is masked with a sauce vin blanc.

Caprice. As for Saint Germain but garnished with banana. The banana is split lengthways and gently tossed in butter with a little demerara sugar and a squeeze of lemon. Flame in rum and arrange each slice of banana on each fillet of sole. Finish with noisette butter, lemon juice and serve with diable or tomato sauce.

Cardinal. Poached fillets in white wine and masked with an adjusted béchamel incorporating lobster butter.

Cardinal is also featured as a timbale, a more elaborate preparation where the fillets are garnished with a salpicon of lobster or crawfish and truffle.

Carême. Fillets filled with a fish forcemeat, rolled and poached, dressed as a crown in a round dish, garnished with poached soft roes, button mushrooms and sliced truffle and the whole preparation masked with a sauce vin blanc. The fish forcemeat or 'farce' is prepared as for a quenelle preparation. There are several variations of this preparation, one which includes chopped truffle.

Carlton. Poached fillets, garnished with sliced mushrooms, truffle, asparagus tips, sauced over with its fumet flavoured with dry vermouth and glazed.

Carmen. Poached fillets garnished with diamonds (or strips) of red pimento, masked with a sauce vin blanc and glazed.

Casanova (Paupiettes de sole à la). Whole poached fillets set in a dish, garnished with oysters and mussels cooked in a light court bouillon, and masked with sauce vin blanc. Indicate the fillets with truffle blades and garnish with triangle-cut croûtons.

Cecilia. Fillets sauté as for meunière, garnished with asparagus tips and finished with butter and a sprinkling of grated parmesan. Gratiné under the grill and serve.

Cendrillon. Rolled, poached and dressed in a whole baked potato in sauce vin blanc loaded with sliced mushrooms stewede in butter. The topping is lightly glazed.

Chablis. Similar to vin blanc with the fish velouté flavoured with Chablis.

Chambertin. Fillets poached in red wine and garnished with button mushrooms, fish quenelles and masked with a sauce chambertin. The cooking preparation consists of a fish fumet with the addition of red wine.

Champagne (Timbale de Sole au). Poached fillets masked with a fish white velouté flavoured with dry Champagne touched with brandy. A truffle blade and two fleurons indicates each fillet.

Champignons (aux). Whole fish or fillets poached, well garnished with sliced or button mushrooms and masked with sauce vin blanc.

Cherubin. Folded and poached fillets in croustades garnished with sliced mushrooms in cream. Fillets are masked with a vin blanc sauce loaded with a fine purée of smoked salmon.

Cléopâtre. Goujons of sole, floured and sauté in butter, garnished with sauté soft roes and shrimps, and cucumber turned in olives and cooked in salted water and butter. Finished with noisette butter and chopped parsley.

There are several versions of the Cléopâtre; sauté sliced aubergines are an additional garniture.

Colbert. The whole fish, cleaned and trimmed, is used. Place point of knife on the backbone just below the head, white skin side up, and make an incision following the bone down the centre. Press and fold the fillets back on either side and break bone in two places. Breadcrumb and deep fry. Drain, season and serve with maître d'hôtel butter. The correct mode of service at table is to lift out the backbone and place the butter in the cavity.

Condorcet. Poached fillets topped with sliced cooked tomato and cucumber garniture, masked with vin blanc sauce and sprinkled with chopped parsley.

Court Bouillon (au). Whole fish or fillets poached in water with the addition of salt, peppercorns, white wine, sliced carrot, onion and a bouquet garni. Served with a melted butter sauce.

Crevettes. Poached fillets masked, with an adjusted fish velouté tinted with anchovy essence or tomato purée, checked for seasoning, strained and loaded with shrimps.

D'Antin. Similar preparations as dugléré.

Derwent. Poached fillets in white wine sauce garnished with diced tomato and chopped parsley.

(Speciality of Midland Hotel, Derby.)

Dieppoise. Poached whole fish or fillets garnished with soft roes, shrimps, mussels and oysters, masked with a white wine sauce and finished with chopped parsley.

Dorchester (Timbale de Sole). Poached fillets masked with lobster sauce, garnished with mushrooms and lobster claw and served with a pilaff of rice.

(Creation of Eugène Kaufler, chef-des-cuisines at the Dorchester Hotel, London.)

Doria. Whole fish or fillets prepared as for meunière and well garnished with cucumber turned in olives and poached in water with lemon juice. Finish with noisette butter, chopped parsley and wafers of rinded lemon.

Dugléré. The sauce for masking the poached fillets is prepared in one of two ways: by loading an adjusted béchamel with diced tomatoes and chopped parsley; or by loading an adjusted fish velouté with diced tomatoes, chopped parsley and adding a little dry white wine.

Fines Herbes (aux). Whole fish or fillets poached in a fish stock with white wine and mushroom parings. Served masked with a sauce vin blanc loaded with chopped fines herbes.

Florentine. Fillets of sole as for mornay, but resting on a bed of butter-tossed and seasoned cooked leaf spinach.

Fried Fillets of Sole (Filets de Sole Frit). Two fillets to the portion. Trim, season, breadcrumb or batter, and deep fry. Drain, salt and dress with a bouquet of fried parsley. Serve with tartare sauce and lemon wedges.

Gastronome (Filets de Sole Frappé). The fillets are folded, poached in a white wine-flavoured court bouillon, cooked, drained and masked with a sauce américaine checked for setting, as required, with fish jelly. They are dressed on a mousse of mushrooms and the whole piece glazed with aspic, flecked with chopped or a julienne of truffle.

Grand Duc. The fillets are folded, poached, garnished with asparagus tips and truffle blade, masked with mornay sauce and glazed.

Gratin (au). The fish or fillets are cooked in a fireproof dish in butter, white wine, minced onion and chopped mushrooms. The preparation is then garnished with whole mushrooms, sprinkled with white breacrumbs and chopped fines herbes, dotted with butter and gratiné in a hot oven.

Grilled (Grillée). Whole fish seasoned, floured, oiled and grilled. Served with lemon wedge or sauce diable.

Grimaldi. The fillets are spread with fish forcemeat, rolled and poached, dressed on a bed of spaghetti, garnished with collops of lobster and truffle blades, and masked with a fish velouté combined with lobster butter and cream. The pasta is dressed with butter, cream and seasoning.

In the original version, the whole preparation is dressed in a timbale of puff paste (a giant vol-au-vent).

(Grimaldi is the name of an ancient Genoese family.)

Goujons (Sole frit en). The goujonade is a noted deep frying feature. Cut the fillets diagonally into strips, a sort of king sized julienne, breadcrumb, roll, deep fry, drain, salt and serve with tomato or tartare sauce and lemon wedges.

Goujons of Sole and Scampi. Equal quantities of sole cut as for en goujon and whole scampi of the same size. Breadcrumb, mingle, deep fry, drain, salt and serve with a tomato ketchup-flavoured tartare sauce with lemon wedges.

Goujons of Sole Mirabeau. Cut as for en goujon, season flour and sauté in butter, dress with anchovy fillets, pitted olives and capers, and finish with noisette butter and chopped parsley.

Héléna (Paupiettes de sole). Fillets stuffed and rolled and poached in court bouillon. Arrange on a foundation of spaghetti seasoned and dressed with butter and grated cheese. Set a truffle blade on each fillet, mask the whole with mornay sauce and glaze to a golden brown in a hot oven.

The stuffing consists of a purée of soft white fish, i.e. whiting, seasoned, lié in cream and flecked with truffle. May be extended with white breadcrumbs soaked in milk.

Héliopolis. Folded and poached fillet dressed in a half lobster shell with a salpicon of lobster, mushroom and truffle, and a rondel of lobster on the fish. Mask preparation with vin blanc sauce mounted with egg yolk and loaded with a julienne of truffle and mushroom and glaze.

Hollandaise. Poached fillets masked with hollandaise sauce, garnished with fleurons and finished with chopped parsley.

Hongroise. Poached fillets masked with a fish velouté flavoured and coloured with paprika, corrected with butter and reduced cooking liquor, and glazed.

Hôtelière. Fillets floured and sauté in butter and masked with cooked sliced mushrooms and chopped fines herbes in a demi-glace sauce

Indienne. Poached fillets dressed on a bed of boiled rice and masked with a lightly creamed and well flavoured curry sauce. Serve with chutney, Bombay duck and poppadums. This preparation can also be served cold.

Jeanette (Paupiettes de sole au chaudfroid à la). Rolled poached fillets of sole filled with a purée of whiting mixed with a purée of foie gras, seasoned and lié in cream. Mask with white chaudfroid prepared from a fish fumet basis. Top each fillet with a truffle blade, mask the whole preparation with aspic, pick out the fish and the border around the dish with piped chopped aspic.

Joinville. Fillets mornay with medium sized prawns or large shrimps incorporated in the sauce. The dish is piped with duchesse potato.

Julienne. Cut fillets in large julienne strips, season, flour and deep fry. Drain, salt dust and dress with a bouquet of fried parsley. Serve with lemon wedges.

Marguery. As for vin blanc with the sauce loaded with poached mussels and shrimps. Glaze under a grill or in a hot oven.

Marinière. As for vin blanc with the sauce loaded with poached mussels, shrimps and chopped fines herbes and glazed.

Mercia. Poached in madeira, butter and cream sauce garnished with a brunoise of vegetables.

(Speciality of Midland Hotel, Derby.)

Minute (à la). Fillets of sole, seasoned, floured, and sauté in butter, served masked with their cooking juices.

Mirabeau. Fillets of sole meunière garnished with olives filled with a purée of anchovy flecked with chopped tarragon.

Monte Carlo. Poached fillets masked with an adjusted fish velouté coloured with tomato purée and reduction of cooking liquor, checked for seasoning, strained and corrected to a smooth rich sauce with cream and butter. The preparation is garnished with fleurons. Sauce is sometimes enriched with a touch of brandy.

Montmorency (Paupiettes de sole). Rolled, poached, masked with sauce vin blanc and garnished with a salpicon of shrimps and mushrooms in a shrimp sauce. The preparation is served with parisenne sized balls of poached potato, masked with vin blanc sauce and sprinkled with chopped parsley.

Montrachet. Similar to vin blanc with the fish velouté flavoured with montrachet.

Mornay. A serving dish is piped with duchesse potato. Poached fillets or a whole fish arranged in the centre. The preparation is masked with mornay sauce, sprinkled with grated cheese and glazed.

Mousse of Sole Américaine. The mousse is similar to the preparation of quenelles. Prepare equal amounts of sole and whiting, rub through a sieve or pound in a mortar. Place the purée in a pan resting in cracked ice. Work salt, cayenne and lemon juice into it with a wooden spoon. Bind with egg white and combine with half-whipped cream. Beat thoroughly to a smooth paste and fold into a buttered mould. Cook in a bain-marie for 35 to 40 minutes. Unmould, mask with a brandy-flavoured sauce américaine. Decorate with a crown of truffle blades. There are several variations to this elaborate preparation, such as flecking the sauce with chopped truffle and garnishing it with whole lobster claws cut in collops. The mousse may also be wholly prepared with sole.

Murat. Equal amounts of fillet cut as for en goujon, fonds d'artichauts and raw potatoes cut as the fish. Season and flour the fish and cook the three components in butter in different pans. Combine the preparations and finish with noisette butter, lemon and chopped parsley. Toss together and serve.

Nantua. Poached fillets garnished with crayfish tails masked with a nantua sauce, prepared with a fish velouté and crayfish butter. Where crayfish is unobtainable, lobster or crawfish is employed and the garniture consists of the diced meat or scampi.

Newburg. Poached fillets garnished with lobster collops, masked with lobster sauce prepared from an adjusted fish velouté, lobster butter and a salpicon of lobster, loaded with flecked truffle. It is usual to serve a rice pilaff as an accompaniment, but it may also be dressed on a bed of rice.

Niçoise. Grilled whole fish or fillets well garnished with concassed tomato, capers and black olives with anchovy fillet coils. Finished with noisette butter and chopped fines herbes.

Normande. Similar to dieppoise. Fillets of sole au vin blanc with poached soft roes, mussels, oysters and shrimps in the sauce as a garniture, plus a topping of a few fried whitebait and an 'N' cut out of thin sliced bread and butter fried as a croûton to indicate the number of portions.

Normandy. Fillets shallow fried and garnished with sauté soft roes, anchovy fillets, glazed button onions, concassed tomato and peeled lemon rondels. Finished with noisette butter and chopped parsley.

Orly. Fillets of sole battered and deep fried, served dressed with fried parsley and with orly or tomato sauce.

Pacha (à la). Poached fillets dressed on a foundation of rice à la turque, masked with adjusted béchamel sauce, sprinkled with parmesan and glazed in a hot oven. The rice is cooked as for risotto and dressed with saffron and concassed tomato.

Paillard. Fillets cooked as for meunière and dressed with thin, peeled, sliced lemon. Garnished with sauté morilles, shrimps and diced croûtons, finished with noisette butter and chopped parsley.

Palace. Poached in fish stock with white wine on a bed of chopped onion and mushroom, dressed with sliced truffle, and masked with a reduction of the cooking liquor mounted with butter and glazed.

Or, poached in a fumet with chopped shallot, tarragon and white wine, dressed with sliced mushrooms and tomato and masked with a reduction of the cooking liquor mounted with butter, flavoured with brandy and glazed.

Parmentier. Fillets of sole mornay, *without* a border of duchesse potato. The fillets are dressed on a bed of creamed potatoes and finished mornay style.

Paupiettes (en). Term given to the process of dressing the fillets with a fish forcemeat and poaching them in a fish stock. The fillets are then garnished and masked with a sauce. Paupiettes are usually arranged in a crown (en couronne) in a round dish or in a timbale of puff paste. The paupiettes are named after the predominating garnish, i.e. carême, nantua, normande, joinville and the many garnishings associated with fish dishes. These preparations are listed as Paupiettes de Sole Carême, and so on.

Poached Fillets of Sole with Parsley Sauce. The fillets are poached and masked with a fine parsley sauce prepared by loading freshly chopped parsley into an adjusted béchamel.

Portugaise. Poached fillets masked with a light tomato sauce touched with brandy, finished with a sprinkling of chopped parsley.

Princesse. Poached fillets dressed with asparagus tips, a truffle blade on each bouquet and a band of red pimento, masked and glazed mornay.

Richelieu. Identical preparation as for sole colbert with the addition of a line of truffle blades in the cavity with the maître d'hôtel butter.

Ritz (à la). Fillets poached in a fumet, white wine and mushroom cooking liquor, set in a dish and garnished with oysters, shrimps and mushrooms. Masked with mornay sauce, lobster butter added, sprinkled with grated parmesan and glazed.

(Creation of Louis Diat.)

Riviera. Fillets are floured, sauté in butter, garnished with a salpicon of mushrooms, fonds d'artichauts and truffles and finished with noisette butter and lemon juice.

Saint Germain. Season fillets, pass in flour and melted butter and coat with white breadcrumbs. Place in buttered dish and bake in oven or under the salamander. Dot with additional butter if required. Finish with noisette butter, lemon juice and chopped parsley. Serve with béarnaise sauce.

Savoy. Poached fillets dressed with sliced mushroom and truffle and garnished with asparagus tips and concassed tomato arranged each side of the fish in bouquets. The preparation is masked with sauce vin blanc, sprinkled with grated parmesan and glazed.

Soufflé of Sole. Pound the required amount of sole fillet in a mortar or rub it through a sieve. Mix the purée into a stiffish cold béchamel and season with salt, cayenne and lemon juice and flavour with brandy. Place over heat and work in 2 or 3 beaten egg yolks to bind. Stiffly whisk the egg whites and fold into the preparation, combine well and fold into a buttered soufflé dish. Top with truffle blades, and cook in a hot oven for 20 minutes, by which time the soufflé should have risen out of its dish. Serve immediately.

It could be advisable to arrange a collar of greaseproof paper around the soufflé dish to prevent the preparation swelling over the sides instead of rising upwards.

Star Fried Sole (Filet de Sole Frit en Étoile). Have 2 fairly large fillets. Cut each down in tapered strips about 5cm (2 in) from the top of the fillets octopus style. Breadcrumb and roll each strip separately. Deep fry, drain, salt and serve with tomato or tartare sauce.

Sully. Breaded, deep fried fillets dressed with a bouquet of fried parsley and served with béarnaise sauce and anchovy butter.

Suprême. Poached fillets dressed on a foundation of rice pilaff and masked with a fish sauce suprême, a velouté adjusted with poaching liquor checked with cream and touched with dry white wine or sherry.

Talleyrand (Paupiettes de Sole à la). Poached, set on a foundation of spaghetti dressed in butter, masked with white wine sauce loaded with chopped truffle and glazed in a hot oven.

Tout-Paris. Folded and poached fillet dressed in a half lobster shell and masked with sauce nantua combined with sauce vin blanc.

Vendôme. Identical preparation to grimaldi with the sauce incorporating crayfish butter.

Vénitienne. Poached fillets masked with sauce vénitienne.

Vermouth (Sole au). Arrange a prepared whole fish in a buttered dish, season and dot with butter. Add a tablespoon of dry vermouth and the juice of a lemon. Bake in oven until cooked and browned, basting frequently. Add 3 tablespoons cream, reheat and serve. Fillets, 2 to the portion, may be treated identically.

Véronique. Poached fillets of sole garnished with pitted grapes and masked with a sauce made from the fumet, in which the fish has been cooked, mounted with butter and incorporating the grape juice, and glazed. Poach the fish in a court bouillon with white wine and set in a serving dish. Strain cooking liquor, add the juice in which the grapes are cooked, and reduce the preparation to a fumet with a consistency of syrup. Add butter and mount the sauce, checking it with salt, cayenne and lemon juice. Dress each fillet with a line of grapes, mask with the fumet and glaze.

(Escoffier created this dish at the Carlton Hotel, London, naming it after a play and featuring it at a first night theatrical supper party held at the hotel.)

Vin Blanc. Fillets or whole fish poached, masked with a delicate velouté flavoured with dry white wine, and garnished with fleurons (2 per serving).

There are several derivatives to this preparation using various white wines. In all cases the sauce, a fish velouté mounted with fish stock, should be nicely flavoured and well creamed.

This dish is not glazed.

Vin Rouge. Proceed as for vin blanc, but using a full bodied red wine, such as a Burgundy or a Spanish red wine. Check colour as required. Garnish with fleurons.

Waleska. (Filets de Sole Marie Waleska). Fillets are poached in a court bouillon containing white wine, arranged in a dish, garnished with collops of cooked lobster arranged alternately with truffle blades, masked with mornay sauce, sprinkled with grated parmesan and glazed. It is often seen garnished with long sliced cooked scampi instead of the lobster meat.

(Noted dish named after the Polish Countess Marie Waleska (1810–1868), friend and confidante of Napoleon. Sometimes spelt Walewska.)

Yvette. Poached fillets garnished with shrimps, truffle blades, masked with a shrimp sauce and lightly glazed.

Sprat

Small fish not dissimilar in size to the sardine. Served deep fried with lemon wedges and tartare sauce. Also smoked for hors-d'œuvre feature.

Sturgeon (Esturgeon)

The flesh of this fish resembles veal and it is usually prepared in the same ways as the escalope and cutlet of this meat. It is also usual first to prepare and cut the fish as required and then to marinate it in white wine with aromates.

Baked Sturgeon. Cut the fish into escalopes and marinate for several hours in white wine, sliced onion, carrot, salt, peppercorns and a pinch of mixed herbs. Place in a buttered fireproof serving dish, paint with melted butter and bake in the oven for 30 minutes. Finish with noisette butter, chopped parsley and peeled sliced lemon rondels.

Vin Blanc. Marinate and poach the fish in a court bouillon. Mask with a vin blanc sauce which incorporates the reduced strained marinade liquor.

Trout (Truite).

A soft water fish with a delicate flavour. Trout is available fresh or frozen but like salmon there is a marked difference between the two. The frozen is more amenable for shallow frying in the meunière idiom. For one particular preparation, the noted Truite au Bleu, the fish must be alive. For this, live trout are kept in special tanks in the kitchens of famous restaurants. In some the tank is on show and guests may actually select their own trout.

Amandine. The trout is cleaned, seasoned, floured and sauté in butter. A few split almonds are tossed in butter in a separate pan and salt-dusted. The trout is set upon a serving dish, the almonds thrown over it and the preparation finished with noisette butter, a squeeze of lemon and chopped parsley. Some chefs add a dash of fresh cream and a pinch of mixed spice to the almonds prior to garnishing the fish, an operation to be recommended.

Au Bleu (Truite au Bleu). For the desired effect and required flavour the trout must be freshly caught. It is retrieved from the tank and killed with a sharp blow at the back of the head. The gills and entrails are immediately removed in one operation and the fish put on a dish and sauced over with vinegar when the skin will turn blue. It is plunged into a special kettle (fitted with a loose inside tray) containing boiling court bouillon with a little white wine added. It is simmered for about 6 minutes and served as soon as it is ready accompanied by melted butter sauce and steamed new potatoes (pommes vapeur). The fish is sent to the table in its kettle, lifted out on its tray and the skin removed.

Cléopâtre. The prepared fish is seasoned, floured, sauté in butter and garnished with shrimps, soft roes and cucumber turned in olives cooked in water and butter. The preparation is finished with noisette butter and a sprinkling of chopped parsley.

Doria. The prepared trout is seasoned, floured and sauté in butter. It is garnished with balls of cucumber cut with the aid of a parisienne cutter and poached in a little salted water and butter. The preparation is finished with the cucumber liquor or melted butter. The garnish is sprinkled with chopped parsley.

Frites. Small size trout are prepared, seasoned, breadcrumbed, deep fried and served with lemon wedges.

Grenobloise. The prepared fish is seasoned, floured and cooked in butter. It is served garnished with rinded lemon rondels and capers, and finished with noisette butter and chopped parsley.

Hollandaise. The prepared trout is poached in a court bouillon and served dressed on a serviette with steamed new potatoes, a bouquet of parsley and hollandaise sauce.

Maître d'Hôtel. The prepared trout is seasoned, floured, oiled and grilled, and served with maître d'hôtel butter.

Mantoue (à la). The fish is split open, the backbone removed, the cavity filled with a fish stuffing loaded with chopped truffle, poached and served masked with a brown fish sauce incorporating chopped mushrooms (sauce italienne).

Meunière. The prepared trout is seasoned, floured, sauté in butter, garnish with rinded lemon rondels and finished with noisette butter, lemon juice and chopped parsley.

Meunière with Sweetcorn. Cooked as for meunière and garnished with buttered sweetcorn kernels mixed with shredded red and green peppers. Dressed with peeled lemon rondels and finished with noisette butter and chopped parsley.

Nantua. The prepared trout is poached in a court bouillon and served with nantua sauce passed separately.

Turbot

Large flat sea fish with a delicate flavour. It freezes well and may be used in the same ways as salmon and halibut. It deep fries and grills well and is good for most fish entrées. In many respects turbot is in a class with salmon; this should be remembered as there is a tendency to depreciate its status.

On the menu turbot is sometimes designated turbotin which would imply a smaller and therefore younger fish. The fillet is often termed a filet, suprême or medaillon. When cut across the bone it is known as a steak or tronçon.

Béarnaise. A 360g (12 oz) steak, seasoned, oiled and grilled with a bayleaf or two, served with béarnaise sauce.

Dieppoise. Poached fillet garnished with shrimps and mussels and masked with vin blanc sauce.

Diplomate (Suprême de Turbot). Poached fillet in court bouillon with write wine, dressed in a purée of mushrooms, shrimps and smoked salmon, masked and glazed à la mornay.

Florentine. Poached fillet cleared of all skin and bone and set on a foundation of cooked leaf spinach seasoned and tossed in butter. Masked with mornay sauce, sprinkled with grated cheese and glazed. Additional piping of the dish with a border of duchesse potato enhances appearance of the preparation.

Fried. Fillet, seasoned, breadcrumbed or battered and deep fried. Dressed with bouquet of fried parsley and served with tomato or tartare sauce and lemon wedges.

If frozen fillet is used it is advantageous to give it a short brining—fresh water with addition of rock salt (gros sel)—to reconstitute the sea-fresh flavour, before cooking.

Grand Duc. Poached fillet garnished with asparagus tips and truffle blades, masked with mornay sauce, sprinkled with grated cheese and glazed.

Gratin (au). Poached turbot portioned in small pieces, dressed in a buttered dish piped with a duchesse potato, masked with mornay sauce and glazed. Usually presented in scollop shells.

Grillé. Turbot steak seasoned, floured, oiled and grilled. Served with maître d'hôtel butter.

Grilled Turbot Steak and Caper Sauce. The service of grilled fish, in this instance turbot, with caper sauce is a traditional British Fare country custom.

Indienne. Flaked cooked turbot dressed with curried rice in alternating layers and diced hard-boiled egg. Sprinkled with melted butter and finished off in a hot oven. Similar preparation to a kedgeree.

Joinville. Poached fillet arranged in buttered fireproof dish piped with duchesse potato. Masked with mornay sauce loaded with prawns, sprinkled with grated cheese and glazed.

Meunière. Fillet seasoned, floured and sauté in butter. Garnished with peeled lemon rondels and finished with noisette butter, lemon juice and chopped parsley. May be garnished belle meunière and other similar preparations as for sole cooked à la meunière.

Poached Turbot and Shrimp Sauce. Steak cut across the bone, poached and set in serving dish. Masked with an adjusted fish velouté or béchamel, loaded with shrimps and checked for seasoning and colour with anchovy essence.

Whitebait (Blanchailles)
Small fry of herring and sprat found in river estuaries. Sold fresh or frozen. Prior to use the whitebait should be tested for freshness and washed thoroughly.

Devilled Whitebait (à la Diable). Pass in milk and flour, place in a basket and fry to a crispy brown in two dippings. Drain and season with salt and cayenne. Dress piled upon a doily. Garnish with fried parsley. Serve with lemon wedges and brown bread and butter.

Fried. The fish are passed in milk and flour, placed in a basket and immersed in hot deep oil. Remove when cooked, allow the oil to recover and redip. Finish frying to a crispy golden brown. Drain, dust with salt, dress piled upon a doily, garnish with a bouquet of fried parsley and serve immediately with lemon wedges and cut brown bread and butter.

Whiting (Merlan)
Sea fish with a white, delicate and soft texture making it ideal for quenelles, soufflés, mousses and fish stuffings. For these preparation it is often mixed with sole or turbot.

En Colère. In a fit of pique the whiting siezes hold and bites its tail—it is deep fried thus! The fish is cleaned and trimmed with a pair of scissors, the eyes removed but the head left on. The body is incised, seasoned, breaded and the tail placed in its mouth. The whole piece is deep fried, dressed with a bouquet of fried parsley and served with béarnaise or tartare sauce and lemon wedges.

Fried. The fish is seasoned, breadcrumbed or battered, deep fried, drained, salt-dusted, dressed with bouquet of fried parsley and served with tartare sauce and lemon wedges.

Gratin (au). Whole fish or fillets cooked in a fireproof dish in the oven with chopped shallot, mushroom and parsley, white wine, breadcrumbs, butter and lemon juice. Served in dish in which it is cooked.

Maître d'Hôtel. The fish is split open, the backbone removed, seasoned, breaded, deep fried and served with a portion of maître d'hôtel butter in the cavity. Similar preparation as sole colbert, by which name the whiting dish is also known.

Orly. Fillet of whiting seasoned, dipped in batter, deep fried and served with tomato or orly sauce.

SPECIALITY DISHES

Bouillabaisse
Speciality fish stew from Marseilles which embodies, as principal ingredients, fish only found in the Mediterranean.

Bouillabaisse combines the flesh of firm and soft fish and saffron, and the secret is in their blending and rapid cooking process. As with most traditional fare of local origin there is no real standard recipe; the following one is representative.

Chop very finely equal amounts of celery, leek, onion and tomato, add a shallot, garlic clove and piece of pithless lemon peel. Stew in olive oil, season with salt, pepper, ground clove, bayleaf and good pinch of saffron. (This is an important ingredient for both colour and flavour of end product.) Dredge in a little flour, add a bouquet garni and glass of dry white wine.

The firm fish is now cut into smallish pieces of equal size. It consists of crawfish, conger eel, lobster, prawns, turbot and baby octopus, all previously prepared and cleaned. Moisten well with fish stock or water, bring to the boil fiercely for 5 minutes.

Now add the soft fish, cleaned, prepared and cut in smallish pieces of equal size. It consists of red mullet, smelts, whiting, rascasse (a Mediterranean fish similar to mullet) and shelled mussels. Cook over a fierce fire for a further 10 minutes.

Take out the bouquet garni and bayleaf and dress the fish on rounds of fried French bread moistened in the cooking liquor. Sprinkle with chopped parsley.

It is usual to serve the cooking liquor first as a soup, followed by the fish. The entire preparation may also be offered together with the fried bread.

This dish is also exported from Marseilles in cans and requires heating and then serving.

Coulibiac
Russian fish pie prepared with salmon or sturgeon and shaped like a sandwich loaf. It is cut into thick slices and served with melted butter.

Prepared with 6 ingredients: fish, cabbage, mushrooms, pancakes, rice and paste as follows.

Fish: About 2 kilo (4 lb) trimmed, cut in fillets, seasoned and stiffened in butter in the oven.

Cabbage: Large, trimmed, boiled whole, drained, chopped, seasoned and dressed in butter and flattened out between two dishes.

Mushrooms: Eight large, washed, seasoned, baked in butter and then sliced.

Pancakes: Large, flat, flecked with chopped visega and fines herbes.

Rice: About 500g (1 lb) washed, spread on buttered tray, seasoned, moistened with water, dotted with butter and baked without coloration.

Paste: About 1 kilo (2 lb) of brioche.

To make paste: 40g (1½ oz) yeast, milk, 750g (1½ lb) flour, 360g (12 oz) butter, 3 eggs, salt, water.

Make a ferment by dissolving yeast in sufficient warm milk in a bowl, sprinkle with flour, cover with cloth and prove until flour coating cracks. Warm flour and slowly add ferment. Add melted butter, beaten eggs, pinch of salt and sufficient water at blood heat to form stiff dough. Knead until paste clears hands, cover with cloth and prove again in warm place. Knead again, roll out and use as required.

To Assemble: Have all the prepared ingredients ready and ample melted butter on hand.

Roll out pastry and cut a portion for the base. The pie is built up on this foundation in layers, each well brushed with melted butter: pancakes, allowing ample overlapping, rice, mushrooms, cabbage and fish; rice, mushrooms, cabbage and fish. Enclose the whole wrapped up in the pancakes. Actual sequence of layers is optional, as long as they alternate and are enclosed in pancake.

Cover the sides, ends and top with the remaining pastry. Seal, smooth edges, leave 3 vents at intervals along the top and brush the whole with egg. Make a little simple decorating for appearance. Set the piece on an oiled tray, ferment, protect with greaseproof and bake at 200°C. (375—400°F.) for an hour. Remove paper protection after 40 minutes to allow pie to colour. When cooked, pour little more melted butter into the vents.

For service à la Russe offer sour cream and beet juice as well as melted butter sauce.

Kedgeree
Indian breakfast dish.

Mix about 500g (1 lb) cooked rice with 250g (8 oz) flaked cooked haddock. Season with salt, pepper and teaspoon curry powder. Add 75g (3 oz) butter and 2 diced hard-boiled eggs and reheat. Sprinkle with chopped parsley and serve very hot with mango chutney.

Kedgeree may be prepared with any type of flaked fish or mixture of fish: salmon, cod, prawns, shrimps and so on.

Eggs

The ways with eggs are almost limitless. Over and above their numerous culinary uses in the kitchen they may be soft- or hard-boiled; shallow and deep fried; poached or baked; scrambled; made into omelettes; featured hot or cold, garnished, for hors-d'oeuvre.

With so big a subject some classification is needed. They are therefore listed under three methods of presentation: general egg dishes, omelettes and eggs for cold.

COOKING EGGS

By eggs in the kitchen, and unless otherwise stated, we mean chicken eggs. There are the de luxe eggs of certain game birds, which are noted separately, and duck eggs which are larger with a greenish shell, and richer in flavour. Turkey eggs, though larger, resemble duck eggs; both must always be well cooked and are safest hard-boiled for 10 minutes. Ostrich eggs were apparently once popular with the ancient Egyptians, Greeks and Romans.

Dried Eggs. The original was the dehydrated commodity introduced by the Ministry of Food in the Second World War (1939–45). Despite critical comments, if properly handled a good quality end product could be achieved. The advances made in drying foods have resulted in a superior commodity. The new instant powders result in a product a quarter of the weight of the original egg and a convenience line useful for omelettes and scrambling, plus other uses in the kitchen and in confectionery and bakery.

Boiled egg. Plunge into boiling water for 3 minutes. When boiling a quantity, place in cold water, bring up to the boil and maintain this heat for 2 minutes.

Lightly boiled egg. Plunge into boiling water for 2 minutes.

Coddled egg. Plunge into boiling water, remove from heat and stand for 10 to 12 minutes.

Hard-boiled egg. Plunge into boiling water for 8 minutes and refresh immediately in cold water to prevent discoloration.

Soft-boiled (oeuf mollet). Plunge into boiling water for 3 minutes, remove, crack and shell with care.

Poached egg (oeuf poché). Break into boiling water containing vinegar and a little salt, simmer for 2½ to 3 minutes, remove, drain and trim if required. The vinegar assists the white to envelope the yolk.

Scrambled egg (oeufs brouillés). Two or three per portion. Break into a bowl, add salt and pepper and whisk well. Pour into a hot small deep pan containing heated butter at the frothing stage, cook slowly, stirring with a wooden spoon. The eggs should be moist, have a creamy consistency and should be served at once. Preparation may be enhanced with the addition of a small amount of warmed cream.

Fried egg. Eggs are fried in three ways: pan fried in a frying pan or shallow fried on a griddle, à la poêle; shallow fried in a ceramic serving dish or metal skillet, sur le plat; deep fried in hot olive oil, à la française.

Shallow frying is performed in butter, bacon fat or lard and the pan or dish should be pre-heated.

Cocotte or baked egg (oeuf en cocotte). The cocotte is a ceramic receptacle large enough to contain one egg. The cocotte is pre-heated, a piece of butter dropped in and when melted the egg is broken in, seasoned with salt and pepper and baked bain-marie style in a tray of hot water in a hot oven for 3 to 4 minutes. The preparation is featured as it is, au naturel, or garnished.

GENERAL EGG DISHES

Aline. Poached, dipped in batter, deep fried, drained, seasoned and served with tomato sauce.

Alsacienne. Poached, dressed on a sauerkraut foundation and garnished with fried bacon, sliced frankfurter and rondels of cooked carrot.

Anchois (aux). Scrambled eggs with chopped or pounded anchovy fillets, checked as required with anchovy essence, served on buttered toast.

Andalouse. French fried in olive oil and dressed alternating with deep fried rondels of aubergine. Served with tomato sauce.

Aurora. Poached, served on buttered toast, masked with a creamed tomato sauce and garnished with chopped or julienne of ham and truffle.

Bacon and Eggs. Two fried eggs garnished with two rinded bacon rashers, one back and one streaky.

Balzac (à la). Scrambled egg loaded with chopped tongue and truffle, dressed with a cordon of tomato sauce and garnished with small triangles of butter fried croûtons.

Béarnaise. Poached, dressed in vol-au-vent case, masked with béarnaise sauce and truffle blade.

Beauvilliers. Break two eggs in a skillet lined with sliced ham. Cook and serve masked with madeira sauce.

Belle Hélène. Poached eggs on buttered toast, masked with suprême sauce and garnished with asparagus tips.

Belle Otéro. Baked potato with the top sliced off and the pulp removed and dressed with butter, milk, salt and cayenne. A foundation of the preparation is piped back into the potato shell, a poached egg is inserted and the piece decorated with the remainder of the prepared and piped potato, topped with a truffle blade, masked with mornay sauce and put in a hot oven till golden brown.

Bénédictine. Poached, arranged on small toasted muffin and rondel of ox tongue, masked with hollandaise sauce, glazed and dusted with chopped parsley.

Bercy (à la). Two fried eggs garnished with a grilled chipolata placed between the yolks and finished with a tomato sauce cordon.

Bergère. Poached, dressed on a preparation of minced cooked lamb in demi-glace, masked with mornay sauce and gratiné in a hot oven.

Beurre Noir. Fry two eggs and place in serving dish. Empty soiled fat from pan and replace with fresh butter. Let it brown, add chopped gherkins, capers and parsley, brown with a dash of vinegar, sauce preparation over the eggs and serve sizzling.

Bombay. Soft-boiled (mollet) on rice and curry sauced.

Carême. Fried eggs dressed on a purée of chicken with chopped truffle and masked with sherry flavoured sauce suprême.

Chantilly. Soft-boiled (mollet) dressed on a purée of lentils and velouté sauce masked.

Chartres. Poached, on croûton, decorated with tarragon leaves and sauced with a tarragon fumet, i.e. essence.

Chasseur. Poached eggs on buttered toast masked with chasseur sauce with addition of sauté chicken livers.

Châtelaine. Poached eggs arranged in tartelettes filled with a savoury purée of chestnuts, masked with sauce suprême. Two per portion.

Churchill (à la). Two poached eggs on sliced York ham. (Favourite breakfast dish of Sir Winston Churchill.)

Cingalèse. Poached eggs on rice pilaff, masked with curry sauce and served with chutney.

Clamart. Poached in tartelettes containing a purée of peas, cordon of jus lié.

Cocotte à la Crème (oeuf en). When ready, sauce with hot cream.

Cocotte au Jus (oeuf en). Sauced with hot demi-glace or madeira sauce.

Cocotte Monte Carlo (oeuf en). Line buttered cocotte with concassed tomato, break in egg, season and cook in the usual way.

Cocotte Parisienne (oeuf en). Line buttered cocotte with a preparation of minced ham, chicken, mushroom and truffle bound in cream.

Break in the egg, cook bain-marie fashion for 3 to 4 minutes, top with a truffle blade.

Cocotte à la Reine (oeuf en). Line buttered cocotte with minced white of chicken in cream, break in egg, season, cook bain-marie style and finish with topping of hot cream.

Colbert. Two poached eggs on a foundation of vegetable macédoine, masked and glazed à la mornay.

Coque (à la). French for boiled egg.

Curried. Whole hard-boiled, dressed on bed of boiled rice and curry sauce masked.

Daumont. Poached, dress in croustade with minced chicken, mask with suprême sauce, top with truffle blade.

Diable. Soft-boiled masked with sauce diable.

Divette. Scrambled eggs with shrimps. (Derivative of Yvette, a more elaborate preparation.)

Duchesse. Poached and dressed in nest of duchesse potato, masked with béchamel and glazed.

Fines Herbes (oeufs brouillés aux). Scrambled eggs on toast loaded with chopped fines herbes.

Florentine. Poached, dressed on cooked leaf spinach sauté in butter, mornay masked and gratiné. May also be dressed on a purée of spinach.

Foies de Volaille (oeufs brouillés aux). Scrambled eggs garnished with a sauté of chicken livers lié in madeira sauce. Serve on buttered toast.

Forestière. Scrambled, garnished with sauté diced bacon and sliced mushrooms.

Française (oeufs frits à la). Deep fried in hot olive oil, drained, dressed on fried bread and served with tomato sauce.

Grand Duc. Poached eggs on fried bread, garnished with asparagus tips, truffle blade, masked and glazed à la mornay.

Gratin (au). Poached on toast and gratiné à la mornay.

Georgette. Poached egg dressed in a large baked potato with shrimps and shrimp sauce, topped with piped duchesse potato prepared with the pulp which has been removed. Similar to Belle Otéro.

Indienne. Sliced hard-boiled eggs on baked rice and curry sauce masked.

Italienne. Poached on spaghetti dressed with butter, cheese and seasoning. Tomato sauce masked.

Jambon (oeuf sur le plat au). Line a skillet with sliced ham or grilled gammon rashers, melt in some butter, break in 2 eggs, season and cook in the oven.

Maison Blanche (oeufs à la). Poached on a foundation of creamed sweetcorn, masked with suprême sauce and topped with truffle blades.

Masséna. Poached in fond d'artichaut lined with béarnaise sauce, masked with madeira sauce with poached bone marrow topping.

Metternich (oeufs à la). Poached eggs arranged in fonds d'artichauts, topped with a julienne of tongue lié in cream, masked with mornay sauce and glazed in a hot oven.

Mirabeau. Fried and dressed with anchovy fillets, pitted olives and capers.

Miroir (au). Term for fried egg, i.e. sur le plat.

Montmorency. Poached on fried croûton rondels masked with a tomato sauce suprême, and garnished with fonds d'artichauts filled with asparagus tips lié in cream sauce.

Mornay. Poached eggs on toast masked with mornay sauce, sprinkled with grated parmesan and glazed to a golden brown in a hot oven.

Opéra. Fried and garnished with a sauté of chicken livers in madeira sauce and asparagus tips.

Pacha (à la). Poached eggs dressed on a pilaff of rice à la turque, masked with mornay sauce, sprinkled with grated cheese and glazed in a hot oven. The pilaff is dressed with concassed tomato and saffron.

Païva. Soft-boiled, arranged in croustade case lined with mushroom purée, truffle blade topped, masked and glazed à la mornay.

Pastourelle. French fried eggs garnished with grilled bacon, kidney and cèpes sauté in butter and lié in a bordelaise sauce.

Patti (à la). Poached eggs dressed in small, cooked, short-paste tartelette cases, masked with a suprême sauce incorporating a light purée of fonds d'artichauts, sprinkled with sieved hard-boiled eggs, reheated and served.

Périgourdine. Poached, on croûton masked with madeira sauce flecked with chopped truffle.

Piémontaise (à la). Poached, arranged on a risotto with a cordon of tomato sauce. The risotto is dressed with butter, saffron, gruyère and parmesan cheese.

Polonaise. Poached, on minced lamb and chopped mushrooms, demi-glace sauced and gratiné.

Princesse. Scrambled eggs lightly loaded with diced chicken and chopped truffle, dressed on buttered toast, garnished with asparagus tips and topped with truffle blade.

Provençale. Fried and garnished with concassed tomato and sauté sliced aubergines.

Rossini. Poached, dressed on croûton spread with foie gras purée, topped with a collop of foie gras surmounted with a truffle blade and masked with périgueux sauce.

Sarde (ouefs à la). Small poached eggs. Peel the required amount of tomatoes, slice off the tops, empty the contents and set the eggs into the tomatoes. Breadcrumb and deep fry with care. Dress with fried parsley and serve with a demi-glace sauce flecked with chopped fines herbes.

Shirred Eggs. American preparation cooked and served in a skillet. Butter the dish, sprinkle with crushed cracker biscuit or breadcrumbs, season with salt and pepper. Break in the eggs, add more crumbs, a little cream and bake slowly until the crumbs brown.

Soyer (à la). Two poached eggs on grilled bacon or slice of ham on buttered toast masked with a sauce prepared with cream and butter and seasoned with salt, pepper and a little sugar.

(Created by Alexis Soyer who, as a variation, would sauce the preparation with hot maître d'hôtel butter.)

Stanley (à la). Poached eggs arranged on a foundation of rice pilaff, masked with a purée soubise tinted and flavoured with curry powder. The purée is prepared with boiled onions rubbed through a sieve, checked for seasoning and for consistency with cream.

Turbigo. Cooked sur le plat (in a skillet), garnished with grilled tomato, chipolata and diced sauté kidneys in madeira sauce.

Victoria. Poached and dressed in tartelettes or in a vol-au-vent containing a salpicon of truffle and lobster and masked with lobster sauce.

Yvette. Scrambled and garnished with shrimps, asparagus tips and truffle blade.

OMELETTES

Omelette making is representative of the manipulative and sensory skills inherent in cookery. Proficiency comes with practice after theoretical tuition and practical demonstration have highlighted the critical factors.

To make an omelette, break and beat 2 or more eggs well. (Eggs should always be well beaten so that the yolks blend with the whites and do not separate in cooking.) Take a clean, pre-heated iron omelette pan, drop in a piece of butter and pour in the beaten eggs, seasoned with salt and pepper, as it is on the point of browning. Mix the contents with the aid of a fork (it is at this point the garnishing/ingredients are usually added), allow the preparation to start setting, roll up the omelette away from you, shape and turn out on a warmed plate or dish. Can be served plain or garnished.

(It will be noted that the French spelling has been adopted in place of the English omelet; this is, of course, quite optional.)

Américaine. Fines herbes omelette filled with concassed tomato and topped with a grilled rasher of bacon.

Anchois (aux). Egg mix is loaded with chopped anchovy fillet, made up in the usual way and decorated with criss crosses of anchovy cut in julienne.

Archiduc. Filled with a salpicon of truffle and sauté chicken livers, topped with a truffle blade.

Arnold Bennett. Garnished with diced smoked haddock cooked in cream and touched with cayenne. Left flat, masked with mornay sauce, sprinkled with grated parmesan, flashed to a golden brown under a grill.

(Dedicated to Arnold Bennett while he was staying at the Savoy Hotel, London, collecting material for his book *Imperial Palace*.)

Asparagus Tips (aux Pointes d'Asperges). Add to the raw egg mix and when omelette is made up garnish with whole asparagus tips.

Bénédictine. Stuffed with a purée of cod. The fish is cooked, sieved, combined with béchamel, corrected with butter and cream, and seasoned with salt and pepper.

Café Parisien. As for à la reine but masked and glazed à la mornay. (Café Parisien was once the name of the Savoy Grill, London.)

Croûtons (aux). Egg mix is loaded with crispy croûtons of diced bread and served with a cordon of demi-glace sauce.

Espagnole (Spanish Omelette). Sliced button onions stewed in butter, concassed tomato, cooked peas and fines herbes. The omelette is cooked on both sides, not folded, served flat. May include sliced sauté onion and diced red peppers.

Fines Herbes (aux). Chopped parsley, chervil and tarragon are added to the raw mix.

Foies de Volaille. Filled with sauté and seasoned chicken livers with chopped parsley added and bound in a demi-glace.

Fromage (Cheese Omelette). Grated parmesan, gruyère or cheddar added to the raw mix.

Italienne. Fines herbes omelette stuffed with a concassed tomato preparation combined with a sauté of chicken livers in demi-glace sauce.

Ivanhoe. Filled with diced smoked haddock cooked in cream and touched with cayenne.

Jambon (Ham Omelette). Diced or julienne shredded lean ham.

Joinville. Filled with shrimps in a fish velouté pinked with tomato purée.

Lard (au). Egg mix loaded with crispy sauté diced bacon and made up in usual way.

Lorraine. Beat 2 eggs, season, sprinkle with shaved gruyère, add a few pieces of diced, crispy grilled bacon, enrich preparation with cream and make up omelette in usual way.

Lyonnaise. Egg mix loaded with sliced and fried button onions and made up in usual way.

Parmentier. Egg mix loaded with diced and sauté potato and made up in usual way.

Patti. Egg mix loaded with salpicon of fonds d'artichauts and truffle and made up in usual way.

Paysanne. Flat fines herbes omelette, garnished with small blanched and sauté lardons, diced sauté potatoes and a chiffonade of sorrel.

Poulard. Famous omelette of Mère Poulard. Mont-Saint-Michèle, France. Reputed to be prepared from a secret formula. It is said the eggs are separated, the beaten yolks are poured into the pan, followed by the beaten and seasoned whites with cream. The two are combined and the preparation is then made up in the usual way.

(The original Miss Annette Poulard was a country servant girl who married a baker's son and opened a restaurant.)

Princesse. Omelette aux fines herbes garnished with asparagus tips and truffle blade topped.

Reine (à la). Filled with minced chicken and chopped truffle in cream sauce and garnished with asparagus tips.

Richmonde (à la). Stuffed with mushrooms in a cream sauce, glazed with mornay sauce and surmounted with an 'R' cut in cheese.

Rognons (aux)—**Kidney Omelette.** Filled with a sauté of diced kidney in madeira sauce.

Rossini. Filled with a salpicon or foie gras and truffle and served with a cordon of sauce périgourdine.

Russe (à la). Filled with caviar. (Reputed favourite of the Duke of Windsor when Prince of Wales.)

Soyer (à la). Beat 3 eggs, season with salt and pepper, garnish with chopped parsley and a little very finely minced raw onion, cook very slowly before rolling it up.

Tomato (aux Tomates). Filled with concassed tomato, dressed with a topping and sprinkled with chopped parsley.

Trouvillaise. Fines herbes omelette filled with peeled pink shrimps lié in a salt and cayenne seasoned butter and cream sauce.

Truffes (aux). Chopped truffle in the raw mix, line of sliced truffle when made up, cordon of demi-glace sauce.

Tsarine. Filled with consommé-poached cucumber cut in balls and lié in cream.

Suissesse. Load egg mix with grated gruyère. When cooked, sprinkle with more cheese and flash under a grill to brown.

Vichy (à la). Filled with thin sliced rondels of carrot simmered in butter, moistened with stock. Served sprinkled with chopped parsley.

COLD EGG DISHES

Jellied Eggs (Oeufs en Gelée)

Eggs for cold are usually poached or soft boiled, i.e. mollet. They are either sauced in a chaudfroid, decorated and glazed, or decorated and aspic masked. The eggs are dressed on a foundation of mousse or other preparation and given a final aspic glazing. It is usual to present jellied eggs in services of 6, but they may be prepared individually in short paste tartelettes in a similar manner to the multi-portioned presentation.

Where a mousse foundation is indicated this is prepared from a fine purée of the cooked main ingredient combined with half-whipped cream, seasoned with salt, cayenne, spice and lemon juice as required, checked for colour and flavoured as indicated with port, sherry, madeira or brandy. Chicken jelly is added to aid the setting of the mousse.

Decoration is achieved with coloured white of hard-boiled egg, truffle, chervil pluches, tarragon leaves, radish, gherkin, olive, pimento, paprika fingerprints, flower petals and various juliennes.

Bolonaise (oeufs rafraîchie à la). Poached eggs on a rice risotto, masked with a brown chaudfroid flavoured with red wine and loaded with minced beef stewed in butter, aspic glazed finish. The risotto is set with the aid of aspic.

Californienne (oeufs en gelée à la). Poached eggs on a mousse of apricot, garnished with apricot quarters and a julienne of ham, and masked with a limpid brandy flavoured aspic.

Cantaloupe (Mousse de, aux oeufs pochés). Mousse of cantaloupe melon, enhanced with ground ginger, sugar and port, is used as foundation for the poached eggs. Decorated with scooped balls of melon and glazed with port-flavoured aspic.

Chasseur (oeufs pochés glacé). Poached eggs well masked with sauce chasseur incorporating a sauté of chicken livers. Aspic glazed.

Clamart (oeufs en gelée). Poached eggs on a mousse of peas, garnished with cooked peas, diced carrots and turnips, masked with aspic.

Favorite (oeufs pochés sur une mousse). Poached eggs on a mousse of French beans, glazed with an aspic loaded with a colourful julienne of mixed vegetables.

Gentilhomme (oeufs pochés à la). Poached eggs on a mousse of

101

game, masked with a chopped truffle loaded aspic. The mousse is prepared from a grouse, pheasant or partridge.

Jambon (oeufs à la gelée au). Poached eggs dressed with alternating rounds of ham, decorated and well masked with aspic.

Marinière (oeufs poché à la). Poached eggs with a mussel à la marinière preparation with the addition of button onions, mushrooms and chopped fines herbes. The preparation is made up with a good fish jelly.

Maryland (Jellied Eggs). Canned sweetcorn, drained, checked for seasoning, with cream and softened gelatine added and run into a serving dish to set. Set poached eggs, masked with white chaudfroid, flavoured with brandy and tinged with meat glaze, on the corn foundation. Mask with aspic jelly loaded with a julienne of ham and chicken. Alternatively, glaze eggs in brandy flavoured aspic.

Montrouge (oeufs en gelée). Poached eggs on a mousse of mushrooms, decorated with diced tomatoes and aspic glazed.

Reine (oeufs en gelée à la). Poached eggs on a mousse of chicken, masked with chaudfroid, decorated and glazed.

Rose de Mai (oeufs glacés). Poached eggs masked with white chaudfroid on a mousse of fresh tomatoes, decorated with small pressed tomato boulets and aspic glazed.

Stanley (oeufs pochés glacial). The eggs are poached and masked with a white chaudfroid lightly coloured and flavoured with curry powder. They are dressed on a risotto of rice set in aspic, garnished with poached button onions and mushrooms and finished with aspic glazing.

Strasbourgeoise (oeufs glacés à la). Poached eggs on a foie gras mousse, well masked with a brandy flavoured aspic loaded with chopped truffle.

Tarragon (oeufs pochés à la). Poached eggs decorated with tarragon and set in a rich aspic flavoured with tarragon.

Yorkaise (oeufs en gelée). Poached eggs on a mousse of ham, garnished with a julienne of ham and aspic masked.

Stuffed Eggs for Hors-d'œuvre and Garnishings

Hard-boil, refresh, shell, cut through centre with point of a knife in zig-zag pattern. Separate halves, remove yolk, mask with equal quantity of softened butter, season with salt, cayenne anchovy essence or Worcester sauce and lemon juice. Pipe back into the white halves in a fancy pattern, top with a caper and glaze, as required, with aspic.

Cold Omelette

Prepare a 3-egg omelette with fines herbes and cooked minced onion. Cook but do not fold; leave flat and let it get cold. Fill with dressed crabmeat, fold over, arrange on lettuce and mask with tomato sauce. Decorate with rondels of hard-boiled egg, tomato and cucumber.

Scotch Egg
Hard-boiled egg, shelled, wrapped in a good layer of sausage or forcemeat, breadcrumbed and deep fried. Served sliced with salads, or hot with tomato sauce.

De Luxe Eggs
The eggs of the plover, gull, pheasant, partridge and lapwing are presented hard-boiled with brown bread and butter and celery salt as an hors-d'œuvre de luxe as well as for aspic and other show-piece work.

These eggs may also be scrambled and served on toast, dressed with chopped truffle and a little cream.

Pasta and Pastry Entrées

PASTA

Term given to fare classified in cookery books as farinaceous foods, known to chefs as 'Pâtes Alimentaires' or 'Pâtes d'Italie'. The modern term 'pasta' is more apt and indicative with new eating habits.

Pasta was introduced to Italy from China by the Venetian traveller Marco Polo and was brought to France by Marie de Medicis when she became Queen to King Henry IV.

There is also a link between Russian and Italian cookery, sponsored no doubt by the former aristocracy, and pasta figures in certain types of Russian fare, notably the varenkis, a variety of sweet and savoury ravioli.

Pasta is versatile, sustaining, interesting, inexpensive and, because of its specialized manufacture, a high grade product. This indicates that pasta is 'bought in' ready made and a large pasta industry exists in Britain.

It is basically prepared from Durum Semolina, milled Canadian Durum wheat, to which water is added to form a dough. For tube shaped pasta the dough is extruded through dies, for flat types it is rolled. The product is then dried by a special process. There are some 200 varieties of pasta; the ingredients, size, shape and colour determine the type. There are cubes, dice, letters, numerals, pipes, rings, ribbons, rondels, shells, stars, strings, wheels and so on.

Usually white, pasta is coloured green with spinach juice; red with beet; yellow with saffron or egg yolk; and flecked with truffle, pimento and herbs.

The big four pasta are noodles, spaghetti, macaroni and vermicelli.

The preparation and presentation of pasta relies upon the variations on a theme idiom; this means it is cooked identically and variety is injected by the garnishing ingredients from which the dish takes its name.

Pasta is cooked in salted boiling water for 15 minutes. For preparations requiring further cooking, i.e. baking, 10 minutes pre-cooking should suffice. When cooking long spaghetti or noodles, place one end in the boiling water and as it softens, slowly coil it around the pan. When cooked, drain well in a collander or conical strainer and finish as required. Some like it crisp and underdone, 'aldenti', in which case cooking time is suitably reduced.

When cooked, the pasta is tossed in butter and seasoned with salt, pepper from a mill, a suspicion of nutmeg and ample grated cheese. There is really only one cheese—parmesan; next comes gruyère, a half and half; and then the more fully flavoured cheddar. Pasta is eaten au naturel as above—seasoned and butter and cheese dressed—or joined with other foods, i.e. tomatoes, mushrooms, sauté chicken livers, minced beef, ham or veal, seafoods, poultry, diced hard-boiled eggs, leaf spinach, peas, broccoli, shredded green and red peppers and various sauces. Additional grated cheese is offered separately with all pasta dishes.

The preparations listed indicate and apply to noodles, spaghetti, macaroni and all large pasta unless otherwise stated.

Alsacienne. Dressed pasta combined with a julienne of ham lié in tomato sauce.

Al Sugo. Cook pasta for 5 minutes in boiling salted water, drain, toss in butter, check seasoning and add grated cheese. Moisten well with veal stock, bring up to the boil and simmer slowly until the pasta acquires a nice gloss. Serve with grated cheese.

Bolonaise or Bolognese. Cooked and dressed in butter, cheese and seasoning, and combined bolonaise sauce. Possibly the best known pasta preparation.

Bourgeoise. Cooked and dressed with butter, cheese, seasoning and combined with cream.

Bressane. Dressed pasta combined with a sauté of chicken livers in madeira sauce.

Cannelloni. Long and thick tubes of stuffed pasta, featured in the same ways as ravioli.

Charcutière. Cooked and dressed with butter, cheese, seasoning and tomato purée, and garnished with rondels of frankfurters, thin rondels of gherkin and julienne of ham. Mix well over heat. As an alternative, it may be garnished with grilled baby frankfurters and diced ham.

Dominicaine. Spaghetti dressed in butter and cheese, seasoned, loaded with chopped anchovy fillets and sliced cooked mushrooms. Generously garnished and well blended over heat.

Florentine. Prepare spinach en branches, toss in butter, chop and combine with dressed pasta.

May also indicate Pâtes Gratiné Mornay with the addition of a foundation of en branches spinach sauté in butter.

Foies de Volaille. Dressed pasta combined with a well seasoned and sauced sauté of chicken livers which includes a good binding of tomato purée and the addition of chopped parsley.

Genoise. As for bourgeoise with the addition of sliced mushrooms cooked in butter.

Lasagne. Pasta rolled into thick ribbons 2cm (¾ in) wide and usually coloured green. Prepared in any of the ways indicated for pasta.

Macaroni Cheese. Cooked macaroni, seasoned, butter dressed, arranged in buttered dish, masked with mornay sauce, sprinkled with grated cheese and put in hot oven till golden brown.

Maison Blanche. Dressed in butter, seasoned and loaded with sweetcorn kernels, cooked peas and peeled shrimps, mixed well, arranged in a buttered dish, masked and glazed with mornay sauce till golden brown.

Marie Jeanne. Dressed with butter, cheese, seasoned and combined with chopped tomato and diced grilled bacon.

Milanaise. The dressed pasta is garnished with a garniture milanaise lié in tomato sauce. This consists of a julienne of white of chicken, ham, tongue, gherkin, mushroom and hard-boiled egg white in about equal amounts. Truffle may be added sparingly. The pasta and its garniture are well cohered and tossed together over heat for service.

Mornay. Cooked and dressed with butter and seasoning, arranged in a buttered dish, masked with mornay sauce, sprinkled with grated cheese and put in a hot oven till golden brown.

Napolitaine. Cooked pasta dressed with butter, cheese and seasoning and combined with rough chopped and seeded fresh tomatoes. Mix well together, cohere over heat and serve very hot. Tomato sauce may be used in the place of the fresh tomatoes.

Noodles (Nouilles). 'Bought in' as a commercial pasta or kitchen made.

Method. 500g (1 lb) flour, salt, 2 eggs, 8 yolks, 50g (2 oz) milk. Sieve flour, add salt, make a well in the centre, add eggs, yolks and milk and knead until the preparation clears the hands and the paste is tough, smooth and crack free. Rest for 30 minutes. Divide the paste and roll out. Partly dry the paste and cut in strips or ribbons, or stamp to required pattern (for ravioli). Complete the drying process on a floured board or hang in strips. Use or cook as required.

Ravioli. Stuffed rondels or squares, kitchen made or 'bought in'. If raw, it should be poached in boiling salted water, drained, arranged in a buttered dish and baked with butter, bolonaise, madeira or tomato sauce and grated parmesan.

Stuffing: Chopped shallot melted in butter and made up with cooked minced chicken, chopped spinach and parsley, oatmeal or breadcrumbs. Other ingredients for ravioli include minced beef, cooked brains, game, veal and tomatoes.

Sicilienne. Cook and dress pasta with butter, seasoning and cheese and combine with a sicilienne garniture; stew chopped shallot in olive oil, add minced raw beef, sliced aubergines, rough chopped red pimento and tomato. Season with salt, pepper and pinch of mixed herbs, add more oil and stew slowly. Combine with pasta and let preparation cohere over heat.

Tomato. Cooked and dressed with butter and cheese and combined with tomato sauce. Check flavour with a touch of sugar and colour with carmine if required.

Varenikis. Russian version of ravioli with sweet and savoury fillings. One popular filling consists of a preparation of cream (or cottage) cheese worked with egg yolk and seasoned with salt, sugar, paprika, lemon juice, nutmeg and grated cheese. The filled varenikis are poached with care in boiling water, drained, arranged in a buttered dish, baked in butter and cheese and served masked with sour cream and beetroot juice or just with grated cheese.

As a sweet, the pasta is poached in milk, baked in butter and served sauced with apricot, cherry, raspberry or strawberry purée or syrup.

VARIETIES OF PASTA

Alfabeto: letters of the alphabet. **Ave Maria:** short cut. **Bavette Fine:** thin spaghetti. **Bucatini:** very thin macaroni. **Capellini:** angels hair. **Casarecce:** egg nest noodles. **Cavatelli:** little caves, wavy shape with one side open. **Chiocciole:** shells. **Coquillettes:** cockle shells. **Denti de Cavallo:** horses teeth, cut pasta. **Ditali:** largest macaroni size cut tubes. **Ditalini:** small macaroni size cut tubes. **Diteline:** finest spaghetti, nested. **Farfalle:** butterfly bows. **Farfarllette:** small bows. **Fusilli:** rifle twisted macaroni, example of pasta artist. **Lasanga:** ribbon. **Linguine:** flat ribbon type spaghetti. **Macaroni:** generic term for larger pasta varieties, tubular. **Maltagliati:** twists. **Manicotti:** similar to cannelloni. **Maruzze:** large shells. **Napoletani:** a thick spaghetti. **Noodles:** ribbon, the French nouilles. **Numerals:** numbers. **Occhi di Lupo:** small rings. **Pastini:** very small round forms. **Peperini:** very small cut, used as mock rice. **Reginette:** very thin ribbon. **Rigatoni:** ribbed macaroni. **Semini:** little seeds. **Spaghetti:** little strings, long, round and solid pasta. **Spaghettoni:** large spaghetti. **Stellette:** little stars. **Tagliatelle:** large flat ribbon noodles. **Tortellini:** doughnut shaped rings. **Tripolini:** small butterfly bows. **Tubetti:** small cut tubes. **Tubettini:** tiny cut tubes. **Varenikis:** Russian version of ravioli. **Verdi:** green pasta. **Vermicelli:** small worms. **Yolanda:** noodle twists. **Ziti:** cut macaroni tubes. **Zuppa Reale:** soup nuts.

PASTRY ENTRÉES

Gnocchi (Gnokis)
Classified as farinaceous goods. May be prepared from a choux paste, semolina or potato. The first is known as French gnocchi and the other two as Italian gnocchi.

French or Choux Gnocchi. Cubes of poached choux paste. Heat ½ litre (1 pint) milk with 120g (4 oz) butter, salt, pepper and nutmeg.

Take off heat and slowly work in 300g (10 oz) flour. Reheat and cook flour. Remove from heat and blend in well beaten eggs. Return to heat but do not boil. Add 120g (4 oz) grated parmesan. Fill mixture into a piping bag filled with a plain bit, press out into oblongs, cutting off each one with a knife at 1cm ($\frac{1}{2}$ in) and allowing the gnocchi to fall into boiling salted water to poach. As they rise to the surface and are cooked, remove, drain and use as required.

Italian or Semolina Gnocchi. Heat 1 litre (2 pints) milk and season with salt, pepper and nutmeg. Add 300g (10 oz) fine semolina and cook for 20 minutes. Take off heat, thicken with 2 egg yolks, spread on a wetted tray to thickness of 1cm ($\frac{1}{2}$ in) and allow to cool. Stamp out in 5cm (2 in) rondels, or cut into squares or lozenges.

Potato Gnocchi. Purée of cooked potato worked while hot into a paste with butter, beaten egg, a little flour, salt, pepper and nutmeg. Scale off into olive or ball shapes, press with a fork to form a criss-cross pattern and poach in boiling water. Drain well, place in buttered serving dish, sprinkle with grated parmesan and gratiné in a hot oven.

Gnocchi à la Parisienne. French gnocchi, poached, drained, arranged in buttered dish, masked with suprême sauce, sprinkled with gruyère and gratiné in a hot oven.

Gnocchi à la Piédmontaise. Italian or semolina gnocchi baked in a buttered dish with diced tomatoes and ample grated parmesan.

Gnocchi à la Romaine. Italian gnocchi arranged in a buttered serving dish, painted with melted butter, sprinkled with grated parmesan and gruyère and gratiné in a hot oven.

Note. All gnocchi may also be featured masked and gratiné with bolonaise, madeira, suprême and tomato sauces.

Polenta

Often classified (and misnamed) as Italian gnocchi.

Cook 300g (10 oz) maize flour in 1 litre (2 pints) boiling water for 25 minutes. Season with salt, pepper and dash grated nutmeg. Add 50g (2 oz) butter and 50g (2 oz) grated parmesan. Handle and serve as for Italian gnocchi.

Vol-au-Vents

Individual puff paste case, an all-purpose affair, for filling with a wide variety of foods in sauces.

To make cases. Roll out paste to thickness of 3mm ($\frac{1}{8}$ in), stamp into 8cm (3 in) rounds with a grooved pastry cutter. Remove centres from half of the rounds with a 4cm (1½ in) plain cutter for the lids. Turn all the paste upside down (this aids rising in baking). Moisten the plain rounds and set the paste rings evenly in position on the rounds. Prick the centres over, rest for 20 minutes in the cool, bake cases and their lids on lightly oiled tray at 246°C. (475°F.). Clear cases of any crumbs.

Another method. Roll paste to 1cm (½ in), stamp out with an 8cm (3 in) plain cutter and turn over. Make grooves around the edges and cut small circle on the top for the lids with the point of a knife. Eggwash and bake at 246°C. (475°F.) on a moistened tray. The cases must rise well, the lids be detached and the cases cleared of any flaking.

Filling. Nothing can be cooked in the cases, therefore the fillings must be ready and very hot. They are not filled in advance as the cases might become soggy. The cases are filled with the aid of a spoon, topped with their lids, flashed quickly in a hot oven, garnished with a sprig of parsley and sent immediately to the table. Fillings may consist of any poultry, game, fish or meat, singly or combined, with or without mushrooms, but always in an appropriate sauce.

Cardinal (Vol-au-vent). Flaked poached sole fillet and button mushrooms in américaine sauce topped with truffle blade. Sauce is a fish velouté with tomato purée and brandy.

Cervelles (Vol-au-vent de). Diced poached brain, button mushrooms, truffle in sauce madère or suprême, truffle blade topped.

Chicken (Vol-au-vent de Volaille). Diced chicken, veal quenelles and button mushrooms in a velouté sauce topped with a truffle blade.

Financière (Vol-au-vent à la). Diced sweetbread, veal quenelles, mushrooms, truffle, cocks combs and kidneys and pitted olives in madeira sauce.

Foie Gras (Vol-au-vent au). Diced foie gras and truffle in sauce périgourdine.

Godard (Vol-au-vent). As for financière without the olives.

Lobster (Vol-au-vent d'Homard). Diced lobster meat, mushroom and truffle in sauce américaine, topped with truffle blade.

Mogador (Vol-au-vent). Veal quenelles, diced chicken and truffle in a demi-glace sauce.

Morue (Vol-au-vent de). Diced poached cod, sliced mushrooms and chopped parsley in béchamel sauce, truffle blade topped.

Quenelles (Vol-au-vent de). Chicken and veal quenelles and button mushrooms in suprême sauce, truffle blade topped.

Seafood (Vol-au-vent de Fruits de Mer). Wide term indicating any fish or shellfish in combination, usually diced lobster, cooked mussels, oysters, and button mushrooms in a well creamed fish velouté.

109

Shrimps, prawns, scampi and crab are all subjects for vol-au-vents in various fish sauces, i.e. américaine, dugléré, vin blanc.

Sweetbread (Vol-au-vent de Ris de Veau). Cubed cooked sweetbreads, veal or chicken quenelles, truffle and mushroom in suprême sauce. Truffle blade topped.

Toulouse (Vol-au-vent de). Diced sweetbreads, chicken and button mushrooms in suprême sauce with truffle blade topping. Also termed Toulousaine (à la).

Victoria (Vol-au-vent). Diced lobster and truffle in a fish velouté combined with lobster butter.

Other Varieties. Useful line for vegetarian fare: filled with mushrooms in cream sauce, pasta in tomato sauce, savoury rice and nutmeats. Also sweet vol-au-vents filled with various fruit pulps, purées and custards.

Bouchees, Bonne-Bouches or Patties

Small puff pastry cases filled with a savoury fish, meat, poultry or game stuffing. Served hot for hors-d'œuvre, cocktail parties or to accompany such dishes as bortsch.

They are prepared from a puff paste stamped out into round, square, oblong or diamond shapes, egg washed and baked on a greased tray. When cooked, the selected stuffing is inserted with the aid of a piping bag.

Fish. Sieved cooked fish, seasoned, bound with half-whipped cream, flecked with chopped fines herbes.

Foie Gras. Sieved, mixed with chopped truffle, salt, lemon juice and touched with port or sherry.

Game. Sieved and cooked, lié in espagnole sauce and half-whipped cream. Well seasoned.

Lobster. As for fish stuffing. Crab may also be used similarly.

Meat. Minced, combined with little chopped cooked onion, sieved hard-boiled egg, chopped parsley, well seasoned, made pliable with stock or demi-glace sauce.

Poultry. Minced, mixed with velouté sauce, well seasoned, chopped parsley.

Quenelle. Raw quenelle mixture, any type, piped into the centre of rolled out puff paste, folded over, secured, cut, egg washed and baked.

Croustades

The terms Croûte, Croustade, Timbale and Feuilletée are now all used for puff paste cases filled with various savoury fare in sauce for one or more portions. Croûtes and croustades were once prepared out of rolls and bread complete with lid; the term timbale also indicates a round metal or ceramic service dish, while feuilletée is the French

term for puff paste. Croustade is often used as another term for
vol-au-vent. Larger than individual pastry cases, they are seldom
seen except at certain gastronomic occasions. Since there could be
some confusion or overlapping of terms and functions over vol-au-
vent, croustades, timbales, bouchées and other puff paste goods, it is
best to relate them to portioning or size from small patties, individual
to multi-servings.

Meat

Meat has the distinction of bearing two name tags; a generic one for the live animal, and another—a culinary term—for the carcass after slaughter. In this context the meat of the oxen—bull, bullock or cow—becomes *beef*, that of the young calf is *veal*, the sheep according to age is known as *mutton* or *lamb*, and pig's meat is either *pork* or (processed) *ham* or *bacon*.

French is the origin of the culinary terms and there is a similarity between beef and boeuf, veal and veau, mutton and mouton, lamb and agneau, and pork and porc. The glandular and other by-products of meat are termed *offal*.

BEEF

Roasting Cuts—Loin (Aloyau) and Ribs (Côte de Boeuf)

The loin and the ribs of beef are the leading roasting cuts: the ribs correspond to giant cutlets; the loin or saddle, when cut along the backbone, produces two sirloin cuts. The ideal joint is the one turning the scales at around 6½ kilo (14 lb).

For the oven the piece is chined of surplus bone and excess fat and all gristle should be suppressed. Roasting joints should be trimmed for ease in carving, and at the same time they require protecting with fat in the form of a thickish bard. The piece is then tied at intervals with string. Prior to roasting, the joint should be well seasoned with salt.

For traditional presentation, roast beef is accompanied by Yorkshire pudding, pan gravy, horse-radish sauce, roast and parsley potatoes and dressed savoy cabbage. Other presentations are named after their predominant accompaniments.

Jardinière (à la). Roast beef accompanied by peas, diced French beans, turned carrots and turnips, asparagus tips, lima beans and cauliflower sprigs.

Primeurs (Côte de Boeuf Rôti aux). Roast rib of beef with spring vegetables (primeurs): glazed green peas, new carrots and turnips, French beans, asparagus tips and rissolée potatoes, Yorkshire pudding, pan gravy and hot horse-radish sauce.

Primeurs à la Crème. As for aux primeurs with the vegetable garnish masked in an adjusted béchamel sauce enriched with cream.

Racines (aux). Roast beef accompanied by glazed and turned carrots and turnips, celery hearts, small braised onions and parsley potatoes.

112

Richelieu. Roast beef garnished with duxelle stuffed tomatoes and mushrooms, braised lettuce and château potatoes.

Roast Beef, Rib Room Style. American glamour presentation of traditional Roast Beef of Old England. Special feature of the Rib Room, Carlton Tower Hotel, London, and other speciality restaurants.

Thick slice of roast rib of beef, served on a platter with individual Yorkshire puddings, accompanied by peas, baby carrots, savoy cabbage, baked jacket or parsley new potatoes, pan gravy, horse-radish sauce and dressed green or mixed salad. The baked or jacket potato is in foil, offered with a chive and butter dressing.

Chined ribs of 12 kilo (25 lb) are used and plate portions of 360g to 380g (12 to 13 oz) are served. The joint is carved in the room.

Grilling Cuts of Beef

These come from the fillet, sirloin and rump.

The *fillet* gives four grilling steaks: the fillet proper, fillet mignon, tournedos, and châteaubriand, a multi-portioned cut taken from the thick end of the fillet.

The *sirloin* gives three cuts: the minute or mini steak, entrecôte, and double entrecôte.

The *rump* gives two: the rump proper, and the point taken from the end.

The *porterhouse,* a multi-portioned cut and kind of giant chop, has the sirloin on one side, the fillet on the other and the centre bone in the middle. There is a smaller and individual porterhouse known as a T-bone steak.

In speciality restaurants the 'big three' steaks, i.e. fillet, sirloin and rump, are usually listed as standard, medium and large.

Steaks are grilled to order as underdone, medium and well done, to taste.

Aberdeen Angus. A 60g (2 oz) grilling cut of beef, usually fillet, seasoned, griddle cooked and served in soft roll with maître d'hôtel butter.

Grilled Bone. Beef bone to which meat adheres for grilling. May be raw, though are usually pre-cooked, taken from a roast joint. The 'devilled' or 'spatchcook' method generally applies: paint with melted butter or oil, roll in breadcrumbs seasoned with dry mustard, salt and cayenne, grilled till well charred.

Sirloin Steak (Entrecôte)

One of the most versatile cuts of beef, since it may be roasted whole and served hot or cold, or be cut into steaks of various thickness; according to size they are the minute, sirloin, double sirloin and the giant porterhouse. Sirloins are sold in the boneless and trimmed strip.

The following entrées, unless otherwise indicated, prescribe a 250g (8 oz) trimmed sirloin steak. Surplus fat is suppressed and the vein or yellow ligament of gristle removed. The cooking of these dishes is by shallow frying, grilling, or braising. Unless otherwise requested, steak should always be underdone.

Barbecued Steak. Season and sauté a single or double sirloin steak in butter, place in a serving dish, mask with barbecue sauce and heat.

Béarnaise (Sauté à la). The steak is seasoned, sauté in butter, finished with noisette butter and chopped parsley and served with béarnaise sauce.

Bismark Steak. Hamburg steak shaped as a tournedos, breaded, sauté in butter, topped with a fried egg, garnished with parisienne potatoes, finished with noisette butter and chopped parsley, served with tomato sauce.

Bordelaise. The steak is seasoned, sauté in butter, garnished with rondels of consommé-poached bone marrow and masked with a bordelaise sauce.

Braised Sirloin Steak and Onions. Season and lightly sauté the steak in butter in a deep pan. Smother with sliced blanched Spanish onions, season with salt and pepper, add a piece of butter, moisten with stock, cover the pan and braise slowly in the oven for an hour. Serve sprinkled with chopped parsley.

Carpet Bag Steak. Fillet or thick cut rump steak stuffed with oysters lié in a mushroom sauce and grilled. Served with béarnaise sauce.

Cecelia. Sirloin or minute steak seasoned, sauté in butter, garnished with grilled mushrooms, asparagus tips, finished with noisette butter and chopped parsley and served with soufflé potatoes.

Colchester Steak. Very similar to carpet bag. Thick cut fillet steak filled with oyster, secured with needle and thread, seasoned, wrapped in strips of bacon, grilled (usually underdone to medium), bacon and thread removed and steak served with béarnaise sauce.

Diana. Steak Diana or Diana is a popular dish prepared at table. There are several versions of the dish, we reproduce two.

1. Prepare a minute steak, season with salt and pepper and sauté in butter. Cook quickly on each side and sprinkle with Worcester sauce. Flame in brandy and serve with maître d'hôtel butter.

2. Melt a small quantity of minced onion in butter. Add tomato purée and chopped mushrooms and make up a short sauce, adding more butter as required. Place the steak in the pan, season with salt and pepper, sprinkle with Worcester sauce and cook. Flame with brandy and serve sauced over with the contents of the pan.
Note: May also be prepared with a fillet steak.

Eros. Prepared at table. Season and sauté a minute steak in maître d'hôtel butter, sprinkle with Worcester sauce and serve masked with the contents of the pan.

Hamburg Steak. Select pieces of pure meat from the fillet and chop finely. Season with salt, pepper and Worcester sauce, add small quantity of minced onion stewed in butter and bind with egg yolk. Shape in flour as a large rissole, fry in butter, top with a fried egg and finish with noisette butter and chopped parsley.

Fore-runner of the hamburger and referred to in old cookbooks as Steak à la Hambourgeoise, and à la Viennoise. Not to be confused with the Bismark Steak which is breaded and fried.

Note: Hamburger is written up under Snacks.

Hamburg Steak Mirabeau. As for Hamburg steak with the fried egg topping decorated with criss-crossed anchovy fillets, capers, pimento stuffed olives dotted in a pattern. Finished with noisette butter and chopped parsley.

Hôtelière (Sauté). Season and sauté a sirloin steak in butter. Dress with watercress, finish with noisette butter and serve with a French dressed lettuce salad and maître d'hôtel butter.

Lyonnaise. Sirloin steak seasoned, sauté in butter, masked with demi-glace sauce and garnished with rondels of fried onions.

Marchand de Vin. As for bordelaise but without the bone marrow garnish.

Minute Steak au Poivre Flambé. Season the steak with salt and with plenty of crushed peppercorns. Sauté in butter and flame in brandy. Serve sauced over with the juices from the pan.

Minute Steak Sauté au Beurre. Prepared at table. The steak is seasoned, sauté in butter and finished with noisette butter and chopped parsley.

Another version of this preparation prescribes topping the steak with a fried egg.

Mirabeau. Grilled steak garnished with pimento stuffed olives, anchovy fillet coils, tarragon leaves and finished with noisette butter and chopped parsley.

Moelle (à la). The steak is seasoned, sauté in butter, garnished liberally with consommé-poached rondels of bone marrow, finished with noisette butter and chopped parsley and dressed with a bouquet of fresh watercress.

Monkey Gland Steak. Prepared at table. Season and sauté a minute steak in butter. Serve with spaghetti seasoned with salt and pepper and dressed at the table with tomato sauce, butter and grated parmesan. May be prepared with a flattened rump steak. There are several versions of this preparation.

Montgolfier. Grilled steak garnished with soufflé potatoes.

Pepper Steak (Steak au Poivre). Score a sirloin or rump steak with a knife and rub in freshly crushed peppercorns and salt. Sauté in butter, serve sauced over with the contents of the pan. This preparation is also served flambé with brandy.

Fillet of Beef (Filet)

The fillet, which nestles under the sirloin separated by the backbone, is the most tender cut of beef. Like the sirloin, the fillet is also sold in the long strip, but unlike the sirloin, it is thick at the head and thins down gradually to the tail. The piece is almost pure meat and because of the lack of fat is inclined to dry out when cooked; it should therefore be larded. The fillet in the piece is not usually straight roasted but 'poêlé', a cooking process similar to braising.

In the following preparations the piece is presented with various garnitures, from which the dish takes its name. The fillet should be underdone, well glazed, sliced on the thick side, accompanied by its garnish and a demi-glace sauce prepared from the poêlé liquor.

Américaine. Sweetcorn kernels, lima beans, glazed baby carrots, whole grilled tomatoes and mushrooms, fondant potatoes. Demi-glace touched with brandy.

Arlequin (Fillet de Boeuf poêlé à l'). Larded fillet, poêlé and garnished with turned or baby glazed carrots and turnips, cauliflower sprigs, rolled leaf spinach and fondant potatoes. Cauliflower sprigs are masked with mornay sauce and browned in the oven.

Châtelaine. Braised whole chestnuts in veal stock, fonds d'artichauts filled with a purée soubise (onions) and noisette potatoes. Demi-glace.

Chipolata. Turned and glazed carrots, braised small onions, grilled bacon, baby chipolatas and whole chestnuts braised in a sauce espagnole.

Dubarry. Fonds d'artichauts filled with balls of cauliflower masked with mornay sauce and glazed. Demi-glace.

Duchesse. Primeurs and individual moulds of glazed duchesse potato. Demi-glace.

Financière. Assorted pitted olives—French, Spanish and pickled—veal and chicken quenelles, cocks combs and kidneys, loaded into a madeira sauce. Fondant potatoes.

Italienne. Duxelle filled whole tomatoes, quartered fonds d'artichauts and grilled mushrooms. Demi-glace.

Jardinière. The garnish indicates an assortment of vegetables, glazed and neatly arranged with new potatoes. Demi-glace.

Macédoine. Macédoine of vegetables, fondant or cocotte potatoes, Demi-glace.

Mireille. Grilled mushrooms, spinach purée and quartered fonds d'artichauts. Demi-glace.

Montgomery. Grilled mushrooms, duxelle filled whole braised tomatoes, quartered fonds d'artichauts and braised lettuce. Demi-glace.

Nemrod. Similar preparation to périgourdine and wellington. The piece, taken from the middle fillet, is larded with lardons, ham and truffle. It is marinated in white wine, brandy and aromates. The piece is roasted for 10 minutes, cooled, spread with liver pâté, wrapped in puff paste and cooked in a hot oven until the pastry is golden brown. The preparation is cut into thick slices and served with a demi-glace incorporating the marinade, and loaded with a julienne of ham, carrot, mushroom and truffle.

Périgourdine. Similar to wellington. The piece of middle fillet is part roasted, cooked, spread with a liver pâté loaded with chopped truffle sandwiched between thin barding fat, wrapped in puff paste and baked in a hot oven until the pastry is golden brown. The piece is sliced thickly and served with périgourdine sauce.

The term 'sous la cendre' or 'sous la croûte' is given to this type of preparation.

Primeurs. Glazed and turned carrots and turnips, peas, French beans, asparagus tips and fondant or noisette potatoes. Demi-glace.

Primeurs à la Crème. As above, but with the vegetable garnish masked with a creamed béchamel or reduced double cream. Demi-glace.

Provençale. Whole grilled tomatoes and mushrooms. Demi-glace.

Renaissance. Primeurs and duxelle stuffed whole tomatoes, fondant potatoes, demi-glace.

Richelieu. Braised duxelle stuffed tomatoes and mushrooms, braised lettuce, château potatoes, demi-glace.

Talleyrand. Spaghetti dressed in butter with a salpicon of ham, truffle and foie gras. Demi-glace loaded with chopped truffle.

Wellington. The fillet is wrapped and cooked in pastry and served with a rich sauce. A piece from the middle fillet is selected. It is larded, seasoned and set to roast in butter for up to 10 minutes. It is then wrapped in thin barding fat, spread fairly thickly with liver pâté and wrapped in a second layer of fat. The piece is enclosed in puff pastry, sealed, decorated and vents provided. The preparation is egg-washed and roasted in a hot oven until the pastry is golden brown. It is served in thick slices with a madeira sauce.

Tournedos

Cut from the thin end of the fillet in the shape of a cylinder 5cm (2 in) diameter and 4 to 5cm (1½ in to 2 in) deep. The cut is trimmed and should carry no fat at all. It will weigh about 120g (4 oz). It is prepared in similar ways to the sirloin and fillet, the dish taking on the name of the garniture. In each instance the cut is seasoned with salt and pepper, sauté in butter or grilled and left on the underdone side. In certain presentations the tournedos is dressed on a rondel of fried bread or croûton, usually spread with a pâté preparation.

Alsacienne (à la). Grilled tournedos dressed on croûton and garnished with braised sauerkraut and thick sliced ham.

Béarnaise. Grilled tournedos dressed with watercress and served with Béarnaise sauce.

Cendrillon. Grilled tournedos on croûton and garnished with fonds d'artichauts filled with mushroom purée.

Champignons à la Crème (aux). Season and sauté the tournedos in butter, remove and keep hot. Throw prepared whole button or sliced mushrooms into pan, add salt and lemon juice and cook by stewing in butter. Add fresh cream to form a sauce, let it cohere and mask the tournedos.

Chartwell. Seasoned and sauté tournedos dressed on a croûton spread with pâté de foie gras, and topped with a whole grilled mushroom surmounted by a rondel of horse-radish butter. Garnished with minted garden peas, whole baked tomato stuffed with sweetcorn kernels and fondant potatoes. Finished with noisette butter and chopped parsley.
(Dedicated to Sir Winston Churchill.)

Chasseur. Season tournedos, sauté in butter and keep hot. Add 2 chopped shallots, 3 sliced mushrooms and a little olive oil to the pan, cover and let the preparation sweat. Add a glass of dry white wine, a cup of demi-glace tomatée (tomato half-glaze), a piece of butter, chopped fines herbes, salt and pepper. Let the sauce cohere and mask it over the tournedos.

Clamart. Grilled tournedos on croûton garnished with fonds d'artichauts filled with glazed peas.

Concarde. Sauté in butter, dressed on a croûton, topped with foie gras rondel and truffle blade, masked with madeira sauce, garnished with halves of tomato stewed in butter and arranged in fonds d'artichauts top side up, and served with parisienne potatoes.

Façon du Chef (à la). Tournedos dressed on a croûton spread with liver pâté, topped with a grilled mushroom filled with béarnaise sauce. Garnished with whole grilled tomato, baby chipolata or frankfurter, asparagus tips and a sauté of chicken livers lié in demi-glace. Finished with noisette butter and chopped parsley.

Favorite. Sauté tournedos garnished with asparagus tips and truffle blades.

Forestière. Tournedos sauté in butter, dressed on a croûton, garnished with braised morilles and sauté bacon lardons.

Frank Harding. Season and sauté the tournedos in butter and dress on a croûton spread with pâté de foie. Garnish with asparagus tips, sweetcorn kernels, garden peas and parisienne potatoes. Finish with
118

noisette butter and chopped parsley. At the point of service, top with a rondel of maître d'hôtel butter.

(Created for and dedicated to F. D. M. Harding when managing director of the Pullman Car Company. Frank Harding had this preparation served when he entertained guests on the Brighton Belle.)

Frascati. Sauté in butter, dressed on a croûton surmounted with a collop of foie gras, garnished with button mushrooms, asparagus tips and truffle.

Gabrielle. Sauté, dressed on a small round croquette made with minced chicken, chopped truffle and duchesse potato fried in butter. Topped with a rondel of consommé-poached bone marrow and truffle blade, garnished with braised lettuce.

Grand Duc. Tournedos sauté, dressed on a croûton, topped with poached bone marrow, masked with périgourdine sauce and garnished with asparagus tips and truffle blades.

Judic. Tournedos sauté masked with demi-glace, loaded with cocks combs and kidneys, topped with a truffle blade and garnished with braised lettuce.

Lucullus. Tournedos sauté, dressed on a croûton, masked with périgueux sauce, topped with small grilled mushrooms and truffle blade and garnished with bouquet of asparagus tips, cocks combs and kidneys.

Madras. As for maître d'hôtel with the tournedos topped with a thick rondel of curry butter.

Maître d'Hôtel. Dressed on a croûton topped with thick rondel of maître d'hôtel butter, finished with noisette butter, dressed with bouquet of watercress and served with straw potatoes and French dressed green salad.

Maréchale (à la). Tournedos sauté, garnished with cocks combs and kidneys in demi-glace, topped with truffle blade.

Maryland. Dressed on a croûton, topped with a whole grilled mushroom and garnished with corn and banana fritters and whole grilled tomato. Escorted with creamed sweetcorn, peas, fondant potatoes and maryland sauce.

Mascotte. Tournedos sauté, topped with truffle blade and garnished with diced sauté potatoes and fonds d'artichauts in demi-glace.

Masséna. Season, sauté the tournedos in butter and keep hot. Swill out the pan with madeira sauce, reduce and correct with butter. Load with chopped truffle and flavour with brandy. Mask the tournedos with the sauce and garnish with quartered fonds d'artichauts tossed in butter, a bouquet of concassed tomato and consommé-poached rondels of bone marrow. Touch the garniture with chopped parsley. (The croûton is optional for this preparation.)

Moelle (à la). Seasoned and sauté tournedos, dressed on a liver-pâté-spread-croûton and garnished generously with rondels of consommé-poached bone marrow. Finished with noisette butter and chopped parsley.

Niçoise. Tournedos sauté and dressed on a croûton. Surmount with a rondel of peeled lemon and a pimento stuffed Spanish or pickled black olive with anchovy fillet coil. Garnish with a whole grilled tomato, French beans and parisienne potatoes. Finish with noisette butter and chopped parsley.

Ninon. Grilled or sauté, dressed on pâté-spread-croûton and garnished with braised whole endives, grilled mushrooms and small baked tomatoes filled with béarnaise sauce.

Opéra. Asparagus tips and a sauté of chicken livers garnish, masked in madeira sauce, finished with chopped parsley.

Parisienne (à la). Grilled, dressed on a croûton, topped with béarnaise sauce and garnished with fonds d'artichauts, asparagus tips, noisette potatoes and truffle blade.

Périgourdine (à la). Sauté and masked with périgourdine sauce.

Peronne. Sauté in butter, dressed on a liver-pâté-spread-croûton, masked with madeira sauce and garnished with fried whole banana, braised green peppers stuffed with rice and a whole grilled tomato.

Persanne. Sauté, dressed on a croûton, masked with madeira sauce and garnished with banana fritters, braised green peppers stuffed with rice and a grilled whole tomato.

Petit Duc. Same as grand duc but without the poached bone marrow.

Pompadour. Tournedos sauté, masked with périgueux sauce and garnished with fonds d'artichauts and parisienne potatoes.

Portugaise. Grilled, dressed on a croûton, cordon of tomato sauce and garnished with whole duxelle stuffed braised tomatoes.

Princesse (à la). Grilled tournedos dressed on a fond d'artichaut with asparagus tips and madeira sauce.

Provençale (à la). Sauté, dressed on a croûton, with a preparation of chopped tomato, onion and fines herbes stewed and reduced in olive oil and sauté cèpes.

Rachel. Tournedos sauté, dressed on a fond d'artichaut topped with truffle blade and masked with a bone marrow sauce.

Richelieu. Grilled and garnished with duxelle-stuffed tomatoes and mushrooms, braised lettuce and château potatoes.

Rita (à la). Tournedos sauté, dressed on a liver-pâté-spread-croûton and surmounted with a rondel of paprika butter. Garnished with whole baked tomato filled with chopped red pimento and cooked rice and topped with an olive stuffed with a purée of anchovy fillet, parisienne potatoes and asparagus tips. Finished with noisette butter and chopped parsley.

Rossini. Tournedos seasoned and sauté in butter. The pan is swilled out with madeira sauce, reduced and finished with butter. Tournedos is dressed on a croûton, masked with the sauce and topped with a rondel of foie gras surmounted with a truffle blade.

Rouleau de foie gras truffle is sold in cylindrical shape for rossini and other medaillons of beef preparations. The rondel should be passed in flour and very lightly sauté in butter.

Escoffier suggested the rossini be accompanied by noodles dressed in butter and parmesan cheese and seasoned.

Sarah Bernhardt. Tournedos sauté, topped with consommé-poached bone marrow, masked with madeira sauce and garnished with small stewed tomatoes.

(An Auguste Escoffier creation.)

Savoy (à la). Garnished with asparagus tips, truffle blade, whole grilled tomato and pommes noisettes, finished with madeira sauce.

Smitane. Season and sauté the tournedos in butter and keep hot. Add 2 chopped shallots and 3 sliced mushrooms to the pan and stew in butter. Add cream, allow some reduction and thicken with butter. Season with salt and cayenne and sour the sauce with lemon juice and a dash of vinegar. Mask the tournedos with the sauce.

Strasbourgeoise. Butter-sauté tournedos masked with a well creamed velouté loaded with foie gras purée flavoured with brandy and topped with a truffle blade. The sauce is prepared in the pan and the piece is cooked.

(Auguste Escoffier creation dedicated to Marie Ritz, wife of noted hôtelier and native of the capital city of Alsace. Most Escoffier à la strasbourgeoise and à l'alsacienne preparations are similarly inspired.)

Talleyrand. Sauté, dressed on croûton, masked with périgourdine sauce and garnished with anna potatoes and fonds d'artichauts filled with foie gras.

Truffles (aux). Tournedos sauté, dressed on a croûton well garnished with sliced truffle and masked with a good madeira sauce.

Vert Pré. Grilled tournedos topped with maître d'hôtel butter rondel and garnished with straw potatoes and bouquet of watercress.

Planked Steak

The planking of food, an American contribution to the culinary repertoire, is reserved for juicy cuts of meat and fish with the objective of capturing the essential escaping juices from the fare. Planking is now almost exclusively reserved for steak, notably the double sirloin or other similar large, juicy cuts. The focal point of the operation is the plank, made of hard wood with grooves to catch the juices. Stainless steel planks are also made but wood is better. It should be 'seasoned'; paint the plank with olive oil and place it in a moderate oven, repeating the process several times.

For the cooking operation the plank is oiled, sprinkled with salt and pepper and heated in the oven. When hot it is piped with duchesse potato to serve as a trap for the juices. The potato is left unglazed. The piece for planking, the steak for example, is seasoned and grilled for 5 minutes to seal and placed in the centre of the plank. Paint the meat and potato with melted butter and place in the oven for 15 minutes. This will brown the potato and fill the grooves with gravy.

Garnish with primeurs: glazed carrots, turnips, button onions, mushrooms, peas, asparagus tips and whole tomato—for colour and eye appeal. Flash in the oven to heat through, sprinkle with chopped parsley, arrange rondels of maître d'hôtel butter on the steak and send to the table where the meat is divided up on the plank and served with the escorting vegetables.

The steak may also be garnished with poached bone marrow or rondels of grilled fat.

Note: A grilled salmon steak may be given the plank treatment; the board piped with duchesse, the fish garnished with new potatoes, olives of poached cucumber, peas and asparagus tips and served with mousseline sauce or parsley butter.

Other Beef Preparations

Beef à la Bourguignonne. Similar preparation to the à la mode, prepared with a larded point of beef or with pre-cut steaks. The final sauce is loaded with glazed baby mushrooms, pitted olives and blanched and sauté bacon lardons.

The red wine used in the marinade, which is added to the braising operation, should be a Burgundy.

Beef à la Mode. Comprehensive braising operation prepared with a joint of beef taken from the rump at about 3 kilo (6 lb). The piece is stuck with thick lardons and marinated for 6 hours. It is then sealed in hot olive oil and placed to braise in a deep closed pan for 4 hours with its marinade, calves feet, sliced onion, carrot, celery and leek previously sauté in hot dripping, and sufficient stock to cover.

The meat is removed, glazed and its sauce prepared from the strained and suitably corrected braising liquor loaded with diced calves feet, glazed baby carrots and turnips—or turned roots—button onions and mushrooms. The sauce should be rich, thick and glossy and the meat is sent to the table in its sauce for carving in thick slices.

The à la mode is also prepared from beef cut into steaks or collops; the procedure is identical.

When prepared from the whole piece it is also presented for cold buffet service. While still hot the larded piece is pressed into a

122

terrine, masked with its garnished sauce, finished with a good topping and allowed to cool and set. For service it is thickly cut and offered with dressed salad.

Beef Bourgeoise. Identical preparation to the à la mode and the bourguignonne, but the sauce is garnished with glazed baby carrots, turnips, onions, mushrooms, pitted olives and blanched and sauté bacon lardons.

Note: There is an overall similarity between these three classic braised beef preparations i.e. the à la mode, bourguignonne and the bourgeoise. All three prescribe the meat in the piece or in steaks; only the marinade and final garnishing really differs. It is now more usual to present these dishes with the beef cut into braising steaks.

Beef Olives. Thin cut stewing steak, stuffed, rolled and braised with aromates in brown stock and served in their corrected and checked braising liquor.

Braised Steak and Onions. Prepare required quantity of well trimmed beef cut into steaklets. Season and toss to seal in hot dripping. Smother with sliced blanched onions, season, dot with butter, moisten with stock, cover pan and braise in the oven for 2 hours. Sliced mushrooms may also be added.

Carbonnade of Beef. Collops or diced stewing steak braised with onions in brown sauce incorporating beer. The preparation is stewed together and corrected for service in the usual way.

Étuvé de Boeuf. Original recipe prescribed fillet but other lean and well trimmed cuts may be used. The meat is cut into large cubes and sauté in butter with button onions, turned carrots and minced celery. The preparation is sauced over with white wine and made up with stock. It is then braised in a covered pan. The meat is served in its strained and reduced cooking liquor with the addition of tomato purée. Accompanied by dressed spaghetti.

Faggots. Country style preparation made with liver, beef and onion. Chop liver, mince beef (equal amounts), mix together, add sauté chopped baked onion, season with salt, pepper, dash of ground nutmeg and a pinch or so of mixed herbs. Bind with egg, scale off and roll into balls of equal size. Arrange in a greased baking tray and bake in the oven until cooked. Additional bulk may be provided by white breadcrumbs moistened with stock. Faggots are eaten hot with a rich brown gravy or cold with salad and bread and butter. They are sometimes prepared individually wrapped in pigs caul and baked as indicated.

Note: Not to be confused with faggot, the English term for a bouquet garni.

Goulash. The basis of this Hungarian dish is a sweet type of pepper from Central Europe called paprika.

Sauté required quantity of sliced collops of stewing meat in butter. Remove from pan and keep warm. Set minced shallot, celery and carrot to stew in butter, add salt, pepper tomato purée and paprika, stir, thicken with flour and make up with stock. Add bouquet garni and simmer for 30 minutes. Strain, check seasoning and consistency and load the sauce with the sauté beef. Let the preparation cohere and serve with gnocchi parisienne.

This basic formula indicates beef, but it is also applicable for veal, lamb and chicken goulash.

Hot Pot of Beef with Dumplings. Cubed stewing steak cleared of all fat and gristle, seasoned and sauté to seal in dripping. Place in deep pan on sliced onion, carrot and turnip. Season and moisten with stock. Cover pan and braise in oven for 2 hours. Add handful of peas and dumplings and braise for another hour. Serve sprinkled with coarsely chopped parsley.

Dumplings are prepared from suet dough; a pinch of mixed herbs may be incorporated into the dough for added flavour.

Kromeskis, Cromeskis (Cromesquis). Made from raw or cooked minced beef, lamb, veal, chicken or game. Minced main ingredient is seasoned with salt, pepper, pinch of mixed herbs and bound with egg. It is shaped in flour as a cone or an egg, battered or breadcrumbed and deep fried to a golden brown.

Cromeskis are also made into quite elaborate preparations with sweetbread, brain, chicken livers, foie gras, lobster, sole, oysters and various permutations of fish, meat or poultry and game. Chopped truffle, mushrooms and various salpicons also come into play: they are diced and lié in sauces related to the main ingredient, battered and deep fried.

Lobscouse or Scouse. A variety of sea pie and another favourite of seafolk. It consists of a meat and potato or root vegetable pie or stew covered with ships biscuits to form a crust topping. Made with all kinds of stewing meat, including corned beef; it has been made with such varied meats as bear, walrus and whale. A more contemporary version is prepared with stewing cuts of mutton cooked with carrots, onions and seasoning. When potatoes are added it's similar to an Irish stew. Lobscouse is usually accompanied by pickled red cabbage.

Sea Pie. Originally a sea-faring dish. Prepare and cube about 1 kilo (2 lb) lean stewing beef, place in pan with 2 chopped onions and season with salt and pepper. Cover with stock and stew for 35 minutes. Arrange in pie dish with an equal amount of cubed or sliced raw potatoes. Sprinkle with chopped parsley, cover as a pie with suet pastry crust rolled fairly thickly and bake in the oven at 175°C. (350°F.) for 2 to 2½ hours. Serve with a rich brown gravy.

Note: Roots such as carrot, turnip, leek and parsnip may be added, forming a type of meat and vegetable pie covered with a suet crust.

Shepherds Pie. Prepared with lean raw beef or mutton well minced, combined with chopped baked onion, seasoned, moistened with stock and cooked slowly. Arranged in greased dish, topped with creamed potato, forked over, dotted with butter and baked in the oven until a crisp brown topping forms. Served with a thick brown sauce. May also be prepared with minced cooked meat.

Steak Puddings. There are various types of steak puddings and all are similarly prepared. It may be prepared just with steak though it is usual to combine the meat with other ingredients such as kidney, mushrooms and oysters.

Steak, Kidney, Mushroom and Oyster Pudding. The proportions are based on 750g (1½ lb) cubed stewing steak cleared of fat and gristle, to 250g (½ lb) cubed beef kidney. These ingredients are seasoned and tossed together in butter to seal and lightly brown the meat. The preparation is then placed in a bowl with chopped cooked onion, sliced mushrooms, tomato purée, chopped parsley, seasoned, moistened with stock and a few drops of Worcester sauce and mixed well. The pudding basin is greased, lined with a suet dough allowing some overlapping. The basin is then three-quarters filled with the meat preparation, which should be moist, the lid of dough is placed in position and sealed down. Perforations are made to allow steam to escape and the pudding is sealed with greaseproof paper or foil, wrapped tightly in a cloth and steamed for 5 hours.

When cooked, the pudding is unwrapped, the oysters and their cooking juices are added, and also any stock (consommé) lost by evaporation. Serve from the basin, boiling hot.

Six to eight oysters are allowed to the 500g (1 lb) of pudding. They are poached in sufficient consommé with butter. To cook them in the pudding would toughen the shell fish.

Steak, Kidney, Oyster and Lark Pudding. A traditional dish. On the scale of 2 per 500g (1 lb) beef and kidney, the larks are cleaned, skinned and boned and cooked in with the pudding.

Strogonov. Beef Strogonov is a famous Russian fare preparation.

Slice the tail of the fillet in collops, season and toss in butter. Remove from pan, keep hot. Add minced shallot and sliced mushrooms to pan and allow the preparation to stew in butter. Add cream to make up a sauce and allow some reduction. Sour the sauce with lemon juice and a dash of vinegar, check seasoning and consistency with butter. Load the sauce with the sauté beef, let the preparation adhere and serve with a pilaff of rice. Preparation may also be prepared with a velouté.

Note: In recent times another ingredient has been added to the strogonov sauce—tomato. The reason for this is possibly to improve appearance or on account of the British love of tomatoes. The original is a white sauce.

Salt Beef

The salting of beef is an ancient practice of food preservation. It has associations with the days of sail when hard tack and sea biscuits formed the diet of mariners. Salt beef was always popular among the less wealthy members of the community since it was cheap and wholesome when cooked with root vegetables. As with the case of many other foods of humble origin, salt beef has graduated into the annals of gastronomy. Well prepared, it is very acceptable and worthy of its food fashion status. The silverside, topside and brisket are the salting pieces. At one time, salting was performed on the premises, now salt beef is 'bought in' ready processed. It is also sold pressed and ready cooked for slicing and hotting up in stock as a convenience food.

Salt Silverside of Beef with Dumplings and Root Vegetables. Brined meat is still raw meat and requires cooking. It is washed, soaked in several waters, plunged into boiling light stock and simmered at 15 minutes to the 500g (1 lb). It is served with dumplings, a selection of poached vegetables, hot horse-radish sauce and gravy. The gravy is prepared by well reducing and defatting some of the cooking liquor. The vegetable selection consists of cabbage, celery hearts, leeks, whole onions, carrots, turnips and potatoes sprinkled with chopped parsley. The dumplings, prepared from a suet dough, are poached in stock for 40 minutes. Also offered with this substantial preparation is a dish of coarse baysalt (gros sel), a point well appreciated by gourmets.

Pressed Beef. Pressed, corned, preserved and bully beef is equally a member of the salt beef family. Here again is a humble commodity with associations going back to two World Wars when it was the lot not only of the soldier but also the civilian.

Pressed beef is salt beef which has been brined, cooked by boiling, pressed into a mould and cooked. It is eaten cold with salad or made into hot preparations.

Bully Beef Pie. Equal amounts of minced corned beef and cooked potato, seasoned, chopped cooked onion added, well mixed and folded into a greased baking dish. Smoothed and forked over, dotted with butter, baked till a golden brown in the oven and served with thick brown gravy.

Corned Beef Hash. Popular American dish. Chop half an onion, set it to melt in butter. Add equal quantities of diced corned beef and sauté potatoes. Mash together with a fork, season with salt, pepper and Worcester sauce, shape as an omelette and arrange on a hot serving dish. Finish with noisette butter and chopped parsley.
Note: The name corned is a derivative of salt cones used in brines.

Corned Beef Steak. Equal quantities of corned beef and cooked potato passed through a mincer, seasoned with salt, pepper, Worcester sauce, a small amount of minced onion previously stewed in butter, bound with egg yolk, shaped as a hamburg steak and fried in butter on both sides. Served topped with a fried egg, finished with noisette butter and chopped parsley.

Fried Corned Beef. Thick slices of corned beef, dipped in batter, deep fried to a golden brown, dressed with fried parsley and served with tomato sauce.

VEAL (VEAU)

Veal is calves meat. It remains veal until the calf is a year old. Our home-killed veal varies in quality; French, Dutch and Italian veal is often better as the calves are usually slaughtered at an earlier age. If the carcass is too big the meat is inclined to toughness. Veal can therefore be a difficult meat and needs to be carefully selected.

The best culinary cuts are the escalopes, taken from cushions of pure meat from the thigh (the noix), or from the boned cutlet, best end, or loin. These pieces are sliced in collops and flattened out with a wetted butchers bat. The larger joints—loin and shoulder—are best braised and other cuts stuffed and braised. The knuckles, feet and large bones are wealthy in gelatinous substance and are ideal in the preparation of stocks and aspics; they were once the source of jellies for sweets.

Escalope of Veal
The escalope should be thin and flat. Some preparations prescribe breading, for others the piece is just floured prior to cooking, which is usually shallow frying.

Anglaise (Escalope de Veau à l'). Seasoned, breaded, sauté in butter and garnished with grilled bacon, parsley new potatoes and tomato sauce.

Beaulieu. Breaded sauté in butter, garnished with pitted black olives, quartered sauté tomatoes, fonds d'artichauts and parsley new potatoes, and finished with noisette butter and chopped parsley.

Bocconcini. Season, flour, pass in beaten egg and olive oil and coat with a preparation of mixed grated gruyère and parmesan cheese. Flatten, sauté carefully in butter and finish with a dash of noisette butter.

Champignons (aux). Floured, sauté in butter and masked with a madeira sauce loaded with cooked sliced mushrooms.

Champignons à la Crème (aux). Speciality prepared at table. The escalope is seasoned and sauté in butter with sliced mushrooms. The preparation is flamed in brandy and cooked in marsala or dry sherry. Fresh cream is added and the sauce allowed to cohere. Serve the escalope masked with sauce.

Cordon Bleu. Prepare 2 equal size escalopes and make up a sandwich with 2 slices of parma ham and a slice of gruyère in the centre. Press down, season, breadcrumb with care, secure with cocktail sticks if required, and sauté in butter. Remove the fastenings and top the preparation with rinded lemon rondels and finish with a dash of noisette butter.

There are several variations to the Cordon Bleu, one of which suggests york in place of the parma ham.

Endives (aux). Season, flour, sauté in butter and garnish with whole braised Belgium endives. Finish with noisette butter and lemon juice.

Flamande (à la). Seasoned, floured, sauté and garnished with whole braised endive, turned carrots and turnips, grilled bacon and chipolata.

Flambé. Prepared at table. The escalope is seasoned with salt, pepper and lemon juice and sauté in butter. It is flamed in brandy, well sauced with cream, heated through and served. Sliced mushrooms may also be added and cooked with the veal.

Flambé Normande. As for flambé but with thin slices of eating apple sauté with the escalope and the flaming performed with calvados. Finished with cream.

Gismonde. Breaded, sauté arranged on leaf spinach sauté in butter, masked with madeira sauce loaded with a julienne of truffle.

Holstein. Seasoned, breaded, sauté and topped with a fried egg, decorated with criss-crossed julienne of anchovy fillet dotted with capers. Finished with noisette butter and chopped parsley. Served with sauté potatoes.

Liègeoise. Another name for viennoise. Adopted during World War One in commemoration of the Belgium city sacked by the Kaiser's armies. Since Austria fought on the side of Germany, Vienna was out of favour.

Milanaise. The escalope is seasoned, breaded, sauté in butter and dressed with spaghetti milanaise.

Olives (Escalope de Veau aux). Season, pass in flour, sauté in butter and place in fireproof cocotte. Add dry sherry, lemon juice and a quantity of chopped mixed French and Spanish olives. Allow to heat through and cohere with the lid on in the oven. Finish with noisette butter and a little chopped parsley.

Orloff. Seasoned, floured, sauté in butter, dressed with purée soubise and sprinkled with truffle cut in half moons.

Ostend. Another name for Holstein.

Princesse. Seasoned, breaded, sauté in butter, dressed with a bouquet of asparagus tips secured with a strip of red pimento and a truffle blade, finished with noisette butter.

128

Pointes d'Asperges (aux). Floured or breaded, sauté and garnished with buttered asparagus tips.

Smitane. Season, pass in flour, sauté in butter, mask with sauce smitane with sliced or button mushrooms.

Viennoise. The noted Wiener Schnitzel. The escalope is seasoned, breadcrumbed and sauté in butter. It is set on a serving dish, lightly brushed with melted butter and dressed with a thin rinded rondel of lemon surmounted by an anchovy fillet coiled round a pitted Spanish olive. The preparation is then generously garnished with chopped parsley, sieved white and yolk of hard-boiled egg, capers and golden fried breadcrumbs arranged in a colourful pattern. Finish with noisette butter and serve sizzling hot.

Zingara. Season, pass in flour and sauté in butter. Sandwich between two thin grilled gammon steaks the same size as the veal. Press down, place in a serving dish and mask with madeira sauce loaded with chopped truffle and sliced mushrooms.

In recent times the zingara is presented as a sauté escalope masked with madeira sauce loaded with a julienne of ham and mushrooms.

Veal Cutlets

The cutlets, taken from the best end, should be well trimmed. They are seasoned, breaded or not, sauté or grilled, and served garnished or straight.

Côte de Veau Dauphine. Fairly thick cutlet cooked in consommé or a blanc and cooled. The kernel is removed and diced, to it are added equal amounts of diced lean ham, truffle and cooked mushroom. Bind in a reduced allemande sauce. Reshape kernel and place back in position in cutlets. Breadcrumb and sauté in butter. Serve with a demiglace and tomato sauce.

Fritto Misto. Noted Italian dish. For 4 portions, prepare 4 each of the following, all uniform in size: small raw collops, raw calves liver, cooked calves brain, blanched sweetbread, balls of leaf spinach, cauliflower sprigs. Season, dip in batter and fry quickly in olive oil to a crispy golden brown. Drain, salt dust, pile upon a doily, serve immediately with tomato sauce and lemon wedges.

The batter is prepared with flour, egg yolks, grated parmesan, salt and sufficient milk for a creamy consistency and left to stand for 30 minutes. Variations include breading the ingredients and coating them in equal quantities of breadcrumbs and grated parmesan.

Grenadins

Term given to a thickly cut oval shaped escalope of veal. Because of the 'dryness' of veal, especially when thick cut, grenadins are usually larded and then braised. They are then featured with any garniture as for escalopes and other veal preparations.

129

Veal Joints

There are three joints: saddle (selle), loin (longe) and breast (poitrine). Veal is seldom plain roasted as it is inclined to dry out; it is usually braised or poêlé.

The prepared joint, usually boned, is salted and set to roast in hot dripping in a braising pan for about 10 minutes. Veal bones, sliced onion and carrot, a bouquet garni and stock are then added. The preparation is brought up to the boil and braised in the oven. When ready the piece is glazed, accompanied by a good brown sauce prepared from the strained, reduced and corrected cooking liquor and the appropriate garniture. Jus lié sometimes replaces brown sauce. For an elaborate service the veal sauce is enriched by madeira.

In other preparations the joint is boned, rolled, stuffed and braised.

Anglaise (à l'). The joint is boned, sage and onion stuffed, rolled and tied and then braised. Served with a good jus lié.

Bourgeoise. Braised veal accompanied by glazed baby onions, mushrooms, carrots and turnips.

Braised Dressed Breast of Veal. The piece is boned, stuffed, rolled and tied up. It is placed in a deep pan and cooked in hot dripping for 10 minutes. Veal bones, sliced onion, carrot and a bouquet garni are added plus sufficient veal stock. The preparation is braised in the oven, with the lid on, for about 2½ hours. The piece is glazed and served with its braising liquor strained, reduced, corrected and flavoured with madeira. Accompanied by primeurs and fondant potatoes.

Note: Sage and onion stuffing is indicated and it should be bound with egg.

Espagnole. Braised veal garnished with whole baked tomatoes filled with rice, braised button onions and rissolée potatoes.

Flamande. Braised veal accompanied by glazed carrots and turnips, braised Belgian endive, cabbage, sliced gammon, chipolatas and parsley potatoes.

Française. Braised veal accompanied by purée of spinach au jus and anna potatoes.

Italienne. Braised veal garnished with duxelle-filled whole tomatoes, braised fonds d'artichauts and grilled mushrooms.

Jardinière. Braised veal garnished with baby carrots and turnips, peas, French beans, asparagus tips and cauliflower sprigs.

Orloff. Elaborate dish prepared with the saddle of veal. The piece is poêlé and the loin meat detached from the bone, sliced and replaced in position sandwiched with a purée of onion, i.e. soubise, spread between each slice and a truffle blade to indicate each portion. The reconstituted joint is then masked with a well buttered soubise sauce and glazed quickly in a hot oven.

Piémontaise. Braised veal accompanied by risotto à la piémontaise and tomato sauce. The risotto is seasoned, dressed with parmesan, gruyère, butter and a pinch of saffron.

Primeurs. Braised veal accompanied by glazed baby or turned carrots, turnips, peas, braised endive and fondant potatoes.

Richelieu. Braised veal accompanied by dressed whole tomatoes and mushrooms, braised lettuce and château potatoes.

Other Veal Preparations

Bitoke. Preparation made with a raw veal, chicken and mixtures thereof. Chop, pass through a mincer, work to a smooth paste, season with salt and pepper and bind with cream and egg yolk. Shape as a rissole or cutlet, fry in butter.

Bitoke à la Crème. Cook in butter, remove from pan and keep hot. Swill pan out with cream, season, touch with lemon and allow some reduction over heat. Mask bitoke with this sauce.

Bitoke aux Champignons. As for à la crème with the addition of sliced mushrooms cooked in the bitoke pan before swilling out with cream.

Bitoke Monsolet. As for à la crème with the addition of glazed button onions and mushrooms in the prepared sauce. Garnish with fondant potatoes, parsley sprinkled.

Bitoke Sauté au Beurre. As described, finish with noisette butter.

Bitoke Smetana. Cook in butter, remove, keep hot, add minced shallot and sliced mushrooms to pan and stew in more butter as required. Add cream, heat and sour with lemon juice. Let sauce reduce, season with salt and cayenne and mask over bitoke.

Bitkis. Small size bitoke, three to the serving. All preparations for the larger bitoke go for the smaller bitkis.

Marengo (Petit Sauté de Veau à la). Season small veal collops and brown in olive oil with chopped onions. Remove from pan and keep hot. Swill pan out with white wine, allow some reduction and make up sauce with brown stock, tomato sauce, tiny garlic clove and pinch of mixed herbs. Reduce, check consistency and seasoning, load with glazed button onions and mushrooms and mask over the veal. Let the preparation braise together and serve garnished with heart-shaped croûtons.

Meurette of Veal. Rich veal stew with red wine.

Meurette de Veau Bourguignonne. Cut the veal into small lean

131

collops, season, sauté with minced shallot and onion, dredge with flour, coat and brown. Add calves feet, veal bones, tomato purée, red wine and brandy, moisten as required with water or stock and braise with the lid on in an oven for 1½ hours.

Pick out the meat, place in a fireproof terrine, strain in the braising liquor, add the diced calves feet, garnish with glazed button onions, mushrooms and small carrots. Seal the lid of the terrine (which must have a vent hole) with a band of flour and water paste, brown this in the oven and serve very hot.

Note: The veal may be marinated in red wine, brandy and aromate and the marinade added to the meurette preparation, no additional wine or spirit may be needed.

Meurette may also be prepared with beef.

Osso Bucco. Method of featuring rich and gelatinous knuckles of veal. They are placed in a deep pan with sliced onions, seasoned and tossed in butter. Tomato purée, a bouquet garni and sufficient stock or water to moisten is added to the preparation, which is then braised slowly in the oven with the lid on for 4 hours. The bouquet is removed, the seasoning checked and the preparation served thus, accompanied with butter, and parmesan dressed risotto or spaghetti. This preparation is usually termed Osso Bucco à l'Italienne.

Sauté of Veal Chasseur. Prepare, season and sauté veal collops in butter. In a second pan sweat chopped onion, shallot and sliced mushrooms in hot olive oil. Add tomato sauce, chopped fines herbes and dry white wine. Let the sauce cohere, add the prepared veal, blend, reheat and serve.

Veal Stews. They should always be prepared with the basis of a good veal stock, otherwise the end product could be insipid and the whole effect spoiled. It is equally important to trim the meat of all gristle, fat and other so-called inedible parts. There are two basic veal stews: white (blanquette or fricassée) and brown (ragoût).

Blanquette. The veal is sliced in collops and treated by pre-blanching from cold to whiten the meat and dispose of excess albumen. It is moistened with veal stock or water, brought to the boil and garnished with whole carrots and onion piquée. The preparation is allowed to simmer until almost cooked (the vegetables are removed when cooked). The stock is strained and made into a veal velouté with a blond roux, cooked for 30 minutes. The sauce is then added to the veal and slow cooking applied until the meat is tender.

It is garnished with small white glazed button onions and white mushroom heads cooked in a cuisson. It is finished with a liaison of egg yolks and cream and kept au bain-marie for service. Blanquette is usually accompanied by noodles à la crème, i.e. cooked for 15 minutes in salted boiling water, strained, seasoned and dressed in butter and cream.

Blanquette of lamb, chicken and of sweetbreads are prepared identically.

Fricassée. The veal is sauté in butter without coloration, sprinkled with flour and placed in the oven for 10 minutes to cook the flour (as for blond roux). It is then moistened with good veal stock and allowed to simmer, covered, until tender. The garnish is pre-cooked and added at the last moment. The preparation can be finished with cream and butter, i.e. Fricassée de Veau à l'Ancienne Mode.

Ragoût. Slice veal in collops, season, sauté and brown in clarified butter in a braising pan with sliced onion and carrot. Dredge with flour to coat the meat and place in the oven to cook the flour. Add tomato purée and bouquet garni, cover with veal stock and cook in the oven, covered, for an hour.

Prepare equal amounts of carrot and baby turnip (or larger turned in olives), button onions and mushrooms, and glaze.

Prepare the sauce by adding the strained cooking liquor to an espagnole or demi-glace, reduce, season and correct with butter.

Add sauce and vegetables, including cooked peas, to the veal and cook together for 30 minutes. Serve sprinkled with chopped parsley.

LAMB (AGNEAU) AND MUTTON (MOUTON)

Mutton is the meat of the fully grown sheep. Lamb is the culinary name until the young sheep is a year old.

British home-killed lamb requires no introduction—it is the best. The finest imported is from New Zealand and we consume a vast annual tonnage. The quality is consistent and it enjoys a high culinary reputation. From France we have the Pauillac baby lamb, a delicacy.

The term lamb is used here throughout, but the descriptions of dishes are applicable to lamb and to mutton unless otherwise stated.

Roasting Cuts of Lamb

The saddle (selle) and the best ends (carré) are the more recherché roasting pieces. The leg (gigot) is popular but the shoulder (épaule), though sweet, is not very economic or easy to carve because of the excess of bone, unless it is boned and rolled.

Lamb should not be over-cooked but left pink and moist. The gravy is reclaimed by swilling out the roasting tray with water or stock and reducing it so that the coagulated juices which adhere to the pan are incorporated. The meat should be carved on the thickish side. The roast is accompanied by three sauces: pan gravy, mint sauce or jelly, and redcurrant jelly. More recently, different sauces have been used: lemon mint sauce, cranberry and bramble jelly; caper sauce and onion sauce, as well as mint sauce, are usually offered with roast mutton.

When roasting the saddle it should be scored lightly, seasoned and flour-dusted. It is usually cut the French way, in long slices parallel with the centre backbone. For presentation the meat on either side of the centre bone is lifted off the saddle, carved and replaced.

For roast best end of lamb, trimmed and chined pieces in small racks are preferable. The piece is seasoned, floured, roasted in butter and finished with noisette butter and chopped parsley.

The term persillée is given to this roast when it is finished with a coating of fine white breadcrumbs and chopped parsley and browned in the oven.

Argenteuil. With asparagus tips dressed in butter. Usually featured with saddle of lamb.

Bergère. An assortment of vegetables in season.

Boulangère. Famous preparation usually applicable to roast best end. Sliced new potatoes arranged in layers in a fireproof dish with blanched shredded small onions, moistened with stock, dotted with butter and oven baked to brown the topping. Sprinkled with coarse chopped parsley.

Bouquetière. Selection of green and root vegetables au beurre or à la crème.

Bretonne. Purée of well creamed haricot or butter beans. Noisette potatoes.

Café Foy. The main garnish consists of small tartlets of unsweetened short paste filled with a savoury custard or royale and baked. Garden peas, sliced carrots and fondant potatoes.

Devonshire. Buttered broccoli spears, minted new potatoes and garden peas.

Du Barry. Sprigs of cauliflower gratiné mornay.

En Croûte, Gigot d'Agneau. French regional dish. Consists of a small leg of spring lamb boned (but with the shank left on as a handle) and stuffed, wrapped in puff pastry, baked and served with a gratin dauphinoise.

The stuffing consists of diced lamb's kidneys and chopped mushrooms cooked in butter with rosemary, tarragon and thyme.

The leg is stuffed, secured with thread, seasoned and partly cooked to stiffen in a hot oven for about 20 minutes. When cooled it is wrapped in puff pastry and the edges pinched together. It is then brushed over with egg yolk and baked for a further 15 minutes or so until the pastry is golden brown.

The gratin consists of thick rondels of potato baked in a dish in the oven with milk, beaten egg, grated cheese and seasoning. Prior to service gratiné with grated cheese.

Fleuriste. Roast saddle, leg or best end garnished with tartelettes filled with vegetable macédoine dressed in butter, whole baked duxelle-stuffed tomatoes and individual moulds of duchesse potatoe i.e. pommes mont d'or.

Fontainbleau. Roast saddle or best end garnished with glazed nests of duchesse potato filled with a butter dressed macédoine of vegetables.

Gourmande. Boulangère potatoes with the addition of sliced mushrooms.

Malmaison. Roast best end or saddle garnished with duxelle-filled and baked whole tomato and fonds d'artichauts filled with a purée of peas and a potato purée.

Pré Salé. Term given to the meat (lamb) of sheep who have grazed by the seashore in salted meadows. The origin of pré salé comes from the grazing lands by the Mont-Saint-Michèle on the borders of Brittany and Normandy where Agneau Rôtie Pré Salé is a local speciality.

Printanière. New vegetables, baby carrots, turnips, French beans, peas, broccoli spears, minted and rissolée new potatoes. The vegetables are glazed and chopped parsley sprinkled.

Richelieu. Duxelle-stuffed whole baked even-sized tomatoes, grilled mushrooms, and parisienne potatoes.

Sarladaise. Boulangère potatoes with the addition of sliced mushrooms and fonds d'artichauts.

Windsor. Cauliflower mornay and persillé potatoes.

Boiling and Braising Mutton

Boiling and braising is usually left to mutton, although there is nothing to prevent the use of lamb in these preparations. But mutton is better destined because of cost and because it is best prepared in these ways, many of which are of traditional origin.

Boiled Leg of Mutton. The trimmed leg with aitch bone removed to facilitate carving, is simmered in boiling water containing an onion stuck with cloves, carrot, parsley sprigs, a piece of celery, salt and peppercorns. It is served with a vegetable selection of poached cabbage, whole onions, celery hearts, parsnips, carrots, turnips and parsley or whipped potatoes. The roots are masked with parsley sauce and the preparation is served with caper sauce.

Braised Leg of Mutton. The leg is salted, placed in a braising pan with sliced onion, carrot, leek, celery, calves feet or knuckle of veal or beef and roasted for 10 minutes in dripping. A bouquet garni is added, the preparation covered with stock and braised with the lid on in the oven for 4 hours. The liquor is strained, reduced and added to a jus lié, corrected and loaded with glazed baby carrots, turnips and button onions. The piece is glazed and served with its prepared vegetable sauce.

Irish Stew. Trim equal quantities of best and neck end of mutton into even-sized cutlets. Suppress fat, leaving the lean meat attached to the bones. Blanch for 5 minutes, then arrange in a braising pan on a foundation of equal amounts of shredded cabbage and onion, few sliced carrots, celery, and season with salt and pepper. Cover with water, bring to boil and simmer for an hour. Pick out the meat, remove bones and place in another pan. Add even-sized trimmed raw potatoes and half the amount of well blanched medium-sized button onions. Strain the original stewing liquor into this preparation through a coarse strainer, bring to boil, cover pan and simmer for another hour. Test onions, check seasoning and serve sprinkled with rough chopped parsley. The finishing of the operation may be performed in a fire-proof serving dish when it is topped evenly with the potatoes.

Irish Stew should be light, well flavoured and free of fat. Red cabbage and Worcester sauce normally accompany this dish.

Lancashire Hot pot. Required amount of mutton chops, trimmed of fat and leaving just a small centre bone piece. Arrange the chops, sliced kidney, mushrooms, sliced blanched onion, chopped ham and sliced potatoes in layers in a braising pan. Season each layer with salt and pepper and finish with a thick topping of sliced potato. Moisten with stock, dot with butter and braise with the lid on for 3 hours. Brown the potato topping before serving and sprinkle with rough chopped parsley. Pickled red cabbage is the traditional escort to this preparation. The hot pot may also be prepared with beef.
Note: Calculate 500g (1 lb) mutton to 120g (¼ lb) kidney.

Navarin. Brown lamb stew prepared from best and scrag end, cut into even pieces with all fat removed and leaving meat on the bone as in Irish stew. The meat is fried in hot dripping with sliced onion, carrot and bacon oddments and seasoned. When sealed, dredge with flour, shake pan and let coated meat colour. Add tomato purée, bouquet garni, cover with stock and simmer for 30 minutes or until meat clears bones. Pick out the meat and place in another pan with blanched small onions and turned or baby carrots and turnips. Strain original cooking liquor over preparation, bring to boil, cover and braise for another 30 minutes. Add prepared blanched even-sized potatoes and braise for a further 30 minutes. Check that vegetables are cooked, test for seasoning, consistency and colour and prior to service add cooked peas and sprinkle with chopped parsley. Navarin may be prepared from lamb, mutton and goat's meat, as it is often done on the Continent.
Note: Calculate vegetables and potatoes at 120g (¼ lb) each to 500g (1 lb) meat. The important thing in these lamb stews and braises is to clear the meat of all fat and bone and add adequate vegetable garnishings.

Cutlets, Chops, Noisettes and Rosettes
One of the first things a young trainee chef learns is how to dis-
136

tinguish a cutlet from a chop; cutlet from the best end and chop from the loin. The true noisette is traditionally obtained from the boned loin of lamb or mutton. It is also cut from the best end to the thickness of two cutlets, with the fat trimmed and the bones removed, leaving the eye of the meat. They are usually breaded and shallow fried. The rosette is the loin with the skirt left on, rolled into a tight ring and secured with string at intervals. The individual rosettes are cut from the bulk between strings or pre-cut and secured with string or cocktail sticks.

The noisette preparations here are also applicable to cutlets, chops and rosettes. Noisettes were, at one time, always dressed on croûtons; this is now optional.

Alhambra (Côtelettes or Noisette à l'). Breaded, sauté in butter, masked with a light demi-glace flavoured with sherry and garnished with shredded orange and lemon.

Bonne Bouche (Noisette d'agneau). Noisette seasoned, breaded, sauté in butter, garnished with quartered, sauté fonds d'artichauts, parisienne potatoes and truffle blade and finished with noisette butter and chopped parsley.

Boulangère. Seasoned and sauté cutlets or chops, 2 per serving, dressed on boulangère potatoes. Noisette butter and chopped parsley finish.

Champvallon (Côtelettes à la). Trimmed cutlets seasoned and sauté in butter, placed in a pan with shredded blanched onion, moistened with white stock and braised with a cover on in the oven. Towards the end of the cooking process, add thin rondels of potato and finish cooking. The preparation should be well reduced and served sprinkled with chopped parsley.

Chump chops are more commonly used for this preparation. Sliced tomatoes are sometimes included.

Clamart. Breaded noisette, sauté and garnished with small tartlets of short paste filled with peas, straw potatoes, chopped parsley and noisette butter.

Cyrano. Breaded and sauté noisette garnished with fonds d'artichauts filled with a purée of mushrooms and heart-shaped croûtons. Cordon of demi-glace sauce.

Lesdiguières. Sauté in butter, arranged in a large, emptied, blanched Spanish onion resting on a foundation of leaf spinach, masked with mornay sauce and glazed.

Malmaison. Breaded and sauté noisette, garnished with duxelle-dressed whole tomatoes and fonds d'artichauts filled with a purée of potatoes and a purée of peas. Noisette butter and parsley finish.

Mutton Chop with Kidney. Select 360g (12 oz) mutton chop, trim, place a whole kidney on the inside and secure with a metal skewer.

Grill over a fierce fire, turning several times. When half cooked season with salt and pepper and finish the operation.

(Another Alexis Soyer creation.)

Normande. Breaded and sauté noisette garnished with purée of onions, i.e. soubise.

Princesse. Seasoned, breaded and sauté noisette, garnished with asparagus tips, sprue and truffle blade. Parisienne potatoes, noisette butter and chopped parsley finish.

Réforme (Cutlets). Two trimmed per portion. Season, flour, egg-wash and coat in white breadcrumbs with chopped parsley, tongue and ham added. Sauté in butter and mask with Réforme sauce.

The sauce is prepared from a vinegar, salt and peppercorn reduction with tomato purée added, strained, made up with redcurrant jelly, butter, salt, cayenne and nutmeg, strained again if needed and then loaded with a julienne of hard-boiled white of egg, gherkins, ham, tongue, mushrooms and truffle.

(Alexis Soyer's most celebrated creation.)

Savoy. Breaded, sauté noisette garnished with asparagus tips, truffle blade, whole grilled tomato, fonds d'artichauts and parisienne potatoes.

Voisin. Breaded and sauté noisette dressed on a croûton and garnished with tomato balls and fonds d'artichauts filled with spinach purée and purée of peas. Noisette butter and chopped parsley finish.

Zingara. Breaded, shallow fried, masked with demi-glace loaded with a julienne of ham.

Other Lamb Preparations

Baby Lamb—Agneau de Pauillac. The term pauillac is given in French to milk-fed baby lamb—agneau de lait. The lamb is still suckled by its ewe and has not yet grazed in the meadow. It is therefore very small and its meat pinkish white and very tender. The carcass is dissected into seven joints: two legs, shoulders, best ends and a saddle. The pieces are seasoned with salt and pepper, powdered with flour and roasted, well protected, in butter at 180°C. (350°F.) allowing 15 minutes to the $\frac{1}{2}$ kilo (1 lb). Finish with noisette butter and chopped parsley when cooked. Prepare the pan gravy in the usual manner and serve with spring vegetables and redcurrant jelly.

Cornish Pasty. Individual short paste pasty filled with diced mutton or steak, potato, minced onion and seasoning. Sometimes prepared with a puff paste. Eaten hot or cold.

The original Cornish pasty was an elaborate and larger affair; a meal in itself, with one end filled with meat, potato and onion and the other with apple.

Cured Lamb. In Iceland lamb is salted and smoke cured in the manner of pork for hams and bacon. The cured lamb is sliced and eaten raw with potato salad or it may be roasted or grilled.

Moussaka. Preparation of cooked minced lamb and aubergine known throughout Central Europe and the Near East.

Basic recipe for 500g (1 lb) lean minced lamb.

Sauté a minced onion in olive oil, add 250g ($\frac{1}{2}$ lb) chopped mushrooms and cook. Add 4 to 6 peeled, seeded and chopped tomatoes, chopped parsley and the lamb. Stir and moisten with stock. Cut 4 to 6 unpeeled aubergines into oval slices, flour, sauté in oil, drain and line in greased fireproof dish. Build up with alternating layers of meat and aubergine, sprinkling each with grated parmesan, ending with an aubergine topping. Sprinkle with more parmesan, bake in moderate oven until topping is browned. Serve hot or cold.

Note: Garlic may be added if desired. Preparation may also be extended with breadcrumbs and more cheese.

Schashlik. Traditional Balkan dish of meat and rice. The meat is impaled on a brochette or skewer, grilled over a fierce fire and then eaten with rice.

Schashlik is prepared with lamb, preferably the eye of the meat from the best end. Slice in rondels, place in a bowl with sliced small onions, season with salt, crushed peppercorns, lemon juice, pinch of thyme and a few small bay leaves, moisten with olive oil and leave to infuse for several hours. Thread the meat onto a stainless steel brochette with the onion and bayleaves, paint with olive oil and grill or shallow fry in a thick iron pan. Place a whole grilled tomato on the end of the skewer and set the preparation on a bed of pilaff rice. Finish with a dash of noisette butter. The preparation, after cooking, may be flamed at the table in brandy.

The preparation is named after the rice garnishing.

Schashlik à la Caucasian. Chicken livers, peas and red pimento.

Schashlik à la Grecque. The rice cooked for risotto is dressed with butter and grated parmesan and garnished with cooked peas and diced red pimento.

Schashlik à la l'Hongroise. Diced red and green peppers, ham and green peas.

Schashlik à la Russe. Chopped ham, veal and chicken with saffron.

Schashlik à la Tartare. Shredded red and green peppers, chopped ham and saffron.

Note: The brochette is symbolic of the hunter cooking his meat spitted on a sword over a camp fire. The Flaming Sword theme—the flaming of the brochette—has been adapted and developed beyond the cooking of meat to chicken, seafood and other preparations. The fare is spit-roasted on the sword (or a brochette) and served with a variety of rice dishes.

Shish Kebab. The kebab differs from schashlik as it contains other ingredients besides the lamb. The shish part indicates the brochette. The lamb is prepared and infused as for schashlik with small flat mushrooms and bacon pieces added. The skewer is threaded with the lamb, bacon, mushrooms and mingled with the onion and herbs. The piece is painted with olive oil and grilled or shallow fried. It is arranged with a whole grilled tomato stuck on the sharp end on a bed of pilaff à la grecque or other type of rice preparation. Dressing and garnishing of the pilaff may be varied as fancy dictates. Flaming is optional.

PORK (PORC)

The pig is more than a food—it is a veritable industry. Not only does it give us pork, it provides ham, bacon and delicatessen foods. At one time pork was only in season when there was the proverbial 'R' in the month, but the advent of deep freezing and the marketing efforts of pork breeders and promoters have made it an all-the-year-round meat.

One essential key point has to be made clear about cooking pork: whatever the culinary process, it should always be well cooked. It should be roasted at 195°C. (375°F.) allowing 25 minutes to the $\frac{1}{2}$ kilo (1 lb). The boneless loin of pork for whole roasting or grilling cuts is used as an all-purpose convenience joint.

The Roasting Cuts
The roasting joints are the leg and the loin. They are featured with four principal escorts: stuffing, crackling, rich brown gravy and apple sauce.

Stuffing. A light herb and onion stuffing to accompany the rich meat. Prepared with chopped, baked onion stewed in dripping with the chopped cooked pigs liver, chopped suet, white breadcrumbs soaked in milk, salt, pepper, dash of nutmeg, lemon juice, sage and chopped parsley. Well blended and bound with beaten egg. Preparation should be pliable and not too moist. Stuffing is tied into the boned joint, or cooked separately.

Crackling. Prior to roasting, the skin is scored in an even pattern to facilitate its removal when cooked. With the loin the whole skin is lifted, scored and tied back on the joint.

Gravy. Prepared by swilling out the roasting tray, thickened with cornflower or arrowroot, checked for seasoning and colour.

Apple Sauce. Aids digestion. Alternatives are small baked apple, apple fritters, apple jelly or a spiced compote.

The loin and leg are handled identically for roasting once prepared for the oven.

Variety is introduced by the garniture from which the roast will take its name. The basic roast, Home Style or À l'Anglaise, consists of roast potatoes, purée of spinach dressed with croûtons and quarters of hard-boiled egg, stuffing, apple sauce, crackling and thickened pan gravy. Another popular escort is butter beans. Père Antoine indicates a dish of purée of potatoes stuck with grilled baby chipolatas, masked and glazed with mornay sauce.

Boning Joints. Boning, stuffing and rolling joints of leg, loin and ribs of pork is much favoured. It facilitates cooking, carving and portioning. This also applies to lamb, mutton and veal.

Boiled Leg of Pork and Pease Pudding

Select a plump and well meated leg and plunge into boiling water containing sliced onion, carrot, celery, leek, parsley stalks, salt and a few peppercorns. Simmer at 25 minutes to $\frac{1}{2}$ kilo (1 lb). Serve with poached whole onions, celery hearts, parsley potatoes, apple sauce and pease pudding. The gravy will be made up with the well reduced cooking liquor, cleared of fat.

Suckling Pig

Whole roast and dressed suckling pig is a spectacular and traditional preparation for the hot table or the cold buffet. The baby pig is obtainable blanched and oven ready between 5 to 8 kilo (10 to 16 lb). The piece is wiped over, its skin lightly and evenly scored, the stuffing inserted, then brushed with butter, seasoned and roasted in a deep pan with olive oil. The piece should be protected with paper or foil and basted frequently. When ready the piece is set upon a dish, painted with hot olive oil, served with small baked apples, gravy, dressed purée of spinach, other vegetables to choice and roasted potatoes. The piece will usually be filled with a sage and onion stuffing which incorporates the offal of the piglet. Allowance is made when filling the piece for shrinkage of the meat and swelling of the stuffing and it is usual to sew up the animal once stuffed.

For a cold buffet presentation the stuffed and roasted piece is painted over with a brown glaze prepared from a concentration of coloured aspic, the animal is piped with coloured butters, garnished as required and a whole baked orange placed in its mouth.

Pork Chop

The chop cut from the loin and rib is a popular feature for grills and entrées.

Alsacienne. Seasoned, sauté in butter, dressed on sauerkraut, moistened with stock and braised in the oven for about 45 minutes.

Charcutière. Sauté chop masked with sauce diable loaded with sliced or chopped gherkins.

Hawaiian. Sauté chop garnished with butter-tossed pineapple ring with a red cherry in the centre and finished with noisette butter.

Lyonnaise. Sauté chop dressed on lyonnaise potatoes finished with noisette butter and chopped parsley. Apple sauce.

Tartare (à la). Soak 250g (8 oz) pork chop in vinegar for 30 minutes, season, grill, serve sandwiched between equal amounts of shredded fried onion and thinly sliced pickled cucumber. Finish with noisette butter and chopped parsley.

(Alexis Soyer creation.)

Ham (Jambon)

Ham as a culinary term means a leg of pork which has been cured by a specific process according to its place or locale of origin. Curing consists of wet or dry salting, brining or pickling, smoking and maturing. The manner in which the ham is cured and the time taken in maturing determines the ultimate character and quality of the ham. The art of curing is a specialized craft and many of the processes are closely guarded. Hams are described as mild cured, pale dried, dry salted, honey, sugar or treacle cured and others. They vary in size from 3 kilos (6 lb) to as much as 10 kilos (20 lb). Curing should not be confused with cooking. A cured ham is a raw ham and can be eaten as such or cooked.

The best known English ham is the York; others come from Devon, Wiltshire, Worcestershire and Ireland. From abroad, hams come from France, Italy, Central Europe, Canada and the U.S.A. There are the noted sweet hams from Kentucky, Virginia, Georgia and California, where the pigs feed in fruit orchards off windfall peaches and plums which impart a special flavour to the meat. Others are fed on nuts and acorns. Smoking is performed over hickory, apple and oak fires.

Canned hams are produced in great variety, boned, cooked and ready for slicing.

Cooking Ham. Raw ham is cooked by plunging it in boiling water, simmering at 20 minutes to the $\frac{1}{2}$ kilo (1 lb) and allowing to cool in its liquor. The piece is usually pre-soaked in cold water overnight prior to the cooking process. When cooked the thick skin is removed. When cold the fat is trimmed, smoothed over and rolled in toasted breadcrumbs. Gammons, shoulders (fores), and bacon are cooked in a similar manner.

Ham Entrées

The braising and infusing of cooked, and the baking of raw, hams produces the best types of hot entrées.

These modes of preparation are applied either to the whole piece or are simulated with sliced cold ham infused in the appropriate sauce.

Braising Ham (Jambon à l'Étuvé). This is a process of infusing,

142

and heating ham with wine with the objective of enhancing its delicate flavour.

The cooked and trimmed ham is placed in a braising pan with 1 litre (2 pints) consommé or clear stock. The preparation is flavoured with madeira and inserted in the oven at 150°C. (300°F.) with the lid on and allowed slowly to infuse for about 2 hours. The ham is served accompanied by a demi-glace sauce to which is added the reduced infusion, and vegetables.

Ham Braised with Madeira-Velouté Florentine (Jambon à l'Étuvé au Madère). Rich spinach purée, fondant potatoes and madeira sauce. Ham and spinach are good partners.

Variations are introduced with the wine and the garnitures. The wine may be fortified with madeira, marsala, sherry, port, burgundy or champagne, and the wine and infusion embodied in the sauce with which the ham is served. Purées go best with ham: spinach (florentine), green peas (clamart), chestnut (limousine), haricot or butter bean (bretonne or soissonnaise), Brussels sprouts (flamande), French beans (favorite), fonds d'artichauts (rachel), or celeriac (suzette). Straight vegetables such as braised celery hearts and whole endive, baked tomatoes, veal-stock-braised whole chestnuts and primeurs are good accompaniments with fondant and mousseline potatoes.

Ham Braised with Sauerkraut. National dish of Alsace. Sauerkraut is washed, drained, seasoned and arranged in alternate layers in a braising pan with sliced onion, carrot, thickly sliced ham or gammon and frankfurters. The meat should be well encased by the sauerkraut. Add a muslin bag containing peppercorns and a few cloves—the sauerkraut should contain juniper berries. Finish with topping of sauerkraut, dot with butter or dripping, moisten with stock, cover pan and braise for 5 hours. Serve ham and sausages with the sauerkraut. Pass reduced and strained braising liquor separately, and French mustard.

Whole ham pieces may be braised in this manner.

Baked Ham California Style with Peaches. The raw ham is scored in a pattern, stuck with cloves, set in a deep pan with whole peaches and brown sugar moistened with consommé or clear stock, and baked at 177°C. (350°F.) at 20 minutes to the ½ kilo (1 lb). The piece is basted and glazed to acquire a rich brown gloss. Curaçao, brandy or rum may be added. The ham is served with its cooking liquor lightly spiced and corrected into a peach sauce with butter. It may also be served with cumberland or madeira sauce. It is usual to feature a good and colourful selection of primeurs with this preparation, including sweetcorn kernels, lima beans, baked whole tomatoes, braised endive, celery hearts and spinach purée or leaf.

Note: Variations are introduced to this basic baking preparation substituting the peaches by California prunes, cherries, grapefruit, orange, pineapple, pears and apples, with suitable liqueurs to match the fruit.

Mousse of Ham. Hot mousse is prepared with all types of cooked ham and featured with peach, madeira and cumberland sauces or pickled peaches.

Basic preparation: To 360g (12 oz) ham purée add $\frac{1}{4}$ litre ($\frac{1}{2}$ pint) stiff béchamel sauce and 4 beaten egg yolks. Season with paprika or cayenne and colour with carmine. Continue beating in large bowl and fold in 4 stiffly whipped egg whites. Half fill lightly buttered soufflé dish with preparation, top with truffle blade and bake at 200/230°C. (400/450°F.) for 20 minutes.

Bacon

Bacon has many uses in the kitchen. The side divides up into a gammon or fore and the two halves into back and streaky rashers. The gammon and the fore are boiled for hot or cold; gammon is also cut into steaks. Bacon for grilling should be rinded and dry grilled under or over heat. The French name for bacon is lard.

Bacon and Egg. The bacon is grilled and the egg fried in butter or bacon fat. The preparation is finished with a splash of noisette butter. The practice of cooking bacon and eggs together in a skillet is a good one since the components blend well.

Gammon Steak

Popular food featured in many ways. The steaks are cut from the gammon at 175g–250g (6–8 oz) or 360g–420g (12–14 oz). The fat is incised at intervals, the piece grilled and served with a garniture. As with all pork products, the steak should be well and adequately cooked and sauced in its natural juices. In all the ways described, unless otherwise indicated, the preparation is finished with noisette butter and, as applicable, chopped parsley.

Caprice. Grilled gammon garnished with two medium sized bananas baked with demerara sugar, lemon, butter and rum. Dress fruit on the piece and finish with noisette butter.

Creole. Grilled gammon garnished with a compote of peaches in spiced sauce—pitted fresh fruit poached in a light spiced syrup. Canned peach halves suitably treated may be used.

Florentine. Grilled gammon on butter-tossed cooked leaf spinach with fried egg topping.

Florida. Grilled gammon dressed with mandarin, orange and grapefruit segments and pitted red cherries. Finish with noisette butter and fruit juice.

Gammon Sandwich. Grilled gammon sandwiched between two thick slices of toast. Remove crusts, cut into triangles. Serve hot with mango chutney or sweet pickle.

Gammon and Scampi Meunière. Grilled gammon dressed with sauté scampi, topped with rinded lemon rondels and finished with noisette butter, lemon juice and chopped parsley.

Grand Gammon. Grilled gammon on toast topped with a slice of sauté calves liver and a fried egg. Finish with noisette butter and chopped parsley and serve with fried potatoes and cole-slaw.

Grapefruit. Grilled gammon dressed with segments of fresh or canned grapefruit. Finished with noisette butter and grapefruit juice.

Hawaiian. Grilled gammon topped with round of pineapple. Best results are with fresh fruit; the round is trimmed, cored, grilled or sauté in butter. The Hawaiian may be topped with a fried egg.

Holstein. Grilled gammon topped with fried egg and served with sauté potatoes and tomato sauce.

Mirabeau. Gammon Holstein with the fried egg topping decorated with criss-cross of anchovy julienne dotted with capers, gherkin fan and pimento stuffed olive.

Orange. Grilled gammon dressed with segments or rondels of fresh pitted orange. Finished with noisette butter and orange juice.

Southern Style. Grilled gammon dressed with spiced peaches, pitted red cherries and pineapple, heated together and finished with a squeeze of lemon and noisette butter.

Viennoise. Breaded gammon treated and dressed exactly as for the escalope of veal preparation of this name.

Virginia. Grilled gammon dressed with one or two rondels of crystallized pineapple with a centre of candied red cherries, sauced with spiced syrup and garnished with buttered corn kernels, lima beans à la crème, whole grilled tomato and lyonnaise potatoes. Finished with a cordon of tomato sauce and noisette butter.

Virginian. Grilled gammon with whole banana fritter, straw potatoes and sauce diable.

West Coast. Grilled gammon masked with a spiced cherry sauce. Pitted black cherries are cooked in syrup, the syrup drained off, mixed with chopped glacé ginger, thickened with arrowroot, loaded with the cherries, masked over the gammon and flashed in a hot oven to cohere.

Boiled Gammon
Gammon is soaked overnight and cooked. When ready skin, trim and serve with parsley sauce, baby carrots, whipped or parsley potatoes and pease pudding.

OFFAL OF MEAT (ABATS)

Offal is used here to indicate a whole range of the by-products of beef, veal, mutton, lamb and pork.

145

Sweetbreads (Ris de Veau)

The name applies to two glands: the rounded and plump pancreas and the long thymus gland. The former is best for entrées, the latter used more for vol-au-vent fillings, unless deemed plump and suitable for handling otherwise. The breads of veal calf and the pig are the best and most employed; those of the other animals are coarser and are used in fillings.

Sweetbreads are obtained fresh or frozen and should always be handled with care, as they are of a highly perishable nature. Before any process the breads are first blanched: wash and poach for 10 minutes in boiling water containing sliced onion, parsley sprigs, lemon juice, salt and peppercorns. Remove, wash under cold running water and suppress all connective tubes and gristle. Flatten between two dishes with a weight on top. For all the presentations given, the breads are pre-prepared in this manner.

It was originally the practice to lard or dress the bread with fillets of white of chicken, ham, tongue and truffle prior to pressing. This is still indicated in certain special recipes. For important preparations sweetbreads are braised whole in white or brown sauce, velouté and demi-glace. Otherwise they are sliced in collops, breaded or not, and sauté in butter. At one time braised sweetbreads were always featured dressed on a croûton, but this has now become optional.

Alsacienne. Thick bread, blanched, opened, dressed with diced truffle and ham, pressed and braised in white velouté for an hour. Glazed and masked with the braising sauce checked with cream, butter, salt, cayenne and lemon juice, strained, touched with brandy and loaded with a fine purée of foie gras, heated and served.

Demidov (Demidoff). Plump whole bread, blanched, sliced open, larded with ham and diced truffle and then pressed. Braised in espagnole sauce and glaze. Served masked with the braising liquor checked with butter, salt, cayenne, lemon juice and carmine, flavoured with brandy, flecked with chopped truffle. Heated and served.

Financière. Whole sweetbread blanched, braised in espagnole sauce, dressed on a croûton, masked with the corrected and strained braising sauce loaded with glazed button mushrooms, pitted olives, chicken quenelles, cocks combs and kidneys, flavoured with madeira and topped with a large truffle blade.

Note: Bread may be larded with ham, chicken and truffle.

Green Peas (Ris de Veau Braisé aux Petits Pois). Whole plump bread blanched but not pressed and braised in a closed pan in the oven with espagnole and tomato purée. Served masked with corrected braising sauce, flavoured with madeira and loaded with glazed green peas.

Judic. Whole plump bread, blanched but not pressed and braised in a closed pan in the oven with espagnole and tomato purée. Served masked with the corrected braising sauce flavoured with madeira and garnished with whole braised lettuce.

Parisienne. Braised whole sweetbread in espagnole sauce dressed on a croûton masked with the strained and corrected braising preparation, garnished with fonds d'artichauts and parisienne potatoes.

Princesse (pané). Slice into collops, breadcrumb, sauté in butter. Dress with asparagus tips, truffle blade and noisette potatoes. Noisette butter, lemon juice and chopped parsley finish.

Sauté au Beurre. Slice into collops, season, flour and sauté in butter. Noisette butter and lemon juice finish.

Smitane. Blanch and braise plump bread in white velouté for an hour and glazed well. Mince 2 shallots, sweat in butter with sliced mushrooms, salt and cayenne. Strain the braising sauce and add it to the shallot and mushroom preparation. Check with fresh cream. Let preparation cohere, sour with lemon juice and dash of vinegar, sauce over sweetbread and serve.

Suprême (Ris de Veau à la Crème). Whole plump bread, blanched but not pressed, braised in a closed pan in the oven in white velouté for 30 to 45 minutes, basted to gloss then set in serving dish. Sauce is corrected with cream, slightly reduced, checked with salt, cayenne and lemon juice, strained and loaded with glazed button or sliced mushrooms and masked over sweetbread. Preparation left to cohere then served.

Sweetbreads as Garnishes and Fillings. The coarser sweetbreads for these employments are blanched, picked over and cleared of all tubes and connective tissues, and poached with seasoning in cream or velouté.

Kidneys (Rognons)

Kidneys are indicated in the plural, since they are served in pairs. They possess a distinctive flavour and are employed in their own right or used with other foods to which they impart their flavoursome properties. For quality, calves and then pigs are the best; the larger kidney of the sheep and the ox are used in puddings, braises and various garnishings. For preparation the kidneys are skinned, split and opened out or left whole.

Bordelaise. Diced kidneys stewed in butter with minced shallot, then cooked with fines herbes moistened with red wine. Check preparation and serve.

Chez Lui. Peel and parboil 2 large onions, slice off tops, scoop out centres, line with farce, place a whole skinned kidney in each, top with piece of butter and replace lids. Rest the stuffed onions on a bed of sliced carrot in a fireproof dish, season and almost cover with stock. Cover and braise in the oven for $2\frac{1}{2}$ to 3 hours. Finish with noisette butter and chopped parsley.

Farce: Minced shallot, small garlic clove, 4 chopped tomatoes, chopped mushroom parings and ham, salt and pepper stewed in butter.

Devilled (Diablé). Split open, skin, season, brush with melted butter, coat with breadcrumbs mixed with mustard powder and cayenne. Impale on a skewer and grill quickly. Serve with sauce diable.

Kidneys and Bacon (Rognons au Lard). Split open, skin, impale on a skewer, paint with olive oil, grill or sauté in butter. Leave on the underdone side. Serve on thick buttered toast with grilled bacon rashers. Serve with a choice of mustards.

Kidney and Mushroom à la Soyer. Split, open out, skin, impale 3 kidneys on a skewer, season, grill but leave underdone. Sandwich between 6 large mushrooms stewed whole in butter. Finish with noisette butter and chopped parsley.

Madère. Diced and seasoned, sauté in butter, flavoured with madeira and lié in demi-glace sauce.

Maître d'Hôtel. Split open, skinned, impaled on a skewer, seasoned, olive oil brushed, grilled and served with maître d'hôtel butter garnished with watercress.

Petit Sauté. Quickly toss diced kidney and chopped shallot in butter to seal, then add binding agent, i.e. demi-glace or sauce madère. Check seasoning.

The petit sauté is employed as an individual dish, as a filling for omelettes, or a garnish to scrambled or fried eggs.

Turbigo. Two whole skinned kidneys, seasoned, stewed in butter for 10 minutes, demi-glace tomatée added, flavoured with madeira and braised for 30 minutes. Served masked with the reduced and corrected braising sauce, garnished with 2 kidney-shaped croûtons and grilled chipolatas, and finished with chopped parsley.

Vert Pré. Grilled, dressed with watercress, garnished with pommes pailles and served with maître d'hôtel butter.

Liver (Foie)

All ground and feathered animals handled in the kitchen have edible livers. Our concern here is with meat and in order of quality the liver of the calf (foie de veau), pig, sheep and ox are of culinary interest. Calves liver is the best; that of the ox is large and often flabby when cooked. The preparations given are intended for calves but may be adapted to all liver. Like sweetbreads and kidneys, liver needs to be handled with care. It should smell and look fresh; if tainted or clammy destroy it. If fresh it should be used as received, if frozen use as soon as it thaws out. The liver should be wiped over and cleared of all skin, tubes and connective tissues.

Anglaise (à l'). Seasoned and floured escalopes of liver, sauté in butter, garnished with grilled bacon, finished with noisette butter, touch of lemon juice and chopped parsley.

Bordelaise. Larded whole liver, marinated in white wine, brandy and aromates, barded and roasted in the oven. Served with bordelaise sauce.

Braised Liver and Bacon. Prepare, season and flour liver collops, cook quickly in butter or bacon fat, add tomato purée and stock. Cover pan and braise in oven. Remove liver, set in serving dish, mask with rough strained cooking liquor. Garnish with grilled bacon, chopped parsley and serve with whipped potatoes.

Italienne (Foie de Veau à l'). Prepared, floured escalopes, sauté in butter, served masked with italienne sauce i.e. half glaze with added tomato purée, purée of lean ham, minced cooked mushrooms and fines herbes, checked with salt, cayenne and lemon juice.

Liver and Bacon (Foie de Veau Sauté au Lard). Slice into thin collops, season, flour, sauté in butter or bacon fat. Set in a dish, garnish with grilled bacon rashers, even-sized parsley potatoes and finish with noisette butter.

Another method: Cook prepared liver in pan in which the bacon was cooked, dress in dish, swill out pan with stock, allow some reduction and sauce over the preparation. Garnish with bacon, finish with chopped parsley.

Note: The degree of cooking is a matter of personal taste. Unless otherwise requested, cook it à point, neither under nor over cooked. The trend is for slicing liver thinner, allowing three escalopes to the portion and cooking it well done.

Liver, Bacon and Mushrooms. Cook the bacon, mushrooms and liver individually and consecutively in the same pan in butter or bacon fat. Dress on a serving dish. Swill out pan with stock, reduce and sauce over preparation. Finish with chopped parsley. Serve with sauté potatoes.

Lyonnaise. Prepare, season and flour sliced liver, cook in olive oil with minced blanched onion, chopped fines herbes and a dash of vinegar. Dress the liver sauced with its cooking preparation, noisette butter and chopped parsley.

Soubise. Slice two large onions, blanch and cook in olive oil. Add 4 prepared, seasoned and floured escalopes of liver. Cook together. Arrange liver in dish smothered in the onion, finish with noisette butter and chopped parsley.

Brochettes of Kidneys and Liver. This is a composite description of the service of kidney or liver on a skewer, i.e. en brochette.

Whether the main ingredient is kidney or liver—or both—the method is identical. The liver is trimmed and cut into equal sized collops and the kidney into quarters, then placed in a bowl with even-sized pieces of bacon, whole mushrooms, shredded, blanched, small onions, salt, crushed peppercorns and moistened with olive oil. A pinch fines herbes is added and the preparation left for an hour to infuse. The liver and/or kidney is threaded on a skewer alternately with the bacon, mushroom and onions. It is brushed with olive oil and grilled over a bright fire or under a salamander. A whole grilled tomato is placed on the end of the brochette, the whole dressed on a bed of risotto rice, finished with noisette butter and chopped parsley and served with tomato sauce.

Various brochettes can be made up with liver, kidney, bacon, onion, mushrooms and seasonings. May also incorporate fillet steak and, like schashlik, may be served with different rice preparations. For a de luxe presentation, brochettes may be flamed in brandy or other spirit.

Tongue (Langue)

The tongues of all animals under the meat heading are edible. Sizes, however, vary and we go for the largest for most preparations, i.e. the ox tongue (langue de boeuf). Tongue is possibly best known as cold fare, but it presents well braised and there are many hot preparations. Small tongues, those of the lamb, sheep, calf and pig, are used in charcuterie for brawn and for pressing.

Tongues are usually bought ready prepared and dressed for cold or canned whole. For hot entrées the tongue is braised in demi-glace or madeira sauce and served with a purée of vegetables in a similar manner to hams. As the texture of these dishes is delicate, pre-heating cooked tongue in consommé or stock is dispensed with; the sliced meat is simply masked with the sauce selected and heated through. Smaller tongues are braised whole.

Raw ox tongue is heated in a similar manner to salt and canned beef, i.e. the piece is brined, cooked and then pressed. For a cold buffet it must be suitably mounted whole and then glazed.

Bourgeoise. The sliced tongue is garnished with braised baby onions and glazed carrots and masked with a demi-glace.

Écarlate. Term for the whole tongue for cold when it is heavily masked with a red coloured aspic preparation.

Florentine. Sliced braised tongue masked in madeira sauce and served with a purée of spinach.

Italienne. Sliced braised tongue set on butter-and-cheese-dressed noodles and masked with espagnole sauce loaded with chopped ham and mushrooms.

Napolitaine. Sliced braised tongue served with spaghetti dressed with butter, grated parmesan and tomato purée.

Calves Head (Tête de Veau)

The term calves head is used as it is the one most employed, but actually all heads are eaten; that of the ox or bullock is made into brawn, and those of the sheep and pig are processed as for that of the calf.

The whole head is required and taken off the bone complete and intact. The brain and tongue are set aside. The boned head and tongue are wrapped in a cloth and carefully cooked in a blanc for 1½ hours. The brain is cooked separately. The cooked head is now ready for featuring in several ways.

Calves Head Vinaigrette. The head and tongue are prepared as above and served cold with a special dressing made by loading a vinaigrette with chopped cooked brain, chopped parsley and a little lemon juice.

Calves head prepared in this manner can also be shredded, dressed in the brain sauce and featured as an hors-d'œuvre.

En Tortue (Tête de Veau). Cook the head and tongue in a blanc as above, cut into even pieces and set to braise in espagnole and tomato sauce. Add turtle herbs infused in stock. Let the preparation braise with the lid on for an hour. Pick out the meat, place in a serving dish, garnish with pitted olives, veal quenelles and glazed button onions and mushrooms in equal amounts. Strain the reduced and corrected braising sauce over the preparation. Garnish with heart-shaped croûtons and eggs fried in olive oil (à la française), one croûton and one egg to the serving.
Note: The brain is not usually used for the tortue.

Financière. Similar to the tortue, the portioned head and tongue are braised in a demi-glace sauce which is loaded with pitted olives, glazed button mushrooms, cocks combs and kidneys, and truffle blades.

Poached Calves Head (Tête de Veau à l'Anglaise). The poached head is dressed whole in a dish with the tongue and garnished with sprigs of parsley. It is served hot and cut up at table with a brain sauce; prepare a roux and make into a velouté with the liquor in which the head was cooked, season with salt, cayenne and lemon juice and load with the chopped cooked brain and a little chopped parsley.

Calves head is nutritious and easy to digest and is therefore considered suitable where a light diet is prescribed.

Brain (Cervelle)

A very light and easy to assimilate food. All brain is edible, the smaller the better usually. The raw piece should be washed in several waters to remove all traces of blood and the covering membrane carefully cleared. It is then simmered from 10 to 20 minutes, according to size, in a court bouillon consisting of a few onion slices, parsley stalks, salt, peppercorns, lemon juice and water. Leave to cool in its cooking liquor and use as required.

Au Beurre (Cervelle Sauté). Whole poached brain cut in half, floured, seasoned with salt and pepper and gently sauté in butter. Dressed on a thick slice of hot buttered toast and finished with a dash of noisette butter and chopped parsley.

Beurre Noir (Cervelle au). Toss in butter whole poached brain and place in serving dish. Set some butter in a hot pan, allow it to brown and then burn it with lemon juice or vinegar. Add capers and chopped parsley and sauce the preparation quickly over the brain.

Brain on Toast. Poached brain, well drained, served on a thick slice of hot buttered toast, finished with a little melted butter and chopped parsley.

Crème (Cervelle à la). Select a whole poached brain and, according to size, leave whole or slice through. Place in a serving dish. Reduce some cream over heat, add a piece of butter, season with salt, pepper and lemon juice. When the sauce has cohered mask the brain, heat through and serve.

Fried (Cervelle Pané). Whole or sliced uncooked brain seasoned, breadcrumbed and deep fried in hot olive oil. Served with tomato sauce. May also be battered instead of breaded.

Brain in vol-au-vents. Pieces of poached brain suitably heated in hot butter or cream are used for this purpose. Featured straight or mingled with white of chicken, veal or chicken quenelles, or sliced or button mushrooms.

Amourette
Thick end of spinal cord of veal or beef (calf or oxon) prepared as for brain.

Crépinette
Preparation of forcemeat wrapped in pigs caul, breadcrumbed, deep fried, baked or sauté in butter. Made with a variety of fillings from pork forcemeat to chicken, sweetbread and game and usually includes a salpicon of the main ingredient and often chopped truffle. Served with various sauces to choice.

Feet and Trotters
Calves feet are prized for their gelatinous content; they are so delicate they almost wholly dissolve. Calves feet (pieds de veau) are sometimes grilled, either first cooked in a blanc or as they are.

The feet of the pig and sheep are called trotters (pieds de porc, pieds de mouton) and they are also rich and wholesome. In certain de luxe preparations the trotters are made into pâtés with truffle and brandy. They are also grilled, either cooked in a blanc or not. For grilling, all feet and trotters, pre-blanc cooked or not, are split open and surplus bone removed.

The following preparations (except first) apply to all feet and trotters.

Calves Foot Jelly. Place 4 calves feet in a pot with a little sliced onion and carrot, about 120g (4 oz) raw lean minced beef, salt and a few peppercorns. Cover with 2 litres (4 pints) water, bring to boil and simmer for 6 hours. Skim periodically. Replace water as it evaporates. Strain through a fine muslin, check colour with browning.

Fried. The feet are cooked, boned, dipped in batter, deep fried and served with tartare or tomato sauce.

Grilled. The feet are cooked, boned, painted with melted butter, coated with breadcrumbs and mustard powder and grilled. Served with melted butter or tartare sauce. Another method is to coat the pieces in mustard, breadcrumb, dot with butter and grill.

Poached Calves Feet and Pigs Trotters and Parsley Sauce. The trotters or feet are simmered in a blanc for 45 minutes, boned and served with parsley sauce.

Vinaigrette (à la). The feet are cooked, boned, split in half and served cold with vinaigrette or a lemon dressing. The preparation may also be shredded for hors d'oeuvre.

Tripe

Name given to the two stomachs of cud-chewing animals; the first is smooth, the second honeycombed and it is usual to mix both equally for culinary employments. Beef tripe is used most. Tripe is purchased cleaned and blanched from the butcher. It is cut into squares, wrapped in a cloth and cooked for 3 to 4 hours in a blanc containing a whole nutmeg.

Tripe à la Mode de Caen. Noted French regional cookery speciality prepared and served in individual or a large stoneware tureen.

Prepare and cook in a blanc squares of tripe and boned calves feet cut as the tripe. Allow 1 of tripe to $\frac{1}{2}$ of calves feet. Arrange the tripe and feet in layers in the tureen, mingled with shredded blanched onion. Season with salt, pepper and nutmeg. Dot with butter and fill up with stock. Cover and bake slowly for 6 hours. Prior to service, check stock content and dust with chopped parsley.

Tripe and Onions. Cut tripe into squares and cook in a blanc. Shred, blanch and set required quantity of onion to stew in butter without coloration. Load the onion into a béchamel sauce and use this to bind the tripe. Check seasoning with salt, cayenne, lemon juice and grated nutmeg. Let the preparation cohere, serve very hot in a fireproof dish and dust with chopped parsley.

Fried. Cooked tripe cut into squares, seasoned, breadcrumbed or battered, deep fried and served dressed with fried parsley and tomato sauce.

Grilled. Cooked tripe breadcrumbed, grilled and served with sauce diable.

Moutarde. Cooked tripe coated in mustard, breadcrumbed, deep fried and served with sauce piquante.

Parisienne. Cooked tripe well seasoned, coated in maître d'hôtel butter and breadcrumbs, deep fried and served with a sauce robert.

Tripe is also braised in a rich brown sauce, plain cooked and served with parsley sauce.

Heart (Coeur)

One of the lesser offals, for unless that of a young animal the heart is inclined to be large and tough.

Prior to cooking, the heart should be well washed and cleared of the more obvious connective tubes. Small hearts are braised whole in espagnole; larger hearts are split open, dressed with sage and onion stuffing and braised.

Braised Stuffed Heart. The heart is dressed with sage and onion stuffing, wrapped in long streaky bacon rashers or sewn up. It is set in a pan on sliced onion and carrot, seasoned and moistened well with stock and braised with the lid on for 2 hours. Served masked with its strained and corrected braising liquor.

Stuffing: Minced onion stewed in suet or pure dripping, breadcrumbs soaked in milk, pinch of sage, salt, pepper, lemon juice and dash of nutmeg, bound with egg and water into a pliable mass.

Oxtail (Queue de Boeuf)

The thicker part of the long oxtail is employed. It contains a rich gelatinous substance similar to that present in all joints and feet of animals.

Hot Pot of Oxtail. Dissect tail into vertebra, season, and sauté in hot dripping to seal. Dredge with flour and allow the coated pieces some superficial browning. Place some sliced onion, carrot, celery and leek in a pan, season and sauté in dripping. Add the oxtail and tomato purée and cover with stock. Bring to boil, add soaked haricot beans and braise with the lid on for 4 hours in the oven. Pick out the oxtail and set in a tureen. Check braising preparation for flavour, consistency and colour and turn out over the tails. Heat through and sprinkle with chopped parsley.

Note: This is known as the English method and is sometimes called a haricot of oxtail.

Queue de Beuf en Hochepot. Proceed as for the above hot pot preparation, omitting haricot beans. When ready, pick out tails and keep hot in a tureen. Strain the braising liquor, check seasoning, colour and consistency and load with equal amounts of glazed baby carrots, mushrooms, turnips, onion and cooked haricot beans. Sauce preparation over the tails and sprinkle with chopped parsley.
Note: This is known as the French method.

Chipolata (à la). Similar to the hochepot, but the end sauce is loaded with glazed baby carrots, onions, chestnuts and grilled chipolatas.

Daube (en). Oxtail braised as for hochepot and garnished with glazed baby onions, bacon lardons, and calves feet shredded en julienne. (The feet are cooked in with the tails.)

Bone Marrow (Moelle)
The nutritious marrow found in large bones is much sought after and used in numerous dishes. For garnishings the firm type is cut into thick rondels and poached with care in lightly seasoned consommé. The softer marrow is used in sauce work. Short thick marrow bones are employed for a preparation, known as L'Os à la Moelle, tied at the ends firmly with a piece of double cloth and poached in consommé for 2 hours. The cooked marrow is allowed to slide out and is served on thick hot buttered toast.

CHARCUTERIE AND DELICATESSEN PRODUCTS

Grouped under this general heading are the products of the charcutier's art, including sausages and other manufactured meat goods. Nowadays this range is better known as delicatessen (Dutch for delicate eating) and has developed into quite an industry.

Sausages
The enclosing of cooked and raw meat with seasoning and spice in gut and other wrapping goes back through the ages to the early Greek and Roman civilizations. The sausage remains to this day, a staple item of food in an endless variety of shapes and sizes. Some require cooking, others are already cooked.

The Household or Common Sausage. Term given to the beef and pork sausages sold at 6 or 8 links to the ½ kilo (1 lb). The quality is told by the proportion of meat to cereal filler content, coupled with the seasonings used in the mixture. Sausages are grilled or fried and may also be breaded. Blanching in boiling water for 2 or 3 minutes prior to cooking prevents the skins bursting.

Jumbo or king-sized sausages, 4 to the $\frac{1}{2}$ kilo (1 lb), are marketed to the pub trade and other popular catering outlets for snack service.

Sausage Toad in the Hole. The sausages are blanched, arranged in a greased tray with a yorkshire pudding mix and baked in the oven until done. Served with a rich brown gravy.

American Toad in the Hole. As above but using frankfurters.

Vin Blanc (Saucisses au). Chipolatas sauté in butter and dressed on a grooved croûton to contain each one, usually 2 to the portion. Swill the pan out with white wine and demi-glace, allow some reduction and sauce over the preparation.

Assiette Anglaise (Delicatessen Platter). Name given to a variety of cold meats, delicatessen slicing sausages and other products, served sliced and garnished with green, potato and Russian salads and relishes.

Black Pudding. Large black coloured sausage made with ox or pigs blood, suet, oatmeal, onion and seasonings. 'Bought in' ready made, it is thickly sliced, fried in butter or dripping and served with whipped potatoes.

Cervelat, Smoked slicing sausage made with dried, pale meat, finely minced and seasoned.

Chipolata. Long thin French type pork sausage giving 12 or more to the $\frac{1}{2}$ kilo (1 lb). The name is derived from chives once used to flavour them.

Liver Sausage. Made in a variety of types, smoked and unsmoked, mild and rich. One variety is made with foie gras. Slicing sausage and for sandwich spreads.

Mortadella. Large Italian slicing sausage made with milled pork ham, diced pork back fat, flavoured with peppercorns, pistachio nuts and garlic.

Paris Ham. Cured defatted loin of pork, cooked, smoked and strung in casing.

Rauchfleish. Cured, dried and smoked beef silverside.

Rollschinken. Gammon ham cured with spices and smoked.

Salami. Cooked slicing sausage containing pork, flavoured with garlic and other agents. Originals from Italy now reproduced elsewhere. Slice thinly and use sparingly.

Other Sausages. There are ham, tongue, breakfast and luncheon slicing sausages of endless variety.

Bath Chap

Lower half of pigs cheek usually 'bought in' ready made. Bath chap is cured in the manner of bacon and eaten as ham, or it may be boiled and served hot.

Brawn
Preparation made from the head of various domestic animals, bullock and pork being best known. Made from brined and cooked diced meat incorporating the tongue. Moulded, pressed and dressed in écarlate. Served cold with salad.

Haggis
Famous Scottish fare consisting of a sheeps stomach (bag) filled with the chopped liver, lights and heart (pluck), oatmeal, suet, onion and seasonings. Usually 'bought in' cooked and reheated by simmering in boiling water for 30 minutes, pricking it occasionally. Haggis is served with mashed potatoes, swedes and turnips and featured with neat Scotch Whisky.

OTHER MEATS

Other meat besides that of domestic mammals is eaten. Some are classified as ground game (Gibier à Poil), while similar meats are unclassified as goat, horse, whale and other species. Dates are given where the game concerned is in season, meaning when it is permissible to hunt. These dates are of more interest to the hunter than the chef since it is permissible to lay down in the freezer certain game for out-of-season eating.

Hare (Liévre) (*August 1–February 28*)
The hare has larger and more pronounced features than those of its tamer and more domesticated relation the rabbit. Likewise its flesh is gamey, richer and fuller flavoured. The hare is a very active animal and its flesh hardens with age and so becomes tough. Age is told by size and general appearance: the long ears should be soft and the tips tear easily. Hare is usually purchased ready skinned. Chestnut purée and redcurrant jelly are the escorts to all hare preparations.

Grand Veneur. The saddle or 'râble', is larded, marinated and roasted and served with the sauce of this name as well as the usual chestnut purée and redcurrant jelly.

Jugged Hare (Civet de Lièvre). Classic preparation and celebrated salmi applicable to all game whether ground or feathered.

The hare is dissected into 6 or 8 joints according to size; 6 portions: 4 limbs, the breast and the saddle; 8 portions: 4 limbs, and the breast and saddle each cut into halves. The dissected pieces are called the civet and the operation is performed over a bowl to catch the blood. The head and neck are retained for game stock.

The pieces are marinated for up to 48 hours; the marinade will contain port or a full bodied red wine. Pick out the civet and sauté it with a few oddments of bacon, sliced onion and carrot. Dredge with

157

flour, brown the pieces, add the marinade, game stock—prepared with the head and neck—cover the pan and braise for 2 hours in the oven.

Pick out civet and keep warm in a fireproof serving dish. Add the blood to the braising liquor, check seasoning, correct with butter, heat without boiling (the blood might curdle), strain the sauce and load with glazed button onions, mushrooms and bacon lardons and mask over the meat. Decorate with heart-shaped croûtons and serve with the traditional chestnut purée and redcurrant jelly.

Râble de Lièvre à la Crème. Large saddle, skinned and marinated in olive oil, aromates, seasoning, sherry or dry white wine. Stew the râble in butter in a deep pan, add strained marinade and cook for 90 minutes. Take out and keep hot. Make up a velouté from a roux, the strained braising liquor and game stock as required. Add cream, check seasoning with salt, cayenne and lemon juice. Load with glazed button onions and mushrooms and mask over the râble.

Roast Saddle of Hare (Râble de Lièvre Rôti). Country folk dress hare with herb and onion stuffing and roast it whole and the preparation gives rise to the more classical roasted saddle.

Select a large râble, skin, lard with care and marinate for 48 hours. Roast in butter, finish with noisette butter and dress with watercress. Serve with jus de rôti, redcurrant jelly and chestnut purée.

A red wine or port marinade is employed for this operation.

Venison (*July–February 28*)
General culinary term given to the edible flesh of all large ground game. In a more restricted sense venison means deer or 'Chevreuil'. Even so the range is wide and embraces roebuck (chevreuil), fallow deer (daim), red deer (cerf), moose (élan) and reindeer (renne). The male is the buck, the female a doe.

Venison should be young but not too young; it should also be hung for several days prior to cooking. The marinating of venison is a controversial matter—some chefs insist upon it, others say there is no need. The process, therefore, is optional. Venison is judged by the depth of fat which determines the quality of the meat. To hang, wipe over and dust with ground ginger and pepper—to keep the flies off. The legs and particularly the saddle or haunch are the ideal roasting pieces. Whereas marinating is optional, larding, or at least barding, prior to roasting is deemed as essential since, in common with all game, the meat is inclined to dryness.

Redcurrant jelly and chestnut purée should always accompany all preparations.

This meat also supplies chops, cutlets and steaks. It is equally rich in offal, particularly liver and tongue; the tongue of the reindeer when cured and smoked is something of a delicacy.

Civet de Chevreuil. The meat is cut into collops, marinated in red wine, aromates and seasoning. It is then sauté with onion and bacon oddments, flour dredged, browned, moistened with stock and the marinade and cooked with the lid on in the oven. The meat is picked out, the braising liquor reduced, corrected into a sauce, loaded with onions, mushrooms and diced bacon and sauced over the meat. Dressed with heart-shaped croûtons.

Roast Venison. This process applies to the haunch (saddle) or the leg. Hang for a week, wash with a weak solution of vinegar, lard liberally, season well with salt, pepper and ginger and roast, well protected, allowing 15 minutes to the $\frac{1}{2}$ kilo (1 lb). Serve with jus de rôti, cumberland, poivrade or a sweet game sauce.

Sweet Game Sauce. Into $\frac{1}{4}$ litre ($\frac{1}{2}$ pint) game jus de rôti, add 2 glasses of port or claret and 25g (1 oz) lump sugar. Check seasoning and allow preparation to cohere.

Selle de Chevreuil Montmorency. Hang saddle for several days, wash in weak vinegar solution, marinate for 8 hours in olive oil, seasonings, aromates and red wine. Season adequately and roast, well protected, basting frequently with the strained marinade. Dress with watercress and feature with a sauce poivrade prepared from the strained and checked cooking liquor, incorporating redcurrant jelly and candied red cherries.

Rabbit (Lapin)

Two kinds of rabbit exist in a culinary sense; the wild species and the one reared for table. One is gamey and not unlike hare, the other is mild flavoured and tender. Rabbit may be prepared as for hare. For other preparations it should be soaked in salted water to remove all surplus blood.

Blanquette. Dissect, clear all surplus bone and soak in salted water to whiten. Sauté the pieces with onions and carrots in butter, dredge with flour to coat and cook without coloration. Moisten with stock and velouté and stew with the lid on for 2 hours. Pick out the rabbit and keep hot. Strain the braising liquor, correct with butter, cream and lemon juice, and load with glazed baby carrots, mushrooms and onions. Combine with the rabbit, heat together and serve sprinkled with chopped parsley.

Casserole. Dissect and remove all surplus bone. Season and place in hot butter in a casserole. Add sliced onion, carrot, bacon lardons, chopped tomatoes and onions. Season and sauté together. Moisten with stock and stew in the oven with the lid on for 2 hours. Sprinkle with chopped parsley and serve.

Rabbit Pie. Line a pie dish with overlapping bacon rashers. In it arrange some tomato purée, sliced mushrooms, minced pre-blanched onion and chopped parsley. Add the pieces of rabbit, which should be boned, season and moisten well with stock. Fold in the rashers, cover with puff pastry, seal down, decorate and leave a vent. Egg-wash and bake for 2 hours. Replace the stock lost in cooking through the vent hole. Serve hot or cold.

Roast Rabbit.   The saddle is selected and is larded, marinated in white wine and aromates, roasted and served dressed on a croûton with jus de rôti.

Wild Boar (Sanglier)

The young boar (marcassin) makes the best eating and may be prepared in the same way as venison. One of the most noted preparations is the decorated boars head (hure de sanglier) for a cold buffet.

Goat (Chèvre)

Goat is a near relation to the sheep. Its meat is edible and it forms a staple diet of countryfolk in Italy, Spain and parts of France. For eating, the young goat or kid (chevreau) of a few weeks old is selected and treated as for lamb; it is considered something of a delicacy. The roasting joints, saddle and leg, are good and prior to cooking are first blanched for 10 minutes in boiling water and wiped over. The best end is treated the same as lamb cutlets. When it reaches maturity the meat of the goat is inclined, like old mutton, to be coarse and tasteless.

Horse (Cheval)

To a nation of animal lovers and because of close emotional ties, the eating of horse meat has, to the British, always been repugnant. But it is well enough known on the Continent and the horse butchers shop with its gilt head outside is a common sight.

   Horse flesh is very bloody in appearance and stronger in flavour than beef. Steaks taken from the sirloin, fillet and rump are tender and good when properly handled. If and when horsemeat is featured it must be clearly defined as such. In efforts to popularize it in the past it was given the name of chevaline, but all attempts have so far failed.

Squirrel (Écureuil)

Small rodent of which the grey species are best known. Classified as game, it may be prepared as a pot roast with root vegetables, in a pie, or stewed and prepared in any of the ways for rabbit.

Whale (Baleine)

In olden times when whales frequented home waters, their meat was eaten by the poorer members of the community. In recent times 'seabeef' is known to the inhabitants of Northern climes. In the years following the Second World War whalemeat was introduced to supplement a meagre meat ration. The flesh of the younger species of whale is pink and tender, that of older ones inclined to coarseness with an oily and fishy tang about it.

The best way with whale steak is braising with mushrooms, tomatoes or a little onion, which enhances the flavour. Whale meat may also be roasted and prepared into various entrées in the manner of beef.

Poultry and Feathered Game

Poultry is the term given to domestic birds. These indicate chicken, turkey, duck and goose. Feathered game (gibier à plume) indicates the wilder species. This adjective is used for want of a better word because some birds, such as duck, are both domesticated (poultry) and wild (game), and others, like pigeon or quail, are neither really tame or wild. In the culinary sense game differs from poultry. Whereas poultry is popular and, owing to modern production and marketing techniques, is consumed on an ever-increasing scale, game is more of an acquired taste. It is sedate, traditional and more the prerogative of the epicure.

All birds and their eggs are edible, though some are more palatable than others; it depends on how the birds are reared and what they feed upon. Poultry is specially bred for the table but the flesh of a wild bird feeding, for example, on fish or marine growth, may not always be considered good eating. Age and sex are other considerations. Whether the hen eats better than the cock is debatable and depends, so we are informed, upon the actual species of bird. The older the bird, the tougher and possibly the less flavoursome and succulent the flesh.

POULTRY (VOLAILLE)

Volaille is the French for poultry in general and chicken in particular. Poultry is usually 'bought in' weight graded, plucked, eviscerated and oven-ready.

Where a bird is purchased with the feathers on, it needs plucking with care so as not to tear the skin. Once plucked the neck is slit and the bird decapitated. Then, unless otherwise specified, it is drawn through the anus. An incision is made, the fingers inserted and twisted to loosen the innards, which should come away free in a whole mass in one drawing motion.

Care is taken not to perforate the gall bladder which contains a bitter liquid and a check is made to ensure the lights are not left behind. The claws of the drawn bird are trimmed and then it is singed over a flame and picked over with a knife to clear any pieces of feather or stubble left behind. The bird is wiped and trussed.

For special treatment with certain stuffings, the bird is drawn by the neck. This is particularly applicable where rich stuffings, such as foie gras, are indicated. Poultry freezes well; the frozen birds should be thawed before use.

Chicken

Size, hence age, determines the ultimate use. Chicken is marketed weight graded and eviscerated from ½ to 2½ kilo (1 to 5 lb) birds, classified in four types: the *poussin* of a few weeks old, featured as a one or double portion bird; the *roaster* or *broiler* (*grain and reine*), 1 to 2 kilo (2 to 4 lb); the *capon* (*poularde*), 2 to 2½ kilo (4 to 5 lb), a castrated cock table-reared; the *boiler* (*poule*), usually a large fat hen.

The French terms poussin, poulet de grain and poulet reine, and poularde would apply to three sizes of roasting birds. The term broiler to denote the popular battery bred bird could mislead in a culinary sense, when it is intended to identify a tender eating bird. The kitchen term to broil is an old English one, meaning to grill, but it is now synonymous with roasting.

Caterers favour the 600g to 700g (20 to 24 oz) two portion bird and serving half a chicken to the portion, so that all servings are identical. This practice supersedes the old one of serving the breast to the ladies and the leg to the gentlemen. Thus the two portion bird is, in many respects and for a large number of preparations, better and more satisfactory to feature than the larger four and six portioned chickens. But, of course, the final decision of portioning and size of bird must be left to the chef.

Roasters are now used exclusively for all preparations; boilers are more suited for sandwiches and certain cold preparation where the breasts only are featured.

Chicken is a versatile and comprehensive subject since it may be treated to the culinary processes of roasting, poaching, poêling, deep and shallow frying and grilling. This gives rise to innumerable dishes, and necessitates the provision of notes upon basic culinary processes and general points.

Roast Chicken. The bird is trussed, wiped over, salted inside and out and roasted in a pre-heated oven at 150°C. (350°F.) allowing 25 minutes to the ½ kilo (1 lb). The trussing string is removed and the bird finished with a dash of noisette butter and dressed with a bouquet of watercress. It is served with bread sauce and pan gravy.

Poached Chicken. Chicken is poached whole in a court bouillon consisting of sliced onion, carrot, celery, parsley oddments, mushroom parings, salt, peppercorns, lemon juice or lemon pieces and a bouquet garni. It is simmered at 20 to 25 minutes to the ½ kilo (1 lb) and the liquor is used in the preparation of the accompanying sauce. (The term poaching is preferred to boiling.)

The sophisticated culinary process of half roasting and half braising, termed poêlé à blanc, which leaves chicken uncoloured but perfectly succulent gives rise to a number of classic preparations. The process is best suited to large roasting birds, especially capons. The bird

163

is trussed, seasoned and set to roast in a braising pan for 10 to 15 minutes in butter or good dripping. When the process is well under way, sliced onion and carrot are added and the preparation moistened with veal or chicken stock sufficient to cover the pan to a depth of 5cm (2 in). The pan is covered and braised in the oven, allowing 20 minutes to the ½ kilo (1 lb). The chicken is dressed and finished as required and its sauce is made up with the braising liquor, suitably corrected.

Frying Chicken. Fried chicken is an American introduction to the culinary art. The bird is dissected into joints, seasoned and bread-crumbed. The portions are shaped, patted with a palette knife and sauté to a golden brown in clarified butter. The chicken is sometimes flavoured with herbs and spices. Breaded chicken may also be deep fried au friture, a method preferred to shallow frying by most chefs. It may be battered instead of breaded for deep or shallow frying.

Note: Where chicken is jointed, either for cooking or service, great care must be taken to avoid the inclusion of bone splinters, sharp ends, surplus bone and gristle.

Albuféra. The chicken is dressed with a rice stuffing mixed with diced foie gras and truffle. It is poêlé and masked with a sauce suprême tinted with meat glaze and garnished with large chicken quenelles, button mushrooms, truffle blades, cocks combs and kidneys.

Ambassadrice. The bird is larded with lardons and truffle and poêlé. It is then masked with sauce suprême and dressed with asparagus tips, truffle blades and sweetbread collops.

Ancienne (Fricassée de Poulet à l'). The chicken is jointed and cooked in stock, onion and carrot in a closed dish. It is dressed, masked with a sauce suprême loaded with button onions and mushrooms and garnished with heart-shaped croûtons.

Without the croûtons, it is also featured for cold service with its sauce well creamed, accompanied by a cold pilaff of rice.

Archiduc (Poulet Sauté). Jointed, sauté à blanc, i.e. in butter in a closed pan, masked with a white velouté with cream, flavoured with sherry, port or whisky and loaded with chopped truffle.

Another version of this preparation indicates the addition of a brunoise of vegetables.

Argenteuil. The chicken is poêlé, dressed masked with a suprême sauce with white asparagus purée and garnished with asparagus tips.

For the sauce, add a fine purée of white asparagus to about a quarter of the bulk of a well creamed suprême. Add salt, cayenne and lemon juice and colour to a pale green as required.

Aurora. The chicken is poêlé and masked with a sauce suprême tomatée loaded with equal quantities of chopped lean ham and truffle.

Autrichienne (Fritot de Poulet à l'). The chicken is jointed, seasoned, dipped in batter and deep fried. It is dressed with a fried bouquet of parsley and served with a poivrade sauce.

Basket (in the). The chicken is jointed, seasoned, breaded, deep fried, drained, salt dusted, arranged in a basket on a serviette and served with dressed green salad. There are numerous variations of the basket theme, some of which, like Chicken in the Rough, are registered names. Bearing in mind the maryland, the basket may be augmented by corn and fruit fritters and various composite salads.

(Chicken in the Rough was devised in 1937 by an American caterer, Beverley Osborne, and subsequently registered as one of the original franchise foods.)

Beaulieu. Joint, supress all surplus bone and season. Chop an onion and a shallot and set to stew in butter and olive oil. Add the chicken and sauté together. Add white wine and moisten with stock, tomato purée and a handful of pitted black olives. Cover the pan and braise in the oven. When ready, check seasoning, sprinkle with chopped parsley and serve with whole French beans in butter and pommes cocotte.

Bonne Femme. Roast a jointed 2 or 4 portion bird in butter en cocotte. Serve dressed in a cocotte with bonne femme garniture, consisting of equal quantities of glazed button onions and mushrooms, bacon lardons and pommes cocotte. The lardons are streaky bacon, blanched and sauté in half butter, half olive oil. The potatoes are cut and cooked in a similar manner. Combine the 4 ingredients, toss together, sprinkle with chopped parsley and a squeeze of lemon. Mask chicken generously and finish with noisette butter.

Bordelaise. The chicken is jointed, seasoned, floured and sauté in butter. It is dressed sauced over with its cooking liquor with the addition of white wine and garnished with rondels of fried onion, quartered fonds d'artichauts and olivette potatoes. Finished with chopped parsley and noisette butter.

Bouquetière. The chicken is poêlé, masked with sauce suprême and garnished with fonds d'artichauts filled with petit pois, French beans, baby carrots and turnips and cauliflower sprigs.

Bourguignonne. The bird is jointed, seasoned, sauté in butter, moistened with brown stock and red wine and stewed with blanched button onions, mushrooms and diced bacon.

Bristol. The bird is stuffed with rice dressed with grated parmesan and diced foie gras and truffle and poêlé. It is arranged on a foundation of rice pilaff and masked with sauce suprême.

Cardinal. The bird is poêlé, masked with a sauce suprême pinked with tomato purée and dressed with tomatoes filled with shrimps and heart-shaped croûtons.

Casserole (en). The chicken is jointed, seasoned, floured, sauté in butter, moistened with stock and cooked in the oven with the lid on with blanched button onions, mushrooms, diced bacon and fines herbes.

Note: Rather than a dish, casseroled chicken is now more of a term for a culinary process of braising chicken with onions, mushrooms, bacon and fines herbes.

Céleri (au) (Poached Chicken with Celery Hearts). Poached chicken masked with sauce suprême or ivoire, garnished with poached celery hearts similarly masked and sprinkled with chopped parsley. Buttered noodles may escort this preparation.

Chasseur. The bird is jointed, seasoned and sauté in butter with minced onion, shallot and sliced mushrooms. It is moistened with stock, white wine and tomato purée and stewed in the oven with the lid on. It is served in its cooking liquor augmented as required with demi-glace. Concassed tomatoes are sometimes used as an alternative to the purée.

Châtelaine. The chicken is poêlé, masked with a demi-glace sauce and garnished with whole braised chestnuts, celery hearts, whole peeled baked tomatoes and fondant potatoes. Finished with chopped parsley.

Chimay. Two ways of preparing this dish.

1. Chicken stuffed with raw noodles tossed in butter and diced foie gras, poêlé à blanc, masked with sauce suprême and topped with raw noodles sauté au beurre.

2. Chicken is poêlé à blanc, jointed and arranged on noodles dressed in cream and butter, masked with a sauce suprême and garnished with asparagus tips.

Clamart. The chicken is poêlé and dressed in a demi-glace sauce loaded with bacon lardons, blanched and sauté in olive oil, glazed button onions and braised whole lettuce.

Coq au vin. French regional cookery preparation cooked and served in a casserole dish. Joint a young roaster, season and sauté in butter with button onions, mushrooms and blanched bacon lardons. Flame preparation in brandy. Sprinkle with mixed herbs, moisten with a little stock and finish with red wine. Cover dish and braise in oven for 45 minutes. Serve garnished with heart-shaped croûtons.

Demidov (Demidoff). Portioned roast chicken arranged on cocotte and well garnished with a paysanne of carrot, turnip and truffle cut in 8-point stars, julienne of celery and blanched onion, all tombé au beurre and lié in madeira sauce. Finished with noisette butter, lemon juice and chopped parsley.

Derby. Chicken stuffed with rice mixed with diced foie gras and truffle and poêlé, masked with sauce suprême and garnished with tartlettes filled with diced foie gras and truffle.

Diable (à la). The whole trussed bird is cut through along the backbone, opened out and trimmed of all bone splinters. It is then seasoned, spread with mustard, coated in breadcrumbs and grilled. It is dressed with gherkin fans, lemon rondels and watercress and served with sauce diable.

Diva. The chicken is stuffed with rice mixed with diced truffle and foie gras, poêlé, masked with a sauce suprême pinked and flavoured with paprika, and garnished with turned and poached cucumber lié in cream.

(An Escoffier creation dedicated to Sarah Bernhardt, the celebrated actress friend and patron of the famous chef.)

Doria. The bird is poêlé and masked with velouté of cucumber prepared with the braising liquor, checked, strained and well creamed. It is garnished with poached cucumber balls lié in this reduction.

Duroc (Poulet Sauté). Jointed, sauté in butter with minced shallot, chopped tomatoes, sliced mushrooms, jus lié and white wine, and served sprinkled with chopped parsley.

Edward the Seventh (Volaille Poché Edouard VII). Poach a capon in a court bouillon and skin it. Prepare a rice pilaff and add sauté chicken livers. Dress the bird on the rice, mask with a well creamed sauce suprême coloured and flavoured with a hot curry powder, and decorate with strips of red pimento. For a 'grande service' it is usual to stuff the bird with rice pilaff flecked with chopped and sauté chicken livers.

(Escoffier creation at the Carlton Hotel, London, for H.M. King Edward VII. The great chef's Royal patron was a noted gourmet with a considerable capacity for good food.)

Estragon (à l'). The whole bird is poached in a court bouillon containing tarragon sprigs. It is served masked with its cooking liquor well reduced and corrected, decorated with blanched tarragon leaves and served with boiled rice.

Favorite. The bird is dressed with chicken forcemeat stuffing flecked with chopped truffle and poêlé. It is garnished with asparagus tips, cocks combs and kidneys, and truffle blades and masked with sauce suprême.

Fermière. The chicken is jointed and braised in brown stock in a casserole with sliced carrot, turnip, leek, diced bacon and peas.

Financière. The chicken is braised in brown stock with Madeira wine, dressed with glazed mushrooms, cocks combs and kidneys, chicken quenelles, stuffed olives and masked with a demi-glace containing the reduced cooking liquor.

Forestière. The bird is jointed, seasoned and sauté in butter with chopped shallot and morilles, then stewed in brown stock and madeira.

167

It is served masked with its corrected cooking liquor and garnished with diced sauté potatoes, lardons and chopped parsley.

Fritot de Poulet. The bird is jointed, seasoned, battered and deep fried, dressed with a bouquet of fried parsley and served with tomato sauce.

Gastronome. The bird is braised in brown stock and dressed with braised whole chestnuts, truffle, morilles and fonds d'artichauts filled with cocks combs and kidneys in demi-glace sauce, containing reduced cooking liquor, with which the chicken is masked.

Grand Mère. The chicken is roasted, jointed and garnished with bacon lardons, baby mushrooms, diced sauté potatoes and croûtons. Finished with noisette butter and chopped parsley.

Gros Sel. The chicken is poached in a court bouillon and garnished with baby or turned carrots and small onions and masked with a reduction of the cooking liquor. Bay salt (gros sel) is offered separately.

Hongroise (Poulet Poché à l'Hongroise). Poached chicken on rice pilaff masked with paprika sauce. The pilaff may be enhanced with blanched shredded red and green peppers stewed in butter.

Indienne (Poulet Poché à l'Indienne). Poached chicken arranged on boiled rice and masked with a sauce suprême lightly tinted and flavoured with curry powder combined with butter. Serve with chutney.

Ivoire (Poulet Poché Ivoire). Poached chicken dressed on a pilaff of rice or buttered noodles and masked with a suprême sauce tinted to an ivory hue with meat glaze. Sliced or glazed button mushrooms may be incorporated with the pilaff.

Jacques. The bird is dressed with a stuffing of chicken and duck livers sauté with minced shallot and mushroom. It is then poêlé in brown stock and served with a demi-glace sauce to which reduction has been added.

Judic. The chicken is jointed, seasoned, sauté in butter and stewed in brown stock. It is dressed with braised whole lettuce, cocks combs and kidneys, truffle blades and sauced with its corrected and reduced cooking liquor.

Lucullus. The bird is stuffed with a chicken forcemeat dressing flecked with chopped truffle and braised in brown stock. It is garnished with chicken quenelles, button mushrooms, cocks combs and kidneys, and truffle blades and masked with madeira sauce.

Maréchale. The chicken is jointed and sauté in butter and madeira. It is dressed with asparagus tips, truffle blades and sauced over with a reduction of its cooking liquor.

Marengo (Poulet Sauté). The bird is jointed, seasoned and sauté in olive oil with chopped tomato and a crushed garlic clove. Tomato purée and sliced mushrooms are added and the preparation is moistened with white wine and demi-glace and cooked. The dish is dressed with eggs fried in olive oil, heart-shaped croûtons, crayfish tails and chopped parsley. The fried eggs and croûtons denote the number of portions. (Scampi may be used in place of the crayfish.)

Maryland. The bird is portioned, breaded, sauté in butter and garnished with sweetcorn and banana fritters, creamed sweetcorn and maryland sauce. Another version is to deep-fry the chicken.

Note: In common with most regional and traditional fare, a certain amount of controversy arises about the garnishing of this preparation. It is often augmented with apple rings and pineapple fritters, grilled bacon rashers and whole tomatoes. But possibly the main controversy is the question of the sauce; horse-radish is usually substituted for the maryland.

Milanaise. The bird is jointed and cooked in butter. It is arranged on a pilaff of rice dressed with parmesan and garnished with diced ham sauté chicken livers, mushrooms and truffle. The pan is swilled out with madeira, reduced, corrected, and masked over the chicken.

Minute (à la). The bird is jointed, seasoned and sauté in butter with diced bacon, the preparation is masked with madeira sauce and allowed to cohere and served sprinkled with chopped parsley.

Montmorency. The bird is larded, poêlé, garnished with button mushrooms, stuffed olives, diced truffle, cocks combs and kidneys and masked with madeira sauce.

Néva (à la). Cold buffet preparation. Large fowl stuffed with chicken mousse combining purée of foie gras and chopped truffle, poached in white stock. It is then skinned and dressed whole, garnished with suprêmes of chicken, and masked with white chaudfroid. The preparation is then surrounded with tartelettes filled with Russian salad. The whole piece, after suitable decoration with truffle, ham and tongue, is masked with aspic.

Orientale (Poulet poché à l'Orientale). Poached chicken arranged on rice pilaff dressed with saffron, peas, diced red and shredded green peppers and masked with a sauce suprême.

Parmentier (Poulet Sauté). Jointed, seasoned, sauté in butter, masked with demi-glace sauce and served garnished with diced sauté potatoes and chopped parsley.

Patti. Capon dressed with a rice, diced foie gras and truffle stuffing and poêlé. It is set upon a large croûton, masked with sauce suprême and garnished with fonds d'artichauts.

(Named after Adelina Patti (1843–1919), a world famous prima donna.)

Paysanne. The jointed bird is braised in brown stock in a casserole with sliced carrot, turnip, leek, celery, onion, potato, peas and diced bacon.

Peau de Goret. The chicken is roasted whole and at the point of service it is masked with hot suet to crisp the skin. It is served with game chips, bread sauce and pan gravy.

Périgourdine. The chicken is dressed with a foie gras stuffing and poêlé. It is arranged upon a rice risotto flecked with a sauté of chicken livers, and masked with a périgourdine sauce.

For the dressing, clarify 120g (4 oz) chopped suet with an equal amount of pâté de foie gras, add an equal quantity of sauté chicken livers and season with salt, cayenne and lemon juice.

Périgueux. The chicken is jointed, seasoned and cooked in the oven in a sealed cocotte in butter with madeira and chopped truffle.

Pie (Chicken). Pie dish lined with overlapping bacon rashers in which is arranged the jointed and boned chicken pieces with minced cooked onion, sliced mushrooms, chopped parsley, seasoning and stock. The bacon rashers are folded inwards, the pie covered with puff paste, decorated, egg-washed and baked. When ready, the pie is topped up with stock or consommé poured in through the vent hole.

Chicken pie is featured hot or cold. For a cold service it is usual to add whole, shelled hard-boiled eggs. The meat is packed in fairly tightly and veal may also be added to the chicken.

Poached Chicken with Parsley Sauce. Chicken masked with parsley sauce and dressed on boiled rice or noodles au beurre.

Poincaré. The chicken is poêlé, garnished with buttered pasta coquillettes, crayfish tails and truffle blades and masked with a sauce suprême pinked by incorporating a coulis of crayfish. (Scampi may replace the crayfish.)

Another version of the dish indicates replacing the pasta coquillettes by cheese quenelles.

Polonaise. The bird is stuffed with a polonaise dressing, trussed and roasted. For presentation the bird is dressed in a cocotte and masked with a preparation of fried breadcrumbs, chopped parsley, sieved yolk and white of hard-boiled egg and a touch of lemon juice. Finished with noisette butter.

This dish is often featured with poussin as Poussin Rôti Polonaise. Equally suitable for capon.

Polonaise dressing: Chop onion and chicken livers, stew in butter or suet, add breadcrumbs pre-soaked in milk, chopped parsley, sieved yolk and white of egg and seasoning. Bind with egg if required.

Portugaise. The bird is jointed and braised in brown stock with chopped tomatoes and onions. It is served masked with a reduction of its cooking liquor and garnished with whole peeled tomatoes stewed in butter.

Pot Royale. A trussed capon, a piece of stewing beef cleared of fat and tied with string, and a piece of gammon (previously soaked) are cooked together in stock or a court bouillon. They are dressed on a large dish and served with a selection of poached root vegetables: small carrots and turnips, onions, leek, celery hearts, potatoes and cabbage. The preparation is featured with three sauces: suprême, hot horse-radish and a well reduced and corrected braising liquor. The vegetables are dressed in a neat fashion on a round dish, the onion is masked with cream sauce and the whole is sprinkled with chopped parsley.

Note: There is also a Pot Royale of Beef in which the meat takes pride of place. The dish is prepared and featured as for the Royale of Chicken.

Primeurs. This preparation indicates a roasted 2 or 4 portion bird or a capon well garnished with vegetables in season: glazed baby carrots, turnips, petits pois, whole French beans, baby mushrooms, baked tomatoes and parisienne or parsley new potatoes. Finished with noisette butter and chopped parsley.

Primeurs à la Crème. Indicates as aux primeurs with the garniture —except the potatoes—masked with a creamed béchamel sauce.

Provençale. The bird is jointed, seasoned and sauté in olive oil with chopped tomatoes, fines herbes and a tiny crushed garlic clove, dressed with capers and cèpes and finished with chopped parsley and noisette butter.

Richelieu. The whole bird is poêlé in brown stock and dressed with glazed mushrooms, stuffed whole tomatoes, braised lettuce and noisette potatoes. Demi-glace containing reduced cooking liquor is offered separately.

Riz (Poulet au). A de luxe version of chicken suprême. The bird is poêlé and dressed upon a rice pilaff finished with butter. It is masked with a sauce suprême flecked with chopped truffle.

Roast Chicken Américaine. Roast chicken with grilled bacon, whole tomatoes, mushrooms, frankfurters, sweetcorn, lima beans, fried potatoes, spiced bread sauce and pan gravy.

Roast Chicken Country Style. Grilled gammon rashers, stuffed tomatoes, mushrooms, cambridge sausages, sage and onion stuffing, bread sauce, pan gravy and roast potatoes.

Roast Chicken Home Style (Poulet Rôti à l'Anglaise). Two and 4 portion birds and capons. The bird is stuffed, trussed, salted and roasted. It is featured with grilled bacon, chipolatas, fried potatoes or game chips, bread sauce and pan gravy and garnished with watercress. (Herb and onion is the usual stuffing.)

Note: Where bacon rolls appear on the menu this indicates rolling and grilling the bacon. It may also be rolled around baby chipolatas.

171

Roast Poussin (Poussin Rôti). The one portion bird is roasted whole and served garnished with watercress and grilled bacon and accompanied by bread sauce, pan gravy and game chips.

Rose de Mai. Spectacular cold preparation. Large plump fowl poached and when cold the suprêmes are lifted and the centre bones removed. The centre is reconstructed with a mousse of tomatoes. The carcass is masked with white chaudfroid and the mousse decorated and aspic glazed. The piece is flanked by its suprêmes, left whole or sliced, chaudfroid masked, decorated and aspic glazed. The dish is completed with moulded, decorated and aspic-glazed tomato mousse barquettes and darioles shapes, and with wedges of aspic. The whole piece is finished decorated as fancy dictates and with aspic glazing and piping. The centre piece may be dressed upon a rice socle.

Rôti (Poulet). For a plain roast the bird is roasted whole, garnished with grilled bacon, dressed with watercress and served with bread sauce and pan gravy.

Saint Jacques (Poulet en Cocotte). Whole bird stuffed with a preparation of chicken and duck livers lightly cooked in butter with sauté minced shallot and mushrooms and then poêlé.

Saint James (Poulet en Cocotte). Whole bird stuffed with veal forcemeat with added chopped fines herbes. The preparation is poêlé and served masked with the cooking liquor reduced and corrected into a sauce with madeira and brandy. Served with a selection of vegetable primeurs.

Souvarov or Souvaroff. The chicken is poêlé and masked with a madeira sauce flecked with chopped truffle and incorporating a fine purée of foie gras.

Spatchcock. Same as à la diable or devilled. For whole or portioned chicken and poussins.

Stanley. The bird is jointed and braised in white stock. It is dressed masked in a sauce suprême tinted and flavoured with curry powder combined with butter and garnished with a julienne of tongue, ham and truffle. Served with pilaff of rice.

Suprême (Poulet Poché au Riz). Poached chicken dressed on a pilaff of rice and masked with a sauce suprême. For a de luxe presentation the masked chicken is topped with truffle blades to indicate the number of portions.

Trianon. The chicken is poêlé and dressed masked with a sauce suprême. It is garnished with whole fonds d'artichauts stewed in butter and filled with petits pois, whole skinned baked tomatoes and chicken quenelles.

Valenciennes. Jointed, seasoned and poêlé, served dressed on a risotto of rice dressed with butter, parmesan cheese and loaded with peas, diced ham and fonds d'artichauts, concassed tomato and blanched shredded red peppers.

The Suprême of Chicken

The suprême, or breast, being the most tender and exclusively white meat is considered the best part of the bird and as such it is highly glamorized.

When the suprêmes are lifted from the chicken they are trimmed, leaving the small winglet bone tips in place. Care is taken to leave the kernel or noix in place (after removing the nerve). For most preparations the supême is breadcrumbed, seasoned, sauté in butter to a golden brown and finished with noisette butter.

Alsacienne (à l'). Suprême of poached chicken dressed on a collop of foie gras lightly floured and sauté in butter. Masked with suprême sauce loaded with chopped truffle and served with noodles à la crème.

Américaine. Seasoned, passed in flour, egg-washed and coated with white breadcrumbs incorporating chopped ham, parsley and tongue. Sauté in butter and served garnished with grilled bacon, mushrooms, whole tomato, corn and banana fritters and asparagus tips.

Crème (Suprême de Volaille à la). Season, flour and sauté in butter without coloration. Swill the pan out with cream, add butter and check with salt and cayenne. Flavour with sherry or brandy. Let the sauce cohere and mask over the suprême.

Dugléré (Suprême de Volaille). Breaded, sauté in butter, dressed on a fried croûton of equal size, garnished with whole braised endive, grilled mushrooms and whole baked tomato, and finished with noisette butter and chopped parsley.

Hongroise. The suprême is seasoned, sauté in butter, masked with a sauce suprême, coloured and flavoured with paprika butter, and served with a butter-dressed rice pilaff.

Jeanette (Suprême de Volaille). Lift and trim the suprêmes from 2 large chickens poached in stock and mask with white chaudfroid. Decorate with tarragon leaves, pimento strips or truffle. Run some melted aspic along the bottom of a ceramic or glass serving dish, and stick onto it 4 escalopes of truffled foie gras. Set the decorated suprêmes upon the foie gras and finish with a final masking of aspic jelly.

(Well known Auguste Escoffier creation at the Savoy Hotel, London.)

Lard (Suprême de Volaille au). Season, breadcrumb and sauté in butter, dress with 2 grilled bacon rashers and finish with noisette butter.

Maréchal (Suprême de Volaille). Breaded and sauté suprême, topped with a truffle blade, garnished with asparagus tips (sprue) and finished with noisette butter.

173

Polignac. The suprême is seasoned, sauté in butter and masked with a sauce suprême loaded with a julienne of truffle and mushroom.

Porto (Suprême de Volaille au). Season, flour, sauté in butter and keep hot. Swill out the pan with port, allow some reduction, add to sauce porto and mask over the suprême.

Princesse (Suprême de Volaille). Three variations of this dish.

1. Stewed in butter, masked with suprême sauce and garnished with asparagus tips.

2. Poached, masked with suprême sauce and garnished with asparagus tips and heart-shaped toasted croûton with the top dipped in chopped parsley.

3. Breaded and sauté suprême garnished with asparagus tips, truffle blade, parisienne potatoes and finished with noisette butter and chopped parsley.

Rachel (Suprême de Volaille). White chaudfroid-masked trimmed suprêmes, dressed on a mousse of brandy-flavoured chicken. The suprêmes are decorated with sliced truffle, the dish garnished with asparagus tips, and the whole piece masked with aspic jelly.

Réforme. An adaptation of Cutlets Réforme. Prepared and breadcrumbed suprême exactly as for the cutlets, with the identical garnish.

Richmonde (Suprême de Volaille à la). Breaded, sauté in butter and garnished with fonds d'artichauts filled with pitted black grapes. The garniture is brushed with butter and heated in a hot oven. Finished with a dash of noisette butter.

Rossini (Suprême de Volaille). Season and sauté in butter, mask with a sauce suprême with purée of foie gras added, loaded with chopped truffle and slightly flavoured with brandy. Serve with noodles dressed with butter and cheese.

Saint James (Suprême de Volaille). Place a moulded centre piece of Russian salad caught in aspic on a round dish. Line the dish with sliced york ham. Arrange whole suprêmes of chicken on the ham. Garnish with cornets of ham filled with a purée of foie gras flecked with chopped truffle.

Saint Wystan. Sauté in butter with pâté maison and red wine sauce garnished with asparagus tips.
(Speciality of Midland Hotel, Derby.)

Sauté au Beurre (Suprême de Volaille). The piece is seasoned, floured, sauté in butter, dressed on a suprême-shaped croûton and finished with noisette butter.

Savoy (Suprême de Volaille). Breaded and sauté in butter, garnished with whole grilled tomato, asparagus tips and parisienne potatoes and finished with noisette butter and chopped parsley.

Sous Cloche (Suprême de Volaille). Season and flour suprême, sauté in olive oil and butter to seal without colouring. Add sliced white mushrooms and cook 3 to 4 minutes. Place preparation in cloche dish. Swill pan out with sherry, add cream, lemon juice and check with salt and cayenne. Mask the chicken and mushroom preparation with the sauce, cover the dish with its glass cloche, flash in a hot oven for 5 to 10 minutes, top with truffle blade and serve.

Suprême de Volaille et Jambon Lucullus. Suprêmes of chicken masked with white chaudfroid, decorated and dressed on a dish lined with sliced york ham, and the whole piece covered with aspic flavoured with brandy.

Suzanne. The suprême is breaded, sauté in butter and garnished with battered deep-fried scampi, asparagus tips in bouquet with thin strip of red pimento, a heart-shaped croûton and a truffle blade.

Trianon. Braised in white stock, masked with suprême sauce, garnished with nests of fonds d'artichauts filled with buttered peas, poached whole peeled tomatoes and large quenelles of chicken.

Viennoise (Suprême de Volaille à la). Flattened suprême without the wing tip bone prepared exactly as for the escalope of veal of this name.

Stuffing Suprêmes
For this elaborate preparation, the suprême is flattened, stuffed, rolled breadcrumbed and sauté in butter.

The suprême and its kernel are flattened with a butcher's bat, the stuffing piped in a thick ribbon along the centre, the kernel placed over the stuffing and the piece rolled and reshaped, sealing in the filling. The piece is seasoned, breadcrumbed, sauté and finished with noisette butter.

Antonin Carême (Suprême de Volaille). Stuffed with foie gras, poached, masked with sauce smitane and garnished with peas and parisienne potatoes.

Cordon Bleu (Suprême de Volaille). Place thin slices of parma ham and gruyère cheese on the flattened suprême, roll up, breadcrumb and sauté in butter. Top with a truffle blade, serve with a rice pilaff.

Jacques (Suprême de Volaille). The suprême is stuffed with chopped duck livers stewed in butter with mixed minced shallot and mushroom, seasoned with salt, cayenne and a touch of lemon juice, breaded and sauté.

Kiev (Suprême de Volaille à la). The suprême is filled with a savoury butter, topped with a truffle blade and garnished with poached turned cucumber olives and parisienne potatoes. The filling is prepared by working the butter to a pomade and seasoning it with lemon juice, salt, cayenne and a touch of nutmeg. It is now usual to feature the kiev ungarnished with a pilaff of rice.

Another version is to deep fry the pané and savoury butter stuffed suprême.

Opéra. The suprême is filled with a mushroom purée, topped with a truffle blade, garnished with asparagus tips, whole baked skinned tomato and parisienne potatoes, and finished with chopped parsley and noisette butter.

For the dressing, the mushrooms are stewed in butter, pressed through a sieve and the purée reinforced either with a stiff velouté or a béchamel sauce and seasoned with salt, cayenne, nutmeg and lemon juice and worked into a pliable preparation for piping.

Other stuffings include purée of foie gras; veal and chicken forcemeat flecked with chopped truffle; rice; chicken liver and truffle; smoked salmon and ham purée.

Sliced and Minced Chicken Dishes

These dishes are made with sliced (émincé) or chopped (hachis) cooked chicken. The preparation is assembled and prepared in large or individual dishes and gratiné mornay. It is also usual, as applicable, to pipe the dish with duchesse potato.

Américaine (au Gratin de Volaille). Foundation of noodles dressed in butter and loaded with peas and sweetcorn kernels, layer of sliced chicken, criss-crosses of julienne of red pimento, mornay masked, cheese sprinkled and glazed.

Chicken à la King. This preparation has changed over the years. The original recipe prescribes the following procedure.

Breast of poached chicken thinly sliced and heated in butter. In a second pan, cream is heated and then thickened with beaten egg yolk. The preparation is checked with salt and cayenne and flavoured with brandy. The chicken is loaded into the sauce with strips of red pimento, the preparation is allowed to cohere, topped with truffle blade and sent to table where each portion is served piled upon thick buttered toast.

The contemporary method indicates sliced cooked chicken, diced or shredded blanched green or red peppers and sliced mushrooms loaded into a well creamed velouté sauce, checked with salt and cayenne and flavoured with sherry or brandy. Served with a pilaff of rice.

Note: The à la King treatment is also given to other white meats such as turkey and also to lobster, crabmeat and scampi. It prescribes the sliced basic ingredient in a cream sauce with pimento and mushroom and a sherry or brandy flavour. The preparation is served with rice.

Legend has it that one evening a latecomer went into Mrs King's restaurant in Chicago requesting something to eat. Hurriedly Mrs King, who ran the restaurant with her daughter, mixed some chopped pimento in to flavour some left-over minced chicken in white sauce and served it as a snack on toast. From then on the latecomer became a regular and each time ordered the dish he now called chicken à la King. It became a house speciality and its fame spread throughout America to become glamorized in the great hotels and restaurants of the world beyond.

O. G. Goring, the London Hotelier, in his book *50 Years of Service* recounts a slightly different story. He describes the dish as similar to Poulet Sous Cloche with pimento and whisky flavoured. Apparently in 1918 at the Carlton Hotel, London, a certain American by the name of Mr King sent this recipe to the kitchens requesting Escoffier to prepare it. Escoffier obliged and is credited with naming it after the American client.

Chicken Sausages (Boudin de Volaille). Prepared with minced raw chicken, veal, egg, cream and seasoning and the bulk made up with fresh white breadcrumbs soaked in milk. This is filled into sausage gut, scaled, tied off in lengths and blanched. The sausages are then breaded and sauté in butter, served with various vegetable purées—parmentier (potato), clamart (green pea), florentine (spinach), limoisine (chestnut)—and accompanied by madeira sauce.

Boudin de Volaille Mornay. Sauté in butter, dressed on a purée of potatoes, masked with mornay sauce, sprinkled with grated cheese and glazed.

Colbert (Hachis de Volaille Gratiné Colbert). Minced chicken in well creamed béchamel or velouté, topped with poached eggs, mornay masked, cheese sprinkled and glazed.

Florentine (Émincé de Volaille Florentine). Cooked leaf spinach tossed in butter foundation, sliced chicken layer, mornay masked, cheese sprinkled and glazed.

Galantine of Chicken. Preparation resembling a thick sausage served hot or cold. Large raw chicken, skinned whole, boned and the meat passed through a fine mincer with equal amounts of veal and a small quantity of pork fat. This is worked to a smooth paste with egg and cream, and seasoned with salt, pepper, mixed spice, lemon juice and brandy. The preparation is then spread out over the skin to the thickness of 1cm ($\frac{1}{2}$ in). This is then stuck evenly and at intervals with oblong fillets of tongue, breast of chicken, bacon fat, whole truffle, and pistachio nuts, which have all previously been marinated in brandy or sherry. The marinade is sprinkled over the preparation which is rolled and tied up in a damp cloth and poached at 20 minutes to the $\frac{1}{2}$ kilo (1 lb) in stock. It is cooled, re-rolled and shaped in a clean cloth.

For hot, the galantine is sliced and served masked with a madeira sauce. For cold, it may be masked with white chaudfroid and aspic, or (without the skin) rolled in toasted breadcrumbs or masked in

177

écarlate. When sliced, the fillings should show well separated in a neat pattern.

Small sized galantines are prepared identically and are known as Ballotine. They are prepared from chicken, duck, pigeon and other birds and meats.

Italienne (au Gratin de Volaille). Foundation of cooked spaghetti dressed with butter and grated cheese, layer of sliced chicken and glazed with mornay sauce.

Kournick. Russian chicken pie shaped like a bell. Prepare from a brioche paste, similar to that for coulibiac, roll out, fill with sliced cooked chicken in white velouté sauce, sliced mushrooms, quartered or rondels of hard-boiled egg and season well. Fold over in bell or half melon shape, leave a vent, decorate paste as required, egg-wash and bake for up to one hour. Pour in hot cream through the vent, slice like a cake, spoon out filling and serve with a suprême sauce.

Madras (Gratin de Volaille). Foundation of boiled rice, good layer of sliced chicken, glazed with a mornay sauce well flavoured with curry butter.

Moussaka of Chicken Moldave. Minced cooked chicken and chopped onion stewed in butter, chopped tomatoes, seasoned and moistened with stock as required. The preparation is arranged in layers in a buttered fireproof dish lined with butter-sauté, sliced, unpeeled aubergine and finished with aubergine. Dot with butter and bake in an oven till topping is golden brown. Sprinkle with chopped parsley and serve with a demi-glace or a madeira sauce. Parmesan cheese may be added to this preparation as well as a top sprinkling for glazing.

Nouilles (Émincé de Volaille aux). Foundation of cooked noodles dressed with butter and cheese, layer of sliced chicken, topped with rondels of hard-boiled egg, masked and glazed with mornay sauce.

Pain de Volaille. Preparation consisting of a purée of raw chicken mixed with boiled rice, seasoned with salt and cayenne, mounted with cream and eggs and well beaten to a stiff consistency. It is loaded with diced truffle and mushroom and arranged in a lightly oiled mould with a ring of cocks combs. The preparation is poached and when cooked, unmoulded and masked with a sauce suprême.

Podjarsky de Volaille. Russian preparation: a minced chicken cutlet, similar to bitoke. Mince raw chicken, work to a smooth paste with cream, add fresh white breadcrumbs up to half the quantity of chicken, add more cream if needed, salt and pepper. Shape in flour as a cutlet, sauté in butter, dress with fondant potatoes and peas. Finish with noisette butter and chopped parsley over the potatoes.

May also be featured in any of the ways for bitoke. Small piece of chicken bone may be inserted into the piece to represent cutlet bone for appearance.

Savoy (Hachis de Volaille Savoyard). Minced chicken in well creamed velouté sauce, garnished with bouquets of asparagus tips, concassed tomato and truffle blades to indicate the number of portions, mornay masked, cheese sprinkled and glazed.

West Coast (le Gratin de Volaille). Sliced chicken mingled with blanched shredded green pepper stewed in butter, peas, sweetcorn kernels and peeled shrimps or prawns. Seasoned with salt, cayenne and a dash of nutmeg. Arranged in a dish piped with duchesse potato, mornay masked, cheese sprinkled and glazed.

Oyster

Name of two small morsels of plump, oyster-shaped pieces of lean meat embedded at the base on either side of a chicken carcass. Much appreciated by gourmets.

Duck

There are two kinds of duck: the domestic bird (caneton) and the wild duck (sauvage). The former bird is best as a 2 portion 1½ kilo (3 lb) and 4 portion 2–2½ kilo (4—5 lb) eviscerated bird. Wild duck is small and many species exist. It is classified as game and dealt with separately.

Duck is trussed like chicken and is roasted in a similar manner. With the roast, sage and onion dressing and apple sauce are featured. Braised, the duck is presented with peas and poêlé with various fruit.

Duck is sometimes a difficult bird and care should be taken to ensure a minimum both of fat and bone and a maximum of breast meat. In Britain the Aylesbury duckling is the most coveted, while in France the ducklings of Nantes (nantais) and the much prized Rouen species are highly praised.

Braised Duckling and Green Peas (Caneton poêlé aux Petits Pois). The duck is trussed and seasoned, set in a deep pan and roasted in hot dripping for 15 minutes. Add sliced onion, carrot, chopped tomato or purée. Season, add a bouquet garni and moisten with 1 litre (2 pints) stock. Cover pan and braise in the oven for 50 minutes. Remove, untruss, glaze and portion. Make up a half glaze sauce with espagnole and the strained braising liquor, check seasoning and consistency and colour. Load the sauce with cooked green peas, mask over the bird, let the preparation cohere and serve.

The sauce may be mounted from a brown roux and the braising liquor. Apple sauce is optional.

Duckling and Green Peas à la Française. Proceed as for duckling and green peas with the additional sauce loading of button onions and bacon lardons in equal amounts to the green peas.

179

Roast Duckling (Caneton Rôti à l'Anglaise). The bird is dressed, trussed and roasted in a pre-heated oven at 177°C. (350°F.) allowing 25 minutes to the $\frac{1}{2}$ kilo (1 lb). Finished with noisette butter, dressed with watercress and served with pan gravy and apple sauce.

Sage and onion is the usual dressing. As an alternative to the sauce, small baked apples touched with spice and glossed with syrup may be featured.

Roast Duckling on Canapé. Roasted 2 portion duckling, split in half, trimmed and each dressed on a large croûton, cut from a sandwich loaf, toasted on one side and the other spread with duck liver pâté. Finished with noisette butter and watercress and served with pan gravy, apple sauce, game chips, green peas au beurre and orange salad.

Duck Braised with Fruit

Duck goes exceptionally well with fruit such as mandarin, orange, grapefruit, pineapple, cherries and peaches. The bird is poêlé and the juices of the selected fruit are incorporated in the sauce. The most famous preparation is duck and orange.

Bigarrade. Two or 4 portion bird, trussed, seasoned, roasted in butter for 15 minutes then braised in covered pan in the oven for 50 minutes with sliced onion and carrot, tomato purée, bouquet garni and stock. The bird is glazed and portioned, masked with a bigarrade preparation and garnished with orange.

For the bigarrade, have required number of large, juicy oranges. Shred peel en julienne with a cutter and blanch. Dissect fruit in segments or rondels. Collect juice, combine with lemon juice, sweeten and reduce. Strain braising liquor onto the fruit juice and make up sauce with demi-glace. Check seasoning with salt and cayenne, consistency with butter, colour with carmine and flavour with curaçao. Add blanched julienne of peel. Mask over bird and decorate with orange segments or rondels.

Cerises (Poêlé aux). Two or 4 portion bird poêlé as for bigarrade. Select $\frac{1}{2}$ kilo (1 lb) red or morello type cherries and pit them. If fresh, poach in light syrup. Conserve cherry syrup, add to it orange and lemon juice ($\frac{1}{4}$ of citrus juice to 1 of cherry) and let it reduce over heat. Strain braising liquor onto sweet sauce preparation and make up with demi-glace. Correct seasoning, colour with carmine, check as required with butter and flavour with cherry brandy or curaçao. Load sauce with pitted cherries. Glaze bird, portion and mask with sauce.

Montmorency. Poêlé and garnished with orange segments and cherries. Prepared as for aux cerises with equal quantities of orange segments and pitted cherries and the juices of the fruit. (Allow 6 oranges and 250g (8 oz) cherries per bird.)

Orange (à l'). Same as bigarrade but without julienne of peel.

Note: A certain amount of poetic licence occurs with these duck à l'orange preparations and often bigarrade appears as à l'orange and vice versa. The critical factors however are: adequate meat on the bird, absence of fat, good sauce work and generous garniture.

Pêches (Poêlé aux). Two or 4 portion bird poêlé as for bigarrade or aux cerises. Ten minutes before it is ready, add 4 skinned peaches to the preparation. When ready remove fruit with care. Glaze and portion bird. Strain braising liquor, make up with demi-glace or beurre manié into a sauce. Check seasoning and colour and flavour with peach brandy. Mask duckling portions with the sauce, well loaded with the peaches.

Note: May be prepared with canned or bottled whole, halved or sliced peaches when fresh fruit is unavailable. The peach syrup is employed in the sauce.

Variations on the Duckling with Fruit Theme. Duckling may be braised with pineapple (Caneton Hawaiian); with mandarin segments (Caneton aux Mandarines); with grapefruit and orange segments (Caneton Jaffa); with prunes (Caneton California); or prunes and figs (Caneton West Coast).

In each instance the juices of the fruit concerned are used. The fruit may be fresh, canned or dried (i.e. prunes or figs) and the syrup of the cans used. A liqueur flavouring may be added: curaçao, cherry brandy, grand marnier and other fruit brandies and liqueurs. The julienne of peel is usually confined to the bigarrade, but it may be used in the jaffa.

Other Duckling Preparations

Chipolata (à la). The bird is poêlé, glazed and portioned, masked with a demi-glace sauce loaded with carrots, glazed button onions, braised whole chestnuts, diced bacon and pitted olives, and dressed with grilled baby chipolatas.

Nivernaise. Braised duckling with button onions, mushrooms and baby carrots. Similar preparation to duck and green peas but with different garniture.

Olives (aux). Braised duckling with pitted olives. Similar to duck and green peas with a different garniture.

Paysanne. Similar preparation to duck and green peas but with a different garniture. The duckling is braised and garnished with glazed button onions, peas, diced bacon and a paysanne of carrot, turnip, leek, celery and mushrooms.

Goose (Oie)

The popularity of goose has been eclipsed by other poultry. But at one time it reigned supreme and adorned the festive board at Christmas and other occasions.

181

The young gosling (oison) eats best. It is bought eviscerated and is most acceptable sage and onion dressed and roasted. The wishbone is removed, the bird stuffed, trussed, seasoned, floured and roasted in a deep pan at 177°C. (350°F.) allowing 20 to 25 minutes to the ½ kilo (1 lb). It is featured with pan gravy and apple sauce.

Swan (Cygne)

It may seem sacrilege to consider this majestic bird for the table, yet it was once treated with due reverence and only eaten at banquets for special occasions. The flesh of the fully grown bird is tough and tasteless; only the cygnet (cygneau) is selected for eating and should, rough plucked, not turn the scales over 7 kilo (14 lb). Because of the texture of its flesh the bird is treated in a special way.

Roast Cygnet. The bird is plucked, drawn, the wishbone removed, stuffed, trussed, and rubbed over with salt, pepper and powdered mixed herbs. It is protected with a flour and water dough, and roasted in a deep pan at 190°C. (375°F.) for 3½ hours, the dough removed and finished roasting to colour for 40 to 50 minutes. Dressed with watercress and served with a special gravy and a sweet apple sauce.

Gravy: Swill out roasting tray with stock prepared from the neck and crop. Reduce and strain. Add redcurrant jelly, check seasoning, correct consistency with butter and flavour with port.

Stuffing: Add 4 chopped baked onions to 1 kilo (2 lb) raw minced beef, 120g (4 oz) chopped suet and the bird's chopped offal. Season with salt, cayenne, mixed spice, herbs and lemon juice. Moisten with stock and half cook by braising. Add sufficient breadcrumbs soaked in milk to make up the bulk and knead well.

Cygnet may also be larded with bacon and roasted with sage and onion stuffing, but the above traditional method gives the best results.

Author's Note: I had no intention of writing up swan for this work, but while compiling the poultry and game section I received an enquiry about it. Since apparently there is still an interest, I decided to include it.

Turkey (Dinde)

Turkey is a native of America and according to Brillat-Savarin 'the New World's greatest gift to the Old'. Once it was just associated with Christmas. Then it became acceptable in collations with salads in summer. Now it is also featured at Easter. So turkey has become almost an all-the-year-round bird.

Like chicken, it is marketed eviscerated and it freezes quite well. Turkey varies in size; the most practical are considered to be the 4, 6 and 8 kilo eviscerated birds (8, 12 and 16 lb). Prior to cooking, the wishbone should be removed and the leg sinews should be drawn; these precautions facilitate the carving. The latter operation is performed by breaking the foot joints, affixing them in turn to pieces of string cord and giving a few sharp tugs.

For cooking, the bird is trussed in the same way as chicken. Stuffing is inserted through the vent and sealed in by a flap of skin left for this purpose. Stuffing should always be partly cooked and loosely packed to allow for its expansion and the shrinking of the carcass during cooking.

Roast Turkey. The prepared bird is trussed, stuffed or not, salted, smeared with dripping and set to roast in a deep pan in a pre-heated oven at 163°C. (325°F.) allowing 20 minutes to the ½ kilo (1 lb). The piece should be well protected with foil and greaseproof paper; this will be removed towards the end of the roasting process to colour and the heat increased to 190°C. (375°F.) for 20 to 30 minutes accordingly.

Turkey is best dressed with chestnuts and forcemeat but may also be stuffed with sage and onion. Roast turkey is accompanied by bread sauce, pan gravy and cranberry sauce or jelly. Other garnishing may include grilled bacon, braised ham, grilled pork, frankfurter or chipolata sausages, mushrooms and whole tomatoes.

Derby. The bird is dressed by the neck with a derby stuffing and roasted. It is served with pan gravy, braised celery hearts and fondant potatoes.

(An Escoffier creation.)

Périgourdine. Prepare a small turkey and stuff with derby dressing. Poêlé the bird. When ready, strip off the skin and mask with a sauce périgourdine flecked with chopped truffle and tinged with brandy or sherry.

Poultry Offal

The main offal of poultry is the liver. Though chicken livers predominate, those of the duck, turkey and the livers of other birds are edible. Livers are used in various garnishings and are prepared in brochettes, pilaff and for pâtés.

Other offal includes the heart, used in sautés and risotto, and the cocks combs and kidneys, used in garnitures. The neck and crop are used in chicken stocks and gravies. All offal should be used for making stock.

Brochette de Foies de Volaille. Trim and stiffen the livers in butter, place in a bowl with blanched sliced onion, small mushrooms and squares of bacon rashers. Season with salt, crushed peppercorns, add a bayleaf and sprinkle with olive oil. When preparation has macerated, thread ingredients alternately on the brochette. Paint with olive oil and grill. Stick a whole grilled tomato into the brochette and dress on a risotto of rice dressed with butter and grated parmesan. Set a cordon of madeira sauce around the base of the rice.

Risotto aux Foies de Volaille. The livers are picked over and trimmed, sauté in butter with minced shallot, seasoned, and lié with demi-glace touched with madeira. The livers are dressed in the centre of a moulded ring of risotto of rice and sprinkled with parsley.

Sauté of Chicken Livers. Trim and season the livers and sauté in butter with minced shallot, sliced mushroom and concassed tomato. Moisten with stock as required and check seasoning. Let the preparation cohere and serve sprinkled with chopped parsley, accompanied by boiled rice.

FEATHERED GAME (GIBIER À PLUME)

There are several common factors between all feathered game. It is usually sold by the brace, a cock and a hen bird, and this provides the opportunity of comparing the eating merits between the male and female of the species. Game should not be eaten too soon—the flesh of freshly killed birds is inclined to toughness and lacking in flavour. It should be hung by the feet for a few days in a cool place, when it acquires a gamey (faisandé) flavour. Some birds are eaten whole, others are 2 portioned and this, with the larger species, is the ideal portioning.

Most game is in season only during certain times of the year, meaning when shooting is permitted.

Since the birds may be bought in feather they require plucking and drawing with care, without tearing the skin or damaging the bird. As game is shot, the pellets are often found in the flesh, but as this shot is quite small it is harmless, although any found in cleaning is obviously removed.

If the bird has hung and some putrification has occurred, its preparation for the oven becomes a delicate operation as there could be sharp and jagged edges of bone to be avoided. Wishbones are usually removed. The innards are searched for the liver, heart and crop and the rest disposed of. The neck and crop go to make the jus de rôti. The livers are prepared into spreading pâtés for the croûtons upon which many birds are mounted.

The croûtons are cut either from French bread or from a sandwich loaf. Some are toasted on one side only, others fried in butter; it is usual to toast one side and spread the other with pâté. Sandwich bread croûtons which are fried are also grooved for appearance.

Feathered game is procured fresh. Freezing may dry the bird, spoiling the end product. Certain made-up entrées do freeze without loss of quality; this applies particularly to pheasant.

Game chips are synonymous with roast game and so are such salads as japonaise and plain orange.

Blackbird (Merle)
One-time traditional British fare, excellent in pies, pâtés, terrines, may also be roasted.

Blackbird pie in particular was once a very famous dish. The birds are plucked, drawn, boned and stuffed with veal forcemeat. They are set in a pie dish lined with thin collops of beef steak, minced onion, sliced mushroom, whole hard-boiled eggs, seasoning and chopped parsley, moistened with stock, covered with puff paste and baked. Lost stock is replaced and pie served hot or cold.

Black Game (Coq de Bruyère)
Black game or cock is a member of the grouse family, though less valued than its aristocratic cousin. Best roasted and treated as for grouse with the usual escorts.

Capercaillie or Capercailzie
Member of the grouse or rasores family, treated as for grouse but best roasted.

Curlew
Maritime bird, like an outsized woodcock with a long curved beak. Since this bird feeds off the seashore its flesh is inclined to be rank, so it is usually stuffed with a herb and onion stuffing and roasted. Said to be best in late summer and early autumn when it feeds inland.

Wild Duck (Canard Sauvage)
Wild duck is in season from August to March. There are many species throughout the world. In Britain most culinary birds belong to the Mallard family of ducks, others to the Teal and Pintail. The wild are smaller than the domesticated birds. All duck is edible, but the taste of the flesh varies and depends upon the fowls' diet and habitat. In common with all game it improves with hanging and it should be roasted quickly and, unless otherwise specified, left on the underdone side.

Roast Wild Duck (Sauvage Rôti). The bird is roasted at 232°C. (450°F.) for 20 minutes. It is dressed on a croûton spread with liver pâté, garnished with watercress, finished with noisette butter and sent to the table with the traditional escorts—bread sauce, jus de rôti, apple sauce and fried breadcrumbs. It is served with game chips and orange salad. The apple sauce should be lightly sweetened. Salad japonaise may be featured.

Bigarrade. A preparation identical to the duck recipe with a 2 portion sauvage.

Petits Pois (Sauvage Poêlé aux Petits Pois). As for the duck recipe with a 2 portion sauvage.

185

Presse (Sauvage à la). This much vaunted culinary tour de force which many restaurants have made their house speciality—and which a wit once dubbed squashed duck—may be applied both to the tame and the wild bird. The latter rather than the former is now the usual candidate reserved for this spectacular feature which calls for skill and a press: a plated or stainless steel article of equipment. The operation is a two-staged affair: the mise-en-place in the kitchen and the assembling and presentation at the table. The sauvage is a 2 portion bird.

Kitchen Work. The duck is seasoned and roasted for 10 minutes, a jus de rôti is prepared, the raw liver and heart are chopped, the duck, gravy and offal are dispatched into the room.

Table Work. The duck is impaled on a fork, the legs removed, the breasts carved in long thin aiguillette fillets, placed on a silver flat and kept warm. The legs are sent back to the kitchen where they are devilled or grilled. For devilling they are painted with butter, seasoned with salt, cayenne, mustard or curry powder, rolled in breadcrumbs and grilled. They are returned to the table by which time the dish is ready.

The duck's carcass is placed in the press, crushed and the juices placed in a receptacle. A flambé pan is placed over the lamp with a piece of butter, the chopped offal is added and sauté, the juices pressed from the carcass and the jus de rôti are added, the preparation is seasoned with salt, cayenne and a glass of brandy. Heat the sauce, let it cohere but *do not boil*. Correct consistency as required with more butter—it should be creamy in consistency and chocolate in colour. The sauce is now strained evenly over the fillets of duck, the silver flat placed over the stove, shaken and heated together. The preparation is served accompanied by the devilled or grilled legs.

The escorts to the preparation are soufflée or mousseline potatoes and orange or japonaise salad.

(The japonaise was created by Escoffier as a compliment to this dish.)

Salmis. Famous preparation for all game. This procedure indicates wild duck, but it is applicable to all game, ground and feathered, not only singly but in various computations.

Roast the duck for 10 minutes, dissect into portions and suppress all bone. Melt minced shallot in butter, add the birds neck, giblets, liver and carcass, all rough chopped. Add tomato purée, a bouquet garni, salt, pepper, port or burgundy and make up the bulk with game stock. Bring to boil, simmer and reduce. Strain the preparation, check with butter and seasoning and garnish with glazed button onions and mushrooms. Arrange the cooked game in a cocotte and mask with the prepared sauce. Heat through with the lid on for 15 minutes. Serve garnished with heart-shaped croûtons.

Salmis may be further enriched with a small quantity of chopped truffle.

Fig Pecker (Becfigue)
Small bird found in South of France and Italy, feeds off figs which give its flesh a sweetish flavour. It is roasted or prepared in any of the ways as for quail.

Grouse (*August 12–December 12*)
Grouse is unique since it is exclusive to the British Isles. All attempts at breeding elsewhere have so far failed. It frequents the moors of Scotland and Yorkshire and is also found in parts of Wales and Ireland.

Roast Grouse. For roasting, the breast is barded with a vine leaf and unsmoked bacon fat. Tie down the bard, salt inside and out and set to roast at 232°C. (450°F.) for 10 to 20 minutes according to size. A few minutes beforehand, remove the bard to allow the breast to colour. Dress the bird with its bard in place on a croûton spread with liver pâté, finish with noisette butter and a bouquet of watercress. Serve with pan gravy, fried breadcrumbs, bread sauce and game chips.

Crème (à la). Two portioned bird roasted for 20 minutes. Lift the suprêmes and place in fireproof dish. Mask with a sauce suprême prepared from a roux and game stock, strained, seasoned with salt, cayenne and lemon juice, enriched with cream and flavoured with brandy.

Flamed with Pineapple (Flambé à l'Ananas). Two portioned bird roasted for 20 minutes. The suprêmes are lifted, flamed in brandy at the table, dressed on rounds of fresh pineapple and sauced over with their juices.

Guinea Fowl (Pintade)
Not unlike chicken, but the guinea fowl is usually handled and treated as game. It is best roasted; 1–1½ kilo (2–2½ lb) bird will take 40 to 50 minutes. Since the flesh is inclined to dry, the bird should be barded. Roast guinea fowl is presented with pan gravy, fried breadcrumbs and redcurrant jelly which replaces bread sauce, though both these sauces are sometimes offered.

May also be split open, grilled, served with diable sauce, maître d'hôtel butter and garnished with bacon, mushrooms and tomatoes.

Hazel Hen (Gelinotte)
Handled in similar ways to grouse and pheasant. The bird is plucked, decapitated, fully drawn and trussed. It is best roasted or casseroled à la crème. Since the flesh is inclined to dry in cooking, the breasts should be larded.

Roast Hazel Hen. Season with salt, wrap in a bard, roast at 232°C. 450°F.) for 20 minutes. Dress on a croûton spread with liver pâté, watercress and serve with bread sauce, fried breadcrumbs and pan gravy.

187

Crème (à la). Roast 2 portion bird, cut in half, suppress backbone, arrange in a cocotte, mask with a sauce suprême and heat.

Smitane. As for à la crème but masked with a sauce smitane loaded with sliced mushrooms.

Lapwing (Vanneau)

Similar in type to woodcock, snipe and plover and presented accordingly. Prepared like the woodcock, only the gizzard is removed and the neck and head skinned.

Roast Lapwing (Vanneau Rôtie). Season well with salt, wrap in vine leaf secured with a bard and roast at 246°C. (475°F.) in butter for 8 minutes. Finish with lemon juice, dress on a plain croûton with its bards and serve with a short, well reduced jus de rôti.

Lark (Mauviette: Alouette)

Small perching bird with tiny beak and white legs. Has many culinary uses. May be prepared as any of the ways for quail, also employed in pâtés, terrines and pies. Lark pâtés and terrines are elaborate affairs with foie gras, truffle and brandy.

In company with thrush, also a feature in steak, kidney and oyster pudding.

Roast Lark. Two birds to the serving. Pluck, draw, wipe over, season, wrap in a bacon bard, impale on a skewer and roast in butter in a quick oven or on a grill for about 10 minutes. When ready, squeeze half a lemon over the birds, remove skewers, dress on a croûton spread with liver pâté and serve sizzling hot escorted with bread sauce, fried breadcrumbs, jus de rôti, game chips and watercress garnish.
Note: Opinions sometimes differ as to the drawing of these small birds for roasting. Some suggest only the gizzard be removed in a similar manner to quail.

Lark Pie. The birds are plucked, drawn, boned with care and arranged in a pie dish lined with bacon rashers, chopped onion, sliced mushroom, tomato pulp and chopped parsley and seasoned with salt, pepper, lemon juice and Worcester sauce, moistened as required with good game stock, covered with puff pastry and baked. When ready, finished with more stock and served hot or cold.

Moorhen

Frequenter of ponds and inland waters. Good to eat, usually roasted as for game. The eggs are equally considered a delicacy.

Ortolan *(May 15–September 15)*

The most exclusive of all feathered game. Ortolan is very rare and is only featured for special occasions. It is prepared as the woodcock, snipe and quail, i.e. partly drawn, only the gizzard removed. It is not decapitated; the head and neck are skinned and the eyes taken out. Prepared in any of the ways prescribed for quail and woodcock.

At State Banquets and similar functions the ortolan is presented roasted and escorted by quail.

Roast Ortolan. Season well with salt, wrap in a vine leaf held in place with a bard. Roast in butter for 8 minutes at 246°C. (475°F.). Finish with lemon juice. Dress with its bards on a plain croûton, touch with noisette butter and serve just with its pan gravy, well reduced. The pan is swilled with consommé and allowed to reduce well into an essence.

Ananas (à l'). Salt, bake in a closed service cocotte in butter for 8 minutes. Moisten with fresh pineapple juice and bake again for 3 minutes. Serve very hot, touched with beurre noisette.

Brochettes (en). Small ortolans speared on a skewer with small pieces of bacon and charcoal roasted. Served dressed on a plain croûton.

Lucullus. The prepared bird is encased in a large, hollowed out truffle, roasted in hot charcoal and flamed in cognac.

Partridge (Perdreau) *(September 1–February 1)*
Found throughout Europe. There are also American and Asiatic species. In common with grouse, the most popular and best method of appreciation is the straight roast. Proceed exactly as for grouse with the identical accompaniments.

Bonne Femme. Season and roast a large-sized bird in a deep pan for 5 minutes. Add sliced onion and carrot, tomato purée and seasoning and moisten with stock. Cover the pan and braise in the oven for 1½ hours. Remove bird, split in half, remove backbone and place halves in a cocotte. Strain the braising liquor, reduce, correct with butter and seasoning, load with equal amounts of glazed button onions, mushrooms and bacon lardons. Sauce preparation over the bird and reheat together.

Chartreuse (en). The bird is braised with diced ham and bacon, chopped onion and carrot, white wine, peppercorns, salt, bouquet garni and stock in a closed pan. It is jointed and packed into a mould with braised cabbage, cooked sliced carrot and onion and rondels of French sausage. The preparation is cooked off in a brain-marie, turned out and dressed with a cordon of demi-glace.

Choucroute (à la). The bird is part roasted, halved and then braised in a deep pan with sauerkraut, thickly sliced gammon and sausage, moistened with stock. It is served well juiced with the braising liquor.

Choux (Braisé aux). Roast bird for 5 minutes, halve and suppress backbone. Blanch a large, sound and trimmed savoy cabbage for 8 minutes. Slice it through, cut away the major part of hard stalk, open out the leaves, arrange a half bird in each portion of cabbage and wrap up in long, thin bacon rashers. Brush a large fireproof dish with butter and line with sliced carrot and onion. Set in the stuffed cabbage and half cover with stock. Add tomato purée, bouquet garni and seasoning. Dot with butter, bring to the boil, cover dish and braise for 2 to 2½ hours. Remove bouquet, garnish with baby grilled chipolatas and fried rondels of large French sausage.

Cocotte (en). The bird is roasted for 20 minutes, halved, and then braised in a cocotte in the oven with button onions and mushrooms, diced bacon and stock.

Crème (à la). The bird is part roasted, halved and then braised in a cocotte with onion, carrot and stock. The preparation is finished with cream and lemon juice and allowed to cohere.

Étuvé. The bird is part roasted, halved and braised in a closed pan with diced bacon and ham, chopped onion and carrot, salt, pepper-corns, bouquet garni, stock and white wine. It is served masked with a reduction of the braising liquor.

Peacock (Paon)

Popular and colourful feature of medieval banquets when the birds were roasted and served dressed with all their feathers. But peacocks are better to see than to eat and they are not very often featured now, except on very rare occasions. The flesh is reputed to be tough and tasteless, though the peahen is said to eat better than the peacock. May be featured in any of the ways suitable for pheasant.

It is on record that in May 1952 Alexandre Douheret, Chef-des-Cuisines, Cumberland Hotel, London, created Le Paon à l'Oriental as a speciality dish. This novel creation consisted of boned peacock stuffed with goose, goose with pheasant, pheasant with young hen, young hen with wild duck, wild duck with partridge, partridge with squab (young pigeon), squab with grouse, grouse with snipe, snipe with figpecker and figpecker with oysters. At a lavish State Banquet in Teheran in October 1971 given by the Shah of Persia, roast peacock was served escorted by quail, the birds being dressed 'en volante', i.e., with their colourful plumage.

Pheasant (Faisan) (*October 1–February 1*)

Originally from the East, pheasant is now found all over Europe and elsewhere. Game is always better for being hung, but this is especially applicable to pheasant. As with grouse and partridge, the pheasant is best plain roasted and this is the most popular treatment, though there are many other ways with the pheasant. Since the flesh is inclined to dryness the bird should be well barded. Many chefs say barding is insufficient and that the breast should be larded as well. Since when performed neatly and evenly larding also enhances appearance, this view is supported.

Roast Pheasant (Faisan Rôti). The bird is barded, trussed, seasoned inside and out and roasted at 177°C. (350°F.) for 30 to 40 minutes. It is set on a large croûton spread with liver pâté, dressed with watercress and finished with noisette butter. The roast is accompanied by bread sauce, pan gravy, fried breadcrumbs and game chips.

Casserole (en).   The bird is seasoned, set in a deep casserole with stock and diced bacon, small mushrooms and blanched onions and cooked in the oven with the lid on.

Périgourdine.   The bird is jointed, seasoned, sauté in butter and masked with a sauce suprême loaded with purée of fois gras, chopped truffle and flavoured with brandy. It is garnished with poached celery hearts.

Podjarski.   Chopped cooked pheasant meat seasoned and mixed with a stiffish velouté, worked and shaped as a cutlet. It is then breaded or battered and deep fried and garnished as required.

Souvarov.   The bird is jointed, seasoned, sauté in butter, set in a casserole and masked with a sauce suprême loaded with a purée of foie gras, chopped truffle and flavoured with brandy.

Truffé.   The bird is stuffed with pork forcemeat and diced truffle, roasted and served with a périgeux sauce.

Pheasant with Fruit.   The fruits selected are of the citrus and colourful types: mandarin, orange and grapefruit segments, pineapple wedges, and pitted red cherries. The dish takes on the name of the fruit concerned in a similar manner to duck.

The bird is jointed, seasoned and sauté in butter. The fruit is prepared and the juices collected. The sauté pan is swilled out with the fruit juice and corrected into a sauce with demi-glace. The sauce is flavoured with brandy, loaded with the selected fruit and masked over the bird.

Pigeon

Seasonal in autumn and winter. The young and plump-breasted birds are tender and of good flavour. The birds are drawn and trussed in the same way as poultry and go either 1 or 2 to the portion, according to size. The smaller and younger birds (squabs) are roasted, while the large are best braised. In France, the Bordeaux pigeon is the most sought after.

Roast Pigeon.   Draw, truss and season inside and out. Bard the breast with bacon fat and roast at 200°–232°C. (400°–450°F.) for 10 to 12 minutes. The birds are better left on the underdone side. Dress on a croûton with watercress and serve with bread sauce, pan gravy and game chips.

Compote (Pigeon en).   Proceed as for aux petits pois, loading the sauce with equal amounts of bacon lardons, button mushrooms and onions, and pitted olives. Flavour with red wine and heat together.

Olives (Pigeon aux).   The bird is braised as for aux petits pois. The prepared sauce is loaded with pitted French and Spanish olives, flavoured with red wine, masked over the pigeon and heated through. *Note:* The combination of pigeon and olives is an excellent one, especially when enhanced with a full bodied red wine.

Birds for braising are left whole or halved with the backbone suppressed, according to size.

Petits Pois (Pigeon aux). Pigeon braised with green peas. Roast for 5 minutes with butter in a deep pan. Add sliced onion and carrot, tomato purée and seasoning. Add bouquet garni and moisten with stock. Braise in a covered pan for an hour. Remove bird and keep hot. Strain braising liquor, correct with butter and thicken with arrowroot or cornflower. Check colour with carmine. Load with cooked green peas and sauce over the bird in a cocotte. Heat together.

Petits Pois à la Française (Pigeon aux). Proceed exactly as for previous recipe, loading the sauce additionally with equal amounts of bacon lardons, button mushrooms and onions.

Polonaise. Exactly as for the chicken and poussin dish of this name.

Plover (Pluvier) (*October 1–March 15*)
Several species exist, the golden plover being the most featured. A frequenter of marshlands, it feeds off pond life which imparts a sweet flavour and makes this bird much in demand. It is partly drawn, only the gizzard being removed. Prepared in any of the ways indicated for quail and woodcock, but probably best appreciated as a plain roast.

Roast Plover (Pluvier d'Or Rôtie). The prepared bird is well salted, roasted in butter for 10 minutes at 246°C. (475°F.), finished with lemon juice and noisette butter, dressed with watercress on a plain croûton and served with a concentrated jus de rôti. The roasting pan is swilled with consommé and well reduced into an essence.
Note: Plovers are not barded.

Marrons (Pluvier d'Or aux). Roast in butter for 8 minutes, place in a closed cocotte with brandy to infuse in the oven. Add 6 whole chestnuts poached in veal stock. Swill the roasting pan with stock, reduce and check with salt, cayenne and lemon juice. Strain over the plover and chestnut preparation and heat together.

Vigneronne (Pluvier d'Or). Roasted in butter for 10 minutes, placed in a closed cocotte with brandy to infuse in the oven. The pan is swilled with veal stock, sweetened with grape juice, checked with salt, cayenne and lemon juice and thickened if required. The prepared sauce is loaded with pitted and skinned grapes, masked over the bird and heated together.
Note: For a richer preparation infuse the plover in champagne and brandy.

Quail (Caille)
Small plump bird with white flesh and a distinctive aroma, the subject

of a number of recherché gastronomic preparations. Main source of supply was originally Egypt. Quail is now home bred for the table and marketed fresh, plucked but not eviscerated. It is decapitated but not entirely emptied, only the gizzard is removed. Too small to truss, the legs at the knee joint are slit and then tucked into the sides of the bird. Quail is either roasted for 10 minutes in butter or braised for 20 minutes in veal stock.

Roast Quail (Caille Rôtie). Seasoned, wrapped in a vine leaf secured with a bard and roasted at 246°C. (475°F.) for 10 minutes, dressed on a croûton, finished with squeeze of lemon and noisette butter, garnished with watercress and served with a jus de rôti. The croûton is cut from a crisp French roll 12mm ($\frac{1}{2}$ in) thick, fried on both sides in the roasting pan. The jus is obtained by swilling out the pan with stock, allowing it to reduce and slightly thicken.

Poached Quail. For this, the bird is stuffed with a fine purée of foie gras flecked with chopped truffle, using a piping bag fitted with a small bit. The purée is previously worked over with a palette knife and touched with salt, cayenne and lemon juice. The stuffed bird is simmered in veal stock for 20 minutes.

Alexander. The stuffed, poached quail is masked with a demi-glace flecked with chopped truffle, flavoured with brandy and surmounted with a truffle blade.

Broche (à la). Season, wrap in vine leaf and bard, impale on a brochette, paint with butter and grill for 15 minutes over a bright fire or under a grill. Remove bard and sauce over with lemon juice.

Canapé (sur). Roast quail, dressed on croûton, garnished with watercress and served with jus de rôti.

Casserole (en). Braised quail with diced bacon in madeira and veal stock.

Cendre (sous la). Boned, foie gras stuffed, barded, wrapped in thin short paste and oven baked. Served with a brandy flavoured demiglace sauce flecked with chopped truffle.

Cerises (Caille Rôtie aux). The bird is roasted and placed in a hot sealed fireproof cocotte with cherry brandy to infuse. The pan is swilled out with stock, seasoned with salt, cayenne and lemon juice and thickened with arrowroot or cornflour. It is loaded with pitted red cherries, masked over the quail and served very hot.

(When available, fresh cherries poached in a light syrup are used.)

Cognac (Caille Rôtie au). The bird is roasted and placed in a hot sealed fireproof cocotte with a liqueur glass of cognac to infuse. The pan is swilled out with stock, seasoned with salt, cayenne and lemon juice and thickened with cornflour or arrowroot. Bird masked with prepared jus lié and served very hot.

193

Crème (Caille Rôtie à la). Vine-leaf-barded bird roasted for 15 minutes, arranged in a cocotte, touched with lemon juice and masked with cream, heated together with the lid on.

Feuilles de Vigne (aux). Wrapped in vine leaves, barded, roasted, served on croûtons accompanied by jus de rôti.

Flambée à l'Ananas (Quail Flamed with Pineapple). The bird roasted for 10 minutes is sent to table with a round of pineapple. The fruit is sprinkled with sugar and sauté in butter, the quail is placed in the pan and the preparation is flamed in brandy. The bird is dressed on the fruit, sauced over with the contents of the pan and served.

Fruit (Roast Quail with). Quail may be garnished with any fruit. The bird is roasted, infused with a liqueur in a sealed cocotte and masked with a jus lié loaded with the selected fruit.

As well as such standard preparation as pineapple, cherries and grapes with brandies, other combinations are: curaçao and grand marnier and orange segments; rum and banana; calvados and apple compote; peach brandy and sliced halved peaches; curaçao and mandarin segments.

Liqueurs (Roast Quail infused with). The au cognac preparation may be infused with other spirits and liqueurs such as armagnac, grand marnier, curaçao, chartreuse, liqueur whisky, rum or calvados, the dish taking its name from its infusion.

Marrons (aux). Braised in demi-glace and whole consommé-poached chestnuts in a cocotte.

Périgourdine. The stuffed, poached quail is dressed on rice risotto dressed in butter with a little parmesan cheese and chopped sauté chicken livers. The quail is masked with a velouté prepared from the braising liquor, a roux mounted with butter, cream, purée of foie gras and touched with brandy.

Raisins (aux). Braised in cocotte with madeira and pitted grapes.

Rôti au Lard (Caille). Roasted and dressed with its bard on a croûton with a grilled rasher of back bacon, finished with lemon juice and noisette butter and served with orange salad.

Singapore (Caille Rôtie). Roast vine-barded bird for 10 minutes and then infuse in a sealed cocotte with brandy. Swill out roasting pan with veal stock, season with salt, cayenne and lemon juice and thicken with cornflour or arrowroot. Dress infused bird on a rondel of pineapple and mask with the prepared jus lié.

For preference use fresh pineapple.

Suprême (Caille Rôtie). Similar to à la crème but masked with a well creamed sauce suprême.

Veronique (Caille Rôtie). The bird is roasted and placed in a hot sealed fireproof cocotte with brandy to infuse. The pan is swilled out with stock, seasoned with salt, cayenne and lemon juice and thickened. It is loaded with pitted grapes, masked over the quail and served very hot.

When available fresh grapes poached in a light syrup are used.

Aspics of Quail. For cold table work there are 2 basic preparations, one with white, the other with brown chaudfroid. The actual decorating and presentation is, of course, limited only by the creativity of the chef. For cold it is usual to work with several birds, say in units of 6. The birds are stuffed, poached in veal stock and allowed to cool in their poaching liquor.

Belle Vue. Generic term to describe quail for cold where the birds are boned, stuffed with a truffled purée of foie gras, poached, masked with white or brown chaudfroid, decorated as fancy dictates and finished with an aspic coating.

Bigarrade (Caille Frappé à la). The quail are boned, stuffed with purée of foie gras, wrapped in bards and poached. They are masked with brown chaudfroid loaded with a julienne of orange peel and flavoured with curaçao, decorated with orange segments and finished with a masking of aspic.

Lucullus (Caille Frappé). The quail are stuffed with truffled foie gras, poached and masked with a brandy-flavoured brown chaudfroid and dressed on a mousse of foie gras. The preparation is decorated with hard-boiled quail eggs and masked with aspic flecked with chopped truffle.

Parisienne (Frappé à la). The quail are stuffed with truffled foie gras and poached. They are masked with white chaudfroid, decorated with truffle and tarragon leaves dressed with collops of foie gras, and masked with brandy-flavoured aspic.

Souvarov (Frappé à la or Souvaroff). The birds are boned, stuffed with a truffled foie gras purée, wrapped in bards and poached. They are unwrapped, masked with brandy-flavoured brown chaudfroid, decorated with hard-boiled egg white, dressed on a macédoine of fresh vegetables in aspic and finished with a masking of aspic.

Rook (Freux)

At one time, quite common British fare. For the table, young and tender birds are selected. They are very suitable in pies, prepared as for larks and thrushes, and may also be roasted.

Roast Rook. Pluck, draw, skin, split open and remove the backbone, season, wrap in barding bacon, impale on a skewer and roast for 10 to 12 minutes in a fierce oven. Sauce with fresh lemon juice, dress on a pâté-spread croûton with watercress and serve accompanied by bread sauce, jus de rôti and game chips.

Snipe (Bécassine)
Prepared and handled exactly as for woodcock.

Roast Snipe (Bécassine Rôti). Prepare bird, season, wrap in a vine leaf secured with a bard and roast in butter at 246°C. (475°F.) for 10 to 12 minutes. Finish with a squeeze of lemon and dress with its bards on a croûton spread with liver pâté, garnish with watercress, sauce with a dash of noisette butter and serve with bread sauce, jus de rôti, fried breadcrumbs and game chips.

Starling (Étourneau or Sansonnet)
These small, active, noisy birds were once fairly common fare during the Second World War to help out with the rationing. May be prepared in pies as for lark, thrush or rook; may also be roasted.

Thrush (Grieve)
Similar to lark, seasonal in autumn and winter, distinguished by its black legs. Treated as for quail or used boned in pies, pâtés and terrines.

Roast Thrush. Pluck, draw, wipe over, place 2 or 3 juniper berries inside each bird, season, wrap in barding bacon and roast quickly for 10 to 12 minutes in a fierce oven. Serve dressed on a croûton fried in the roasting tray, with a small bouquet of watercress, accompanied by its short and concentrated jus de rôti.

Note: For a plain roast some chefs suggest only the gizzard be removed.

Woodcock (Bécasse) *(October 10–March 15)*
Medium-sized bird with a long curved beak and neck. Often paired with its cousin the snipe, mainly on account of the similarity of name in culinary French: Bécasse and Bécassine. Snipe is the smaller of the two, with a shorter beak and neck. Both birds are held in high esteem because of their full flavour. Both improve with hanging. They are not emptied, only the gizzards are removed; the neck and heads are skinned but not removed; the eyes are taken out. The object of not decapitating is to conserve the brains, which are much coveted. The birds are not trussed; their legs are secured to the body by the sharp, long beaks. Both are wrapped in vine leaves and bards and roasted quickly for 10 to 15 minutes in a hot oven. Woodcock is considered the superior and is the subject of the noted Bécasse au Fumet, a preparation not unlike the Sauvage à la Presse.

Roast Woodcock. The prepared bird is salted, wrapped in a vine leaf secured with a bard and roasted for 15 minutes in butter in an oven pre-heated to 246°C. (475°F.). It is set with its bards upon a croûton spread with liver pâté, garnished with watercress, finished with a squeeze of lemon and a dash of noisette butter and served with bread sauce, fried breadcrumbs, jus de rôti and game chips.

Armagnac (Bécasse Flambé à la). The bird is roasted for 12 minutes, sent to table and flamed in armagnac. If a 2 portion bird, it is split, dressed on liver-pâté-spread croûtons, sauced with the contents of the flambé pan and served with bread sauce, fried breadcrumbs, jus de rôti, game chips and orange salad. If a single portion, the bird is left whole.

As a refinement, the pan may be swilled out with jus de rôti, reduced and corrected.

Bécasse au Fumet. A spectacular preparation performed in 2 stages: the kitchen mis-en-place and the lamp work finishing at table. The woodcock yields 2 portions.

Kitchen Work. The prepared bird is roasted for 8 minutes in a fierce oven and sent to table with its jus de rôti, 2 liver-pâté-spread croûtons and a small quantity of foie gras purée.

Table Work. The bird is speared with a fork and the 2 suprêmes are lifted with a sharp knife, flamed in brandy, placed in a cocotte and kept hot. The skull is fractured, the brain removed and set aside. The carcass is then flamed in brandy to draw the juices and the pan swilled out with the jus de rôti. It is reduced, thickened with butter, a little purée of foie gras and the bird's brain are added, and the sauce checked with salt, cayenne, lemon juice and flavoured with port. It is blended, heated but not boiled. It should be smooth, creamy and chocolate coloured. Dress each suprême on the croûtons, mask with the strained prepared sauce and serve with game chips or soufflé potatoes and salad japonaise.

Notes on procedure: The entire operation must be performed quickly so no heat is lost. Care must be taken not to boil the sauce or it will curdle. In this authentic recipe the carcass is flamed. There is an alternative method where the carcass is not flamed but crushed in a press (as for the sauvage) for the juices which are collected in a receptacle. When this method is employed the dish strictly speaking becomes Bécasse à la Presse.

Montmorency (Bécasse à la). Roast for 10 minutes, set in a closed cocotte with curaçao or cherry brandy to infuse in a moderate oven. Swill out the roasting pan with veal stock, reduce, make up a sauce with orange and cherry juice, sugar, salt, cayenne and a touch of lemon. Thicken as required with arrowroot or cornflour. Load with orange segments and pitted red cherries, mask over the infused woodcock, heat together and serve.

Veronique (Bécasse Étuvé). Roast for 10 minutes and infuse with brandy in a sealed cocotte in the oven. Pit and skin and poach required quantity of grapes in a light syrup. Swill out the roasting pan with stock, reduce, add the grape syrup, check the sauce with salt, cayenne and lemon juice, thicken if required and strain. Load the sauce with the grapes, mask the woodcock with the preparation and heat through.

Vegetables

In the kitchen vegetables are classified as green, root, pulse and edible fungi. They are received fresh, frozen, canned or dried. The advent of modern transportation and the techniques in the preservation of food have superseded the seasonability of most vegetables—what was once seasonal is now an all-the-year-round feature. Convenience foods have perhaps made their biggest impact with vegetables.

Artichoke (Artichaut)
There are two types: the globe and the Jerusalem (topinambour).

The base of the globe is edible and provides the fonds d'artichauts (artichoke bottoms) much employed as a garniture and purchased ready in can or jar. To prepare, the whole globe is stripped right down to the base and gently poached in water, salt and lemon juice. Served quartered and dressed in butter and chopped parsley; in cream à la crême; sauté in butter; or as a purée, seasoned and butter and cream dressed.

For service as a globe, the outer leaves are supressed, the piece tied with thread and then poached for 30 minutes in boiling water, salt and lemon juice. The base of the leaves are eaten and the artichoke served hot with hollandaise sauce or melted butter, or cold with French dressing.

The Jerusalem artichoke is cleaned and separated, turned and poached à 'blanc' (water, salt, lemon juice, boiled and thickened with a diluted flour and water paste). It is finished with butter and served cream sauce or béchamel masked. Also featured poached and sauté or glazed à la mornay.

An excellent ingredient for vegetable soups.

Asparagus (Asperge)
Though this aristocratic vegetable cans and freezes well, nothing quite equals the quality and flavour of the fresh. Of the greats there are the Lauris and the Argenteuil from France, and the best English from the Vale of Evesham. There are also the tips, points, spears, sprue or parisienne for garnishing purposes. The finest asparagus should be edible almost right the way down.

Poached Asparagus. Trim loose and surplus ears and scrape the stems clear of coarse fibre. Tie in bundles of 6 and poach in lightly salted water for 20 minutes. Drain and serve hot with melted butter, hollandaise or mousseline sauce. Serve iced with French or chantilly dressing.

Tips are also featured hot polonnaise, mornay and au beurre noisette.

Polonaise: Hot tips masked with hot butter and fried breadcrumbs to which sieved hard-boiled white and egg yolks and chopped parsley are added.

Beetroot (Bettegrave)
Raw beet is cooked with care lest the juices escape, so the skin must not be punctured. Wash well, plunge into boiling salted water and simmer for 2 hours. When the skin wrinkles to the touch, the beet is cooked. Their main use is in salads, but there are a number of hot beet dishes either sliced or turned in olives, served with melted butter and cream or béchamel masked. Whole beets may be roasted in a dish with fat and a little water.

Broad Beans (Fèves)
A large podded bean. Fresh, canned and frozen are used, the processed are packed whole or skinned. They are cooked in boiling, salted water.

Béchamel. The usual service, masked with adjusted béchamel sauce.

Beurre (au). Cooked, drained, tossed in butter and served sprinkled with chopped parsley.

Crème (à la). Lié in butter and cream, finished with chopped parsley.

Fines Herbes (aux). Sauté in butter and sprinkled with chopped fines herbes.

Purée. Cooked, pressed through a sieve, corrected with cream and butter and checked for seasoning.

Broccoli (Calabress)
Purple, Cornish broccoli is now almost exclusively handled frozen. Ready cleaned and prepared, it just requires simmering in salted water till cooked, about 20 minutes. Accompanied by hollandaise, mousseline or butter sauce. Is also featured masked with cream sauce, glazed à la mornay, or à la polonaise as for asparagus.

Brussels Sprouts (Choux de Bruxelles)
Sort of miniature cabbage. Remove outer leaves, score the base of the stalks with a criss-cross, wash, drain well, place in a pan with minimum of cold salted water, bring to boil, cover pan and simmer for 20 minutes.

They freeze well and are marketed size-graded; baby size very popular. To cook, plunge in boiling water and simmer for 20 minutes in a covered pan. Drain when done and dress in a little butter.

Crème (à la). Heat cooked, drained sprouts in butter and cream, check seasoning, shake pan well and serve hot.

Purée Bruxelloise or Flamande. Cooked sprouts rubbed through a sieve, rough purée checked with butter and cream and beaten to a smooth green purée.

Rissolée. Cooked sprouts sauté in half hot butter and half olive oil, seasoned with salt and pepper, when browned served with chopped parsley sprinkling.

Bubble and Squeak

Prepared from mashed potatoes, cooked cabbage or sprouts. Mix together, season, then fry in beef dripping, working the preparation with a palette knife and allowing a brown crust to form. The preparation may also be scaled off, shaped on a floured board and shallow fried in dripping.

Butter Beans (Haricots Beurre)

Popular as a second vegetable or as an hors-d'œuvre with dressing.

Prepared from their raw state previously soaked or purchased cooked in cans. Beans are dressed in butter or masked with cream sauce and sprinkled with chopped parsley.

Cabbage (Chou)

When well handled one of the best of green vegetables. Remove outer leaves, halve, quarter, suppress hard stalk and shred leaves. Place in pan with a little water, add salt, bring to boil, cover pan, simmer for 20 minutes, season with salt and pepper, add piece of butter, toss together and serve.

Braised. Trim, halve, quarter, remove hard centre, wash and blanch in boiling water. Place in a deep pan lined with bacon rashers, sliced carrot and onion. Add an onion stuck with cloves and top with more bacon. Start cooking with butter, lard or dripping, on top of the stove. Moisten with stock, cover and slowly braise in the oven for 3 hours. Remove cabbage, free it of its trappings and serve masked with the braising liquor, strained and added to a jus lié or demi-glace.

Poached. The leaves left whole are poached in a covered vessel in the minimum of salted water. When cooked the preparation is not drained but dressed with a little butter, checked with salt and pepper and chopped in the pan with a knife. The cabbage is then pressed between two large soup plates to extract surplus liquid and served cut into wedges like a cake.

Cardoons (Cardons)

Luxury vegetable with combined flavours of endive, artichoke and celery. For preparation they are well washed and carefully trimmed and poached whole in boiling blanc with lemon juice or braised in veal stock. Featured poached and masked with a light béchamel; glazed mornay; braised with veal stock and bone marrow; or cold with a French or lemon dressing.

Carrots (Carottes)

Sweet and colourful root, popular size is the baby purchased ready washed and prepared, canned or dried. Large carrots are sliced or diced.

Crème (à la).   Glazed carrots lié in double cream. Allow preparation to cohere over heat.

Glazed.   Baby size or diced carrots turned in olives, placed in a pan with a little water, butter, salt and pinch of sugar. Covered with foil or greaseproof paper and simmered until the carrots have absorbed their liquid and acquired a nice gloss.

Purée Vichy, Purée Crécy.   Large carrots cooked till tender, pressed through a sieve, and purée bound with butter, cream or milk and seasoning. May be corrected with consommé. Served with golden croûtons.

Vichy.   Thinly sliced and cooked in the minimum of water with butter, salt and a pinch of sugar. Simmered until cooked and glossy and served sprinkled with chopped parsley.

Original recipe prescribes cooking carrots in Vichy mineral water; Vichy salts are marketed and may be used for this preparation.

Cauliflower (Choufleur)
It is better to use fresh cauliflower. Select a small vegetable with a tight centre rather than a large, loose and wasteful one. Individual portion cauliflowers are also grown. The trimmed and washed cauliflower is cooked by poaching for 20 minutes in salted boiling water. It is then served masked with adjusted béchamel or sauce crème.

Cauliflower preparations go under the culinary name of Pompadour after the Marquise Antoinette de Pompadour (1721–64) friend of Louis XV of France.

Dubarry.   Cooked sprigs arranged in fonds d'artichauts and glazed mornay.

Fried.   Sprigs breaded or battered, deep fried and dressed with fried bouquet of parsley.

Gratin (au) **(Choufleur Gratiné Mornay).**   Cooked, arranged in a dish, masked with mornay sauce, sprinkled with grated cheese and glazed to a golden brown in a hot oven or under a grill.

Grecque.   Small sprigs stewed slowly in concassed or chopped tomato, with blanched button onions, olive oil, seasoning and bayleaf.

Hollandaise.   Cooked cauliflower masked with hollandaise sauce.

Polonaise.   Cooked and arranged in a dish, topped with fried breadcrumbs mixed with sieved hard-boiled white and egg yolk and chopped parsley, and finished with noisette butter and lemon.

Celeriac (Celeri-Rave)
Enlarged celery root, resembles a turnip, has bitter-sweet celery taste

May be cooked in any of the ways for celery, but is usually julienne shredded and lemon or cream dressed as a salad and an hors-d'oeuvre.

Cèpes

Small, smooth-shaped, edible fungi, used mainly as a garnish. Sold fresh, dried and in cans. Prepared in same ways as mushrooms.

Bordelaise (Cèpes). Stew minced shallot in olive oil with a suspicion of garlic, add cèpes and cook. Serve sprinkled with chopped parsley.

Russe (Cèpes à la). Stewed in butter, seasoned and lié in a well creamed béchamel sauce.

Chestnut (Marron)

All nuts are nutritious and prized foods; the chestnut in particular has many uses, both savoury and sweet. The large mealy chestnuts from France, Italy and Spain, where they are a staple food among country folk, are the best for culinary purposes. English chestnuts are, in the main, smaller and crisp. Chestnuts may be added to enhance stews and braises, and are also cooked and mashed as potatoes, which they can replace. The nut needs careful and long cooking, an important point to watch. The skins and bitter pith are removed by incising them and placing the chestnuts in a hot oven to open out.

Braised. Drop peeled and pithed nuts into boiling stock and braise, covered, for 3 hours. Serve in the thickened braising liquor sprinkled with chopped parsley. Care must be taken to keep the chestnuts whole.

Jus (Marrons au). Chestnuts braised in veal stock, the braising liquor checked for seasoning and consistency with butter, masked over the chestnuts and sprinkled with chopped parsley.

Purée (Purée de Marrons, Purée Limoisine). Served as a second vegetable or as the correct escort to jugged hare, venison and other ground game.

Chestnuts are either baked in the oven or simmered until tender in stock, sieved or mashed, corrected with salt, pepper and a pinch of sugar, lié in milk or cream and worked to a smooth purée.

Colcannon

Type of bubble and squeak. Boil separately equal amounts of potatoes and cabbage in salted water. Mash the potatoes and cut up the cabbage. Melt butter or dripping in a pan, add the potato and then the cabbage. Season with salt and pepper and mix well.

Dried Peas, Split Peas

Pre-soaked, cooked whole as an inexpensive vegetable, made into purée, or used in soups for which they are really best suited.

Egg Plant (Aubergine)

Exotic vegetable of the marrow species with a smooth, glossy, deep purple skin. Sliced and fried, diced and sauté, aubergines may also be treated in any of the ways as for courgette, i.e. stuffed and baked.

Fried. Wash but do not peel, slice into thickish rondels, flour, pass in milk and deep fry to a golden brown. Drain, season and dress with fried parsley.

Sauté. Wash but do not peel, cut in large dice, season with salt and pepper, sauté in olive oil, add concassed tomato, shake the pan, add a little meat extract and finish with chopped parsley.

Endive

Widely cultivated in Belgium where, as in France, it is known as Endive de Bruxelle. In the U.S.A. it is called endive. In England it was originally called Belgian chicory. In recent times it has been widely marketed as endive, which caused confusion as some insisted on the name chicory and others endive. Also known as Belgian endive.

It may be served raw as a salad or cooked as a vegetable and either way has an attractive bitter tang. For preparation the endive is trimmed, washed, left whole and poached in a shallow tray in salted water dressed with lemon juice for 30 minutes.

Canadian Endive. Poached whole endives in a lightly buttered dish, masked with hot maple syrup, heated together and served.

Crème (à la). Poached and masked with adjusted béchamel sauce or heated in fresh cream allowing the preparation to cohere.

Four (Endive au). Arrange poached endives in a buttered dish, brush with butter, touch with lemon juice, sprinkle with sugar, mask with Jamaica rum and bake in a hot oven until the topping is golden brown.

Iced Endive Parisienne. Arrange poached, cold endives in a glass bowl, dress with lemon dressing, sprinkle with chopped fines herbes and serve ice cold.

Jus (Endive au). Proceed and prepare as for the celery preparation of this name.

Meunière. Cooked whole endive, drained, tossed in butter to brown, arranged in a serving dish and finished with noisette butter, lemon and chopped parsley.

Moelle (Endive à la). As for the celery preparation of this name.

Sucre (au). Whole poached endives arranged in a buttered dish, brushed with butter, sprinkled with demerara sugar, touched with lemon juice and flashed to glaze in a hot oven or under a grill.

French Beans (Haricots Verts)

There are various kinds of these beans from large runners to the small string beans. French beans whole and sliced freeze and dry well and have gone far in augmenting the fresh.

203

They are cooked in a small quantity of salted water, drained and dressed in butter. Tender small French beans look best featured whole.

Lyonnaise (Haricots Verts). Cooked beans sauté in butter and combined with sauté sliced onions. Tossed together and sprinkled with chopped parsley.

Maître d'Hôtel (Haricots Verts). Poached and dressed with maître d'hôtel butter.

Persillées (Haricots Verts). Poached beans dressed in butter and sprinkled with chopped parsley.

Rissolées (Haricots Verts). Poached, sauté and braised in butter, dressed with chopped parsley.

Villars (Haricots Verts). Cooked beans passed in flour and deep fried to a crispy brown, dressed with fried parsley.

Green Peas (Petits Pois)

Possibly the most popular of all green vegetables and handled almost exclusively frozen, dried and canned. Some prefer the small, sweet and very green pea, others like the larger marrowfats.

The frozen are cooked in boiling salted water for about 15 minutes from their frozen state; the canned are pre-cooked and just require heating in butter; the dried are pre-soaked, placed in cold salted water, brought to the boil and simmered. A sprig of mint and a pinch of sugar enhance the flavour of peas. Green peas mingle well with other vegetables, i.e. sweetcorn kernels, sliced, cubed and baby carrots.

Crème (à la). Cooked peas finished with butter and cream.

Française (à la). Peas cooked with blanched button onions, blanched and sauté diced bacon and lettuce hearts in a little stock with salt and sugar. The peas are served without the onion, bacon and lettuce. The cooking liquor is corrected and thickened with beurre manié.

Laitues (aux). Cooked as for à la française and garnished with the lettuce hearts.

Lard (aux). Cooked with button onions and blanched and sauté diced bacon, served without the onions. The cooking liquor is checked with half glaze.

Mangetout Peas. Small, young and tender green peas cooked and eaten whole in their pods. They are topped and tailed and set in a pan with salt, sugar, butter and minimum quantity of water. Covered and simmered until cooked and glazed, served sprinkled with chopped parsley.

Ménagère (à la). Cooked with blanched button onions, lettuce hearts, butter, salt and sugar. The cooking liquor is thickened with beurre manié.

Minted Garden Peas. Cooked peas simmered in butter, chopped mint, salt and a pinch of sugar, until they acquire a nice gloss.

Paysanne (à la). Peas cooked with blanched button onions, blanched and sauté diced bacon and lettuce hearts in a little stock with salt and sugar. Cooking liquor is thickened with beurre manié.
Note: Some confusion exists between the paysanne and the à la française: the former is garnished with the onions, diced bacon and lettuce; the latter is ungarnished.

Petits Pois Illinois. Mingle equal amounts of cooked green peas with sweetcorn kernels, cohere in butter and check with salt, sugar and a mere touch of ground clove, nutmeg and cinnamon. Toss together in a pan over heat.

(Author's creation in 1964 when Catering Manager, Pullman Division of British Transport Hotels. Named after the great Illinois corn belt.)

Purée Clamart, Purée de Petits Pois. Large green peas cooked and rubbed through a wire sieve, the purée corrected with butter and cream, checked with salt, sugar and colour compound to a light green.

Haricot Beans (Haricots Blancs)
Smaller kidney beans prepared as for butter beans or as a purée. There are several types of white haricot bean, like the pea bean and others. Like all pulses, they are employed in soups, stews and braises. They are also baked in sauces—the commercial baked bean in tomato sauce needs no introduction; as a snack it has few peers and is the most successful line of all time.

Boston Baked Beans. Soak overnight, simmer in water with sliced onion, carrot and bouquet garni for 20 minutes. Drain, remove bouquet and mix in small amount of English mustard made up with vinegar. Place in fireproof dish, sprinkle with brown sugar, add thick cut bacon rashers, bake covered for 20 minutes in the oven.

Japanese Artichokes (Crosne)
Not unlike Jerusalem artichokes, but more delicate. To prepare, place in a cloth with baysalt, shake, wash, peel, blanch in salt water and cook in a blanc or stew in butter. May be prepared à la crème, au jus, sauté au beurre, glazed à la mornay, or in fritters dipped in batter and deep fried.

Also known as Chinese artichokes, though the French term of crosne is possibly more acceptable.

Leeks (Poireaux)
Trimmed, well washed leeks are cooked by poaching whole in salted boiling water for 20 minutes in a shallow tray. They may be presented in the same ways as celery and endive.

Leeks are usually masked with adjusted béchamel or cream sauce, but may be treated mornay, polonaise, braised au jus and so forth.

They also eat well cold with a lemon dressing, a presentation once known as Poor Man's Asparagus.

Lentils (Lentilles)
Seeds of a plant, brown and yellow, used for lentil soup; also employed as a second vegetable left whole or mashed into a purée.

Lettuce (Laitue)
Mainly used as a salad, may be braised in the manner of cabbage.

Lima Beans (Flageolets)
Small green kidney bean, sold raw and treated as for butter and haricot beans, or obtainable cooked and canned. Useful as a second vegetable; in soups; stews; cold with salads; partnered with sweetcorn in succotash; or panaché, mingled with French beans.

Mixed Vegetables
The terms primeurs or bouquetière indicate an assortment of vegetables featured as accompaniments to roasts and entrées. The vegetables are dressed on a large serving dish and sprinkled with chopped parsley. The selection would include carrots, turnips, French beans, peas, button mushrooms and onions, cauliflower and asparagus tips. The root vegetables are glazed and all are neatly arranged in groups. *Primeurs à la crème* indicates the vegetables are each and separately bound in fresh cream.

Moreilles or Morels
Type of crinkled mushroom, marketed fresh, dried and in cans. Fresh they need thorough washing. To cook, they are seasoned and cooked in butter. Featured as a garniture and may be prepared in the same ways as mushrooms or cèpes.

Mushrooms (Champignons)
Unique for flavour and versatile on account of their many uses. Always in season. They are virtually wholly edible so there is no waste. There is the firm, white button mushroom and the open or flat variety. Mushrooms can well and are useful, since their liquor may be added to stocks and sauces.

To prepare, one is now advised not to peel mushrooms as the peel contains flavour and nutritious mineral salts. All that is required is to wash well in ample water to remove all grit.

To grill, season with salt and pepper, dot with butter, lard or pure bacon fat and cook. To fry, season, touch with lemon juice, fry in butter or bacon fat; do not overcook. To stew, slice, season, start in butter and finish in hot cream, chicken or veal stock and simmer for 5 minutes.

Crème (Champignons à la). Prepare the whole button or sliced larger mushrooms, season and stew in butter, add fresh cream and let some reduction take place. Touch with sherry. Serve as a vegetable or dressed on toast as a savoury.

Duxelle. All parings, stalks and oddments are used in duxelle, a preparation for stuffing tomatoes, pancakes and marrows, and garnishing scrambled eggs and grilled meat.

Mince and stew shallots in butter, add chopped mushroom oddments and increase bulk with chopped tomatoes. Season with salt, pepper and a dash of ground clove and nutmeg. Allow preparation to cook and use as required.

Flambées (Champignons). Prepared at table. Sauté even-sized mushrooms in butter, season with salt and cayenne, add sherry and cook until moisture is almost absorbed. Flame in brandy, shake pan, add a little cream and let preparation cohere.

Glazed Button Mushrooms. Proceed as for glazing button onions or carrots.

Maître d'Hôtel (Champignons). Large grilled mushrooms on toast, each topped with a rondel of maître d'hôtel butter.

Purée (Velouté de Champignons). Simmered in stock, butter and seasoning and pressed through a sieve. Preparation is stiffened with sufficient béchamel sauce and checked for consistency and seasoning.

Onions (Oignons)

The most useful of all vegetables. There is the small button and the large Spanish. Onions require a lot of cooking and care must always be taken of this critical factor. They are reputed to have certain medicinal properties and are ideal as cold weather fare.

Baked Onions. Bake in their jackets in the oven for about 1½ hours, peel, mask with adjusted béchamel and sprinkle with chopped parsley.

Braised Onions. Peel, blanch for 5 minutes, set in a deep pan with sliced carrots, celery and bacon oddments, season, dot with butter or dripping, heat and then moisten with stock. Bring to boil, cover pan and braise in oven for 2 to 3 hours. Remove, strain and correct cooking liquor, mask onions and finish with chopped parsley.

French Fried Onion Rings. Peel and slice large Spanish onions into rings. Separate, pass in milk and flour, deep fry rings to a crisp golden brown. Drain, dust with salt, pile up upon a doily and garnish with fried parsley.

Poached Onions. Peel, plunge into boiling salted water, simmer up to one hour, remove, drain, mask with adjusted béchamel sauce and dust with chopped parsley.

Purée Soubise (Onion Purée). Mince, scald and dry 1 kilo (2 lb) onions, stew in butter and add ¼ litre (½ pint) of thickened béchamel sauce. Season with salt and a little sugar. Cook for 30 minutes, pass through a tammy cloth and finish with cream and butter.

(Known after the Prince de Soubise (1715–87), a Marshal of France of King Louis XV.)

Parsnips (Panais)
Root vegetable with a distinct flavour, cooked by poaching in salted water for 20 minutes. Featured buttered; masked with adjusted béchamel or cream sauce; glazed mornay; or in a purée seasoned and dressed with milk and butter.

Peppers
Capsicums or green, red and yellow peppers are popular raw in salads or cooked as vegetables and garnishings. Green is the colour most seen. Peppers are full of seeds and need to be emptied: the tops are sliced, the seeds removed and the cavity cleaned.

Fried Peppers. Prepare and blanch in boiling water, shred or dice, season and sauté in butter.

Green Peppers Carlton. Raw, cleaned and blanched peppers stuffed with diced lobster and flaked crabmeat lié in mayonnaise and dressed on lettuce leaves.

Stuffed Peppers. Seed and blanch, stuff with cooked savoury rice, place in buttered dish, moisten with stock or a brown sauce and braise in the oven.

Rice for stuffing is best cooked risotto style, loaded with peas and diced red pimento; other stuffings can be used i.e. forcemeat, sage and onion, and so forth.

Potatoes (Pommes de Terre)
It is to a French scientist Antoine-Augustin Parmentier (1737–1813) that we owe the popular introduction to Europe from South America of the 'apple of the earth'. The ubiquitous and versatile potato figures on all menus, usually in several ways. Potatoes are always seasonal fare and we know two main kinds, i.e. the small 'new' and the large 'old' potato.

The potato is subjected to most of the culinary methods and processes, i.e. boiling, roasting, deep and shallow frying, and from these basic operations the derivatives are many and various—indeed the ways with potatoes are almost endless.

Boiled Potatoes. Peeled, washed, placed in cold salted water, brought to the boil, simmered for 20 minutes until cooked, drained and served sprinkled with chopped parsley. New potatoes are scraped, placed in cold salted water with a sprig of mint, brought to the boil, simmered until cooked, drained and dressed with butter and chopped parsley.

Roast Potatoes. Cut to even size, turned into shape of large olive, dried, salted, set in a roasting tray with hot dripping, started on top of the stove and finished in a hot oven for 20 to 25 minutes. Finished with chopped parsley. Potatoes are also roasted in with the joint, the best method when time permits.

Deep Frying. The popularity of the fried potato has never faltered; indeed it has become enhanced and the demand now is for chips with everything.

Deep frying is one of the foremost classes of potato cookery; the basic method of cooking is the same but variations are made by cutting the potatoes in divers shapes and sizes. The first point to consider is the media, the second the method of frying.

Various animal and vegetable fats are used, olive oil being the best vegetable oil. Pure beef dripping is generally agreed to be the best animal fat, producing the finest results and being the easiest one to manipulate. All media should be clean and well clarified. The modern frying pan is fitted with a built-in strainer and equipped with visual thermostatic temperature controls. Temperatures are important and whatever media is used, it should conform to certain specification. Deep frying is performed in fat at 180°C. (350–375°F.). The fat selected should have a minimum smoke point of 220°C. (430°F.) and a flash point of 300°C. (600°F.). A good margin between smoke and carbonisation is essential. Chefs judge the fat as ready when a blue haze rises off the surface, but temperature check by instrument is preferable. Fat must always be treated with respect and care as it presents a fire risk, especially if it is allowed to burn and break down, thereby lowering the flash point to danger level.

All articles for frying must be quite dry as moisture spoils the friture. When potatoes are immersed they sink to the bottom of the pan. They rise to float on the surface when cooked, but they may not be browned (i.e. coloured) so they are allowed to fry off and colour. (Most but not *all* fare behaves in this manner when deep fried.) When ready, the potatoes are drained, salted and served. Frying is performed loose or in a wire basket. If loose the articles are retrieved with the aid of a wire spider. After each service, the fat should be strained and all equipment cleaned.

Shallow Frying. Known as sauté potatoes; explained separately below.
Prepared Potatoes: Potatoes are factory processed and are available to caterers peeled and packeted. They are peeled by one of three processes: by abrasive, the potato peeling machine; in a caustic solution; or by steam process. They are washed and passed in a bleaching solution which retards oxidation (browning). They are packed dry in film bags and keep up to 7 days in a refrigerator. Whole and cut potatoes for deep frying are processed in this manner.

Allumettes. Matchstick potatoes, the next size up from pommes paille. Potatoes are cut in strips and deep fried.

Alsacienne (à la).   New potatoes cooked with blanched button onions and sauté diced bacon, served sprinkled with chopped fines herbes.

Amandines.   Preparation of half pommes duchesse and choux paste, rolled into ball shapes, breadcrumbed with splintered almonds and deep fried.

Anna.   Peel and slice potatoes as for game chips but thicker. Arrange in layers in a buttered round anna mould. Build up in layers, seasoning each one with salt and pepper. Moisten with clarified butter or beef dripping and bake in the oven for 35 minutes. Turn out on a serving dish and finish with noisette butter and chopped parsley.

Preparation may also be prepared individually in dariole moulds.

Baked Potatoes, Jacket Potatoes.   Select large, floury potatoes. Wash, dry, rub with butter, make a few perforations in the skin and bake on a tray of coarse salt or wrap in foil for an hour at 218°C. (425°F.). To serve, make 2 incisions in the skin and open out to expose pulp. Season with salt and a dash of cayenne and drop in a piece of butter.

Also offered with a number of dressings:

Olive: Half-whipped cream, salt, cayenne and chopped olives.
Cheese and Nut: Cream or cottage cheese, chopped nut and seasoning.
Pickles: Any variety of pickle, chutney or relish.
Cheese: Grated parmesan, butter and seasoning.
Sour Cream.

Bataille.   Diced deep fried potatoes.

Bercy.   As for croquettes, but shaped into balls about 3 or 4 times the size of a marble. Floured, egg-washed and rolled in white breadcrumbs mixed with splintered almonds. Deep fried and dressed with fried parsley.

Berrichonne.   Turned into large olives, poached in consommé with blanched button onions, sauté diced bacon and served sprinkled with chopped parsley.

Biarritz.   Dressed purée of potatoes loaded with diced ham and chopped green peppers and lightly flecked with chopped fines herbes.

Boulangère.   Well known garniture to roast lamb preparations.

Line a buttered serving dish or shallow pan with alternating layers of sliced potato and blanched onion, season each layer, dot with butter, moisten with consommé or stock, cover with foil or grease-proof paper and bake in an oven for an hour. Before the end of the cooking process, remove protection to brown the topping. Serve sprinkled with coarsely chopped parsley.

Byron.   Grease an anna round pan, fill with a dressed potato purée from baked potatoes, brush with melted butter and bake until a crisp topping forms. Turn out, mask with mornay sauce, sprinkle with grated parmesan and glaze.

Château. Roast potatoes shaped as large olives. Season, roast in dripping, finish with noisette butter and chopped parsley.

Chatouillard. Large peeled waxy type potatoes cut with care into a long whole ribbon and deep fried in the one piece as for soufflé potatoes. Well drained and salt dusted.

Chester (Pommes Croquettes). Duchesse preparation loaded with grated parmesan, shaped as required, breadcrumbed and deep fried.

Proportions of mix are 50g (2 oz) grated cheese to 500g (1 lb) potato.

Cocottes. Very small château potatoes, turned to olive shape, blanched and roasted in butter.

Collerette. As chatouillard.

Croquettes. Duchesse potato rolled into small 50g (2 oz) cylinder shapes about 19mm ($\frac{3}{4}$ in) diameter and 38mm ($1\frac{1}{2}$ in) long. Bread-crumbed, deep fried to a golden brown, drained, salt dusted and dressed with fried parsley.

This method indicates the cylinder or cork croquette; other shapes include balls, olives or squares.

The duchesse preparation may be loaded with various chopped ingredients, i.e. ham, chicken, truffle, turkey and so forth.

Darphin. Prepared as pommes anna, cut into short julienne, seasoned with salt and pepper and cooked in clarified butter.

(Named after Claude Darphin, one-time maître d'hôtel of the London House Restaurant, Nice.)

Dauphine. Croquette potatoes prepared with half appareil pommes duchesse and choux paste, shaped, breaded and deep fried, well drained and garnished with fried parsley.

Delmonico. Diced cooked potato, seasoned with salt, pepper and nutmeg, placed in a serving dish, finished with butter, milk and cream, sprinkled with grated cheese and browned in the oven.

Delysia. Pommes sautées à cru with a suspicion of garlic.

(Preparation dedicated to Alice Delysia, celebrated French actress.)

Duchesse. The piping potato. Dressed purée touched with ground nutmeg and bound with beaten egg yolk and butter, whisked well to obtain a smooth, stiff and well cohered yellow paste. Place preparation in a piping bag fitted with a rosette nozzle and use as required.

The potato for bordure duchesse is piped out in a fancy scrolled pattern on a lightly buttered surface, brushed with egg-wash and flashed under a grill till golden brown, then painted over with a thin coating of melted butter for a glossy finish.

Proportions of ingredients: 3 egg yolks and 50g (2 oz) butter to each $1\frac{1}{2}$ kilo (3 lb) mashed potato.

Florentine (Pommes Croquettes). Duchesse preparation loaded with chopped cooked leaf spinach, shaped as required, breadcrumbed and deep fried.

211

Fondante. Shape even-sized new or old potatoes as for château, set in a pan, season, add butter and moisten with consommé. Protect with foil or greaseproof paper and allow the potatoes to cook slowly in the oven. They are ready when the butter preparation is absorbed and the potatoes have a nice gloss. Sprinkle with chopped parsley.

Four (Pommes au). Same as baked jacket potatoes.

Fried (Pommes Frites). With the pont neuf, allumettes and pailles, we have the classic deep fries; today we have the mignonettes, cut smaller than pont neuf and larger than allumettes. The potato is deep fried to a crispy brown, drained and salted.

Ready 'oil blanched' frozen deep fried potatoes are marketed in two main types, the straight sided and the crinkle cut. These are crisped and browned by dipping in the friture in small batches as required.

Game Chips. Best known example of the fancy cutting of potatoes. Sliced into blades on a mandoline slicer, well washed, fried to a crispy brown, drained and salted.

Traditional escort to roast game and the only potato the orthodox kitchen calls a chip. Since, however, the game chip has been highly commercialized and sold in packets, as well as in a variety of flavours, it has become the crisp.

Gaufrettes. Cut across diagonally, large and thin, on a mandoline with the corrugated cutting edge, fried to a crispy brown, drained and well salted.

Gratin (au). As for gratiné but using sliced cooked potatoes.

Gratiné. Dressed mashed potato in a dish, smoothed, masked with mornay sauce, sprinkled with grated cheese and glazed.

Hash Brown. Similar to delmonico, but shaped as an omelette.

Impériale (à l'). Similar to macaire potatoes. The pulp well dressed with cream and butter, flecked with chopped truffle, piped back into the case and the topping lightly glazed.

Italienne (Pommes à l'). Rissolée large, diced, cooked potatoes in olive oil, minced blanched onion, chopped tomatoes and sliced red pimento stuffed olives tossed together over the stove.

Lard (au). Sliced quartered potatoes cooked in stock with sauté diced bacon and blanched button onions, seasoned with salt, pepper and nutmeg and served sprinkled with chopped parsley.

Lorette (Pommes Croquettes). Pommes dauphine mixture, cigar-shaped and deep fried.

Lyonnaise. Sauté potatoes mingled with sliced and sauté onions. Cook each separately, combine and finish with chopped parsley.

Macaire. Stuffed baked potatoes. Potato is baked, the top sliced and the pulp scooped out. It is placed in a bowl, dressed in butter, seasoned with salt, cayenne and a dash of nutmeg and bound with egg yolk. The preparation is piped back into the potato shell, forked over, brushed with melted butter and the topping browned in the oven. May also be glazed à la mornay.

The macaire provides several variations, i.e. other fare combined with the dressed potato, such as: grated cheese; chopped cooked leaf spinach; baked and chopped onion; chopped parsley or fines herbes; chopped lean ham; diced chicken; and divers flavouring agents like anchovy essence, chilli sauce, mushroom or tomato ketchup, or one of the branded extracts like Bovril or Marmite.

Macaire potatoes are also served another way; instead of dressing the skin shells, the prepared purée is piped in oblong portions in a fancy pattern on a greased tray, brushed with butter and glazed.

Maire. Whipped potatoes served with a topping of fresh cream and sprinkled with chopped parsley.

Maître d'Hôtel. Rondels of cooked potatoes, cut as for sauté, seasoned and reheated in butter and milk. Sprinkled with chopped parsley.

Marquise. Individual oblong cake shapes of dressed potato purée incorporating tomato purée, brushed with melted butter and browned in the oven. Or pommes duchesse with centre filled with concassed tomato.

Mignonettes. Deep fried potato cut as large allumette, a size which would correspond to slim fried potatoes.

Mireille. Sauté and combined with sauté fonds d'artichauts cut like the potatoes. Each one cooked separately, combined, seasoned with salt, pepper and lemon juice, tossed together and sprinkled with chopped parsley.
Note: Some recipes indicate the addition of truffle.

Mirette. Butter a round anna pan, line with entwined potatoes cut in long, thin julienne (as for allumettes) and truffle cut identically. Season with salt and pepper, dot with butter and bake in the oven. Turn out and finish with noisette butter and chopped parsley.

Mont-Doré. Duchesse potato arranged in a dish, smoothed and shaped as a dome. Sprinkled well with grated parmesan and browned under the grill or in a hot oven.

Mont d'Or. Individual piped coils of duchesse potato. Piped out on lightly greased tray, egg-washed, browned by flashing in a hot oven or under grill and brushed over with melted butter.

Nana. Same as pommes anna.

Natures. Same as pommes vapeur.

Neige (Pommes à la). Boil large, floury potatoes in salted water for 20 minutes. When cooked, drain well and lightly press through a wire sieve. Preparation should be white, dry and served very hot.

213

Nids (Pommes aux). Individual nests of piped duchesse potato, glazed and filled with petits pois au beurre.

Noisette. Identical mode of preparation as for pommes cocottes, but the potatoes are cut larger.

Pailles. Straw potatoes, one size smaller than allumettes. Shredded into long tapered straws, crisply deep fried and well salted.

Parisienne. Scooped out into balls with a parisienne cutter, seasoned, roasted in butter and olive oil, rolled in meat glaze and sprinkled with chopped parsley.

Parmentier. Diced, seasoned and sauté in butter, served sprinkled with chopped parsley.

Persillées (Parsley Potatoes). Boiled new potatoes finished with butter and chopped parsley. (Name given to all boiled potatoes served sprinkled with chopped parsley.)

Polonaise (à la). Even-sized, cooked in jackets, peeled, sliced in rondels, set in a dish with butter and cream added, heated together and then served sprinkled with chopped capers.

Point Neuf. The original deep fried potato. Large cut potatoes 7cm (3 in) long and 12mm ($\frac{1}{2}$ in) wide. Deep fried in two operations, i.e. one to cook and the other to colour once the fat has recuperated.

Purée (Mashed Potatoes). Select large floury type, peel, place in water with salt, bring to the boil and cook until tender. Turn out, drain well and mash. Place the purée in a pan, season with salt and pepper, add butter and a little warmed milk and whisk thoroughly over heat to a creamy consistency. The resultant purée should be white, light and creamy.

There are excellent complete instant potato mixes now on the market which reconstitute in milk or water as indicated. When made up, the purée may need correcting with seasoning, butter, milk or cream as required.

Mashed potato lends itself to a variety of preparations and these are listed separately under the standard names.

Purée à la Crème. Arrange purée in a serving dish, smooth to a dome shape with a palette knife, sauce with hot cream, dust with chopped parsley.

Reine (Pommes Croquettes à la). Duchesse preparation flecked with chopped white of chicken and truffle, shaped in cylinders, breaded and deep fried.

Riced Potatoes. Same as pommes à la neige.

Rissolées. Shaped as large olives, seasoned and sauté in butter and olive oil. Finished with chopped parsley.

Robe de Chambre (Pommes en). Same preparation as jacket potatoes only steamed.

Sablée. Roasted new potatoes mingled with fried breadcrumbs and sprinkled with chopped parsley. Another version consists of pre-baked sliced and sauté potatoes with breadcrumbs.

Salt Baked. Large floury potatoes, washed and simmered in heavily salted water in their jackets for 20 minutes and then baked in an oven at 177°C. (350°F.) for 30 minutes. Served with any of the dressings for baked jacket potatoes.

Sauté. Boil medium-sized or new potatoes in their jackets, cool, skin, slice into rondels of medium thickness, season with salt and pepper and sauté in half butter and half olive oil until well browned, crispy and dry. Serve sprinkled with chopped parsley.

Sauté potatoes are also prepared from their raw state, i.e. no pre-boiling, otherwise the operation is identical. This preparation, which many chefs claim is the correct way, is known as Pommes Sautées à Cru.

Savoy (Pommes Croquettes). Chopped truffle is combined in the duchesse preparation, rolled into balls, breaded and deep fried.

Saxonne (Purée). Equal amounts of cooked potatoes, onions and turnips rubbed separately through a sieve (mashed), combined and dressed with butter, milk and seasoning.

Scolloped. Thickly sliced potatoes seasoned and baked in dripping, served sprinkled with chopped parsley.

Sicilienne (Pommes Purée). Whipped potatoes flavoured with orange juice and coloured with grated orange peel.

Snow Potatoes. Same as pommes à la neige.

Soufflées. These potatoes are fried in two immersions at different temperatures and their production relies upon practical experience at manipulating the fat. Select waxy variety of potato, peel and slice in 3mm (⅛ in) thick ovals. Dry well. Throw into the friture at 177°C. (350°F.) and when the potato rises to the surface remove. Let the fat recuperate and heat up to 190°C. (375°F.), re-dip the potatoes when they should swell out. Let them colour, drain, dust with salt and serve.

Sunset. Same as sicilienne.

Vapeur. Plain boiled or steamed new potatoes, cooked with a sprig of mint, sprinkled with chopped parsley (*not* dressed with butter).

Voisin. As for anna but with each layer of potato sprinkled with grated cheese and ground nutmeg and gratiné à la mornay.

Whipped. Light purée of potatoes. Sometimes termed Pommes Zephir.

Yorkaise (Pommes Croquettes). Duchesse preparation loaded with chopped lean ham, shaped as required, breadcrumbed and deep fried.

215

Potato Basket

With practice basket, and other work in potato, is quite straight-forward. Work with the aid of a skeleton basket in wood or metal, as in sugar basket making.

Select large waxy type of potato, wash and remove skin. Peel in long, even ribbons and soak in a strong salted water. Make the base of the basket by arranging criss-cross ribbons of potato between the holes (there should be an odd number) of the skeleton, plait these from the centre and work outwards until the base is made. Place the wooden or metal supports in position and plait the body of the basket with potato ribbons working from the base upwards until made. Fix the overlaps in position with pins, trim with scissors. Place piece of shaped wood in the bottom of the basket to retain size and shape in cooking.

The piece is fried in two operations. Stand on a wire slice and deep fry without coloration. Drain, take out the centre wood and side supports and deep fry again. In the second dripping, the basket is allowed to colour. Remove and drain well. With the aid of a spatula remove the piece from its original wooden or metal base support. Trim and remove all fastening pins.

Shape the handle out in thin wire, thread with blanched macaroni, bind with potato ribbon and deep fry to the required colour. Side supports may also be similarly made if they are required. When fried remove wire and fix handle (and supports) onto the basket. Decorate with bows and ribbons in fried potato.

The basket base may, if desired, be made of a fried bread croûton in place of the latticed and plaited potato.

It is usual to fill the basket with a selection of deep fried potato, soufflées, gaufrettes and so on, in various shapes and sizes.

Potato may also be coloured.

Pulses

Term given to dried vegetables of the bean and pea family. They are rich in vegetable protein. They are inexpensive and at one time formed the staple diet of the under privileged when they were known as 'poor man's meat'. Pulses include butter, haricot, lima and red kidney beans, lentils, green and split peas. Each is described separately in this chapter.

Pulses may require pre-soaking prior to cooking. They are soaked overnight in cold water, washed and then placed in clean water with salt, sliced onion (or a bouquet garni), brought to the boil and simmered until soft.

Some improved pulses are manufactured which may be cooked direct from the packet without pre-soaking.

Pumpkin (Potiron)

The pulp of this great gourd is sweetish. It is seasonal in the autumn, but is always available canned. Continental folk use it in soups and in purées as a vegetable. The pulp is diced and cooked for 20 minutes in salted water; for purée it is mashed, seasoned with salt, pepper and dash of mixed spice and dressed with butter and hot milk.

Gratin (au). Cooked and dressed pulp is placed in a fireproof dish lined with bacon, smoothed, brushed with butter, topped with white breadcrumbs and placed in a moderate oven till golden brown.

Red Beans (Haricots Rouges)
Small red kidney bean used as for other dried beans.

Red Cabbage
Usually pickled for hors-d'oeuvre and salads and for the traditional accompaniment to Lancashire Hot Pot. May be cooked in same ways as green cabbage.

Rice (Riz)
One of the most valuable and versatile cereal grains and the staple diet of millions of people.

In the kitchen, rice has many employments, both savoury and sweet; it is featured in place of potatoes or pasta, as an essential dish or an escort to other foods, it is the recognized accompaniment to curry, and it may be featured in salads and hors-d'oeuvre. It combines well and is acceptable with almost every kind of food. When cooked it swells to almost 4 times its original size.

Rice is usually classified by grain size and we know the Patna, Carolina and Piedmont types from the Indies, America and Italy. Some chefs favour the small grain, others the long; the American long grain is very popular, especially with curries.

American Rice. Grown in Arkansas, Louisiana, Mississippi, Texas and in California, the 'long grain' deserves a special mention. There are four varieties marketed: the *regular* standard milled rice; the *parboiled*, which is steam or water treated prior to milling for vitamin and mineral salt retention; the *instant* and pre-cooked, where the moisture content is extracted so the rice subsequently requires a shorter time (this type is normally used in 'cook-in-the-bag' packeting); and the *brown*, which retains the bran and most of the germ and is, therefore, a health food of some importance (ideal for genuine risotto).

American long grain rice needs neither pre-washing nor post refreshing. It should be cooked on the basis of 1 of rice to 2 of water i.e. 500g (1 lb) to 1 litre (2 pints) water. Place rice direct from the pack into a pan, add water and salt, bring to boil, stir occasionally with a wooden spoon, slacken heat, cover the pan, simmer for 15 minutes (without stirring or removing lid) on a low heat or in the

217

oven at 177°C. (350°F.). Fork over and use as required. The rice will be fluffy, plump, glossy and well grained.

The four main ways with rice are risotto, pilaff, boiling and frying.

Risotto or Rizotto. The Italian way. Chop half an onion, set to melt in 75g (3 oz) butter or olive oil, season with salt, pepper and a dash of ground nutmeg, add rice and stir until translucent. Slowly add 1 litre (2 pints) boiling stock or consommé, bring to boil, cover with foil or greaseproof and finish in oven for 18 to 20 minutes. Dress with butter, grated parmesan and check seasoning.

Pilaff, Pilau or Pilaw. Processed exactly as for risotto, but without the butter and cheese dressing. The pilaff should be nice and moist and the grains well separated. If required add additional stock.

Boiled. Rain required quantity of rice into fast boiling water to which salt and lemon juice are added. Boil until rice is cooked, 18 to 20 minutes. Strain, refresh with cold water if required, drain well, place in a dish in a cloth and warm slowly in an oven. Rice should be well separated, very white and firm.

Note. This method differs from the American way as described above.

Fried Rice. May be prepared from raw or pre-cooked rice, but it is preferable to cook first by boiling. Then wash well, drain and dry. Mince a small onion, set to cook in olive oil, add more oil as required and the rice, season and fry to a golden brown.

Another method omits the onion; the rice is seasoned and straight fried in olive oil and butter.

Américaine (Ritz à l'). Risotto garnished with buttered sweetcorn kernels, lima beans and diced tomato.

Espagnole (à l'). Pilaff dressed with a salpicon of chicken livers, ham, mushrooms, fonds d'artichauts, peas, concassed tomatoes and red pimento.

Italienne (Risotto à l'). Mince an onion, stew in 120g (4 oz) olive oil and stir in 250g (8 oz) rice. Season with salt, pepper and dash of nutmeg. Stir and when translucent slowly pour in 1 litre (2 pints) boiling chicken stock. Bring to boil and cook, covered, in the oven for 20 minutes. Dress with butter and grated parmesan and gruyère in equal amounts. May be saffron flavoured.

Milanaise or Milanese (Risotto). Risotto with tomato purée, diced or julienne cooked mushrooms, ham and truffle, well dressed with butter and grated parmesan. Cordon of tomato sauce around the preparation.

Mornay (Risotto). Risotto with added concassed tomato (and any oddment of meat or poultry), moulded in a fireproof dish, masked with mornay sauce, sprinkled with grated cheese and gratiné in oven.

Napolitaine (Risotto). Diced fresh tomatoes added to risotto.

Nature.   Cooked by boiling as for curry.

Parisienne (Risotto).   Sliced or diced cooked mushrooms. Cordon of tomato sauce.

Piémontaise or Piémontese (Risotto).   Risotto coloured and seasoned with saffron. Preparation dressed with butter and grated parmesan and gruyère. May also be flecked with chopped truffle.

Pilaff à la Grecque.   Pilaff dressed with diced ham, peas, red pimento and plumped seedless raisins. Colour with saffron if required. Other versions include à l'orientale, à la turque, à la caucassienne, where saffron is usually included.

Pilaff Valenciennes.   Garnished with diced raw ham, tomatoes, red peppers, peas and mushrooms.

Risi Bisi.   Italian dish indicating a risotto well garnished with peas and diced red pimento lié in butter.

Risotto Preparations.   Rice cooked and dressed as for risotto, arranged in a fireproof dish with a well in the centre, or moulded in a ring. The main ingredient is dressed in the centre and the preparation sprinkled with chopped parsley. The principal ingredient can be a sauté of chicken livers, grilled baby chipolatas or frankfurters, minced chicken or veal, mussels and mushrooms, and so forth. The preparation takes its name from the main commodity, e.g. Risotto aux Foies de Volaille, Risotto aux Chipolatas.

Riz au Gras.   Blanch rice in boiling water, cook in seasoned chicken bouillon until the rice has cooked and absorbed all its cooking liquor.

Tampico (Risotto à la).   Risotto dressed with butter and cheese, seasoned and loaded with sliced mushrooms, red and green peppers, cooked peas and sweetcorn kernels.

Turque (à la).   Pilaff dressed with saffron, butter and purée of tomato.

Salsify (Salsifis)
Thin white vegetable with a long root known also as oyster plant because its taste is said to resemble oysters. The piece is scraped, parboiled in water and lemon juice to preserve colour and then cooked as required.

Crème (à la).   Poached and finished in a cream sauce, usually velouté or suprême.

Fried.   Poached, dipped in batter and deep fried to a golden brown.

Gratin (au).   Poached, masked with adjusted béchamel sauce, sprinkled with grated cheese and gratiné. May also be featured glazed à la mornay.

Poulette (à la).   As for à la crème, but masked with a velouté lié with beaten egg-yolk.

Samphire
Species of seaweed found on beaches and marshlands along the sea-shore. Sort of bright green and thickish grass. Appreciated for its salt tang, it is served raw as a salad or poached and served hot with butter or cream.

Sauerkraut (Choucroute)
National Central and Eastern European speciality. Pickled white cabbage, usually 'bought in' and just needing correcting for service.

Sauerkraut is prepared from finely shredded and washed white cabbage, well drained, separated and packed in a wooden vessel or bowl with coarse salt and spiced with cloves, onion and juniper berries. The preparation is sealed down and pickled for 3 weeks. Properly stored it will keep in good condition for 12 months.

To prepare sauerkraut: Separate, wash well but conserve cloves and junipers. Line a braising pan with bacon rashers and pack in the sauerkraut with sliced carrot, onion stuck with cloves, bacon oddments and peppercorns in a muslin bag. Moisten with stock or water, little white wine, few pieces of butter and top with more rashers. Braise in a moderate oven slowly for 5 hours. Remove peppercorn bag and whole onion and serve sauerkraut as a garniture to boiled ham, frankfurters or any mild slicing sausage.

Ready prepared sauerkraut is sold in cans as naturel, garni with sausages, and as weinkraut, i.e. with white wine. Also marketed as a juice to be served chilled as a starter.

As well as braising, sauerkraut can also be featured plain boiled.

Sorrel (Oseille)
Prepared and cooked in same ways as spinach.

Spinach (Épinard)
Leaf spinach freezes well and is the most convenient form to handle as it needs just cooking in a small quantity of water with salt. Fresh leaves need picking over and washing thoroughly to remove grit.

Crème (à la).   Purée of spinach dressed with butter and sauced with hot cream at the point of service.

En Branches (Leaf Spinach).   Leaves are poached for 20 minutes in a little salted water, drained and tossed in butter. This is known as garniture florentine.

Jus (au).   Purée dressed with butter and veal stock, served with a cordon of demi-glace or jus lié.

Purée Florentine.   Cooked, rubbed through a wire sieve and the resultant purée seasoned and dressed with butter and cream or milk into a smooth preparation. As a vegetable, purée of spinach is garnished with fried croûtons and quarters of hard-boiled egg.

Canned purée just requires correcting for seasoning and consistency.

Split Peas
Dried peas, yellow and green. May be cooked and served as a purée of vegetable, made into soup, but their main employment is in pease pudding.

Pease Pudding. Cook equal weights of yellow and green split peas in sufficient boiling salted water till tender. Strain, mash and season with salt and pepper. Bind with beaten egg, 1 per 500g (1 lb) of preparation, tie up in a damp pudding cloth or greased metal sleeve, and steam or boil for about 45 minutes.

Swede (Rutabaga)
Small young swedes, peeled, diced, cooked till tender in salted water and mashed, make a most acceptable purée. Consistency is checked with butter, cream or milk. The larger swedes are inclined to be woody and bland and give this good vegetable a poor reputation.

Sweetcorn (Maïs)
Culinary name for maize or Indian corn. A noted and attractive American contribution to gastronomy. Main supply comes in cans from Illinois. In the kitchen we know of it in three ways: kernels, creamed and on the cob.

Corn on the Cob. Cobs come fresh, canned or frozen. The canned just require heating in their own liquor, the frozen are simmered in salted water for about 20 minutes. Fresh cobs give best results. To prepare, remove the outer leaves and inner silk and simmer in salted water for about 20 minutes. The cobs are eaten out of hand, with special holders fixed at each end, with a melted butter sauce. This consists of clarified butter seasoned with salt and a dash of mixed spice.

Other preparations indicate baking the cob in seasoned butter and serving them well sauced in their liquor.

Cream Sweetcorn. Purchased canned. To serve, drain, check seasoning with salt and paprika and dress with half-whipped cream. Featured hot as a vegetable or cold for salads and hors-d'oeuvre.

Fritters. Prepared from the creamed variety. Drain, season, thicken with a little flour and bind with beaten egg yolk. Shape in oblong or round shapes and shallow fry to a golden brown on both sides in lard or olive oil.

Required garniture for à la maryland preparations.

Succotash. Equal quantities of sweetcorn and lima beans, heated in butter, seasoned and with a dash of cream added.

(Famous American cookery preparation.)

Sweetcorn Kernels. Usually canned, has a tangy flavour and presents

221

well. To serve, toss in butter and check seasoning with salt, pepper and a touch of finely ground clove, nutmeg and cinnamon.

(Kernels are graded—the king size is the most sought after.)

Zesty Corn Kernels.   Heat in butter, dress with a French dressing and serve very hot.

Sweet Potatoes

There are two varieties of sweet potato: the Batata or Patate Douce, the true sweet potato which originates in South America, and the Yam, a native of the Far East. Both are employed identically in the kitchen. Their flavour resembles artichoke. They are served baked in their jackets or candied.

For baking, the potato is washed and baked for about 50 minutes at 160°C. (325°F.). Care should be taken not to puncture the skin lest the sweet juices escape. The mashed pulp is served with maple syrup, honey, thin golden syrup or treacle sauce.

For Creole style the sweet potato is poached in sweetened water for 25 minutes, drained and served whole with honey.

Sweet potatoes can also be deep fried and sugar dredged, sauté and dressed in maple syrup or brown sugar, mashed, whipped or duchesse with sugar or syrup.

Usually featured as a second vegetable, sweet potatoes are sometimes served as a sweet, such as à la creöle.

Tomato (Tomate)

One may argue whether the love apple is fruit or vegetable, but few would dispute the vast usage of the tomato in the kitchen. Tremendous quantities, all through the year, go in making soups, sauces, salads, juices and garnishings.

Concassed.   Mince shallot stewed in butter or olive oil, add chopped tomatoes, season and allow preparation to simmer and reduce over heat.

Grilled.   *Whole grilled:* core, brush with butter and grill slowly. *Grilled halves:* core, slice through the middle, season with salt and pepper, brush with butter or olive oil and grill.

Tomatoes may also be oven baked.

Provençale (à la).   Peeled, chopped, seasoned and sauté in olive oil with a tiny crushed garlic clove and chopped parsley.

Sautée.   Core, plunge into boiling water to skin, quarter, season and sauté in butter. Serve sprinkled with chopped parsley.

Stuffed.   Core, blanch, peel, slice off the top, scoop out the pulp, pipe in the prepared stuffing, brush with butter, top with white breadcrumbs, brown the topping in a hot oven, replace lid and serve.

Tomato halves can be treated similarly.

Stuffing: Chopped shallot stewed in butter, add tomato pulp, minced cooked beef, chicken or ham and make up bulk with breadcrumbs soaked in milk. Season with salt and pepper and add chopped parsley. Mix well and use in a forcing bag.

Truffles (Truffes)
The black diamond of cookery and the aristocrat of the mushroom family. Two kinds exist: the black, the best known; and the lesser known white species. White truffle, which has a hint of garlic flavour, comes from Italy and is eaten raw in salads. The black and real truffle comes from France, Italy, North Africa and elsewhere. The finest French truffle comes from the Perigord, the Dauphiné, Burgundy and Normandy in that order of merit. In Italy the best are found in the Piedmont. Truffles are also found in England, notably on the Sussex Downs where they favour the chalky and limestone soil. At one time they were gathered by trained dogs, but truffle gathering in England on any scale appears to have lapsed. They grow under the ground on an approximate depth of 20cm (8 in), are a natural growth, and so far attempts at controlled cultivation have proved to be unsuccessful; therefore they command a high price. On the Continent pigs, especially sows, are trained at finding truffles and since the growth gives no surface indication of its presence below, pigs who are fond of the fungus, smell and nose them out.

Truffles vary in size from that of a walnut to a large apple. The outer surface is rough and warty and when sliced through reveals small whitish veins. The colour varies from jet black to grey. They are best employed raw, though they are mainly seen canned and bottled. For processing, the fungus is washed, peeled, seasoned, spiced and cooked in madeira and brandy. Canned truffles are marketed as peeled or pelée, the whole truffle, brushed or brossée, pieces or morceaux, and the peelings or pelures. So valuable is the product that the pieces, scrubbings and peelings are used, and so is the canning or bottling liquor. Truffles may be kitchen bottled as above and as for any fruit or vegetable bottling process.

The truffle has 3 main employments: as a flavouring agent; for decoration; and as a dish in its own right. It has a strong and penetrating odour and should be used sparingly. The blade of truffle (lame de truffe) is an oft-repeated theme in decorating, often used to indicate the number of portions to a dish.

Country people used to boil and eat them with spiced melted butter. The landed gentry discovered a better way; the truffles were seasoned, wrapped in bacon bards and greaseproof paper and roasted in wood ash. Expert opinion has it that this is the best way of preparing them.

Two classic preparations are Truffes à la Serviette and Truffes à la Crème. Fresh whole truffles are sealed in a ceramic dish with a mirepoix, madeira and brandy. The sealing is performed with a flour, water and egg paste. The preparation is cooked in an oven. The truffles are dressed in a serviette and the braising liquor, suitably corrected to a sauce with demi-glace and butter, is offered separately. For the à la crème, the whole cooked truffles are bound with fresh cream and served very hot.

Truffles are also served whole or sliced in beignets or fritters, sauté in butter, made into a purée for dressing on a croûton or canape, or for the preparation of a truffle soufflé. The jet black truffle in cold work has no equal and glazed in limpid aspic or presented upon a white chaudfroid has beauty and charm.

Turnip (Navet)
Partner root to the carrot, prepared as for carrots, glazed and à la crème. The small or baby turnip is better than the large.

Purée. Select the larger turnips, peel, dice and cook till tender in salted water. Press through a sieve, check seasoning and correct consistency with butter and cream or milk. If too thin, it may require bulk by the addition of potato purée.

Vegetable Marrow (Courgette)
There is the large vegetable marrow, green and white and the smaller courgette. The best size for the vegetable marrow is 23cm–30cm (9–(12 in), and for the courgette 10–15cm (4–6 in). There are also two types of courgette: the cocozelles, which has a smooth, dark green skin with lighter green to yellow stripes; and the zucchinia, which is medium green with greyish green mottling.

Vegetable marrow, properly prepared, is most acceptable, but it needs careful handling on account of its high water content. It is cut into large squares, peeled and pipped, poached in a shallow tray in boiling salted water for 15 to 20 minutes, drained, sauced with seasoned melted butter, and masked with adjusted béchamel or glazed mornay.

The smaller courgettes just need washing—should not be peeled or scraped. Cook whole by simmering for a few minutes in salted boiling water. Drain, toss in butter and sprinkle with chopped parsley. Courgettes may also be deep fried, sauté, baked in butter or stuffed with various dressings.

Provençale (Courgettes). Small-sized marrows are poached, cut open, pipped, stuffed with a preparation of chopped shallot or onion, mushroom and concassed tomato, gratiné and served in a half glaze sauce.

Turque. (Courgettes à la). Small marrows are stuffed with a pilaff of rice containing saffron, cooked peas and diced red pimento, finished by braising au jus.

Note: Large marrows may also be stuffed and braised; the vegetable is cut through the centre, pipped, dressed and glazed.

Vegetarian Fare
There are many thousands of vegetarians and they are catered for by their own speciality restaurants, food shops, societies and periodicals. While it is admitted that there are different kinds of practitioners of the cult, a genuine vegetarian eats neither fish, flesh nor fowl, i.e. no dead meat. Eggs are permitted but only butter, vegetable oils and fats may be used to cook them.

Vegetarians argue that there are many preparations besides the egg and pasta dishes which they are invariably offered. There are made-up dishes, roasts and stews using nuts and pulses, and many dishes using salad foods and fruits.

Health stores market special nut meats from which dishes can be prepared, a wide variety of nuts, special vegetarian fats and other branded foods, including dried fruits and vegetarian jellies.

Vegetarian cookery need never be dull or uninteresting if good use is made of the many herbs, spices and other seasoning agents available.

Vegetable Macédoine (Macédoine des Légumes)
The term macédoine means a mixture or combination of vegetables (or fruits) all cut to even size.

The macédoine is an important garnish. Take equal amounts of carrot, turnip, parsnip and French beans and dice or cut in wedges or diamond shape. Add peas and sweetcorn kernels. Cook each separately in salted water and then combine. Serve hot with chopped parsley or use for cold in salads or as hors-d'oeuvre suitably dressed.

White Cabbage
Generally utilized in the preparation of sauerkraut, cole-slaw and other salads rather than cooking it as for cabbage.

Sweets (Entremets)

Hot and cold sweets represent a comprehensive and a specialist branch of cookery. Collectively this field of kitchen work is known as the Pastry. Possibly the most significant factors of recent times to influence the sweet scene are the developments of ice cream into an industry and the increasing role played by fruit.

Almond (Amande)
There are two kinds, the bitter and the sweet. Almond as an essence is also a flavouring agent. Sweet almond is the basis of marzipan or almond paste and the original and genuine blancmange, from which its milk content was extracted. Bitter almonds are used for salting for cocktail savouries; they are blanched, peeled, sauté in hot olive oil, well salted and served hot or cold.

Apple (Pomme)
The most abundant of all fruit. The species are many and varied, both eating and cooking. It is with the cooker, the large and medium sized acid fruit, that the chef is primarily concerned.

Bonne Femme. The homely baked apple. Select large cookers, core, score round the middle or four times from top to tail. Fill cavity with demerara sugar, a clove and top with a nut of butter. Set in a dish with a little water, bake at 177°C. (350°F.) for an hour. Baste to glaze in their cooking liquor and serve hot with custard or vanilla sauce or cold with dairy or ice cream.

Variety is introduced by various fillings: plumped sultanas, candied cherries, ginger in syrup, various preserves, sliced apricots or mincemeat (Mincemeat Dressed Baked Apple).

Charlotte. Charlotte mould lined with savoy sponge fingers or sliced bread dipped in melted butter, filled with sweetened and spiced apple purée, topped with sponge fingers or sliced bread and baked in the oven until topping browns. The preparation is unmoulded, masked with apricot syrup and served hot or cold with preserve sauce or double cream.

Compote. Peel, halve, quarter, core, slice into half moons and place in a pan with sugar, clove and pinch of grated nutmeg. Moisten with water. Bring to boil and simmer gently until cooked. Serve well chilled.

Dumpling (Baked apple). Peeled and cored whole apples filled with demerara sugar, clove, plumped sultanas and butter or with mincemeat and butter. Wrapped and sealed in square of short pastry, eggwashed and baked. Served with custard or preserve sauce.

Dutch Apple Pie. Single or double crust apple pie incorporating plumped sultanas and mixed spice.

Flamed (Pommes Flambées). Small peeled, cored apples poached in a light syrup. When cooked the apples are removed and the syrup reduced. The fruit is sent to table together with the syrup in a fireproof dish and flamed in rum.

Meringue Pie (Apple). A 20cm (8 in) cooked shallow short pastry case filled with sweetened and spiced apple pulp, covered generously with meringue piled in pyramid, smoothed, lightly dredged with icing sugar and baked at 210°C. (420°F.) until the meringue has a crisp brown crust. Served hot or cold.

Paillard. Peel, core, halve, quarter and slice in even half moons. Arrange in a uniform pattern and overlapping sequence in a buttered fireproof dish. Dredge with sugar, moisten with a little water and bake at 177°C. (350°F.) until the apple is cooked and the edges are coloured. Serve cold with cream. The addition of plumped currants or sultanas and a touch of ground clove makes for variety.

(House speciality created at the Restaurant Paillard, Paris.)

Pie (Apple). Peel, core, halve, quarter and slice apples, arrange in buttered pie dish. Sweeten with sugar, cinnamon and a clove or two. Moisten with a little water. Brush edges with egg-wash and top with covering of short paste. Decorate and finish, leaving a vent hole. Egg-wash and bake protected with foil or greaseproof paper for about 30 minutes at 204°C. (400°F.).

The apple is often mixed with other fruit, e.g. cranberry, blackcurrant, blackberry and cherry; blackberry and apple is a popular combination, using fresh, canned or frozen berries. There are also several fruit pie fillings on the market.

Shallow 20cm (8 in) plate pies are prepared with a top and bottom layer of short paste filled with sliced, sweetened and spiced raw, canned or cooked apple, or apple mixed with berries. These pies are egg-washed and baked at 204°C. (400°F.) in the usual manner. For cold service, dredge with icing sugar.

Pudding (Apple). This type of pudding is best prepared, cooked and served in basins. Fillings are straight apple or apple mixed with other fruit, e.g. blackberry, blackcurrant, cranberry and cherry.

The basin is greased and lined with a sweet suet pudding dough about 6mm ($\frac{1}{4}$ in) thick. The lined basin is filled with the prepared sweetened and spiced fruit, sealed with a suet topping, tied down with foil or greaseproof paper, wrapped in a cloth and steamed for 2 hours. Served with hot custard.

Strudel. Traditional Viennese sweet prepared in 2 separate operations, the paste and the filling.

Sift 250g (8 oz) flour into a slab, make a well, add a tablespoon olive oil, a beaten egg and a pinch of salt. Work with a palette knife adding sufficient water to form a stiff dough. Knead for 20 minutes until it clears the hands. Rest it for an hour on a floured surface covered with a basin. Prepare a clean linen cloth or a sheet of strong greaseproof paper, spread on a table and dredge with flour. Roll out the dough, lift carefully on the linen (or paper) and stretch without tearing until it covers the surface as a wafer thin paste. Trim the edges, brush with melted butter, sprinkle with butter fried bread-crumbs, and arrange sliced apple and a handful of plumped currants and raisins on top. Dredge with cinnamon sugar. Roll up the paste like a sausage. Bend and set it on a greased baking tray. Paint with melted butter. Bake at 204°C. (400°F.) until golden brown. Dredge with icing sugar. Serve hot with kirsch-flavoured apricot syrup or cold with cream.

Note: Strudel is also made in individual portions. While apple is the original filling, other fruits may be used.

Whip (Apple). Fine sweetened and spiced apple purée whipped to a froth with egg whites, checked and flavoured with vanilla essence.

Apricot (Abricot)

Valuable fruit whose flavour blends well with other sweet prepara-tions. Apricot sauce is used in binding almond paste to cakes and featured with fritters and many other sweet dishes.

Colbert. The fruit is pitted and stuffed with rice cooked in vanilla flavoured milk, dipped in fritter batter and deep fried to a golden brown. Drained, dredged with icing sugar and served with hot apricot sauce.

Compote. The fruit is poached in a light syrup with a vanilla pod until tender and served with its cooking liquor.

Condé. Cooked apricot halves dressed on a foundation of rice condé preparation. Masked with thickened apricot syrup flavoured with maraschino or kirsch and decorated with crystallized angelica, violets, rose petals and glacé cherries. Pipe with crème chantilly. For an elaborate preparation the rice may be moulded.

Banana (Banane)

Because of its characteristic and attractive flavour, banana is much featured sliced in rondels in trifles, fruit salads and certain pastries. Discoloration is prevented by saucing the fruit with lemon juice.

Creole. Melt a piece of butter in a fireproof dish, place in 2 whole peeled bananas, sauce with lemon, sprinkle with brown sugar and add 2 tablespoons of water. Bake in the oven until the fruit is soft and a rich brown syrup has formed. Sprinkle with rum and serve. Alternatively, the dish may be flamed in rum at the table.

Whip. Mash 2 bananas with a fork, sprinkle with sugar and work to a smooth, thick cream with condensed milk. Fold into a coupé, top with crystallized violets and rose petals and serve with pompadour wafers.

Bavarois
High grade moulded cream preparation, like the blancmange and the mousse, is made in various flavours, colours and permutations.

Basic recipe for vanilla bavarois: 12 egg yolks, 500g (1 lb) sugar, ¾ litre (1½ pints) milk, vanilla pod, pinch of salt, 30g (1 oz) gelatine, ¾ litre (1½ pints) cream.

Beat egg yolks with sugar, place milk to heat with vanilla pod and bring up to just below boiling point. Add scalded milk to egg preparation, add pinch of salt and apply heat. Stir with wooden spoon until preparation thickens. Remove from heat add gelatine softened in water. Let it blend then pass through conical strainer into a clean basin. Combine with the cream, beat well and pour into mould wetted with syrup or lightly oiled. Set in a freezer. Unmould and decorate if required with whipped cream.

While different flavours may be introduced in a similar manner to blancmange, where fruit is concerned in bavarois it is best to use real purées. The following is a basic preparation for raspberry bavarois:

½ litre (1 pint) raspberry (or other) purée, ½ litre (1 pint) syrup, juice of 3 lemons, 30g (1 oz) gelatine, 1 litre (2 pints) cream.

Combine fruit purée with syrup and heat to blend. Remove from heat and add lemon juice and softened gelatine. Mix, strain, combine with cream, beat together, and pour in mould to set under cold.

Other suitable fruits include banana, cherry, greengage, loganberry, peach, pineapple and strawberry.

Berries
There are several lesser known, but none the less interesting, berries which may be grouped collectively.

They are mainly of American origin and are used in salads, compotes, pies and preserves. All are colourful and flavoursome. The tangy red cranberry, used as a jelly or preserve with roast turkey and lamb, is attractive as a pie filling, compote, and blends well with apple.

The deep coloured and flavoured blueberry and bilberry are also used in pies, puddings, compotes and preserves. Others are the whortleberry, huckleberry and the long red mulberry.

Blackberry (Mûre Sauvage)
Seldom used singly in the kitchen. Usually partners apple pie in compote, pies, puddings and charlottes. Fresh are in season in the

autumn, but canned and frozen are available all the year round, either on their own or mixed with apple.

Blancmange (Blanc-manger)

The original blancmange was made with almond milk; the modern blancmange is made with cornflour.

Original Method. To 500g (1 lb) sweet almonds add a few bitter. Blanch, skin, soak overnight in water to whiten, drain, pound to a pulp, combine with ½ litre (1 pint) water working slowly to obtain a good milk and then strain. Add 500g (1 lb) sugar, apply a gentle heat and cohere preparation. Add 30g (1 oz) gelatine, let it dissolve and then add ⅛ litre (¼ pint) cream. Pour to set in an oiled mould.

Modern Method. 60g (2 oz) cornflour to ½ litre (1 pint) milk, pinch salt, 60g (2 oz) sugar, essence and compound.

Mix cornflour to smooth paste with little cold milk and add salt. Heat rest of milk with the sugar. Add cornflour, mix slowly as preparation comes to the boil, maintain heat to cook and thicken. Add flavour and colour as required, i.e. for plain blancmange, vanilla or almond. Set in a mould wetted with syrup or faintly oiled.

Cornflour Blancmange a Victorian recipe courtesy of Brown and Polson Ltd.

4 level tablespoons cornflour patent quality, 2–3 level tablespoons sugar, ½ litre (1 pint) milk, pinch salt, nut of butter, flavouring.

Mix cornflour and sugar with little cold milk, heat the rest of milk to boiling point, pour onto cornflour preparation, stirring well. Return to the pan and boil for 3 minutes. Add salt, butter and essence to taste. Pour into a fancy mould to set. Turn out and serve with stewed fruit, jam or marmalade.

Convenience Blancmange is a packeted affair marketed in various flavours, chocolate being the most popular. Made up by mixing the prepared cornflour and sugar to a smooth paste with cold milk, adding this to boiling milk, cooking for 3 minutes and then moulding.

Originally vanilla, blancmange is reproduced in other flavours either with the ready mix or by correcting the basic recipe.

Banana. Flavour with essence and tinge yellow with compound.

Chocolate. Add 60g (2 oz) cocoa powder to ½ litre (1 pint) milk.

Coffee. Flavour and colour with essence.

Liqueur. Add liqueur and colour to match, i.e. crème de menthe and green colouring, curaçao and orange, apricot liqueur and yellow, anisette and pale green, kirsch or marashino and cherry, rum and coffee, and so on.

Minted. Flavour with peppermint and tinge light green with compound.

Pineapple. Pine essence and yellow colouring.

Rainbow. An assortment of colours and flavours in layers. Build up one colour and flavour at a time allowing each one to set before pouring in the next.

Raspberry. Essence and carmine compound.

Strawberry. Essence and pink compound.

Bouchées

Sweet bouchées are vol-au-vent cases or puff paste croustades, filled with preserves or sweetened fruit purées and served hot with custard or a crème patissière.

Mincemeat Bouchées à la Mode. Filled with hot mincemeat and served very hot with ice cream of any flavour.

Candied, Glacé and Crystallized Fruits

Many fruits and flowers are sugar processed for various uses. Large fruit such as apricot, cherry, fig, greengage, pear, plum, peach, pineapple and strawberry are candied or glacé for confections and frandises. Small pieces like angelica, acacia, lavender, pink and mauve lilac, rose petals, violets and mixed flowers are crystallized for decorative employments. Candied peel and chopped peel and fruit have many culinary uses. Mention should be made of preserved ginger in syrup and glacé ginger, glacé cherries and cherries in syrup for cocktails, made in three flavours: red maraschino, green crème de menthe and orange curaçao.

All these lines are useful; quality and freshness are critical factors.

Cape Gooseberry (Physalis)

Cherry type of berry cultivated in South Africa and in semi-tropical climes elsewhere. Used in preserves and featured as a friandise whole, coloured and fondant icing glazed.

Charlottes

Group of spectacular cold sweets prepared in a charlotte mould lined with sponge fingers, packed evenly with a bavarois preparation, unmoulded when set, tied with ribbon and decorated. There are different types of cold charlottes, the russe being the best known, and there are hot versions, e.g. apple charlotte. The charlotte is said to be a Carème creation.

Fruit. Charlotte surrounded and topped with sponge fingers, filled with a fruit bavarois, piped with whipped cream and decorated with fruits.

Moscovite. Charlotte surrounded and topped with alternating white and rose coloured sponge fingers, filled with a vanilla bavarois incorporating apple purée, decorated with piped whipped cream and glacé fruits.

Opéra. Similar to the russe with the vanilla bavarois filling incorporating a purée of marrons glacé (to the proportion of a ¼ of its bulk), loaded with diced candied fruits and then decorated.

Plombière. Charlotte lined with sponge fingers and filled with kirsch-flavoured vanilla ice cream loaded with diced candied fruits. Can also be filled with a vanilla bavarois.

Russe. The top and sides of the preparation are lined with sponge fingers, the filling consists of a vanilla bavarois, the preparation is tied with red ribbon and the piece piped with crème chantilly.

Note: Some recipes indicate the addition of apple purée to the bavarois filling.

Cherry (Cerise)

A colourful and refreshingly cool fruit. It is in season from May to July and available in cans at all times.

There are sweet dessert and sharp cooking cherries in many varieties, ranging in colour from white to red and black. Cherries are canned, crystallized, processed in cocktails in three colours, bottled in brandy and employed in the flavouring and making of liqueurs. Cherry flavouring, as well as the soothing properties of the fruit, is used extensively in medicine. Cherry stalk tisane is a well known diuretic.

Cherry Pie, Cherry Pudding. Prepared identically as for the apple versions but with cherries.

Compote. Pick over, stalk, wash and place in a pan. Just cover with water and add sugar as required. Bring slowly to the boil. Simmer until tender.

Jubilée (Cerises). Cook pitted cherries in a light syrup and set in a fireproof dish. Reduce cooking liquor, thicken with arrowroot, mask over cherries and flame in kirsch at the table. Cherries are marketed in jars of brandied syrups for flaming.

(Escoffier creation in commemoration of H.M. Queen Victoria Diamond Jubilee in 1897.)

Melba. Foundation of vanilla ice cream garnished with pitted fresh dessert cherries, masked with melba sauce and piped with a border of crème chantilly.

Summer Compote. Stew equal quantities of pitted cherries and stalked red, white and black currants in a light syrup. When tender, cool and touch with maraschino.

Chestnut (Marron)

The best known sweet preparation is the fabulous Marron Glacé, marketed foil wrapped and whole for friandises. Marrons and Debris de Marrons au Sirop (whole pieces canned in syrups) are used in confectionery and as garnitures for gâteaux and iced confections. The purée (Crème de Marrons) is used in special sweets.

Crème de Marrons (Sweet). Prepare chestnuts, cook in a light vanilla-flavoured syrup and press through a sieve into a purée. Work into a smooth cream, check sweetness and flavour with vanilla and maraschino. Serve as a sweet with cream or ice cream.

The canned product, suitably checked, may be used for this preparation.

Mont Blanc, Monte Bianco. Famous preparations presented in 2 ways.

1. Large chestnuts, peeled, skinned and simmered until soft in a light syrup with a vanilla pod. Passed through a sieve and combined with half-whipped cream sufficient to produce a smooth paste. Moulded as required and generously decorated with crème chantilly. (Ready crème de marrons may be used for this recipe.)

2. Cook prepared chestnuts in a light vanilla-flavoured syrup. Remove and place on a wire sieve, press through and let the preparation fall in short threads on a dish. Pile up, but do not mash, pipe up generously with crème chantilly.

Crème Caramel

Light baked custard cream preparation with a caramel topping, usually individually moulded. Prepared in 3 operations; the caramel, the custard, and the cooking. Popular sweet lending itself to a variety of mouldings.

The caramel: Cook 75g (3 oz) lump sugar with a little water to a caramel colour. Line the base of the moulds with this preparation.

The custard: Beat 8 eggs and 120g (4 oz) sugar in a basin. Heat 1 litre (2 pints) milk with a vanilla pod, bring to boil and slightly cool. Whisk the milk into the egg preparation, strain and pour into the caramel lined moulds almost to filling point.

The cooking: Cook in a bain-marie in an oven at 204°C. (400°F.) until set. When cold, unmould into a glass serving dish.

Note: Several complete mixes are marketed. The actual crème caramel mix is accompanied by a tube or sachet of ready made caramel for lining the moulds. Mixes are reconstituted with milk or water as indicated and may be enriched by the addition of eggs or yolks.

The crème caramel idiom is extended into various fruit and other flavours with syrup toppings to match, e.g. raspberry, strawberry, chocolate, coffee. It is usual to serve additional syrup separately.

The following sweets may be individually dariole moulded or prepared in large fluted moulding.

Baked Egg Custard. Beat 6 eggs and 120g (4 oz) sugar into 1 litre

(2 pints) milk heated to boiling point with a vanilla pod and slightly cooled. Strain into a fireproof dish, sprinkle with grated nutmeg and bake bain-barie style at 204°C. (400°F.) until set. Preparation is served in its dish.

Crème Brulé. Heat 1 litre (2 pints) cream with a vanilla pod. Mix 12 egg yolks with 175g (6 oz) sugar. Pour the cream over the egg preparation, mix, strain and pour into small serving dishes. Cook bain-marie style in the oven at 180°C. (360°F.) until set. Dredge with icing sugar and glaze under a salamander.

Crème Caramel Savarin. Preparation moulded in a savarin ring, filled with fruit salad—raspberries, strawberries, fraise des bois and similar soft fresh fruits—and piped with whipped cream.

Crème Florentine. Similar to crème caramel, but without the caramel preparation. The moulds are buttered and lined with praline (chopped grilled almonds), filled with the custard preparation and baked bain-marie style. When cold, the creams are unmoulded and decorated with whipped cream.

Crème Regence. Custard prepared as for crème caramel, poured into moulds, without caramel lining, and cooked bain-marie style. When cold the creams are unmoulded, masked with a caramel sauce and decorated with restrained whipped cream piping.

Crème Renversée. One-time alternative name for crème caramel, though more recently applied to crème viennoise.

Crème Saint Clair. Similar to crème regence but masked with a fruit syrup and decorated.

Crème Viennoise. Derivative of crème caramel. The custard and caramel are prepared separately, then combined, poured into moulds and cooked bain-marie style. Unmoulded when cold and decorated with whipped cream.

Petits Pots de Crème. Individual ceramic pots filled with a crème patissière preparation or custard. Made in various flavours: vanilla (Petits Pots de Crème à la Vanille), chocolate (Petits Pots de Crème au Chocolat), strawberry, banana and other fruits and also liqueurs. The made-up preparation is poured slowly into the pots, covered and baked bain-marie style in an oven at 204°C. (400°F.). Served cold in the moulds and eaten with a teaspoon.

Basic preparation: Bring 1 litre (2 pints) milk with a vanilla pod to the boil. Mix 3 eggs, 6 yolks and 175g (6 oz) sugar in a bowl. Pour slightly cooled milk over the egg preparation and mix well. Strain mixture into the pots without any frothing.

Croûtes

Name given to a variety of preparations consisting of slices of savarin dressed with various fruits, masked with liqueur-flavoured apricot and other syrups, decorated with whipped cream and candied fruit, i.e. croûtes à l'ananas, à l'orange, à la parisienne. Could also describe a whole fruit-filled and decorated savarin.

Currants (Cassis)

The term currant is used here to indicate blackcurrant and the white and red species. Blackcurrant is a popular flavour and, like the blackberry, is used to accompany apples in pies and other preparations. On its own, as a compote, both red and blackcurrants are very attractive.

Summer Pudding. Line a pudding basin or a mould with sliced bread and soak well in the juices of the fruits to be used in the filling. Fill the lined dish with a mixture of sweetened, stewed and sieved soft fruits and their juices, i.e. red and blackcurrants, blackberries, raspberries, pitted black cherries, blueberries, bilberries, loganberries and cranberries. Finish with sliced bread and place a weight on top to press down the preparation. Stand overnight, chill well and unmould when required. Serve with dairy or ice cream.

Damson

Small and dark coloured member of the plum family admired for its sharp flavour. Used in pies, tarts and preserves.

Dried Fruit

Drying in this context is not to be confused with dehydration. Dried fruit presents a wrinkled and shrivelled appearance, while dehydrated food is either an instant powder or in the form of a brittle shell.

There are 2 kinds of dried fruit, small and large: small dried fruit includes such things as currants, raisins, sultanas and dates; large dried fruit includes apple rings, pears, apricots, peaches, prunes and figs. Because of its competitive price and nutritional value dried fruit was once the fare of the less wealthy, but it returned to favour in a new guise, as a food fashion.

Dried apple, pear, apricot and peach are packeted as a fruit salad. For reconstitution by plumping dried fruit is washed, placed in a pan, covered with sufficient cold water and left to soak with a piece of lemon or orange for 12 hours, then brought to the boil and stewed very slowly. Sugar need not necessarily be added, depending upon the quality and sugar content of the fruit. When ready it should have produced its own syrup.

Éclairs, Puffs and Profiteroles

These lines are made from a choux paste.
Basic recipe: ½ litre (1 pint) water, 250g (8 oz) butter, 50g (2 oz) sugar, pinch of salt, 500g (1 lb) flour, 10 eggs.

Heat water, add butter, sugar and salt. When blended, remove

235

from heat and slowly rain in flour. Whisk well, return to heat and gradually allow flour to cook and blend. Remove from heat, add eggs, one at a time, working to a smooth and pliable paste with a wooden spoon. Use when the paste has cooled. Choux paste goods are dipped in soft or water icing flavoured and coloured as required to glaze.

Icing: Pass 500g (1 lb) icing sugar through a fine sieve and slowly work in ⅛ litre (¼ pint) of boiling water. Work to a smooth hot paste and add lemon juice to prevent granulation. Flavours and colours achieved by using different essences.

Vanilla: plain icing flavoured with essence.

Chocolate: melt 60g (2 oz) ground chocolate or cocoa powder in the preparation.

Coffee: flavour and colour with essence.

Strawberry: flavour with essence and colour with compound.

Lemon: lemon juice and colour with well grated zest.

Orange: orange juice and colour with well grated zest.

Filling is performed by piping it inside through a small hole at the base with a bag fitted with a pointed bit.

Alaska (Profiteroles à l'). Glaze with soft vanilla icing, fill with soft vanilla ice cream, serve with a chocolate sauce flavoured with kirsch.

Éclairs. The choux paste is piped with a plain nozzle into éclair lengths on a baking tray, rested, egg-washed, baked at 218–230°C. (430–440°F.) for 20–25 minutes, cooled on a wire rack, glazed with chocolate or coffee soft icing and filled with whipped cream or a crème pâtissière.

Most éclairs are too long and too big; 7cm (3 in) is sufficient.

Éclairs, also puffs and choux, can also be filled with soft vanilla ice cream as frozen éclairs and served with chocolate, butter-scotch or maple syrup sauce.

Profiteroles. Small choux paste balls at 3 or 4 to the portion, fondant glazed and filled. Featured as Profiteroles au Chocolat or Souchard, masked with a hot chocolate sauce.

Puffs. Round éclairs: the French choux, which is fondant glazed; and the unglazed cream puff. Both are filled with whipped cream. The choux paste is moulded into a medium-sized ball, rested, egg-washed and baked. The puff or choux is fondant glazed and filled. The unglazed puff, prior to baking, is painted with syrup incorporating beaten egg yolk for a nice gloss finish.

Religieuse. Gâteau preparation made up of alternating different flavoured éclairs in a circle slanting inwards, topped with a choux puff. The base is piped with a circle of stars and the components are similarly secured with piped whipped cream. The éclairs and the choux are glazed and filled as desired. The name religieuse is sometimes given to a large choux puff.

Farmers Daughters
Norwegian sweet. Set a portion of full fruit strawberry jam on a
dish or plate, mask with whipped double cream, sprinkle with rusk
or ice wafer crumbs.

Fig (Figue)
Fresh figs are considered a de luxe dessert fruit. Canned green figs in
syrups from California are particularly good as a compote. Best
quality dried figs are a breakfast as well as a sweet dish. The figs are
washed, soaked as required and very slowly plumped in water over a
low heat. The fruit is served in its rich cooking syrup.

Flaming Fruit
Operation performed at table with peaches, bananas, apples, pears,
pineapple and other fruits, in brandy, rum, kirsch, maraschino and
other liqueurs, either singly or in permutations.

Hard fruits, like apples and pears, require pre-cooking; soft fruits,
like peaches and bananas, are flamed raw. The pan is heated, sprinkled
with sugar, browned, the prepared fruit set in the pan, pricked over,
flamed and served sauced with its cooking juices.

Peach. Sprinkle sugar in a warm pan and as it browns set in the
peeled fruit. Prick over, sauce with lemon and flame with kirsch.
Shake the pan, let the flame die out and serve the peaches sauced over
with their cooking juices. Peaches are also flamed in maraschino,
brandy, rum, curaçao and peach liqueurs.

Pear. Proceed as for peaches but with whole, peeled and cored pears
previously poached in a vanilla flavoured syrup.

Pineapple. Rings of fresh pineapple flambé in kirsch with sugar and
lemon juice as for peaches or pears.

Fritters (Beignets)
Fruit dipped in a sweet batter, deep fried, well drained, dredged with
icing sugar, glazed under a salamander and served with a hot kirsch-
flavoured apricot sauce. As an alternative finish, the drained fritters
are not glazed but served dredged with spiced icing sugar.

Apple fritters, with the fruit cut in rondels, are possibly the best
known and most popular. Other fruits for fritters include whole,
halved or quartered and cored pears; pineapple rondels, wedges or
cubes; peach halves; and whole or halved bananas. With banana it is
usual first to dip the fruit in a hot crème pâtissière and allow the
coating to set before the batter and deep fry treatment.

A rum-flavoured apricot sauce may be featured as an alternative
accompaniment, especially good with pineapple fritters.

Bread and Jam Fritters. Bread spread with butter and jam, dipped in
batter, deep fried, drained, glazed and served with a hot jam sauce.

Cream Fritters. Stiff baked custard preparation, cut into strips or rondels, battered and deep fried. Drained and dredged with spiced icing sugar.

Soufflés Beignets (Soufflé Fritters). Choux paste, spooned out and shaped as large-sized quenelles, deep fried with care, placed in a warm friture and the temperature raised. When cooked and coloured, drained, filled with crème pâtissière, jam or frangipane cream and served with a hot jam sauce or custard.

Fruit Condés

Hot or cold sweet; combination of sweetened rice and fruit. The original subject for the condé is thought to be apricot but in recent times pear condé is most frequently seen. It is now featured more as a cold than a hot preparation.

Dish is named after Louis de Bourbon, Prince of Condé (1621–86), a Marshal of France. The original dish was prepared with a savarin base; it is difficult to trace when the base became rice.

Rice for Condé: Bring 1 litre (2 pints) milk to boil with 120g (4 oz) sugar and a vanilla pod or blade of lemon rind. Rain in 150g (5 oz) rice and cook very slowly. Remove from heat, add 60g (2 oz) butter and 2 beaten eggs, return to heat, stir to thicken, but do not boil. If for a cold condé, preparation may be further enriched with half-whipped cream.

Arrange apricots, pineapple, peach, pear and red cherries on a foundation of condé rice. Mask with kirsch-flavoured apricot syrup. Decorate with crystallized angelica, violets and rose petals. For elaborate preparations the condé rice may be moulded.

Individual condés are listed under the fruit concerned.

Fruit Fools

The fool is a traditional British Fare sweet and is made with all types of soft fruit and fruit pulp. Gooseberry Fool is the favourite, followed by rhubarb. Can also be made with apple, loganberry, medlar, blackberry and raspberry.

Basic preparation: Press 1 kilo (2 lb) cooked, soft fruit through a sieve into a purée, heat with sugar to blend. When cold combine with ½ litre (1 pint) double whipped cream. Check colour and sweetness, fold into a glass dish, chill and decorate with chopped nuts or candied and glacé fruits.

Note: The quantity of cream to fruit is ½ cream to 1 of fruit. Fools may also be sweetened with honey when the preparation will not be heated.

Fruits in Liqueur

Various prepared fruits, such as apricots, cherries, nectarines, peaches, pineapple and fruit salad, are preserved in brandy or other liqueurs for special occasions. They are usually packed in glass jars. For a de luxe presentation, they are sometimes featured with ice cream dressed as coupes and sundaes.

Fruit Salad (Macédoine des Fruits)

Possibly the most popular and certainly the most featured sweet. A blend of various fruits, a mixture of colours, textures and flavours. The best and the original is the fresh fruit salad, but when the variety of fresh fruit is inadequate, use is made of canned fruit; indeed, the popular concept of fruit salad is a mixture of fresh and canned. Fruit salads are served well chilled with cream or ice cream, i.e. à la mode. The flavour of fruit salads is enhanced by kirsch, maraschino and other liqueurs. The fruit is allowed to macerate under cold with the selected liqueur, i.e. Macédoine des Fruits Frappés aux Liqueurs.

Fruit Cocktails. Usually a canned fruit salad line consisting of evenly diced peach, pear, pineapple, apricot, red cherry and small peeled grapes, well juiced. May be produced with fresh fruit.

Fruit Macédoine and Glace Panaché Alsacienne. Fresh fruit salad au kirsch d'alsace served with 3 ice cream flavours scooped out into small dishes, i.e. pistachio, vanilla and chocolate, with pompadour wafers.

Fruits Rafraîchis Tsarine. Fruit salad macerated in kummel, arranged on a foundation of pineapple ice, masked with whipped cream, and decorated with candied cherries, violets and angelica.

Timbale des Fruits Nouvelle Année. Various ice cream flavours with fruit salad in liqueurs, masked with marshmallow sauce, and decorated with crème marquise, diced candied fruits in kirsch syrup and crushed nuts.

Gâteaux

Croque en Bouche or **Croquembouche.** Tall preparation constructed with smallish choux paste round puffs into a pyramid. The choux puff balls are cream filled and glazed or iced. May also be made with meringue balls or with puffs and meringues.

Milles Feuilles. A thousand leaves, often misnamed vanilla slice, is one of the most delightful pastry confections. Mille feuilles is a puff paste, multi-deck sandwich filled in alternating layers with crème pâtissière or custard, fruit purée or preserve, masked with apricot syrup, covered top and sides with chopped nuts or just a glazed topping of fondant icing, and prepared as a whole gâteau or individual pastries.

For the gâteau the raw paste is cut into a square, baked and cooled. The pastry layers should be clearly defined, loose and easy to remove with a palette knife. The layers are then spread with their fillings; 2 with the custard preparation and 2 with a fresh purée of sweetened

239

raspberries or strawberries, a purée made from preserves or a fine raspberry jam. The gâteau is reshaped, coated with apricot purée, covered with chopped nuts or the sides nut-coated and the top glazed with vanilla fondant icing; in this case the topping is also traversed with lines of chocolate fondant icing smeared into a 'V' pattern at even intervals with the tip of a knife.

Mille feuilles should always be freshly prepared and served so that the preparation retains its crispy texture and before the filling impregnates and softens the pastry.

Note: In Scandinavian countries and in the U.S.A. this gâteau is usually known as Napoleon's Cake.

For individual pastries the raw paste is cut into oblong cakes, baked and then filled and finished as for the gâteau.

Paris-Brest. Ring of choux paste, baked, glazed with vanilla or strawberry soft icing and filled with crème chantilly or pâtissière.

Pithiviers. Gâteau made with puff paste and filled with frangipane. Prepared with 2 rounds of paste, one cut 25cm (10 in), the other just smaller. Frangipane is piped from the centre outwards on the smaller round, the larger puff paste piece placed upon it, the sides are crimped and the top of the gâteau cut down in a pattern of semi-circles. The piece is egg-washed, baked and given a final glazing with icing sugar.

Saint Honoré. Elaborate French gâteau named after the patron saint of pâtissiers.

Ring of choux paste set on a puff or short paste foundation. The ring or band is surmounted at intervals with small choux puffs. The ring and the puffs are sugar glazed. The centre of the gâteau, the choux ring and the puffs are filled with a light crème pâtissière, i.e. créme St Honoré, incorporating whipped and sweetened egg whites. The gâteau is decorated with crystallized violets and cherries.

Genoise
Light and rich sponge cake, from which a range of gâteau, are prepared.

Basic recipe: Work in a copper bowl resting in hot water bain-marie style. Break in 8 eggs and beat into a sabayon with 500g (1 lb) castor sugar. Remove from heat and beat until cool. Rain in 500g (1 lb) flour and add pinch of salt. Add 250g ($\frac{1}{2}$ lb) melted butter and desired colouring and flavouring. Continue whisking into a smooth, well aerated batter. Pour into a lightly buttered and flour-dredged cake tin or mould and bake for 25–30 minutes in an oven pre-heated to 191°C. (375°F.). Turn out to cool on a wire rack. The genoise may be baked in one mould and split through for a single or double deck gâteau and spread with filling, or baked in 2 halves or 3 layers. The preparation is now ready for filling and decorating.

Fillings are many and various, from preserves, i.e. jams, marmalades and curds, to creams, i.e. fresh whipped, chantilly, marquise or butter cream. Spread the selected filling smoothly and assemble the cake. Spread the top and sides with cream or preserves and coat with chopped nuts, chocolate, desiccated coconut or candied peel. Royal, soft or fondant icings are also employed. The decorating, piping and garnishing are left to the creativity of the pâtissier. Before icing, the cake must be abricoted.

Genoise gâteaux may take the form of large round or square cakes, or as individuals, though the main interest here is the large piece for the service of sweets. All these gâteaux and their fillings may be flavoured with kirsch or maraschino.

Another Method: Warm and sift 120g (4 oz) plain flour with a pinch of salt. Whisk 4 eggs with 120g (4 oz) castor sugar in a bowl over hot water until thick. Slowly fold in the flour, beating all the time. Add 120g (4 oz) melted butter and flavour with vanilla or almond essence. Fold in a buttered and flour-dredged cake tin. Bake for 25–30 minutes at 177–191°C. (350–375°F.). Turn out and cool on a wire rack.

Almond Genoise. Incorporate 120g (4 oz) ground sweet almonds in cake mix, crème pâtissière filling, almond royal icing coating, decorated with walnuts, almonds, glacé cherries and angelica.

Banana Genoise. Mix touched with banana essence and yellow colouring, filled with mashed bananas in whipped cream, coated with yellow coloured banana flavoured royal icing and decorated with glacé fruits.

Cherry Genoise. Mix loaded with rough-chopped glacé cherries, filled with cherry jam, coated with royal icing and decorated with glacé cherries and angelica.

Chocolate Genoise. Add 120g (4 oz) grated chocolate to mix. Crème chantilly filling, chocolate royal icing coating, decorated with sugared violet.

Coconut Genoise. Mix flavoured with coconut milk, crème pâtissière filled, coated with whipped cream or abricoted and covered with desiccated coconut. Coconut may also be toasted.

Coffee Genoise. Mix coffee essence flavoured, coffee cream filling, coffee royal icing topping, glacé cherry decorated.

Genoise Sponge Cake. Mix flavoured with vanilla or almond, baked in 2 halves, spread with raspberry, strawberry or greengage jam, dredged with icing or castor sugar.

Lemon Genoise. Flavour mix with lemon juice and colour with zest, lemon curd filling, soft lemon icing coating, decorated with crystallized lemon halves or candied peel.

Orange Genoise. Flavour mix with orange juice and colour with

241

zest, marmalade filling, soft orange icing coating, decorate with candied orange peel.

Mix may be flavoured with grand marnier or cointreau.

Pineapple Genoise. Pine essence flavoured, crème chantilly and crushed pineapple filled, coated with yellow coloured royal icing and glacé pineapple decorated.

Praline Genoise. Almond essence flavoured, strawberry jam filling, grilled chopped nuts coating.

Raspberry Genoise. Raspberry juice in cake mix, jam filled, soft raspberry icing, glacé cherries and angelica decoration. Also filled with crushed berries in whipped cream, coated with raspberry cream and left rough.

Strawberry Genoise. Mix flavoured with strawberry juice, jam filling, coated with strawberry flavoured and coloured royal icing, decorated with glacé berries. May be coated with strawberry cream and left rough, and filled with crushed berries in whipped cream.

Vanilla Genoise. Vanilla essence flavoured, crème pâtissière filling, royal icing coating, candied ginger decorated.

Gooseberry (Groseille à Maquereau)
Known for its green colour and pleasingly fresh bite. The name of the fruit is said to originate from the fact it was once always served as a sauce with roast goose, a practice which still persists in certain parts of the Continent. Useful in puddings, pies and as a fool.

Compote. The fruit is topped and tailed, stewed slowly in sufficient water to cover and sweetened to taste.

Grapes (Raisins)
Many are the varieties, shapes and sizes of white and black grapes. First and foremost grapes are a dessert fruit. Useful in fruit salads and used in open tarts as a filling masked with thickened syrup.

Greengage (Reine-claude)
One of the most attractive members of the plum family. Excellent as a compote, in a pie or tart, and good fresh in fruit salads.

Jelly (Gelée)
Jellies are made from gelatine, an animal and vegetable mucilaginous almost colourless substance which readily absorbs liquid and swells considerably. It is marketed in sheets, nibbled and in powder form. Powdered gelatine is now more usual, though many chefs still prefer the sheet. Gelatine is measured in blooms and sells in various strengths; the more concentrated the product the less liquid required for breaking down and the higher the melting point when set.

One of its main culinary uses is the manufacturing of sweet table jellies. Ready-made jelly crystals are packeted in end-product packs and also in the convenience ½ litre (1 pint) slab. Commercial crystals and slabs containing gelatine, sugar, glucose, fruit juice, citric acid, colouring and flavouring agents are quickly made up with the addition of very hot water. Ready crystals usually go about 75–120g (3–4 oz) to the ½ litre (1 pint).

On no account should made-up jelly be boiled, an operation which destroys the gel.

Chefs use end-product packs or slabs or make up their own jellies with gelatine.

Note: Gelatine comes from 2 main sources: vegetable, known as agar-agar extracted from certain algae or seaweeds, and animal, being osseine from bones or skin from animal skins. Before the advent of commercial gelatines, jellies were prepared by clarifying jelly from calves feet and veal knuckles, a very laborious process.

Formula for ½ litre (1 pint) Jelly: 250g (8 oz) sugar, ½ litre (1 pint) hot water, 30g (1 oz) gelatine (2 tablespoons), selected essence and colouring, lemon juice or 60g (2 oz) in equivalent citric acid.

If natural fruit juice is used the water is decreased accordingly.

The sugar is placed in a bowl, the hot water added, then the gelatine, flavouring and colouring compounds and the acid. The preparation is stirred to ensure a uniform solution and then poured to set in a wetted mould.

Prepared fruit can be caught in the jelly; other variations include the multi-layered and marbled jellies.

Popular flavour range includes orange, lime, lemon, strawberry, raspberry, blackcurrant, cherry, apple, grape and cranberry. Novelties include liqueur jellies made with various liqueurs; wine jellies made with port, red wines and hock; milk jellies made up with milk, and creamy jellies made with beaten egg yolk, 2 per ½ litre (1 pint). Jellies may be made up in layers, in fancy moulds, in individuals, decorated with whipped cream or left plain.

Junket

For a plain junket heat ½ litre (1 pint) milk to blood heat and sweeten with 60g (2 oz) sugar. Stir in a teaspoon of essence of rennet, pour into glass dish to cool and sprinkle with nutmeg. Junkets may be coloured and flavoured with essences and compounds. Packeted junket mixes in a variety of flavours are marketed.

Kaisersmarren (Emperor's Pudding)

Viennese bread and butter pudding. Butter a large shallow dish and line with overlapping thin strips of bread dipped in melted butter. Sprinkle with plumped currants, icing sugar and cinnamon. Moisten with egg yolk beaten in milk. Bake in the oven to a crispy brown.

Serve hot with apricot sauce, or cold, dredged with icing sugar and served with cream.

Loganberry
American berry said to be produced originally through cross breeding raspberry and strawberry by a certain Judge Logan. An attractive flavoured berry which cans well. Useful in fruit salads, as a compote or made into a fool.

Lychee
Small sweet Eastern fruit not unlike gooseberry with a whitish pulp and a hard reddish covering. Obtainable fresh or in cans. Used in fruit salads.

Lychees Stromboli. Flamed in whisky, heated in crème de menthe and served with vanilla ice cream sprinkled with chopped nuts. Operation performed at table.

Marignans
Individual savarin preparation. Three-quarter line a lightly greased barquette mould with savarin dough, prove, bake and when cool drench with a kirsch-flavoured syrup. Slash diagonally with a sharp knife and fill with whipped cream. Sprinkle with chopped pistachio nuts.

Larger multi-portioned marignans are also prepared but take the form and shape of a savarin; the filling of whipped cream and other type of cream is prepared identically.

Melon
Cantaloup, honeydew and charentais are the best known melons. This fruit is featured as a starter, like the grapefruit. Unlike grapefruit, however, melon is also served as a sweet.

En Surprise. Medium-sized melon with the top sliced off, the seeds and then the pulp removed, diced and mixed in a bowl with prepared raspberries, strawberries and loganberries, sweetened with sugar and sprinkled with kirsch or maraschino. The preparation is macerated under cold and filled into the scooped-out melon.

Changes are rung with various fruit permutations. This is a colourful preparation and as much colour and as many contrasting flavours as possible should go into the surprise filling.

Meringue
The crunchy sweetness of snow white meringue seldom fails to attract. It was 'invented' during the 18th century by one Gasparani, a Swiss pâtissier.

Basic preparation: 1 egg white to 50g (2 oz) sugar. Whisk white as far as it will go, then slowly rain in the sugar and a pinch of salt. Flavour with vanilla or almond essence. For coloured and flavoured

244

meringues add required essence and compound. Spoon or pipe out preparation on a sheet of greaseproof paper and cook slowly in a cool oven. The finished article will be uncoloured by the heat, crispy on the outside and soft within. The preparation may be shaped as desired or piped out in a case or shell for fruit and ice cream fillings.

Note: The critical factors in making meringues are that all utensils, as well as the chef's hands, must be clean, dry and free from any hint of grease. Moisture and fat ruin the end product.

Chantilly. Piped or spooned crème chantilly sandwiched between two meringue shells, decorated with crystallized violets.

Chantilly aux Marrons. As for chantilly and topped with a line of marrons glacés.

Glacées. Vanilla ice cream sandwiched between 2 meringue shells, piped with crème chantilly and decorated with sugared violets and rose petals.

Italian Meringue. Egg whites and syrup in place of sugar. Whisk 8 egg whites very stiffly, add in a slow trickle 500g (1 lb) sugar cooked to the large ball stage. Whisk rapidly.

Lemon Meringue Pie. Contemporary food fashion sweet usually made with a packeted filling. This preparation is packed with a gelatine capsule containing lemon juice. The contents of the pack are emptied into a pan, blended with $\frac{1}{4}$ litre ($\frac{1}{2}$ pint) cold water and a beaten egg yolk, and heated to boiling point, by which time the capsule should have broken. It is blended well and poured in a baked 15–18cm (6–7 in) flan pastry case. The filling is topped and sealed with a liberal quantity of meringue and browned in a hot oven. Serve cold.

Note: The meringued pie gives rise to a number of preparations, e.g. apple, banana, lemon curd meringue pie.

Marquise. Crème marquise piped or spooned between 2 vanilla or strawberry meringue shells and decorated with sugared rose petals.

Napolitaine. A portion of napolitaine parfait, sandwiched between 2 meringue shells and piped with crème chantilly. (Three colours of ice cream: vanilla, strawberry, pistachio or chocolate.)

Milk Puddings

Wholesome and easy to digest, these puddings are made with rice, tapioca, sago and semolina and served straight or with fruit compotes. With these cereal grains, it is often difficult to give exact quantities for recipes; the experienced chef advocates 'know your cereals', especially with the new kinds of processing.

Rice. For a simple pudding place 75g (3 oz) carolina rice in a buttered pie dish, sweeten with sugar and cover with $\frac{1}{2}$ litre (1 pint) milk. Sprinkle with nutmeg and melted butter. Bake in moderate oven for about 40 minutes by which time a golden brown topping will have formed.

For a more elaborate pudding heat 120g (4 oz) sugar, $\frac{3}{4}$ litre (1$\frac{1}{2}$ pints) milk, pinch of salt, slice of lemon rind and vanilla pod together. Let preparation infuse slowly and when at boiling point remove the pod. Rain in 120g (4 oz) rice, add piece of butter and cook carefully for 20 minutes. Remove from heat and add 2 beaten eggs. Turn out into a buttered pie dish, dust with nutmeg and cinnamon and bake in a bain-marie until firm to the touch. Serve hot or cold.

Note: Rice pudding cans well and acquires a creamy texture.

Impératrice (Riz à l'). Elaborate moulded rice preparation served cold.

Bring 1 litre (2 pints) milk with 50g (2 oz) sugar and a vanilla pod to the boil. Rain in 120g (4 oz) rice, bring back to the boil and simmer slowly. Beat 4 egg yolks with 50g (2 oz) sugar, stir into the rice, thicken over heat but do not boil. Let preparation slightly cool, then add 40g (1$\frac{1}{2}$ oz) gelatine melted in a little hot water and 120g (4 oz) small diced crystallized fruit in kirsch and stir over cracked ice almost to setting point. Mix in $\frac{1}{4}$ litre ($\frac{1}{2}$ pint) whipped cream and then 4 egg whites stiffly whisked with 50g (2 oz) sugar. Fold preparation in a charlotte mould lined with raspberry jelly. Allow the preparation to set, then unmould onto a serving dish lined with raspberry jelly.

For preparations not for moulding and where the rice is used as a foundation similar for a condé, it is cooked as indicated, sweetened with apricot purée, enriched with whipped cream and loaded with diced candied fruit in kirsch.

Sago. Cereal taken from a species of palm tree grown in Near East. Sago pudding is prepared as for tapioca.

Semolina. Wheat by-product. For puddings proceed as for tapioca on the basis of 50g (2 oz) to $\frac{1}{2}$ litre (1 pint) milk and 120g (4 oz) sugar.

Tapioca. A gelatinous type of substance extracted from the root of the cassava plant. The whole grains are used. They should not be confused with ground tapioca which is used like cornflour and arrowroot as a thickening agent in soups and sauces.

Heat $\frac{1}{2}$ litre (1 pint) milk with vanilla pod, a piece of lemon rind and 120g (4 oz) sugar. Let preparation infuse and when boiling point is reached remove pod, rain in 50g (2 oz) tapioca, add piece of butter and simmer for 20 minutes. Remove from heat and add a beaten egg. Pour into a buttered dish, dust with nutmeg and cinnamon and bake in the oven, bain-marie style, until firm.

Mirabelle

Small round, yellow plum grown in Eastern France and available in
246

the can when the fresh fruit is out of season. Makes a good compote and is also good for variety and colour in fruit salads.

Mousse
Mousse is a somewhat lighter preparation than the bavarois since most mousse recipes indicate whipped egg whites, sugar, cream, flavourings and no cooking. Made in many flavours, the methods varying according to the main ingredient. They may be moulded, turned out and decorated, in this case, ice well to aid setting.

Chocolate Mousse (basic recipe). Whip 6 egg whites to a stiff froth, beat in 120g (4 oz) powdered chocolate, sweeten with sugar and vanilla essence. Beat in ⅛ litre (¼ pint) fresh cream. Check for sweetness and colour and fold into a serving dish. Top with glacé cherries and chill.

Coffee Mousse. As for chocolate, but using concentrated essence or strong infusion of black coffee.

Crème de Menthe Mousse. As for vanilla, but flavoured with peppermint essence and coloured with green compound.

Lemon Mousse. As for orange, but using lemon zest for colour and juice for flavour, check sweetness with sugar.

Maraschino Mousse. Vanilla mousse, without essence, flavoured with liqueur and coloured a pale pink to simulate cherry.

Strawberry Mousse. Combine 500g (1 lb) purée of fresh berries sweetened with sugar with ¼ litre (½ pint) half-whipped cream, add about 15g (½ oz) softened gelatine to aid setting and whisk well. Pour into dish and chill.

Vanilla Mousse. Whip ½ litre (1 pint) cream with 4 egg whites, sweeten with sugar and vanilla essence, mould and chill.

Nectarine
A delicate fruit produced by crossing peach with plum. May be prepared in the same ways as peaches.

Nuts (Noix)
A distinction should be made between nuts used in confectionery, for decorating and dessert, and those used in the kitchen. The latter are almonds and chestnuts. The former cover such species as beech, brazil, cashew, cob, hazel, pecan, pistachio and the coconut. They are marketed shelled whole, chopped, desiccated or ground. Pistachio is noted for its special flavour and green colour; coconut has many uses in bakery and confectionery; pecan is extensively promoted in the U.S.A.

Orange
Most popular of all citrus fruits and available all the year round. As a beverage it is the best selling of all fruit juices.

Jaffa Salad. As for orange salad, employing grapefruit and orange rondels or segments in equal quantities, sauced with a cooked julienne of peel preparation of both fruits, and flavoured with grand marnier or curaçao.

Orange Salad. Select juicy oranges, wash, slice off the skin with a cutter in long julienne strips, place in a pan with sugar moistened with a little water and simmer over a low heat into a marmalade preparation. Slice fruit into even rondels, arrange in a serving dish and sauce over with the julienne preparation when it has cooked. Flavour with curaçao or grand marnier, serve ice cold.

Surprise (en). Large fruit with contents cut out in even segments, macerated in sugar and curaçao, replaced in the skin case and topped with vanilla or orange water ice. Sliced off lid replaced and stuck with angelica to simulate a green leaf.

Pancakes (Crêpes)

The pancake has gone beyond Shrove Tuesday into other spheres. It has become the subject of speciality restaurants featuring a selection of pancakes sweet and savoury—its varieties are numerous.

Sweet Pancakes. *Basic Recipe:* 500g (1 lb) flour, 250g (8 oz) castor sugar, salt, 4 eggs, 1 litre (2 pints) milk, vanilla essence.

Sift the flour, make a well in the centre and add sugar, pinch of salt and beaten eggs. Slowly beat in the milk until cream consistency is reached. Flavour with vanilla and stand for an hour. This recipe may be enriched with cream in place of milk and flavoured with a liqueur, i.e. curaçao, grand marnier, cointreau, kirsch or rum.

Pancakes are made in a special heavy 16cm (6½ in) top diameter iron pan. The pan is pre-heated, a piece of butter thrown in and as it browns the pancake batter is ladled in to make a cake the thickness of a penny and tossed to cook quickly on both sides. The ideal way is to serve pancakes hot from the pan, folded into 4 or rolled up and accompanied by lemon wedges and castor sugar. They may also be served with brown sugar and citrus juices such as orange or grapefruit; maple or golden syrup; filled with strawberry, raspberry, apricot or cherry jam or lemon curd; or accompanied by ice creams.

Crêpes Suzette. Famous and spectacular preparation with interesting historical background. Joseph, a French restaurateur, created the preparation in 1897 at the Restaurant Marivaux in Paris, naming it after a character in a current Comédie Française production. In one scene a maid, Suzette, served pancakes to her employers; they were supplied by the restaurant for each performance.

When Richard D'Oyly Carte wanted a successor to César Ritz at the Savoy Hotel he bought the Marivaux in order to obtain the services of Joseph. Installed at the Savoy, he introduced Crêpes Suzettes to London.

The original procedure was quite simple: pancakes heated in orange juice, sweetened butter and a touch of curaçao; the preparation was not flamed. Escoffier in *Guide to Modern Cookery* (Heinemann) advocated tangerine juice and Prosper Montagué in *Larousse Gastronomique* prescribes adding curaçao to the pancake mix and stuffing the crêpes with suzette butter flavoured with tangerine juice, zest and curaçao. Both chefs were contempories of Joseph.

Henri Charpentier, a flamboyant Franco-American Chef-cum-Restaurateur, claimed in his book *Life à la Henri* to have invented crêpes suzette at the tender age of 12 when at the Café de Paris, Monte Carlo, and to have served them to the Prince of Wales (later to become King Edward VII). Charpentier heated the pancakes in butter sweetened with vanilla sugar and flavoured with orange and lemon zest and flamed in curaçao, kirsch and maraschino.

Somewhere, somehow, with the passing of time, the 2 basic methods merged and the suzette is now always flamed. It would appear Joseph's original butter is adopted and the cakes flamed in brandy and flavoured with curaçao, or just flamed in curaçao, or grand marnier.

Suzette Butter. Work butter in a bowl with a wooden spoon, sweeten with sugar and flavour with orange juice and curaçao. Rub the zest off some orange rind on a few lumps of sugar and add to the preparation to dissolve. Mix well and use as required.

Another method for Crêpes Suzette: The following seems to be the most popular among maîtres d'hôtels.

Heat the pan and pile in 120g (4 oz) sugar. As it starts to melt and cook, add the juice of 2 oranges and half a lemon, a shaving or two of orange peel and a piece of butter. Let the preparation cook to a syrup and then place in the pancakes one at a time (2 per portion), sprinkle with grand marnier and fold each into 4. Flame in brandy and serve flaming and sauced with their liquor.

Curaçao (Crêpes au). Filled with warmed orange curaçao marmalade, dredged with vanilla icing sugar and served with orange wedges.

Flambées (Crêpes). Flamed pancakes at the table, but quite different from the suzette. Heat the pan, sprinkle with sugar, add butter and as contents combine into a syrup set in the pancakes and fold. Flame in a liqueur or spirit to choice. Shake out flames and serve sauced with their liquor.

Georgette. Filled with diced pineapple in a kirsch-flavoured syrup and dusted with icing sugar.

Hawaiian. Pancakes filled with chopped pineapple in kirsch. Sugared and served in deep plates with orange halves cut in a fancy pattern. The orange juice is sauced over the pancakes.

Mikado (Crêpes). Pancakes filled with kirsch-flavoured full fruit morello cherry jam, arranged in a buttered dish, dredged with vanilla sugar, glazed under a grill and flamed in kirsch. The preparation is prepared in the kitchen and sent to the table flaming.

(A François Latry of the Savoy creation.)

Mincemeat (Pancakes). Filled with warmed mincemeat and folded, dredged with icing sugar and served with lemon wedges.

Royal Lemon. Filled with hot lemon curd, dusted with icing sugar and served with orange wedges.

Verlaine (Crêpes). As for crêpes flambées but the pancakes are flamed in a mixture of liqueurs: 4 parts cognac, 4 parts kirsch, 2 parts mandarine, 2 parts kummel, 1 part maraschino. The liqueurs are pre-mixed and added to the pancakes. Before flaming a measure of absinthe (pernod) is added.

(Marcel Boulestin creation named after the French poet, Paul Verlaine (1844–96), reputed to be a slave to absinthe. Boulestin, an idealist, refused to flame the suzette; if patrons wanted crêpes flambées the verlaines were recommended.)

Pannequets

Thin pancakes, filled, rolled, trimmed, cut into 2 lozenge shapes, dredged with icing sugar and served. The usual fillings consist of preserves, i.e. jam pannequets, and various crèmes and custard preparations.

Crème (à la). Filled with crème pâtissière, cut into lozenges and sprinkled with crushed macaroons.

Peach (Pêche)

One of the premier culinary fruits and the most luscious.

Fresh peaches are skinned by blanching in hot water then quickly cooling in ice water. They are gently poached in a light syrup in which they are allowed to cool, then the stones are removed with care.

The preparations listed are applicable to fresh peaches and to canned sliced, halved and whole fruits.

Américaine (Pêche à la Mode Américaine). Whole peaches poached in kirsch-flavoured syrup, dressed on a coffee ice cream foundation surrounded by a border of crushed pineapple in kirsch. The peaches are masked with chocolate sauce. The preparation piped with whipped cream and decorated with a sprinkling of milled or ground nuts, crystallized whole violets, rose petals and a julienne of angelica. The dish may be assembled in a timbale of several portions or in an individual coupe.

Beauty Queen. Halves of syrup-poached peach dressed on rounds of swiss roll, masked with cream, decorated with angelica and glacé cherries and served with ice cream.

(Featured on the inaugural trip of the former 'Kentish Belle' Pullman train which carried the Beauty Queens from the Thanet towns.)

Dame Blanche. Peaches dressed on strawberry ice cream, masked with half-whipped cream sweetened with vanilla and decorated with flaked milk chocolate.

Marjorie (Gratin de Pêche Marjorie). Blanch, peel and slice 6 to 8 peaches. Place in a soufflé dish and sprinkle with kirsch. Heat ½ litre (1 pint) milk and thicken with 50g (2 oz) cornflour and 4 egg yolks. Remove from heat. When cold, blend with ¼ litre (½ pint) whipped cream and mask the peaches. Spread with 250g (8 oz) brown sugar and brown the topping under a grill.

Mary Garden. Peaches dressed on a foundation of rich custard and garnished with kirsch-flavoured fruit salad. The peaches are stuck with angelica, topped with glacé cherries and the preparation masked with kirsch-flavoured apricot syrup.

(An Escoffier creation.)

Melba. Whole peach, skinned, poached in vanilla-flavoured syrup, dressed on a foundation of vanilla ice cream, masked with melba sauce and piped with crème chantilly.

(Pêche Melba, created by Escoffier for Dame Nellie Melba the Australian-born prima donna, is the most famous sweet of all time. Legend has it that returning very late to the Savoy Hotel after a performance at Covent Garden Opera House, the celebrated singer, tired and weary, expressed a wish for something light and sweet. The staff had gone off duty and so Escoffier went into the kitchens and arranged some peaches on ice cream in a timbale and masked them with a purée of fresh raspberries sweetened with syrup. The singer was delighted and enquired of the chef the name of the dish. Let's call it Pêche Melba! The preparation, made on the spur of the moment, not only immortalised the name Melba but created a whole class of sweets. In *Guide to Modern Cookery* (Heinemann) the chef briefly described the preparation: 'Poach some peeled and ripe peaches in a vanilla flavoured syrup. Dress on vanilla ice cream in a dish and mask with a purée of fresh raspberries.' The cream piping came later.)

All fruit may be made up into a melba; the best known are apple, apricot, pear, pineapple, banana, raspberry, strawberry and nectarine. Melba sauce is now marketed ready prepared.

Princesse. Sliced peaches and strawberries macerated separately in sugar, curaçao and brandy, dressed together and served well chilled accompanied by vanilla ice cream.

Sarah Bernhardt. Peaches dressed on pineapple ice cream, masked with a sweetened purée of strawberries, decorated with crème chantilly.

Pear (Poire)

Fresh or canned whole and half fruits are used. The fresh pear is

251

peeled, cored whole, poached till tender in a light syrup and cooled in the cooking liquor.

Alma. Whole peeled and cored pears poached in a syrup flavoured with port to acquire a red colour, dressed on strawberry ice cream and decorated with crème chantilly.

(Creation of Charles Elmé Francatelli in commemoration of one of the battles of the Crimea war.)

Baked. Large, sound pears, washed, pricked but not peeled. Set in deep dish, topped with pieces of butter, sugar and water to 12mm ($\frac{1}{2}$ in) deep and baked till tender in a slow oven. Served sauced in their syrup. Counterpart dish to the baked apple.

Belle Hélène. Two ways of serving this dish.

1. Poached, peeled, whole pears served with vanilla ice cream, and hot chocolate sauce offered separately.

2. Poached, peeled pears on foundation of vanilla ice cream, masked with cold chocolate sauce, sprinkled with nut splinters, decorated with piped crème chantilly.

Compote. Peel, core, prick and poach fruit in syrup with vanilla pod or essence. Serve well juiced in their cooking liquor. Syrup may be flavoured with kirsch or maraschino.

Condé. Whole peeled, cored and syrup-poached, or canned halves, dressed on rice condé preparation, masked with apricot syrup flavoured with kirsch and decorated with angelica and glacé cherries. Piped with a border of crème chantilly.

Dame Blanche. Poached in syrup, dressed on vanilla or strawberry ice cream, masked with vanilla-flavoured half-whipped cream and finished with a sprinkling of flaked milk chocolate.

Impératrice. Poached in vanilla flavoured syrup, dressed on a well creamed rice preparation loaded with diced candied fruit, masked with apricot syrup, and decorated with candied fruits and crème chantilly. (Similar preparation to condé.)

Joséphine. Poached halves dressed around a dome of rice impératrice, masked with a raspberry syrup and decorated with crème chantilly and candied fruits.

Limousine. Disher of ice cream in a sundae coupe, topped with half a pear, garnished with pieces of marron glacé in syrup and decorated with stars of whipped cream.

Manetta. Whole pears, peeled, cored and poached in vanilla-flavoured syrup, and stuffed with chopped nuts macerated in curaçao or maraschino. Set on a foundation of ice cream, i.e. vanilla, coffee, chocolate or other flavours. Masked with melba sauce, sprinkled with praline and decorated with crème chantilly.

(Dish inspired by Manetta in the thirties when he was manager of the Savoy Grill. Manetta was, in his day, one of London's foremost

252

maîtres d'hôtels. Founded his own restaurant which still bears his name.)

Winter Sport. Poached pears in kirsch-flavoured syrup, stuffed with flaked milk chocolate, dressed on vanilla ice cream, masked with a preparation of half-whipped cream sweetened with vanilla and decorated with crystallized violets and rose petals.

Persimmon
Sub-tropical curiosity orange coloured fruit resembling an over-ripe tomato. Eaten as a dessert fruit, used in jellies, preserves and water ices.

Pineapple (Ananas)
Large tropical prickly fruit with a refreshing flavour cultivated in Africa, Australasia, Malaysia and the Americas. The fresh is always best, but it cans well and is marketed whole, in rondels, cubes, tit bits and crushed. For dessert the fresh pine is cut in 19mm (¾ in) rounds, the rind is removed and the centre core stamped out with a cutter. It is served with sugar, a squeeze of lemon and sprinkled with kirsch. Pineapple is flamed in liqueurs, e.g. kirsch, maraschino, rum or brandy, and prepared in melbas and condés.

Condé. Fresh or canned wedges dressed on rice condé and masked with apricot and pine syrup touched with kirsch. Decorated with angelica and glacé cherries.

Creole. Segments dressed on rice cooked in sweetened milk and dressed with cream, masked with a kirsch-flavoured syrup and sprinkled with diced glacé fruits.

Fraises (Ananas aux). Pine round dressed with strawberries, sprinkled with lemon juice, dredged with sugar and sauced with a mixture of claret and maraschino.

Savoyard. Round dressed upon creamed rice with a half peach in the centre, masked with a light sweetened purée of strawberries and a border of piped crème chantilly.

Sultane. Portion of lemon water ice on a round of prepared pineapple, decorated with whipped cream, sprinkled with crystallized rose petals and veiled with spun sugar.

Plum (Prune)
Common type of soft fruit with centre stone; many varieties. Prepared as a compote, pie, pudding or as preserves. Dried plums become prunes.

Pomegranate
Round Eastern fruit the size of an orange, with a curious flavour. The juice is used in beverages, jellies and water ices. Once popular with children, eaten raw.

Posset
Originally a hot drink, milk sweetened with sugar, flavoured with nutmeg, heated with ale, white wine or sherry until preparation

curdled, or with lemon juice. Now served as a sweet with sponge fingers.

Prunes

Dried plums. California prunes are considered to be the best quality. Prunes are sold size graded from king size 14 to 24; large 30 to 40; the catering pack 75 to 85 fruit per 500g (1 lb).

In common with all dried fruit in the kitchen, prunes are now plumped and not stewed. They are reconstituted by adding an equal quantity of water to the preparation, e.g. 500g (1 lb) fruit to $\frac{1}{2}$ litre (1 pint) water. Sugar is added to taste, lemon or orange for flavour and a touch of cinnamon. Prunes (and all dried fruit) may be plumped au naturel simply by soaking from 24 to 48 hours. In this instance sugar may not be necessary. The just-cook method of normal plumping indicates placing the prunes in a pan, covering with an equal quantity of water, adding the flavourings, simmering gently for 30 minutes and leaving the preparation to stand overnight. For a deluxe compote, a glass of port or burgundy is added. Prunes may be spiced with a mixture of clove, nutmeg and cinnamon, or flavoured with a vanilla pod.

Prunes are also marketed canned in syrup.

A well juiced prune compote is an ideal breakfast dish and a useful sweet for the trolley. A few prunes mingled with fruit salad makes a good colour contrast. Compote of prunes and vanilla blancmange has a black and white visual appeal. Prunes are used in braising ham, casseroling chicken, dressings for turkey, garnishing grilled steak, and for service as a compote with roast duck, goose and veal escalopes.

Mousse. Plump 500g (1 lb) prunes and pass through a sieve. Combine the purée with $\frac{1}{4}$ litre ($\frac{1}{2}$ pint) half-whipped cream. Check sweetness with sugar, flavour with lemon zest and cinnamon. Beat well, fold into a mould, chill, unmould, and decorate with whipped cream.

Victoria. Arrange 500g (1 lb) prunes loosely in a litre (2 pints) jar. Make a $\frac{1}{2}$ litre (1 pint) China tea and infuse for 5 minutes. Strain tea over prunes, cover the jar and leave overnight in the cool. The prunes should be well plumped and require no cooking. Serve well chilled with lemon wedges.

Puddings

Baked, Boiled and Steamed Puddings. Sweet baked rolls and boiled and steamed puddings are true representatives of British Fare—good, wholesome food to sustain and nourish in the cold winter months. This fare, especially boiled puddings, has always attracted the attention of the master chefs from France; Alexis Soyer was much fascinated and so was Auguste Escoffier and both have written them up in their literary works.

These numerous and varied puddings should be light and flavoursome and never heavy, stodgy or over-moist.

Baked Jam Roll. Square of short paste spread evenly with jam, rolled up in the manner of a swiss roll, sealed, egg-washed and baked for about 1¼ hours at 204°C. (400°F.). Dredged with icing sugar and served with preserve sauce or custard.

Note: Any flavoured jam may be used, but preference is given to a full-fruited preserve, i.e. strawberry.

Lemon Curd Roll. As for jam roll, serve with lemon curd sauce.

Marmalade Roll. As for jam roll with a quality preserve, serve with marmalade sauce.

Mincemeat Roll. As for jam roll with a quality mincemeat, serve with custard.

Boiled Puddings. Made from a sweet suet paste, rolled and wrapped in a cloth, tied in greaseproof paper or secured in a metal sleeve and boiled in water till cooked.

Basic mix (upon which variations are introduced):

500g (1 lb) flour, 25g (1 oz) baking powder, salt, 75g (3 oz) sugar, 300g (10 oz) suet, water. (These quantities produce 8 portions.)

Sift flour with baking powder, pinch of salt and sugar, add shredded suet and sufficient water to form a stiff dough. Work until it clears the hands. Add the principal ingredient, i.e. dried fruit, chocolate, and rest for about 30 minutes. Shape and wrap in a scalded, flour-dredged pudding cloth, a greased metal sleeve or 2 thicknesses of grease-proof paper. Secure the ends and centres of the cloth or paper. Plunge into boiling water and simmer from 2½–3 hours. Withdraw, stand for a few minutes and release the pudding from its wrapping. Serve with the sauce as indicated.

Note: Also prepared from a ready mix sweet suet paste.

California Roll. Load dough with equal quantities of diced plumped California prunes, raisins and pitted red canned cherries. Touch with a mixture of ground clove, cinnamon and nutmeg. Serve with vanilla sauce spiced with ginger.

Cherry Roll. Load dough with candied cherries, pink with carmine. Serve with cherry jam sauce or maraschino-flavoured vanilla sauce loaded with chopped candied cherries.

Chocolate Roll. In the basic preparation, add 60g (2 oz) cocoa powder to each 500g (1 lb) flour, check flavour with vanilla and colour with carmine. Serve with chocolate cornflour sauce.

College Roll. Mix is loaded with plumped currants, raisins and sultanas and spiced with cinnamon. Served with custard or vanilla sauce.

Date Roll, Fig Roll, California Prune Roll. The dough is loaded with rough chopped figs, pitted prunes or dates as required and spiced with cinnamon. Served with a sweet sauce.

Ginger Roll. Fleck suet dough with large diced preserved ginger, touch with cinnamon, serve with spiced ginger vanilla sauce.

Marmalade Roll. Plain suet roll with hot marmalade sauce.

Mixed Fruit Roll. The suet dough is loaded with an assortment of large dried fruit: plumped and rough chopped figs, prunes and dates; and small fruits: currants, sultanas and raisins. Spiced with cinnamon, and served with a sweet sauce.

Jam Roll. Plain suet roll served with hot jam sauce.

Roly Poly Pudding. Baked roll made with a variety of preserve fillings, i.e. cherry, raspberry, greengage or strawberry jams, orange, ginger or grapefruit marmalades. The preserve is spread on the dough and the preparation rolled up as a swiss roll, secured and simmered for 2 hours. Served with custard or preserve sauce.

Spotted Dog. Popular name for boiled currant roll.

Sultana Roll, Currant Roll, Raisin Roll. The dough is loaded with plumped sultanas, currants or raisins as required and flavoured with cinnamon. Served with custard or vanilla sauce.

Syrup Roll. Plain suet roll served with golden syrup. Syrup is served cold or hot and slightly thickened with arrowroot or cornflour.

Steamed Puddings. These are lighter in texture than the boiled rolls since the paste contains eggs; it is, in fact, a type of sponge mix. They are described as steamed since they are, or should be, cooked in a pudding basin in a steamer or in a double jacket pot. The puddings are prepared in multi-portioned basins or individual moulds.

Golden Syrup Pudding. For 6–8 portions: 500g (1 lb) flour, 1 teaspoon baking powder, 175g (6 oz) margarine, pinch of salt, milk to moisten, ⅔rd cup Lyles golden syrup.

Sift flour and baking powder, rub in margarine with fingertips, add salt, milk to moisten and then the syrup. Mix well—the batter should fall easily from a spoon. Turn into buttered pudding basin, tie down with greaseproof paper and wrap in pudding cloth. Steam for 3 hours. Serve with golden syrup.

(Original Tate & Lyle recipe. Does not contain eggs.)

Jam Pudding. *Basic recipe:* 360g (12 oz) margarine, 175g (6 oz) sugar, 4 eggs, 1 kilo (2 lb) flour, 50g (2 oz) baking powder, salt, 0.45 litre (¾ pint) milk, 750g (1½ lb) jam.

Cream margarine with the sugar and add beaten eggs. Sift flour with baking powder and pinch of salt, blend the preparations and bind with the milk. Lightly grease basins or moulds, line bottom with jam, pour in pudding mix. Tie down with foil or double thickness of greaseproof paper and steam for 2 hours. Unmould and serve with custard or preserve sauce.

Lemon Curd Sponge Pudding. Similar mix as for jam pudding, replacing the jam with lemon curd (500g, 1 lb). Serve with hot lemon curd sauce.

Lemon Sponge Pudding. Similar to jam pudding. Sift 500g (1 lb) flour with pinch of salt. Cream 250g (8 oz) butter or maragrine with 120g (4 oz) sugar and add 2 beaten eggs. Combine the preparations. Add juice of 2 lemons and zest of one. Moisten with milk as required. Fill basins, tie down, steam and serve with a sweet sauce.

Marmalade Pudding. Prepare as for jam pudding, using marmalade and serve with marmalade sauce.

Syrup Pudding. Prepare as for jam pudding, using golden syrup and serve with syrup sauce.

Christmas Pudding. Elaborate traditional pudding featured once a year at the Festive Season as the focal point of the Christmas dinner. Served with custard, rum or hard sauce; it may also be flamed in brandy at table. Its origins are obscure, but it can be traced to the seventeenth-century when it was known as Plum Pudding, a preparation of stiffened plum porridge.

It is now probably more usual to 'buy in' Christmas puddings than make them on the premises. The ready pudding is already cooked and just needs reheating by steaming for 1½ to 2 hours, or 20 minutes in a pressure cooker. At one time the puddings were shaped as a large round ball and featured crowned with sugar and topped with a sprig of holly. Contrary to belief, the pudding does not improve with keeping beyond a period of 12 weeks or so.

Bread and Butter Pudding

Butter a deep pie dish and line with layers of thinly sliced bread with the crusts shaved. Between each layer of bread dot with butter, sprinkle with plumped sultanas and currants and dust with nutmeg and cinnamon and sugar. Finish with a bread topping and dredge with sugar. Moisten with milk in which 1 or 2 eggs are beaten and add a few drops of vanilla essence. Press down and bake in a moderate oven until the topping turns a cripsy golden brown. Serve hot with custard or preserve sauce.

For a de luxe version the bread is dipped in melted butter, the layers are sprinkled with chopped peel, the preparation moistened with half milk, half cream and eggs, and flavoured with spice and essence. The preparation is dredged with icing sugar and baked and served with hot apricot sauce flavoured with kirsch.

Eves Pudding

Line a buttered pie dish with a layer of jam, then a thickness of sweetened apple purée and top with a sponge preparation. Sprinkle with sugar and bake. Serve with custard.

257

Ground Rice Pudding

To 500g (1 lb) ground rice add 500g (1 lb) sugar and pinch of salt. Mix, make a well in centre and break in 8 eggs. Beat with a wooden spoon for 20 minutes in same direction. Flavour with lemon essence, pour into buttered dish and bake at 177°C. (350°F.) until a firm and coloured meringue top forms.

Queen of Puddings or Queens Pudding

Line a buttered and sugar-dredged pie dish with raspberry jam, arrange a layer of white breadcrumbs on the jam and then a good thickness of custard. Bake in a bain-marie. When cooked, top with a thickness of meringue, leave rough, pipe up or smooth over a sugar dredge. Flash in a hot oven to cook the meringue topping. Decorate with piped raspberry and apricot jam.

Quetch

Oval, purple and sweet plum from Eastern France. Good dessert fruit, also used in an eau-de-vie fruit brandy.

Raspberry (Framboise)

Light and delicately perfumed soft fruit, best appreciated fresh with sugar and cream, as a melba or stewed in a compote. All preparations for strawberries may be applied to raspberries.

Rhubarb (Rhubarbe)

Small, young stems make an excellent compote. Also good in pies and as a fool.

Compote. Cut in 6cm (2½ in) bâtons, cook slowly with ample brown sugar and just sufficient water until soft. Because of its delicate nature, rhubarb should be simmered gently, preferably in a cool oven. A suspicion of bicarbonate of soda helps to neutralize the acid content. Honey may be used as a sweetening agent.

Rum Baba

Prepare a ferment with 15g (½ oz) yeast, a little flour and warmed milk. Sift 250g (8 oz) flour into a bowl, make a well in the centre and add, one at a time, 6 beaten eggs. Blend into a smooth batter and add ferment. Work by hand to a rubberlike consistency and add 120g (4 oz) softened butter. Prove for 30 minutes. Add 60g (2 oz) sugar, a handful of plumped currants (optional) and a pinch of salt and beat well. Half fill buttered baba moulds and prove again for 20 minutes. Bake for 12 to 15 minutes at 218°C. (425°F.). Turn out and serve drenched with a rum or kirsch flavoured syrup.

Babas may be baked in small savarin rings and presented piped with cream and topped with a maraschino cherry.

Savarin

Ring of raised dough with the centre filled with fruit, masked in syrup and piped with crème chantilly.

Basic recipe for 4 rings: 500g (1 lb) flour, 25g (1 oz) yeast, $\frac{1}{8}$ litre ($\frac{1}{4}$ pint) milk, 8 eggs, 360g (12 oz) butter, salt, 25g (1 oz) sugar.

Warm flour and make a well in the centre. Dissolve yeast in luke-warm milk and add to the flour. Add beaten eggs and work paste by hand. Melt butter and distribute over the paste. Cover and prove for 2 hours, by which time it should have doubled its size. Add pinch of salt and knead, add sugar. Pipe the paste into lightly buttered moulds to a third of their height to allow for rising. Prove again and bake at 218°C. (425°F.). Turn out to cool on a wire rack. The rings are soaked in syrup, filled as required and piped with crème chantilly.

The syrup is made with equal amounts of sugar and water heated together and flavoured with lemon peel, touch of spice and finished with rum, brandy, kirsch or maraschino. The fruit fillings should be colourful and it is usual to bind the fruit in thickened syrup.

Abricotine. Sauced with syrup flavoured with abricotine liqueur, filled with a compote of fresh or canned pitted apricots and piped with crème marquise.

Chanzy. Filled with crème chantilly and strawberries.

Creole. Filled with pineapple, avocado pear and melon wedges in rum, sprinkled with shredded coconut.

Équatorial. Filled with orange and mandarin segments, pitted red cherries and pineapple cubes, flavoured with curaçao or rum.

Fraises (aux). Fresh strawberries and whipped cream.

Limoisine. Sauced with maraschino syrup, filled with marrons glacés and decorated generously with sweetened whipped cream.

Milles Fruits (aux). Fruit cocktail filling in thickened syrup.

Printanière. Fresh fruit salad filling macerated in kirsch.

Richelieu (à la). Savarin ring sauced with maraschino-flavoured syrup and filled with a fresh fruit salad lié in redcurrant jelly. Piped and decorated with crème chantilly coloured and flavoured with strawberry juice or essence.

Singapore. Diced fresh pineapple filling in kirsch.

West Coast. Savarin case impregnated with rum, filled with grape-fruit and orange segments, canned green figs, plumped California prunes and pitted red cherries. The fruit is masked with an apricot syrup flavoured with anisette.

Soufflés

Hot soufflés, sweet and savoury, are the lightest of preparations and are always made and cooked to order.

The preparation is mounted with a roux, egg yolks and beaten whites, folded into a soufflé dish and baked. It rises out of its dish when ready and must be served without delay.

Basic recipe for 4 covers: ⅛ litre (¼ pint) milk, 25g (1 oz) sugar, salt, 25g (1 oz) butter, 25g (1 oz) flour, 2 egg yolks and 3 whites, flavouring.

Heat milk and sugar together in one pan and add a dash of salt. In a second pan melt the butter and combine with the flour into a roux. Remove from heat and blend in the egg yolks, previously beaten in a little water. Slowly add the milk to form a preparation the consistency of thick cream. Whisk the egg whites very stiffly in a large bowl and combine with the soufflé mix and continue to whisk. Add the desired flavouring and colouring at this stage. Fold into a lightly buttered soufflé dish; *no more than half fill.* Bake in a pre-heated oven at 191°C. (375°F.) for 20 minutes. Do not disturb more than required lest the even temperature is lost. The preparation should rise well out of its dish and must be served without delay.

For larger quantities the ingredients are increased in proportion. Thus for 8 covers: ¼ litre (½ pint) milk, 50g (2 oz) sugar, 50g (2 oz) butter, 50g (2 oz) flour. Same procedure and cooking time.

For vanilla soufflé, heat the milk with a vanilla pod or essence; for orange or lemon, add concentrated fresh juices or essences for flavour and orange or lemon zest for colouring; for coffee, add essence; for strawberry or raspberry, add appropriate essences and colourings.

Arlequin. Harlequin soufflé, half vanilla and half chocolate, each flavour arrange side by side in a vertical position.

Cheese Soufflé. *Basic recipe for 4 covers:* Blend 25g (1 oz) butter with 25g (1 oz) flour over heat and slowly add 25–50g (1–2 oz) grated parmesan and gruyère mixed. Remove from heat and add 2 beaten egg yolks and then ⅛ litre (¼ pint) warmed milk. Make into a thick preparation and season with salt and cayenne. Fold in 3 stiffly whipped egg whites. Half fill a lightly buttered soufflé dish, sprinkle top with grated parmesan and bake for 20 minutes in an oven pre-heated to 191°C. (375°F.).

Chocolate Soufflé. Add 50g (2 oz) finely grated chocolate to the original mix before the eggs are joined, cooking over slow heat to blend.

Liqueur Soufflés. The basic mix may be flavoured with a liqueur and coloured accordingly. The more usual are kirsch, maraschino, grand marnier, curaçao, crème de menthe and anisette.

Rothschild Soufflé. Preparation is loaded with a salpicon of diced candied fruits, flavoured with goldwasser liqueur and decorated with small candied fruit.

Strawberry (Fraise)

Once a short-lived luxury, strawberries are now available almost the whole year round. As with many good things, strawberries are possibly best appreciated au naturel with sugar and cream. Fashion, however, says otherwise and the berries are presented in a variety of spectacular ways.

For a straight service the berries are picked over, stalked, washed, dried and served chilled in a glass dish with castor sugar and a choice of fresh cream, crème chantilly, Cornish or Devonshire cream or vanilla ice cream.

Cardinal. Timbale of prepared strawberries masked with a purée of fresh raspberries, sweetened and flavoured with liqueur.

Cecil (à la). Macerated in sugar, orange and lemon juice and curaçao. Served with double cream.

Chartreuse (aux liqueurs de). The prepared berries are macerated with sugar and equal amounts of green and yellow chartreuse. Just prior to service, the preparation is masked with double cream and served with sponge fingers.

Creole. Prepared berries macerated in sugar, cranberry, pineapple and grapefruit juices and a touch of kirsch. Served chilled with peach ice cream.

Criterion (à la). Macerated in sugar and kirsch, combined with an equal quantity of fresh raspberry purée and cream.

Flan. Prepare a short paste shell and bake. Line with a foundation of sweetened custard—preferably a crème pâtissière—arrange prepared strawberries on top and finish with a thickened syrup glazing.

Liqueurs (Fraises aux). The prepared berries are macerated in sugar with a single or mixture of liqueurs to choice, e.g. kummel, kirsch, maraschino, cointreau, anisette, cherry brandy, benedictine, curaçao, crème de menthe, cognac, abricotine, drambuie and others. Served escorted by double cream and vanilla ice cream.

Marquise. Macerated in sugar and liqueur and dressed masked with crème marquise.

Melba. Arrange required number of prepared strawberries on a vanilla ice cream foundation, mask with a sweetened purée of raspberries and pipe with crème chantilly.

Mousse. 500g (1 lb) prepared berries, mashed to a purée, combined with castor sugar, flavoured with curaçao and blended with $\frac{1}{4}$ litre ($\frac{1}{2}$ pint) whipped cream. Moulded, chilled in a freezer, unmoulded, piped with crème chantilly and decorated with whole berries.

Orange (à l'). Purée of strawberries, sweetened with sugar, flavoured with orange juice and curaçao. The preparation is arranged in a dish topped with stalked berries, dusted with sugar and served iced.

Porto (au). Macerated in sugar and port and served well iced.

Ritz (à la). Prepared strawberries masked with a sweetened raspberry purée, decorated with crème chantilly and served with ice cream.

Romanov (Fraises à la). The berries are prepared, sprinkled with sugar and grand marnier and macerated under cold. Just prior to service the preparation is masked with crème chantilly and served with sponge fingers.

Sarah Bernhardt. Macerated in sugar, curaçao and brandy, set on pineapple ice cream and masked with a sweetened purée of fresh strawberries.

Shortcake. An American preparation, made with a genoise sponge split through the centre and spread with crème chantilly, crushed strawberries and topped with more chantilly stuck with whole berries.

Sweet Omelette

The omelette preparation is made with 3 eggs per person, sweetened with icing sugar with a touch of salt added.

Blanc de Neige (Snow White). Whip 4 egg whites to a stiff froth, sweeten with icing sugar, flavour with vanilla essence and add a pinch of salt. Spoon out the preparation to the size of an egg. Drop into hot sweetened milk and poach. Dress in a custard or a chocolate sauce. Serve well chilled.

Flamed (Omelette Flambé). Plain sweetened omelette, brandied, placed in a fireproof dish, dredged with icing sugar and flamed in rum or kirsch at table, i.e. Omelette au Kirsch, Omelette au Rhum.

Mincemeat, Christmas Omelette. Six egg omelette sweetened with sugar, with pinch of salt, orange and lemon zest, cream and rum added, filled with warmed mincemeat, sent to table, dredged with sugar and flamed in rum.

Sucre (au). Sweet omelette served plain, dredged with sugar and branded in a pattern with a red hot iron.

Viennoise. Sweet omelette filled with warmed strawberry or apricot jam.

Sweet Sauces

Apricot Syrup. Heat apricot jam and pass through a strainer. Re-apply heat to reduce slightly. If too thick break down to required consistency with syrup. Flavour with kirsch.

Brandy Butter. Hard sauce well laced with brandy.

Butterscotch Sauce. Heat 250g (8 oz) demerara sugar with 50g (2 oz) butter and 1 tablespoon golden syrup until sugar has dissolved. Boil for 3 minutes and moisten with a little boiling water. Cool, add ¼ litre (½ pint) cream and flavour with vanilla essence.

Chocolate Sauce. Grate and dissolve 250g (8 oz) plain block chocolate in 0.45 litre (¾ pint) water. Flavour as required with vanilla essence, sweeten with sugar, add pinch of salt and simmer for 25 minutes.

Correct with a nut of butter and a dash of fresh cream for brilliancy and smoothness. This sauce is also marketed ready-made in tubes.

Coffee Syrup. Place 250g (8 oz) demerara sugar in a pan to dissolve in sufficient water, bring to boil and simmer for 5 minutes until preparation browns. Add ½ litre (1 pint) strong black coffee and simmer for 5 minutes until a good syrup forms.

Crème Chantilly. Whipped double cream sweetened with sugar and flavoured with vanilla essence.

Crème Marquise. Crème chantilly laced with redcurrant, Bar-le-Duc conserve. For another version, flavour and colour the cream with raspberry purée.

Crème Pâtissière. *Method 1:* Heat and infuse ½ litre (1 pint) milk with a vanilla pod. Mix 120g (4 oz) cornflour with 250g (8 oz) sugar, add 2 beaten eggs and 5 egg yolks and work to a smooth creamy consistency. Strain the hot milk onto the preparation, bring to the boil and stir until the custard thickens.

Method 2: Place 8 egg yolks, 1 whole egg and 250g (8 oz) sugar in a basin and mix to a smooth texture. Blend in 120g (4 oz) sifted flour and mix to a smooth paste. Bring ¾ litre (1½ pints) milk with a vanilla pod to the boil and whisk into the egg preparation. Strain into a clean pan, heat to just below boiling point, stirring constantly.

Method 3: Heat ½ litre (1 pint) milk with 120g (4 oz) sugar and flavour with vanilla essence. Remove from heat, rain in 120g (4 oz) flour, mix well, return to the heat and cook flour. Remove from heat and beat in 2 eggs and 5 yolks, re-apply heat to thicken.

Crème pâtissière may be left vanilla flavoured or flavoured with chocolate or coffee.

Cumberland Rum Butter. Beat 250g (8 oz) softened butter with 500g (1 lb) demerara sugar to a smooth pommade. Season with nutmeg and cinnamon and flavour with rum. Traditional Christmas pudding accompaniment.

Custard. There are 3 kinds of custard sauces: (1) the orthodox, (2) custard made from a powder, (3) the instant mix variety.

1. Beat 6 egg yolks with 175g (6 oz) sugar. Heat 1¼ litres (2½ pints) milk and slowly add to the egg mixture. Flavour with vanilla and thicken over heat without boiling.

2. Mix 50g (2 oz) custard powder with 50g (2 oz) sugar. Add a little cold milk taken from ½ litre (1 pint) to the preparation to work to a smooth paste. Heat remaining milk to boiling point, pour over the 'dry mix' and whisk over heat until the preparation thickens. Check for flavour as required.

3. The instant is a complete mix which reconstitutes with the addition of water or milk prescribed by the manufacturer. Needs making up with care and may require checking for sweetness and flavour.

Note: Custard is also canned and reacts well to this process.

Fruit Sauce. Heat ½ litre (1 pint) any kind of fruit purée and add ⅛ litre (¼ pint) syrup. Simmer, strain and check colour with compound.

Hard Sauce. Beat equal quantities of sugar and softened butter together until preparation resembles clotted cream. Touch with lemon juice. Flavour with brandy or rum, arrange in rondels or in a sauceboat and chill well. Should be white and crunchy.

Lemon Curd Sauce. Boil 500g (1 lb) lemon curd with 1 litre (2 pints) water, add 120g (4 oz) sugar and 50g (2 oz) diluted cornflour. Simmer over heat to thicken and check colour with yellow compound. May also be made with orange curd.

Maple Syrup (Érable). The sweet juice and properties of the maple tree in North America were known to the redskins long before it was discovered by the white man. The main supply of maple syrup comes from Quebec, in Canada, where it is widely used. The sap rises in March and April when the juice is collected, refined and packed in glass jars and cans.

As a sweetener it is served with pancakes, waffles, flapjacks, griddle cakes and cereals, and as a sauce with ice cream. It is used to glaze ham, meat and vegetables, i.e. carrots, turnips, parsnips, sweetcorn and sweet potatoes. Maple syrup may be thickened into a sauce with cornflour and butter.

An allied product, maple butter, is used as a sweet spread on pancakes, toast and cakes, as a filling, cake frosting and a hard sauce.

Marshmallow Sauce. Boil ¼ litre (½ pint) water. Sieve 675g (1 lb 6 oz) sugar into a bowl. Dissolve 25g (1 oz) gelatine in a little of the water, pour remainder onto the sugar and beat with a wire whisk. Add the gelatine and continue beating for 25 to 30 minutes until preparation is light and firm. Colour and flavour as required.

Melba Sauce. Warm 500g (1 lb) raspberry jam and pass through a sieve. Bring to the boil, thicken with 50g (2 oz) cornflour diluted to a paste and colour to a rich red with carmine. (This sauce is marketed ready made bottled or packed in tubes.)

Preserve Sauce (Jam Sauce, Marmalade Sauce). Boil 500g (1 lb) jam with 1 litre (2 pints) water and 120g (4 oz) sugar. Allow some reduction and thicken with 50g (2 oz) cornflour diluted to a paste in water. Strain and check colour with compound.

Sabayon. Work 500g (1 lb) sugar with 12 egg yolks until a white mixture is attained. Add 1 litre (2 pints) milk, infuse with a vanilla pod or flavour with essence and bring to the boil. Whisk the preparation in a large copper bowl standing in a bain-marie until it rises to 4 times its original bulk and becomes firm and frothy.

Sabayon is also made with a sweet or medium white wine or equal parts wine and milk. Is served hot or cold in stem glasses with savoy sponge fingers or used as a rich sauce for serving with Christmas and other puddings.

Syrup. Melt 500g (1 lb) sugar in ½ litre (1 pint) water, apply heat, simmer 10 minutes, adding juice of a lemon or 50g (2 oz) glucose. Strain through a muslin. May be coloured and flavoured as required. May also be thickened for glazing purposes with addition of 1 tablespoon arrowroot dissolved in warm water to 500g (1 lb) sugar. Syrup may also be made from glucose when no graincutter is required; 500g (1 lb) glucose to ½ litre (1 pint) water, bring to boil and simmer for 10 minutes.

Tutti-Fruitti Sauce. Mix equal amounts ginger marmalade with crushed pineapple and thin out with sufficient water. Heat together and cool. Load with chopped glacé cherries in 3 colours, i.e. red, green and orange.

Vanilla Sauce. Boil 1 litre (2 pints) milk with 120g (4 oz) sugar and thicken with 50g (2 oz) diluted cornflour. Flavour with vanilla essence and a touch of clove and nutmeg. Bring to boil, simmer and strain. May also be flavoured with almond essence, brandy or rum.

Syllabub

Old English preparation of whipped cream, sugar, spice, port, sherry, brandy and lemon, which has regained a measure of popularity.

Add the juice and zest of 2 lemons to 250g (8 oz) sugar and a little grated nutmeg. Add ¼ litre (½ pint) sherry or port and up to the same amount of brandy. Warm together but do *not* boil. Decant in tall jug and add ½ litre (1 pint) double cream. Whip well until foam rises to the top. Let preparation stand before serving in stem glasses. Pass savoy sponge fingers separately.

Equal amounts of sherry and port may be used in the preparation.

Tangerine

Small member of citrus fruit family with great individuality of flavour. Canned segments are mostly used in the kitchen, for salads, jellies and trifles.

Givrées. Preparation consisting of cutting an opening at the top of the fruit and removing the contents, leaving the shell intact. The juice is pressed from the fruit, combined with syrup and partly frozen. The mandarin is served filled with water ice, the lids replaced and stuck with an angelica leaf.

Tarts and Flans

Open pastry work made in 3 ways: the large, round, multi-portioned tart or flan; the small, round, square or triangle individual tartlet; and the long tart or strip flan. These are filled with various sweet preparations, i.e. fruits, preserves, creams, custards and varieties of made-up mixes. A tart is not to be confused with a pie; one is shallow and the other deep.

Tarts and flans are made with either a short crust or a flan paste. Both are short and do not rise. The flan paste is a short crust improved with egg yolks. Tart, flan and tartlet cases are made in special tins, strips are prepared on a baking tray. For most preparations the pastry case is pre-baked, for some it is baked with its filling.

Fruit flans are masked with plain and thickened syrup or sometimes with a fruit jelly. Syrup is thickened to the proportion of a tablespoon of arrowroot or cornflour to each ¼ litre (½ pint) hot syrup.

Apple Flan. Half to three-quarters fill pre-baked pastry case with well sweetened vanilla-flavoured custard and allow it to set. Prepare apples in half moons and blanch in boiling water. Arrange in neat and overlapping pattern on the custard and flash in an oven at 218°C. (425°F.) to finish cooking the apples and brown the edges. Mask with apricot syrup.

Flan de Pomme à la Baloise indicates a flan or apple tart with the fruit arranged on a bed of custard. This treatment may apply to other fruits, e.g. strawberries. These flans are also featured lined with a sweetened apple purée.

Apple Strip Flan. Prepared as for apple flan or tart, lined with custard or not.

Apple Tart. The fruit is cooked with the pastry. Peel, halve, quarter and slice apples in half moons, arrange in a neat and overlapping pattern in the case. Dredge with sugar and bake protected for 20 minutes. Remove the paper protection about 8 minutes from end of cooking time. The apple should be cooked, soft with lightly browned edges. When cool, mask with an apricot syrup coating.

Apricot Flan. When using fresh fruit, slice through, stone and arrange apricot halves neatly in an unbaked flan case. Dredge with sugar and bake for 20 minutes at 204°C. (400°F.) by which time the pastry and fruit are cooked and the apricot edges are lightly browned. Mask with apricot syrup.

When canned fruit is used, arrange in a ready-baked flan case.

Bakewell Tart. Made as a large tart or small tartlets. Pastry cases are lined with strawberry or raspberry jam, filled with a bakewell preparation and baked for 30 minutes at 218°C. (425°F.) when the filling will be firm and the topping browned.

Bakewell filling: Beat 2 egg yolks in a little water, add 120g (4 oz) white breadcrumbs, 75g (3 oz) ground almonds, 50g (2 oz) melted butter and 75g (3 oz) sugar. Add juice and grated rind of a lemon and a pinch of salt. Beat 2 egg whites stiffly, fold into the preparation and mix well. Sufficient for a 23cm (9 in) tin.

Cheese Cake. Large round American style open tart filled with a preparation of cottage cheese, eggs, cream, sugar, lemon juice and gelatine. Usually 'bought in' ready made.

Cherry Tart. Fresh fruit pitted and sweetened, arranged in flan or tartlet cases, and cooked for about 20 minutes at 204°C. (400°F.), till fruit and pastry are cooked. Cooled and masked with apricot or cherry jelly.

Canned fruit, drained and arranged in pre-cooked pastry case.

Gooseberry Tart or Tartlets. Fresh fruit topped and tailed, arranged in pastry case, sugared and baked for 20 minutes at 204°C. (400°F.), cooled and masked with apricot syrup.

When using canned gooseberries, half-cook the pastry cases, arrange the fruit and finish baking. When cool, glaze with gooseberry syrup tinted a pale green or with apricot syrup.

Grape Tartlets. Fresh green grapes, preferably muscats, arranged in pre-cooked pastry cases and masked with a thickened plain syrup.

Greengage Flan. As for apricot, using fresh fruit baked with the pastry, or canned greengages, drained and arranged in a baked case. Glaze with syrup.

Custard Flan. The original French flan. The pre-baked pastry case is filled with a stiffish custard and sprinkled with cinnamon. The custard may be flavoured and coloured as desired. It is made up, cooled, poured into the case while still liquid and then allowed to set.

Hollywood Pie. American style closed flan paste tart filled with pitted red cherries, California prunes, figs and raisins, sweetened and spiced. Served hot with vanilla sauce or cold with ice cream.

Mincemeat Slice. The term slice indicates an enclosed top and bottom pastry tart. Line a lightly greased and floured 23cm (9 in) tin with flan paste, fill with mincemeat, cover with a pastry topping, seal 2 layers, notch round with a knife, decorate paste, leave a vent, egg-wash and bake at 218°C. (425°F.) for 20 to 25 minutes. Serve hot with custard or cold with dairy or ice cream.

Normande Flan. Flan case lined with apple purée and sliced half moons of apple and baked. Topped with egg custard and baked again. Sprinkled with grated nutmeg.

Peach Flan. Prepare and bake the pastry case—large flan, tartlet or strip. Line with well sweetened and flavoured custard and leave to set. Top with sliced canned peaches evenly arranged in a neat pattern. Mask with peach or apricot syrup.

Peach, Pine and Cherry Flan. Prepare and bake a large flan case and line with custard. Arrange the 3 colourful fruits in a symmetrical pattern around a red cherry centre. Mask with warm apricot, peach or pine syrup and cool.

Pineapple Flan. Half-cook large flan or tartlet cases, cool, then arrange sliced or thin wedges of fresh or canned pineapple. Sugar to taste and finish baking. Mask with a syrup flavoured with pineapple essence.

Pumpkin Pie. 500g (1 lb) pumpkin pulp, either canned or freshly prepared, mixed with a little butter, sweetened with black treacle or brown sugar, spiced with ginger, nutmeg, cinnamon and clove, and touched with a pinch of salt. Combined with a custard prepared with $\frac{1}{4}$ litre ($\frac{1}{2}$ pint) milk, 120g (4 oz) sugar and 4 eggs. Flavoured with brandy and mixed well. Poured into a 23–25cm (9–10 in) cooked short paste shell and baked until the topping firms up. May be lattice topped.

Raisin Flan. An American dish which should, strictly speaking, be listed as Raisin Pie.

Prepare a large flan case and fill with an ample quantity of plumped California raisins, sprinkle with sugar with ground cinnamon and nutmeg added, make a lattice top preparation and bake for 20 minutes at 218°C. (425°F.).

Strawberry Flan. Ripe, sound and stalked strawberries are used in flans, tartlets, or strips. The pastry cases are pre-cooked, cooled, the fruit set in and glazed with a kirsch or maraschino flavoured syrup. For a de luxe presentation, first line the cooked pastry shells with a well-sweetened vanilla or almond flavoured crème pâtissière, or a rich custard. Another method is to mask the berries with thickened syrup or a strawberry jelly.

Tarts made with Preserves. This category employs preserves—jams, marmalades, curds and treacles—made preferably in large and small tarts and tartlets to contain the filling. The pastry cases are usually half cooked, filled and finished cooking. For added appearance large tarts are often lattice-topped finished. They are served hot or cold.

Treacle Tart. Bake pastry case for 5 minutes, cool, pour in adequate quantity of golden syrup, sprinkle with white breadcrumbs and finish baking for 15 minutes, by which time the syrup should partly absorb the crumbs, forming a soft moist pulp. May be lattice topped.

Sponge Flan Cases. Sponge flan is not to be confused with its pastry counterpart. These cases, prepared commercially from a sponge mix, are sold ready-made for filling. The cases are filled with peaches, pitted cherries, pear and other fruit, masked with jelly and finished with whipped cream. The jell is packeted in various flavours including a neutral; it is made up with water and stirred over a low heat until thickened.

American Pie Crusts. Pie and pastry crusts and cases are made with other ingredients besides short and flan pastes; with biscuits, for example. Here are 2 methods.

1. 250g (8 oz) sweet wholemeal biscuits and 75g (3 oz) butter. Crush the biscuits and mix with the melted butter. Press in a 20cm (8 in) flan case, chill and set.

2. 250g (8 oz) crushed wafer biscuits, spice, sugar, and 75g (3 oz) butter. Combine crushed biscuits with sugar, cinnamon and clove

flavouring, add melted butter, press firmly in a 20cm (8 in) flan case, bake in a moderate oven for 8 minutes and chill.

Trifle
There is really no set pattern for this well-known British Fare sweet. It is a combination of sponge, jam, custard and decorating, variations being achieved with different flavoured jams and custards. Trifles are also set in fruit jellies. In the top income bracket, the sherry trifle appears to be de rigueur.

Banana Trifle. As for royal trifle with the addition of banana rondels and banana-flavoured custard.

Elisabeth Trifle. Split sponge cakes filled with apricot jam, arranged in a soufflé dish, soaked in sherry and brandy and covered with a light chocolate mousse, prepared with beaten egg whites, sweetened with sugar and sufficient grated chocolate to colour and flavour.

Lemon Royal Trifle. As for the royal but with lemon curd filling and with lemon curd incorporated into the custard.

Peach Trifle. As for banana trifle but with sliced peaches.

Royal Trifle. Usually as for sherry trifle with milk replacing the sherry for moistening the sponge.

Sherry Trifle. Line a glass dish with a layer of sponge split through and spread with strawberry jam, moisten with sweet sherry, and cover with a thick layer of vanilla flavoured custard. When set, pipe with whipped cream and decorate with glacé cherries, angelica and whole sweet almonds.

Note: Greengage jam may replace the strawberry.

Swiss Trifle. Made up in a glass bowl as for the royal or sherry with swiss roll dressed so that the rolls show through the glass in an even pattern.

Vacherin
Multi-portion meringue case filled with crème chantilly or other cream and various fruits. The vacherin may be vanilla-flavoured or coloured and flavoured with fruit juices. The filling determines the name, i.e. Vacherin Chantilly, aux Fraises, aux Marrons, aux Fruits.

The vacherin case or shell is piped out starting from the base in the centre, working outwards and completing the sides which are usually topped and decorated with small meringue shapes.

Waffle (Gaufre)
A batter cooked to order in a waffle iron. The original was a sweet affair dredged with icing sugar. Now featured savoury with grilled bacon, fried egg, minced chicken or as a cheese waffle, as well as sweet, coloured and flavoured with fruits, or with maple syrup, chocolate, coffee fudge sauces and ice creams.

Prepared from ready-mix or as follows. Scale of ingredients: 500g (1 lb) flour to ½ litre (1 pint) milk and 120g (4 oz) sugar, plus 25g (1 oz) baking powder, 120g (4 oz) butter and 4 eggs.

Sift flour and baking powder, heat milk with sugar and butter and whisk. Rain in flour slowly, whisking to a creamy texture. Separate eggs. Beat the yolks and add to preparation and then the whisked whites. Continue beating and then stand for 30 minutes. Pre-heat waffle iron, brush with melted butter, pour in a ladle of batter and cook.

For the savoury version omit sugar and season with salt and pepper. Brush iron with olive oil.

For cheese waffle load batter with grated parmesan.

Wild Strawberries (Fraises des Bois)
Small and sweet, red wild strawberries may be prepared in any of the ways indicated for the large berries as well as with just sugar and cream. The wild berry cans and freezes well.

Champagne (au). Prepared berries macerated with sugar and champagne. Served with cream. This preparation is also featured macerated in claret.

Rêve de Bébé. Equal quantities of berries and diced fresh pineapple macerated in sugar, kirsch and maraschino, lié in crème chantilly and served en surprise in a hollowed out pineapple.

Yogurt
Cultured milk food originating from Eastern Europe. The yogurt we know is made in a variety of flavours and marketed in throw-away cartons. Prepared from warmed homogenized fresh skimmed milk inoculated with 2 natural lactic cultures, i.e. *Lactobacillus Bulgarious* and *Streptococcus Thermophilus* and incubated when it becomes thick and creamy. Yogurt is stored under cold and served chilled. Varieties include apple, apricot, banana, bilbury, blackberry, blackcurrant, cherry, chocolate, cocktail, coffee, grapefruit, hazelnut, lemon, mandarin, natural, orange, pineapple, prune, raspberry, strawberry and various specialities. Eaten as it is or served with fruit compotes, salad and other sweets. Featured for breakfast and also used as a salad dressing pinked with paprika.

Cultured Cream. Soured or cultured cream, complementary to yogurt. Fresh single cream heated and handled in a similar way to yogurt. Texture resembles whipped double cream.

DECORATIVE AND PASTRY WORK

Icings
Fondant Icing. This is a hard icing. It may be purchased ready-made when it just requires breaking down with syrup, colouring and flavouring.

To prepare, dissolve 1 kilo (2 lb) sugar in $\frac{1}{2}$ litre (1 pint) water. When melted apply heat and skim as impurities rise to the surface. Cook preparation to the small ball stage, 112°C. (236°F.). Remove from heat, colour and flavour as required and work on an oiled slab with a palette knife. A graincutter must also be added, i.e. juice of 2 lemons added to the syrup or 120g (4 oz) glucose added to the original sugar and water preparation.

Fondant icing may be coloured and flavoured almond with essence, chocolate grated with the sugar, coffee with strong essence, lemon or orange with zest and juice, pink, pineapple, vanilla and violet with appropriate essences and colourings.

Royal Icing. Sieve 500g (1 lb) icing sugar, place in a bowl and combine with 4 egg whites. Mix to a smooth preparation with a wooden spoon. Add juice of a lemon. Colour and flavour as required. Beat well, until preparation stands in peaks. Use with a palette knife or in a piping bag.

Rock Sugar. Used in cake decorating to resemble snow, but also coloured as required.

Boil together at 138°C. (280°F.) 2 kilo (4 lb) loaf sugar with $\frac{1}{2}$ litre (1 pint) water. Whisk in 250g (8 oz) royal icing and beat until the preparation starts to aerate. Turn into a coarse sieve and collect the rock sugar as it falls through. Leave to cool.

Gum Paste or Pastillage

Employed in making sugar work for grandes pièces and other displays.

Basic formula: 50g (2 oz) gum tragacanth, 212g ($7\frac{1}{2}$ oz) cold water, $1\frac{1}{4}$ kilo ($2\frac{1}{2}$ lb) icing sugar, 25g (1 oz) cornflour or pure starch.

Soak the gum for 24 hours in the water, stirring occasionally. Work the preparation until it is smooth and slowly rain in the icing sugar. Add a spot of blue colouring to give brilliance and work to a firm paste. Add the cornflour or starch which makes the preparation easy to handle.

Turn out on a marble slab and continue to work with a palette knife. Cover the paste first with a dry and then with a damp cloth to prevent a skin forming. The paste is now ready for use. It may be coloured as required during the preparation or when made up, dry painted with brushes, compounds or culinary paints.

Starch is generally favoured, but this makes the preparation inedible. Gum tragacanth could be replaced by a concentrated solution of gelatine.

Nougatine

Wholly edible sugar paste used in making various decorative pieces.

Basic formula: 500g (1 lb) finely chopped almond nibs, $1\frac{1}{2}$ kilo (3 lb) sugar, juice of $\frac{1}{4}$ lemon.

Lightly roast the chopped almonds. Place sugar and lemon in a pan and melt slowly over heat, stirring with a wooden spoon. When sugar has melted it will turn light brown and start to boil. At this stage add the chopped, roasted almonds, remove from heat and stir well. Turn out on lightly oiled marble slab and work with a palette knife. The nougatine is now ready. It is worked as cooked sugar and may be kept pliable in an oiled tray in a medium oven. It may be rolled out to any thickness with an oiled metal rolling pin or cut and shaped to any pattern.

Almond Paste
Almond paste or icing is prepared with ground almonds made on premises.
Method 1: Blanch, skin and pound 250g (8 oz) sweet almonds moistened with rosewater, or moisten same quantity of ground almonds with rosewater. Beat 2 egg whites to stiff froth and add to the almond preparation with 250g (8 oz) castor sugar. Beat to a smooth paste.
Method 2: Beat 2 egg yolks with a few drops of vanilla essence. Mix 360g (12 oz) ground almonds, 175g (6 oz) castor sugar and 175g (6 oz) icing sugar together. Combine both preparations, add juice of half a lemon, work to a smooth, pliable paste.
Method 3: Beat a little orange and rosewater with 2 egg yolks. Mix 500g (1 lb) icing sugar with 360g (12 oz) ground sweet almonds and combine with the egg preparation. Fold in 2 stiffly beaten egg whites and work to a smooth, pliable paste.

Almond paste is always improved with the addition of brandy or rum.

Marzipan
Similar preparation to almond paste. Heat 250g (8 oz) sweet almonds and 500g (1 lb) bitter almonds, blanch, skin and pound in a mortar with rosewater. Place in a pan with 120g (4 oz) icing sugar. Apply heat and stir till the paste dries. Turn out on a sugar-dredged slab, work well and bind with an egg white.

Or, heat 750g (1½ lb) ground almonds, with 120g (4 oz) sugar and a little rosewater until the paste is smooth. Turn out on sugared slab, bind with an egg white, and knead into a pliable paste.

Marzipan may be coloured and flavoured with brandy or rum. Commercially prepared marzipans (and almond pastes) in various flavours (almond, apricot, nougat, noisette, and so on) are obtainable for 'buying in' for all pastry and bakery work.

Pastry
There are many different types of pastry and various ways of making it. Listed here are the best known basic kinds of paste.

Flan Paste. Scale of ingredients: 500g (1 lb) flour, 50g (2 oz) sugar, 15g ($\frac{1}{2}$ oz) salt, 250g ($1\frac{1}{2}$ lb) butter, 2 egg yolks, water.

Sift flour, sugar and salt together, break in the butter in pieces and rub well into the flour with fingertips. Make a well in the centre, add the egg yolks and sufficient water to form a stiff dough. Knead well and rest in a cool place. Roll out and use as soon as possible.

Note: Flan paste is an enriched short paste.

Puff Paste. Scale of ingredients: 500g (1 lb) flour, 15g ($\frac{1}{2}$ oz) salt, juice of 2 lemons, $\frac{1}{4}$ litre ($\frac{1}{2}$ pint) water, 500g (1 lb) butter.

Sift flour and salt and make a well in the centre. Add lemon juice and cold water and mix into a stiff dough. Rest for 10 minutes. Roll out, place softened butter in centre and fold into a square. Roll out, away from you, till 3 times its length and $\frac{1}{2}$cm (1 in) thick. Fold into a square. Turn paste round to roll in opposite direction and roll out again till 3 times its length and $\frac{1}{2}$cm (1 in) thick. Fold into a square. Rest for 10 minutes. Turn paste round and roll out again till 3 times its length and $\frac{1}{2}$cm (1 in) thick. Fold into a square. Repeat the operation and rest for 10 minutes. Repeat the rolling operation twice more. Rest for 10 minutes. The paste has now been rolled 6 times and folded 18 times and is ready for use.

Note: The paste is rolled *away* frim the chef, reversed at each rolling, worked on a floured slab using ample flour dredging.

Rough Puff pastry prescribes 500g (1 lb) flour to 360g ($\frac{3}{4}$ lb) fat.

Short Paste. Scale of ingredients: 500g (1 lb) flour, teaspoon baking powder, 25g (1 oz) salt, 250g (8 oz) butter, $\frac{1}{8}$ litre ($\frac{1}{4}$ pint) water.

Sift flour, baking powder and salt, break the butter in pieces over the preparation and rub together with fingertips into a fine and granular mix. Make a well in the centre, add the water and mix into a stiff dough. Knead well, rest in a cool place, roll out and use as soon as possible.

Pastry Mixes. A wide variety of these lines are on the market, including short, puff, choux, suet, as well as buns, batter, cake and pudding mixes. In considering mixes, quality and price are important factors. Properly handled, i.e. following the manufacturers' instructions, good results are obtained from these useful lines. In all cases samples should be tested to ascertain quality and end results.

Friandises

Assorted petits fours, a selection of sweetmeats served at the end of a meal with the coffee. Consists of various sweets, glazed and candied fruits, small pastries and marzipan goods. Listed on menus as Frivolités, Gourmandises, Miniardises, Douceurs des Dames. The goods are dressed in paper cases and arranged on a dish.

Chocolates. Liqueur and other de luxe and sometimes branded chocolates.

Fondants. Various flavours: almond, chocolate, coconut, coffee, crème de menthe, lemon, orange, peppermint, pineapple, pink, vanilla.

Glazed Fruits. Whole grapes, pine cubes, orange and mandarin quarters, dipped in or masked with sugar, cooked to the small crack stage, cooled on a marble slab.

Marzipan. Pitted dates and prunes stuffed with plain and coloured marzipan, rolled in sugar or sugar glazed. Marzipan walnuts, coloured, rolled into balls, stuck with halves of walnut, glazed with sugar or rolled in sugar.

Mints. After dinner mints: After Eight, Glacier and similar quality goods.

Nougat. Best quality cut into cubes.

Petit-Four Pastries. 'Small ovens' de luxe choux pastries, mini-size, filled with liqueur-flavoured crème pâtissière and soft fondant ice glazed.

Petits-Fours Sec. Various small pastry goods, e.g. palets de dame and langues de chat, made with a sweet biscuit type of appareil, sometimes with currants. 'Bought in' or kitchen made.
Palets de Dame: Cream 250g (8 oz) butter with 250g (8 oz) sugar, add 4 eggs, one at a time, 300g (10 oz) sieved flour, few currants and vanilla essence. Pipe out in rondels on lightly greased tray. Bake at 204°C. (400°F.) until edges are lightly brown.
Langues de chat are made with a similar mix and baked in the same way, but piped out in short lengths thinning down in the centre.

Other Sweetmeats. Peppermint creams, orange creams, lemon creams, toffee, fudge and turkish delight.

Small Pastry Goods

This term covers a range of individual sized puff pastry lines.

Chausson. Pastry turnover. Round piece of puff pastry filled with apple or fruit purée, jam, marmalade or curd, folded over, egg-washed, sugar dredged and baked. Also made with 2 pieces, filled, sealed and baked.

Conversations. Lattice-topped puff paste tartlets filled with frangipane and glazed.

Florentines. Thin puff paste biscuit filled with diced candied fruits and nuts and chocolate coated.

Galette. Round, puff paste cake made in various sizes.

Jalousies. Croustades of puff paste filled with frangipane, jam or cream filling, lattice topped, egg-washed and baked.

Mirilitons. Puffs filled with a preparation of egg yolk, cream butter and orange water.

Palmiers. Thickness of puff paste, each side folded inwards into a sleeve, cut into portions, turned on their sides to reveal the folds in the pastry, lightly flattened, painted with syrup and baked on a greased tray.

Sablées. Round puff paste biscuit type of pastry filled with frangipane paste.

ICE CREAM AND ICED CONFECTIONS

The origins of iced confections are traced to Asia. Water ices were known in China, India and Persia. In antiquity Alexander the Great was partial to iced drinks and Emperor Nero to frozen desserts. Slaves fetched ice from the mountains to satisfy the tastes of their masters. Marco Polo the Venetian traveller brought back recipes for ices as well as pasta from his Asiatic travels. From then on the story of iced confections is that of gastronomy.

The Italians were the first to make frozen cream. When Catherine de Medicis of Italy became Queen to King Henry II of France she brought her cuisiniers and glaciers with her. Later, during the reign of Charles I, ice cream was introduced to England. Ice cream, like gastronomy, born in Italy during the Renaissance, passed to France, where it was perfected, and thence onto England and the New World. For generations Italians excelled at ice cream, and they were the first to exploit its manufacture on a commercial basis in France, England and the United States of America. The Italian street vendor selling hokey pokey (ecco un pocco) is a sight still within living memory.

By the 1960s ice cream had developed into an industry. From a seasonal commodity it became a year-round one. It is manufactured on a similar scale to bread with equal scientific application in manufacturing, marketing and distributing. It is also subjected to similar control and supervision. Ice cream, defined as 'any frozen confection for sale to the public containing milk or cream', must conform to a number of regulations. Because of this and because the preparation now requires special equipment and know-how, on-premise manufacture is largely relinquished in favour of 'buying in' the ready-made commodity. Just as few now bake their own bread, only a few caterers make their own ice cream. Manufacturers make ice cream, iced confections and specialities in a comprehensive range.

Types

Broadly there are two types of ices: (a) cream ice and (b) water, syrup and fruit ice.

The cream is made from a custard mix of various types, described as standard and dairy ice cream. The second type are made with fruit pulp and syrup with, in certain preparations, cream added. The original cream ice is made with milk or cream, sugar, eggs and

275

flavouring. In the manufactured product new methods and processes are applied and the basic commodities may be simulated according to type, quality and price. This in no way detracts from quality; it is a matter of food technology and economics. The modern factory with a vast output handles such raw materials as butter, cream, milk, vegetable fat, vanilla and chocolate beans, sugar and fruit purées in astronomical quantities.

There are also ready or instant mixes made in various flavours for on-premise manufacture.

The quality of ice cream is told by the texture, appearance and taste. It should be smooth and creamy, of good colour and with a recognizable flavour.

Soft Ice Cream

Soft ice cream has become very popular. It is made from a cold mix and is dispensed from special equipment. Principally vanilla in flavour, the majority of soft ice creams are marketed ready-made, under registered names or by franchise.

The Service of Ice Cream

Ice cream is sold in half and one gallon drums, in bricks and individual portions. The usual flavours are vanilla, strawberry, chocolate and coffee. Many other flavours and combined varieties are sold. Bulk ice cream is dispensed with scoop servers termed 'dishers'. These are made in the following sizes at 12, 16, 20, 24, 30, 40 and 60 servings to the quart basic.

For a straight service the ice cream is presented in a coupe with plain or fancy wafers. The addition of the wafer came from the original custom of serving biscuits with ices to counteract the sudden cold of the confection.

The creation of the wafer is not without interest. A complicated banquet was being planned for an outside function. All details were settled except the provision, disposal and washing-up of plates upon which an elaborate iced dessert would be served. The problem was discussed at some length and in sheer desperation, half joking, someone suggested why not let the guests eat the plates! Thus was born the wafer biscuit and, incidentally, the ice cream cone.

The recipes listed are basic for custard ice cream; they are rich, wholesome and full flavoured. All ices may, as required, be flavoured with such liqueurs as kirsch, maraschino and others.

Vanilla Ice Cream. 2 litres (4 pints) milk, 500g (1 lb) sugar, salt, vanilla pod, 14 egg yolks, $\frac{1}{2}$ litre (1 pint) cream.

Infuse milk, sugar, pinch of salt and vanilla pod and bring to the boil. Remove pod and slowly add beaten egg yolks. Maintain heat, stir, thicken but do not boil. When thick and creamy, remove, strain and cool. When cold beat in the cream and freeze.

Chocolate Ice Cream. Render down 400–500g (14–16 oz) plain chocolate and combine with water into a smooth paste. Add to the milk and sugar preparation and proceed as for vanilla ice cream.

Coffee Ice Cream. Proceed as for vanilla adding coffee essence as required to the milk and sugar preparation.

Strawberry Ice Cream. Proceed as for vanilla, adding up to 1 litre (2 pints) fruit purée to each 2 litres (4 pints) milk. With all fruit flavours the best results are obtained from fruit purée; the true flavour is difficult to produce synthetically by essences.

Water Ices

Syrup and fruit ices are now known as sorbets or by the American term sherbert.

Lemon Ice. 2 or 3 lemons, 500g (1 lb) lump sugar, $\frac{1}{2}$ litre (1 pint) water, $\frac{1}{6}$ litre ($\frac{1}{3}$ pint) lemon juice, orange juice.

Rub lemons with lump sugar to collect zest. Place these and remaining sugar lumps in a pan, add water and let sugar dissolve. Apply heat, bring to boil and simmer for 10 minutes. Strain syrup and let it cool. Add strained lemon juice and a little orange juice, and freeze.

Note: This recipe gives a plain lemon water ice. A $\frac{1}{8}$ litre ($\frac{1}{4}$ pint) cream may be added, prior to freezing, for a richer preparation.

Lemon and Orange Ice. To $\frac{1}{2}$ litre (1 pint) syrup add a little mixed orange and lemon zest, simmer to colour and strain. Add $\frac{1}{4}$ litre ($\frac{1}{2}$ pint) lemon juice and $\frac{1}{4}$ litre ($\frac{1}{2}$ pint) orange juice. Blend well and freeze. If richer mix is required add 0.14 litre ($\frac{1}{4}$ pint) cream prior to freezing.

Lime Ice. Proceed as for lemon ice using lime juice and zest in green compound. Touch with orange juice prior to freezing.

Liqueur Ices. Add juice of 2 lemons to $\frac{1}{2}$ litre (1 pint) syrup. Flavour with a liqueur colour as required and freeze. Suggested liqueurs for these sorbets: kirsch, curaçao, anisette, grand marnier, bénédictine, green and yellow chartreuse, maraschino, crème de menthe, cherry brandy and cointreau. Use ample liqueur so flavour gets through.

Melon and Ginger Ice. Combine $\frac{1}{2}$ litre (1 pint) syrup with $\frac{1}{2}$ litre (1 pint) melon pulp. Add juice of 2 lemons, flavour with ground ginger, colour as required to a pale green or orange, mix well and freeze.

Avocado pear ice is made in a similar manner; check flavour with cinnamon and nutmeg.

Orange Ice. Prepare as for lemon, using orange juice and zest. Zest provides colouring matter. Touch preparation with lemon juice prior to freezing.

Pineapple Ice. Prepare as for lemon ice, using fresh pine juice and a little lemon juice.

Strawberry Water Ice. ½ litre (1 pint) syrup, ½ litre (1 pint) straw-berry pulp, juice of 2 lemons.

Prepare a syrup with equal quantities of sugar and water, boiled for 10 minutes strained and cooled. Add an equal quantity of strawberry pulp to the syrup and strain in lemon juice. Mix and freeze.

Note: This is a basic recipe for all fruit water ices. Lemon juice acts as a graincutter, i.e. prevents crystallization. Other flavours include raspberry, blackcurrant, peach, redcurrant, cranberry and pear. For a richer mix add 0.14 litre (¼ pint) cream before freezing.

Tangerine Ice. Proceed as for lemon ice, using tangerine juice and zest. Touch the mix with lemon juice.

Fancy Ices

Ice cream masked with a sweet sauce and decorated. Some are simple, such as ice cream with chocolate or melba sauce, others are more complex, such as biscuit glacé and the frozen baked alaska.

Coupes and Sundaes

Coupes, sundaes, parfaits and glories are all similar in idea and preparation, but there are slight differences and they have therefore been listed in 2 groups.

They all consist of permutations of cream and water ices, fruits and sauces. Some are standard classified named dishes, others are featured as individual house specialities.

Their assembly and decoration relies upon creative and artistic ingenuity for eye and palate appeal, i.e. colour and flavour contrasts. They are Ice Cream Parlour innovations which have passed into the culinary repertoire.

Where sauces are indicated they should be of sufficient consistency to cling to ice cream or fruit. A wide variety of decorations is used in these preparations, including candied fruits and peels chopped in syrup; coloured cake crumbs; crystallized flowers; coconut, desiccated and toasted; glacé cherries; chocolate, vermicelli, broken pieces, milk flake; hundreds and thousands; broken meringue shells; nuts, whole, chopped, desiccated, roasted and coloured almonds; wafers, plain sugared, fancy pompadour.

The coupe is presented in a shallow coupe jacques and the sundae in a shallow, oblong dish or in a medium-sized long glass. These lines can be interchanged, and so provide a wide variety of choice. Many years ago the sale of ice cream sodas was banned for sale on a Sunday in the Illinois town of Evanston. The local drug stores got around this by substituting syrup for soda and called the preparation a Sunday Soda, the origin of the sundae. Coupe is much older and is of French origin.

Adelina. Chocolate ice cream foundation dressed with strawberries in kirsch, decorated with crème chantilly piping and topped with a whole berry.

Alexis. Vanilla and coffee ice, compote of kummel-flavoured cherries, piped with crème chantilly and topped with a glacé cherry.

American Beauty. Peach ice, crushed pineapple, cherry syrup whipped cream, chopped nuts and glacé cherries.

Banana Coupe. Vanilla and strawberry ice cream, topped with sliced banana masked with chocolate sauce, piped with crème chantilly, sprinkled with chopped nuts.

Banana Split. In a sundae dish arrange 3 dishers of ice cream, vanilla, chocolate and strawberry. Split a banana lengthways and place one half on either side. Mask the ices with chocolate sauce. Decorate generously with whipped cream and glacé cherries.

Banana Sundae. Vanilla or strawberry ice, or mixed ices, sliced banana, chocolate sauce masked.

Carina. Vanilla, strawberry and coffee ice, orange and mandarin segments, whipped cream and a cordon of melba sauce.

(Speciality of former Pullman Car Company, named after car Carina which ran in Golden Arrow service.)

Chocolate Favourite. Chocolate ice, chocolate sauce, whipped cream, crystallized violets and flaked milk chocolate.

Cointreau (au). Fresh orange segments sweetened and mixed with cointreau, arranged on a foundation of standard vanilla ice cream or soft ice cream.

Creole. Diced pineapple and banana in kirsch topped with rum-flavoured lemon water ice. Decorated with diced candied fruit in syrup and topped with a glacé cherry set in a star of crème chantilly.

Edna May. Vanilla ice, candied cherries, masked with melba sauce, crème chantilly decorated.

Elysée. Vanilla ice, marrons glacés in kirsch syrup with crème chantilly piping.

(Speciality of the one-time Elysée Palace Hotel, Paris.)

Fruit Salad Sundae. Mixed ice to choice, fruit salad, melba sauce, nuts and whipped cream.

Hélène. Strawberry and chocolate ice, pear masked with chocolate sauce, crème chantilly and walnut topping.

Hot Chocolate Fudge. Vanilla ice served with hot chocolate sauce. There are also coffee and butterscotch hot fudges.

Jacques. Sweetened and kirsch-flavoured macédoine of fresh fruit with lemon and strawberry ice and a star or restrained piping of whipped cream. Diced candied fruit in syrup may be used in place of fresh fruit.

In recent times, any combination of fruit and ice cream passes under the name of jacques, but the above are the original versions of a popular preparation. Jacques is almost a generic name for sundae.

Java. Pistachio ice cream generously garnished with diced preserved ginger in syrup and piped with crème chantilly.

Mandarin. Tangerine ice, mandarin segments, stars of whipped cream, glacé cherry topping.

Mauna Loa. Kirsch-flavoured ice cream, crushed pineapple, masked with half-whipped cream and decorated with shredded coconut in syrup.

Melbas. Melbas may be featured as coupes and sundaes with various fruits and garnishings.

Melon Split. In a long sundae glass arrange 3 dishers of ice cream, vanilla, chocolate and strawberry. Set a long rinded slice of ripe melon either side, mask the ices with melba sauce, decorate with chopped ginger, desiccated coconut, whipped cream and glacé cherries.

Myrtle. Ice cream to choice garnished with diced candied fruit in syrup, with a predominence of ginger and a border of crème chantilly. *Note*: Diced candied peel and fruit with an equal amount of ginger in syrup is known as Myrtle garnish. There is also a Myrtle Sundae. (Former Pullman Car Company speciality named after car Myrtle.)

Nut Sundaes. Popular sundaes made with vanilla or strawberry mixed ice cream masked with chocolate, coffee, marshmallow or butterscotch sauces and sprinkled generously with chopped nuts.

Palm Springs. Vanilla ice with diced dates macerated in brandy, piped with crème chantilly, coloured and flavoured with melba sauce.

Peach Delight. Coffee ice, sliced peaches, marshmallow sauce, hundreds and thousands and glacé cherries.

Peanut Crunch Nut Sundae. Vanilla ice, marshmallow sauce and chopped peanuts.

Pompadour. Raspberries and strawberries on orange water ice, masked with melba sauce and decorated with crème chantilly.

Royale. Vanilla and coffee ice, diced fruit cocktail, whipped cream and glacé cherry. *Note*: The term royale is sometimes used to describe coupes and sundaes.

Tsarina. Pitted cherries in curaçao dressed on a foundation of lemon water ice, piped with a border of crème chantilly flavoured with lemon essence and topped with a maraschino cherry. The cherries may be canned, or fresh and cooked in a light syrup.

Tutti-Fruitti. Vanilla ice studded with diced candied fruits, garnished with sliced peaches, pineapple and cherry, decorated with whipped cream and glacé cherries.

280

Twin Sundae. Arrange a portion of vanilla ice and another of strawberry side by side in an oval sundae dish. Mask one with chocolate and the other with melba sauce. Finish one with chopped nuts and the other with candied fruit in syrup. Top with glacé cherries and walnuts. Set a star of whipped cream, top with cherry and angelica in the centre.

Venus. Vanilla ice and strawberries, decorated with crystallized violets and whipped cream.

Parfaits and Glories
These are dressed in tall knickerbocker glory glasses.

Crème de Menthe Parfait. Commence with walnuts in syrup, chopped mint jelly, vanilla ice, chopped lime jelly, minted ice, crème de menthe cherries in syrup, lime ice, chopped mint jelly, whipped cream, and top with crème de menthe cherry.

Devon Belle Parfait. Poached pear halves in maraschino syrup dressed on a foundation of vanilla and strawberry ice cream. Garnished generously with Devonshire cream, sprinkled with flaked milk chocolate and topped with a glacé cherry.
(Speciality of the former Devon Belle all-Pullman train.)

Dusty Road Parfait. Layer of butterscotch sauce, chocolate ice, more butterscotch, coffee ice, whipped cream, flaked milk chocolate and maraschino cherry topping.
(Speciality of Weekes Restaurant, Tunbridge Wells, Kent.)

Jamaican Sun Parfait. Build up in a sundae glass a layer of white honey, disher of vanilla ice cream, cordon of rum-flavoured coffee essence, topping of banana rondels, demarara sugar, honey, whipped cream and glacé cherry.
(Speciality of Weekes Restaurant, Tunbridge Wells, Kent.)

Knickerbocker Glory. Commence with strawberries in syrup, vanilla ice, sliced peaches, strawberry ice, ground nuts, whipped cream, chopped nuts and strawberry topping.

Maraschino Cherry Parfait. Disher of vanilla ice cream in a parfait glass, garnished with compote of pitted cherries in maraschino syrup, topped with whipped cream and walnuts.

My Lady Parfait. Start with honey and build up with vanilla ice, sliced peaches in syrup, violet ice cream, raspberries in syrup, peach ice, cherries in syrup, marshmallow, whipped cream, crystallized violets and walnut topping.

Palm Beach Glory. Begin with layer of honey and follow with orange ice, walnuts in syrup, vanilla ice, marshmallow, lemon ice, crushed fruits in syrup, marshmallow topping and glacé cherry.

Strawberry Glory. Build up with chopped strawberry jelly, vanilla ice, cherries in syrup, strawberry ice, strawberries in syrup, fresh

281

cream, chocolate ice, whipped cream, flaked milk chocolate, topped with a strawberry.

Summer Parfait. Build up with cherries in syrup, coffee ice, crushed pineapple, vanilla ice, sliced peaches, chocolate ice, raspberries in syrup, whipped cream, chopped nuts and strawberry topping.

Tia Maria Parfait. In a tall parfait glass, build up with coffee ice cream, crushed pineapple in tia maria liqueur, vanilla ice, candied red cherries in tia maria, coffee ice, whipped cream topping with angelica and glacé cherries.

Bombes

Francatelli, the celebrated Victorian chef, is credited with the creation of the bombe. It was inspired by the Crimea War and the iced confection was cylinder shaped like a bomb and presented veiled with red spun sugar to simulate an explosive force.

Bombes are prepared from rich cream ice mixes and with water ices, usually in different flavours. The mix is packed in a greaseproof-paper lined mould and frozen for about 2 hours. The moulds vary from $\frac{1}{4}$ kilo ($\frac{1}{2}$ lb) to $1\frac{1}{4}$ kilo ($2\frac{1}{2}$ lb) capacity. For service, the bombe is unmoulded and set on a doily on a dish, piped with whipped cream scrolls and decorated, as required, with glacé fruits.

Basic bombe mix: To each pint of syrup add 6 egg yolks and $\frac{1}{2}$ litre (1 pint) cream. Make the syrup with equal parts of sugar and water, boil for 10 minutes, then strain in the juice of 2 lemons per $\frac{1}{2}$ litre (1 pint) syrup. Beat egg yolks in a copper bowl in a bain-marie and slowly add syrup. Beat to a sabayon. Add desired flavouring and fold in the stiffly whisked cream.

For fruit ice creams, use $\frac{1}{2}$ litre (1 pint) fruit purée to each $\frac{1}{2}$ litre (1 pint) of syrup. Bombe mixes must be well creamed to prevent iciness when freezing.

The varieties of bombes are endless; these are the best known.

Alhambra. Strawberry ice coated by vanilla.

Alsacienne. Vanilla and chocolate ice with pistachio nuts.

Américaine. Strawberry ice cream outside with orange water ice centre.

Billet-de-Banque. Pralined vanilla ice cream, kirsch flavoured.

Cardinal. Strawberry and vanilla ice.

Czarina. Vanilla ice cream flavoured with kummel.

Dame Blanche. Vanilla ice piped up with crème chantilly.

Diplomate. Vanilla ice cream flavoured with maraschino, loaded with diced candied fruit.

Hélène. Vanilla ice served with hot chocolate sauce.

Jamaican. Pineapple ice flavoured with rum and orange ice.

Liqueurs (aux). Ice cream to choice flavoured with any type of liqueur.

Marquise. Peach and orange ice creams loaded with glacé cherries.

Medicis. Peach ice flavoured with brandy and loaded with diced candied fruits.

Napolitaine. Pistachio, chocolate and vanilla ices in 3 layers.

Nesselrode. Orange water ice centre, vanilla ice cream coating, kirsch flavoured.

Plombière. Vanilla ice loaded with praline and chopped candied fruits.

Sicilienne. Lemon water ice centre, pralined vanilla ice coating.

Suzanne. Pineapple ice flavoured with rum centre, vanilla ice loaded with redcurrant preserve outside.

Tortoni. Pralined coffee ice cream.

Tutti-Frutti. Lemon water ice centre, strawberry ice cream coating flecked with candied fruits.

Victoria. Strawberry and vanilla ice cream loaded with diced candied fruits.

Cassatas

Specialities of the Sicilienne glaciers. Composite moulded ices consisting of cream ice centres loaded with candied fruits and bonbons, covered by a water or different flavoured ice cream. Usually flavoured with maraschino.

Cassata Denise. Liqueur ice cream centre containing glacé fruits, nuts and biscuits wrapped in shell of milk chocolate ice cream.

Cassata Véronique. Four layer cassata of butterscotch, pistachio and vanilla ice cream with cassata fillings.

Biscuit Glacé

The iced biscuit, Pavé Glacé or Parfait (not to be confused with the sundae), is a similar preparation to the bombe but moulded in squares. The popular biscuit or parfait is the ice cream brick now made in so many permutations of flavours and loadings. Biscuits, pavés (or bricks) and parfaits are presented with care. The simple way is to pipe with whipped cream and decorate with glacé fruit. More elaborate ways indicate enclosing the sides with savoy sponge fingers held in place by butter cream, comb scraping the top and decorating with various fruits. Another way is to coat the sides with chopped nuts stuck with cream and top with glacé fruit.

Biscuit Cecil. Liqueur-flavoured vanilla, strawberry and orange ice creams.

Biscuit Princesse. Pralined vanilla and orange ice cream.

Melon Surprise. Ice cream made into a melon with orange water ice centre, outer cover of vanilla coated with melon green.

Napolitaine. One of the best known biscuits, made in 3 flavours; pistachio, strawberry and vanilla.

Panaché. A biscuit composed of 3 or 4 ice creams.

Pralinée. Any flavour ice cream loaded with chopped grilled almonds or assorted nuts.

Tutti-Frutti. Lemon and strawberry ice filled with diced candied fruits.

Iced Mousses and Iced Puddings

Ice cream mousse, often described as iced soufflé or pudding, is a light and delicate preparation. The mousse is moulded with care in a soufflé dish supported by a paper collar to hold the mix in place during the 3–4 hour freezing operation. These mousses and puddings are made in such flavours as vanilla, strawberry, raspberry and coffee, and are always liqueur flavoured.

Basic recipe: 10 egg whites, $\frac{1}{2}$ litre (1 pint) syrup, $\frac{1}{2}$ litre (1 pint) fruit purée, $\frac{1}{2}$ litre (1 pint) cream.

Whisk the egg whites into the cold syrup, beat in the fruit purée, then beat in the cream. Check flavour as required. Fold into a soufflé dish and freeze.

Sorbet

A light water ice served at a banquet between the entrée and the roast, to act as a digestif and aperitif and prepare the stomach for the courses to follow. In this context the sorbet is usually flavoured with a liqueur or wine. Sorbets are also presented 'en surprise', e.g. orange water ice in a hollowed out orange, lemon water ice in a hollowed out lemon, grapefruit water ice in half a grapefruit shell topped with a cherry. Though these are really specialities, they are often listed as sorbet ices.

Granité

Very light sorbet, thin frozen fruit syrup.

Marquise

Pineapple, strawberry or other de luxe fruit syrup, prepared from the fresh fruit, combined with crème chantilly, flavoured with kirsch, frozen and served in stem glasses. A type of sorbet.

Spoom

Sorbet or sherbet preparation. A light water ice to which twice its quantity of Italian meringue mix is added. The preparation is combined and then frozen. It should be very light and frothy. It is served in stem glasses. Spooms are usually flavoured with champagne or other wine.

Igloo

Unglazed choux paste profiteroles filled with soft vanilla ice cream and dished masked with chocolate or butterscotch sauce.

(House speciality of Golden Egg Restaurants.)

Frozen Baked Alaska

A sensational permutation of flavours and a contrast of temperatures. Despite its American name, it is not of recent origin. The combination of hot meringue crust with iced confection belongs to 'la cuisine classique' and first came to the notice of Baron Brisse in 1866. The Baron, famous gastronome and culinary writer, was introduced to the novelty by a Chinese chef of a Far Eastern Emissary visiting Paris and staying at the Grand Hotel with a trade delegation. The recognized works of French cuisine list several preparations based on the Alaska theme such as Soufflée Grand Succes, Soufflée Mylady, Soufflée Vesuvius, Omelette Norvegienne and Omelette en Surprise.

On an oval dish, place a layer of plain sponge sauced over with fruit juice or liqueur. Then arrange a generous quantity of ice cream (a brick or pavé will do), top with sweetened soft berries—strawberry, raspberry, loganberry, any other soft fruit or a fruit salad—and cover with a good heaping of meringue. Smooth over, pipe up or leave rough, flash in a hot oven for 3 minutes until the meringue browns, and serve immediately.

Variety is injected by various ice cream flavours, different fruits and liqueurs and colouring the meringue topping. Vesuvius is especially interesting: this simulates a volcano complete with eruption effects through a receptacle at the summit containing a spirit which, at the point of service, is ignited for all to admire.

Fried Ice Cream

Sliced portioned napolitaine ice cream brick hardened by freezing to a very low temperature, dipped in spiced sweet batter, deep fried to a golden brown, drained and served with hot chocolate sauce.

EXHIBITION WORK

All work of this nature must be planned with care and attention to detail. The actual working should be performed from sketches or models. The theory can be taught, but proficiency comes only by practical application and experience, by observing a skilled craftsman at work and by the study of the works of others.

Creative artistry and display work is admired on cold buffets and tables and at exhibitions such as the Salon Culinaire Internationale de Londres at Hotelympia, London. It is important this creativity and culinary showmanship be perpetuated and be passed forward from the master craftsman to future generations of chefs and cooks.

285

Sugar Work

Sugar is pulled, blown, spun, modelled and manipulated at various temperatures. The key point of this work is to reach the exact temperature and consistency for the specific purpose required. It can be hand tested but unless very experienced it is best to use a sugar thermometer. *Basic sugar preparation:* 1 kilo (2 lb) lump sugar to ½ litre (1 pint) water. Place sugar in a sugar pan and cover with the water. Let the sugar melt as far as it will go and then apply heat. The water evaporates when the sugar starts to move. Skim away any scum and wipe sides of pan. At this stage the preparation is ready to be raised to the desired temperature, but before proceeding it should be strained through a muslin into another clean and warm pan. Re-apply heat and place thermometer in the syrup. Remove pan from heat and stand in cold water immediately the exact degree of temperature is reached. The whole operation must be performed quickly. Granulation must be avoided and this is prevented by employing a graincutter, i.e. lemon juice—1 lemon to 500g (1 lb) of sugar; cream of tartar used at ½ teaspoon dissolved in 1 teaspoon of water; or glucose—50g (2 oz) to 500g (1 lb) sugar, which also gives the sugar extra gloss. Lemon juice and cream of tartar are added to the syrup just prior to its reaching the required temperature; glucose (indispensable in certain preparations but optional in others) is added to the original syrup preparation. Lemon juice is considered to give the best results; an excess of glucose tends to make the finished article sticky. From the moment the sugar starts to boil it continues to cook, passing rapidly through 12 stages until it caramelizes and burns. For culinary purposes 7 stages are of real importance.

		Degrees		
Stage	Term	F.	C.	Test
1	Small thread	215°	102°	Place index and thumb into the sugar and when parted the fine sugar threads will break.
2	Large thread	222°	106°	Place index and thumb into the sugar and when parted the fine threads will be stronger and hold longer.
3	Small ball	236°	112°	Dip fingers into water, pick out a small piece of sugar and roll it in a cup of water; the ball will be small and soft.

4	Large ball	248°	120°	Repeat operation 3 which should result in a harder and larger ball.
5	Small crack	285°	140°	Place a finger into the sugar and draw out a thread, which will snap off but will stick to the teeth when placed in the mouth.
6	Large crack	315°	155°	Dip a finger in water, draw out a thread which will snap off; it will also snap between the teeth when placed in the mouth.
7	Caramel	350° +	180° +	The sugar starts to darken then burn. It is from this degree of heat that toffee and caramel is made.

Tools for sugar work: 2 sugar boiling pots; palette knife; pliers; scissors; marble slab; sugar thermometer; soft brush to clean side of pan; muslin for straining; metal or wooden basket boards and pegs; thin wire; small spirit lamp.

General rules

1. The sugar must be cooked to the correct temperature.

2. All tools and utensils must be clean, dry and very lightly oiled.

3. All steam and moisture must be avoided and work should not be done on a damp or wet day. Sugar work must not be placed in a refrigerator.

4. Sugar may be coloured to any hue. The compound is added before the final cooking temperature is reached. Only best quality colour ingredients should be used.

5. For advanced sugar work a special lime closet is needed to store the articles in a moisture-proof atmosphere. A hot box oven is required for keeping the sugar to be worked at the exact degree of heat.

Sugar Basket

The average sized basket will take between 2–3 kilo (4–6 lb) sugar; 2 kilo (4 lb) would be an ideal weight. This is prepared and cooked as explained, the required amount placed in a clean copper sugar boiling pan and heated to 149°C. (300°F.) when the lemon juice is added. The heat is maintained to 160°C. (320°F.) when it is withdrawn and the pan placed in water to arrest further cooking.

The preparation is turned out onto a *cold* lightly oiled marble slab and worked with a palette knife until it can be handled. The work is now performed deliberately and with dry hands; some craftsmen like to work with a piece of hessian cloth for temperature control and ease in handling. The mass is kneaded with the palm of the hand over and over again. It is then ready for pulling—similar to pulling chewing gum. Roll out with the palms and draw it with the thumb and forefinger. Meantime, the remaining sugar is kept in a pliable ball in a warm closet.

The basket is woven on a metal or wooden skeleton (this is also used for potato basket work) in which there are holes at intervals with the required number of pegs or sticks, an odd number, inserted in each one. The skeleton should be lightly oiled and if wood, must be seasoned. Take the sugar ribbon and plait quickly basketwise from the base upwards until the frame is complete, taking care to support the inside. Turn upside down and rim the bottom of the plaiting. Turn right side up, remove supports, replace with pulled sugar of equal size and length and then rim the top of the plaiting.

The basket frame now needs a base. This is made by working a small mat of sugar into the required shape, then placing the basket frame bodily upon the base piece.

The sides and ends are trimmed and snipped away with scissors. A handle is made of wire, entwined with a double or treble ribbon of pulled sugar and set into place. Finally, the basket is decorated with ribbons and bows and filled with fruit or flowers of pulled or blown sugar.

Ribbons and Bows. For this work the sugar is pulled at 155°C. (315°F.) and coloured as required; it is possible to pull the ribbons in coloured patterns. These accessories are fixed to the basket by heat.

Flowers. Worked from sugar at 160°C. (320°F.) and assembled petal by petal. Petals are thumbed out and fixed together with the aid of pliers and a lamp. The stems are pulled through the sugar with the aid of a piece of wire. Wire is also used to assemble petals, leaves and stems but in competition work judges disapprove of too much wiring.

Fruit and Vases. Made from blown sugar, similar process to glass blowing. The sugar is worked at 150°C. (310°F.). Good results are given by a straight sugar preparation, but experts prefer to use a basic solution containing 120g (4 oz) glucose to 500g (1 lb) sugar. Various sized tubes, up to 12mm ($\frac{1}{2}$ in), are used for blowing. The sugar is rolled into a small ball, the tube stuck into its centre and then blown. The item is modelled as it swells in size, as in glass blowing. Popular blown fruits are grapes (assembled in a bunch) bananas, oranges, peaches, pears, lemons and apples. Vases are also blown and shaped during blowing, the handles fixed separately. The work is performed with coloured sugar and touched afterwards as required with a brush.

Spun Sugar

Coloured spun sugars, similar to candy floss, are used for veiling certain sweets and iced confections à l'orientale, puits d'amour and voilé en surprise.

The sugar is heated, coloured and taken to 155°C. (315°F.), turned out into a large warmed copper bowl and whisked rapidly in a circular movement with a lightly oiled fork into a fine, light sugar gauze.

Work in Carved Salt

This work is carried out with bar salt, purchased from most grocers through a manufacturer. Bar salt for carving is made specially with an improved density to facilitate the work. The carving is performed with small sculptor's tools of various gauges. The work is left white or coloured.

Fat for Modelling

For modelling purposes mutton fat is selected, the whole piece with the suet in which the kidneys are embedded. All skin, gristle, membrane and blemishes are removed, the fat cubed and well washed and soaked several times in cold salted water until the fat is dead white.

Strain off water, place fat in a pan and melt very slowly. When clarified, strain through a clean, damp muslin. Join the fat with an equal quantity of best quality lard. Melt down both until well blended. Cool slowly, stirring all the time. Prior to setting point, add a small quantity of lemon juice and let piece solidify. Turn out the block and, using a large knife, scrape off a few layers at a time and knead thoroughly in a damp cloth. The fat must be worked until it becomes soft and pliable, when it is ready for use. This is the traditional method of preparation. There are other ways, notably the addition of glycerine to the clarified mutton fat, 25g (1 oz) to 500g (1 lb) fat, according to the degree of pliability. The modelling is carried out as one would work and handle clay or putty, with the aid of tools. For lesser pieces such as socles the fat, without being worked over, is melted down and turned into plaster or metal moulds to be unmoulded and trimmed when set. The fat may be coloured or painted. If left uncoloured, as is usual, it should be very white, resembling marble.

Wax and Stearine for Modelling

Basic formula: ¼ stearine, ½ white beeswax, ¼ pure white paraffin.

Place stearine and beeswax in a pan, melt very slowly in a bain-marie and then add the paraffin. Mix well and strain through damp, clean muslin. When it can be handled with ease, turn out on a marble slab and knead well in a clean cloth like a dough. If the wax becomes too hard, additional paraffin or glycerine may be added. The ingredients are purchased from a manufacturing chemist.

Another formula is ½ stearine, ¼ beeswax and ¼ pure white paraffin.

Cheese (Fromage)

A dictionary definition of cheese is 'the curd of milk pressed into a mass'. Cheese is an interesting subject. The locale, type of pasture and soil where the milk-producing animal grazes, together with the mode and method of manufacture, determines the character of a cheese. There are many varieties; a clear classification would be British, Continental or imported, and processed cheese. In recent years British cheese has come very much into its own, and many varieties exist. France has always been famous for the wide variety, with something like 300 regional speciality types of cheese.

Austrian Cheese.   Name given to a sausage shaped, film covered soft smoked cheese. This smoky flavour is attractive and unusual. Also known as Rupp Kase.

Beaufort.   French Alpine cheese similar in character to the gruyère but without the holes.

Bel Paese.   Mild Italian cheese, large and flat, similar in flavour to port salut.

Bel Paesino.   Smaller version of the larger bel paese.

Bleu d'Auvergne.   French cheese from the Massive Central, the Auvergne country, similar to roquefort. Made from the milk of the goat, ewe and cow.

Bleu Moulds.   Three varieties of blue cheese from France: the large Fourmes, the Haut Jura, and the celebrated Bresse Bleu.

Blue Dorset.   Hard, white cheese, with blue veins. Made in Dorset. Also known as Blue Vinny.

Bluefort.   A species of Dutch blue cheese.

Boursin.   French soft creamy cheese from Normandy. Made in several flavours including ham, garlic and herbs, peppercorns, and a plain or standard boursin. Produced in round and square shapes.

Brie.   One of the finest of all French cheeses. Produce of the Brie district in the ancient province of Ile-de-France. Large flat cheese 20mm (¾ in) thick and 25cm (10 in) diameter. Soft and creamy, similar though more flavoursome than camembert. Whole cheese is presented 'sur le paille', on its straw mat packing. Also sold in wedges of different sizes. Said to be at its best in winter.

(At the Congress at Vienna the notorious diplomat and noted gastronome Prince Metternick created brie the King of Cheeses.)

Caerphilly.   White whole milk cheese from the town of Caerphilly in Glamorgan, now produced in the West of England. Mild and cool in flavour, a favourite cheese with Welsh miners.

Camembert. The best known and most popular of all French cheeses. Produce of the Camembert district of Normandy, it was created in 1790 by Madam Marie Harel in the town of Camembert, where a statue stands in honour of this celebrated fermière. Cheese is soft and round, ½cm (1 in) thick by 10cm (4 in) diameter, and foil wrapped. Also sold in halves and wrapped wedges.

In selecting brie and camembert, or any of this type of fermented cheese, the centre softness is tested with a gentle application of the thumb. The softer the better and it is considered best for eating when 'runny'. Firm, white and chalky, these cheeses should be kept to mellow and ripen in their own good time in a cool place.

There are many imitation camemberts made outside France; all are inferior in breed and character to the genuine one from Normandy.

Cantal. A drum shaped semi-hard cheese from Haute Auvergne, France.

Carré de l'Est. A square soft cheese from Normandy described as a cross between camembert and point de l'evêque. Has a waxy texture and a nutty flavour.

Cheddar. One of the oldest and best known of British cheeses. Straw coloured and nutty in flavour, it originated in the Cheddar Gorge country. Takes nine months to mature. Cheddar is also reproduced in Canada, Australia and New Zealand. There is also an applewood smoked cheddar.

Cheshire. The oldest of British cheeses. Mellow, saline and open textured. Made in white, red and blue. White is the natural, red is coloured, and blue well matured. The saline flavour comes from the salt deposits in the Cheshire pastures.

Comté. Type of gruyère from the Alpine districts of France.

Cottage Cheese. Home-made proprietary English cream cheese made in 2 varieties—natural and with chives.

Cottenham. Blue cheese with a fine creamy texture, not unlike Stilton, but larger and milder in flavour. Made in the Midlands of England.

Coulommiers. Type of small thick brie, similar in flavour and made in the Brie district of Ile-de-France.

Danish Cheeses. Fertile Denmark produces a wide range of cheeses. One group is mild in flavour and similiar in style to gruyère; these are Samsoe, Danbo, Fynbo, Elbo, Maribo and Havati. There is also a Danish Blue and the distinctive Christian the Ninth, a mild processed type flecked with caraway seeds.

Derby. Mild, white, close textured and delicate creamy cheese. Bouquet develops with keeping. There is a natural, and a Sage Derbyshire, a traditional Christmas delicacy.

Dunlop. A cheese made in Scotland, not unlike cheddar.

Edam. Well known Dutch cheese made in the shape and size of a football, 2½ kilo (5 lb) in weight. The rind is red, the cheese mild.

Emmenthal. A cheese with all the characteristics of gruyère but with larger holes. Made in Switzerland, it often passes for gruyère. Marketed as Swiss emmenthal, the cheese with the large holes.

Fourme Bleu. French cheese from the Auvergne, somewhat similar to a stilton.

Gejetosy. Cheese made in Norway from cow's or goat's milk.

Gervais, Petit Swiss, Pommel, Demi-Sel (Cream Cheeses). Cream cheese is made wherever there is a dairy. It is the most natural and probably the first kind of cheese made by man. The process of making cream cheese is simple and consists of skimming the curds off soured milk. The curds are salted, placed in a clean muslin and hung in a cool place to drain. Cream cheeses such as these are made in France and Switzerland and marketed foil wrapped.

Cream cheese is best served ice cold and eaten with sugar and a touch of lemon juice. Some prefer to eat it with salt and a dash of cayenne or paprika.

Gloucester, Double. Deep creamy coloured cheese not unlike cheddar, but fuller in flavour. Shaped as a grindstone.

Gloucester, Single. Soft, open texture and rare variation of the double.

Goat's Cheese. Cheese made from the 'poor man's cow'. France excels in these cheeses, and there are some 40 classified types made in various shapes and sizes. Best known are Saint-Maure, a tunnel shaped cheese from the Touraine, Saint-Marcellin, made in smallish pats, and Valençay, which is pyramid shaped.

Gorgonzola. Famous Italian blue cheese made in the Lombardy. White and creamy with areas shot with blue mould. The genuine is made in and around the village of Gorgonzola where it is allowed to mature; the moulding should be natural.

Gouda. Dutch cheese similar to Edam but made in a different shape and weight. They are large and flat and weigh 5 kilo (10 lb) per whole cheese.

Gruyère. The genuine is made in Switzerland where it is sold under the name of emmenthal. It is a hard cheese which undergoes a cooking process in manufacture. Pale yellow, waxy in texture, and perforated by small holes, gruyère has a very distinctive flavour. It is also a culinary cheese, used in the same way as parmesan, with which it is often mixed.

When made in Switzerland it is marketed as Swiss gruyère, the cheese with the small holes.

Ilchester. A new British cheese introduced by Kenneth Seaton, an hotelier, in 1963. Made from cheddar, herbs and bitter ale at Ilchester, Somerset.

Italian Cheeses. Over and above gorgonzola and parmesan, numerous fancy cheeses are made in Italy, mainly mild, such as Dolcetti, Burrini, with a butter centre, Campanellina, shaped as a bell, Caciocavalli, pear-shaped, and the globe-shaped Provoloncini.

Lancashire. Creamy white, mild, lactic cheese. Well known toasting cheese and ideal topping for soups and hot pots. There is also a Sage Lancashire.

Leicester. Rich russet coloured cheese with a flaky texture, mild yet full of flavour. One of the best British cheeses.

Liptauer. Central European cheese selling in delicatessen stores under many guises. It is a cream cheese flavoured and loaded with chopped anchovies, capers, gherkins, garlic and pimento.

Livarot. Soft round cheese from Normandy.

Maroilles. Square soft, brick red cheese similar in type to camembert.

Monsieur Fromage. Soft and small barrel-shaped French cheese from Normandy.

Mozzarella. Italian cheese made from buffalo milk.

Munster. Famous cheese from the town of Munster, near Colmar in Alsace. Soft and full flavoured. Also made flecked with cumin seed.

Nantais du Curé. Small square soft cheese from Brittany.

Origano. Italian herbal cheese.

Parmesan. Well known hard grating culinary cheese from Parma in Italy. All au gratin mornay preparations are sprinkled with parmesan (or gruyère). It is incorporated in sauce mornay, in pasta and risotto preparations, and passed round grated with soups, notably minestrone. Is eaten, as a cheese, with bread or biscuits by Italians.

Philadelphia. American style foil-packed cream cheese by Kraft. As well as a table cheese, it has many culinary uses.

Pont de l'Évêque. A square camembert type of cheese made in Normandy.

Port Salut. French semi-hard cheese with a horned rind and waxy pulp shot with tiny holes. Made in large flat cakes.

Primula. Rich, creamy manufactured cheese from Norway. Shaped in half rounds and wedges wrapped in foil.

Processed Cheese. Processed or commercial cheeses packed in blocks, ribbons, rondels, squares and wedges wrapped in foil are sold under various proprietary names. These cheeses are manufactured from real and processed cheeses and emulsifying salts. They are generally of

293

high quality, good value, easy to handle, wrapped in sterile packing and pleasing to eat. They can be classified as the petit gruyère semi-hard type, cream cheese spreads, and spreads packed in tubes. As well as plain, these cheeses are marketed flavoured with celery, tomato, shrimp, onion, spice, herbs and other ingredients. Processed cheeses in blocks or in ribbons are useful as sandwich fillings and in the quick preparation of toasted and similar goods, such as cheeseburgers.

Ration Cheese. An historical note rather than praise, if any, of a neutral cheese. In 1940 Britain was deprived of all continental imports. Home-produced and commonwealth imported cheese was controlled and subjected to all the indignities of food rationing. Individual brands and local cheese production ceased and the industry was merged to manufacture a standard 'National Cheese'. National or 'mousetrap' cheese contained all the requisite food values but though admirable, it lacked the individuality and breed of 'peacetime' cheeses. It was more an essential item of food than a pleasure of the table.

Roquefort. Famous French soft and creamy blue cheese from the Languedoc. The genuine is made from ewe's milk and matured in caves hewn from rocks in the locale where it is made. An exceptional cheese with a rich flavour.

Saint-Nectaire. Round, soft and buttery cheese from the Limousin in France.

Saint Paulin. Soft round French cheese prepared by Trappist monks.

Sbrinz. Hard gruyère type of cheese made in Switzerland.

Stilton. Queen of British cheese with a global reputation. The genuine Stilton is made in and around the Melton Mowbray district of Leicestershire by a member of the Stilton Cheese Makers Assocation. Rich, creamy and mellow blue, the whole cheese weighs about 7 kilo (14 lb) and is 22cm (9 in) high and 20cm (8 in) in diameter. Stilton is served from the half cheese and scooped out with special servers. May also be sliced across or cut into wedges. One should not really seek to improve the natural flavour of stilton with the 'adulteration' of port, ale, or anything else.

White Stilton is also made. Crumbly in texture, mild and not dissimilar to caerphilly, though possibly more bland.

Suffolk. Little known very hard cheese from East Anglia.

Super Capricet des Dieux. Oval type of camembert cheese from France.

Tomme. Spectacular variety of cheese matured in wine and grape husks. Grape pips are embedded in the skin of this cheese, illustrating the combination of wine and cheese. Some tommes are made from cow's milk, others from goat's milk; certain varieties combine the curds of both milks. Among the best known are Tomme de Savoie,

Beauges, Bourdane, Romans, Peldoux, au Fenouil and au Marc de Raisin.

Trucklet.   Blue veiny cheese from the West of England.

Wensleydale.   Honey-flavoured white cheese from Yorkshire. Not unlike a cross between cheddar and cheshire. In Yorkshire it is served with apple pie.

Definition of Terms

In all works on cookery it is usual practice to provide a list of key culinary terms and their meaning. This precludes the need for endless and repetitive explanations in the text. To this list of terms are added notes on various culinary adjuncts and other related information.

Abricoter. The lining of a cake with a thin coating of boiling preserve or syrup, so that the icing or other topping adheres. Derivative of apricot syrup since this flavour blends well with all others. Marmalade is also used. The jam selected is heated and rubbed through a sieve into a smooth syrup; it may be flavoured with kirsch or maraschino.

Adjusted. The correcting of a preparation to a prescribed standard, i.e. adjusting a basic sauce to an acceptable product.

Aiguillettes. Long thin fillets, i.e. Aiguillettes de Caneton en Aspic.

Angelica (Angélique). Aromatic plant whose bright green stems are crystallized and used for decorative purposes.

Anglaise. Appareil consisting of well-beaten eggs, salt, pepper and a dessertspoon of olive oil per 2 eggs. For pané à l'anglaise, the fare for breadcrumbing is passed in flour, then the anglaise, and then fresh white breadcrumbs before deep or shallow frying.

Angostura. Aromatic bitters and the basis of pink gin, a long or short drink. Invented as a medicament to combat tropical fevers by Dr Siegert. As well as being a cocktail ingredient it has numerous culinary uses in flavouring jellies, fruit salads, grapefruit, ice cream, trifles, prunes, soups, sauces and preserves.

Aniseed (Anis). Sweet seed used in bakery, sweets, stews and the preparation of certain liqueurs.

Antipasto. An Italian hors-d'oeuvre, sold ready prepared in can or jar, consisting of an assortment of sardine, tuna fish, mackerel fillet, olives, anchovy, capers and selected vegetables.

Antoxidant. Preparation used for keeping potatoes (and other foods) white and preventing discoloration. Most common is sodium metabisulphite. By acting as an antoxidant it is also a food preserver. It is normally marketed under a proprietary name and is most useful in the kitchen, particularly in the production of deep fried potatoes.

À Part. To serve à part, to accompany or escort, kitchen and food service jargon, e.g. Crème Saint Germain, croûtons served à part.

Appareil. A preparation, a combination of various ingredients or components, i.e. quenelle appareil.

296

Aromates. Onion, carrot and other roots and a combination of seasoning agents.

Arroser. French to baste; the basting of roasting joints.

Arrowroot. Root vegetable from the Americas. Pulp is dried, powdered, and refined into a starchy flour. Used in thickening sauces, soups and syrups.

Aspic. A clear, limpid setting jelly to mask food for cold. Prepared from well clarified, fortified stock, thickened with gelatine.

Attelets. Ornate metal (silver, plated, stainless steel) skewers for cold buffet decorative purposes. Used in decorating boars head and meat and poultry grandes pièces. Also known as hatelette pins.

Au Naturel. Food featured and served plain and unadorned. Another term would be standard.

Bain-Marie. Shallow pan of hot or heated water to hold and keep soups and sauces warm without over-heating. The cooking of food in a bain-marie or bain-marie style in the oven.

Baking Powder. Two principal baking powders are bicarbonate of soda and cream of tartar. They are used singly or mixed. The usual mix is 1 of soda bicarbonate to 2 of tartar. Most patent baking powders are made up in this fashion from these ingredients or other chemical substances. The raising gas, carbon dioxide, is given off when heat is applied. Baking is becoming increasingly scientific through the application of chemistry. This approach has passed to pastry and cake mixes in ready or packeted mixes. Some of these products are so good that the results can be considered better than orthodox culinary methods.

Barder (To bard). Wrapping a slice of unsmoked bacon fat around a joint of meat, poultry or game for roasting to protect the piece and increase internal moisture. A bard de lard.

Batter (for deep frying). There are two basic sweet and savoury batters for dipping or coating foods for deep frying: stardard or straight batter, raised or yeast batter, i.e. pâte à frire.

Standard Batter. To 500g (1 lb) sifted plain flour add 2 to 3 well beaten eggs and bring to a creamy consistency with ¾–1 litre (1½–2 pints) milk. Sweeten with 50g (2 oz) sugar and add pinch of salt. Rest for 30 minutes, beat again and use as required. For a savoury batter omit the sugar and season with salt and pepper.

Pâte à Frire (raised batter). 500g (1 lb) flour, 6g (¼ oz) salt, 50g (2 oz) sugar, 12g (½ oz) yeast, ½ litre (1 pint) warm water, 2 egg yolks, 25g (1 oz) olive oil, 2 egg whites.

Sieve flour and salt into a basin. Mix the sugar and yeast in a little of the water. Add the rest of the water to the beaten egg yolks. Mix yeast and egg preparation together and then slowly beat this into the flour. Cover and prove in a warm place until preparation doubles its size. Beat up preparation and add olive oil and whisked egg whites. Use additional flour or water if required. For a savoury preparation omit the sugar and season with salt and pepper.

Note: There are a number of very good batter mixes on the market which are reconstituted with water or milk according to the directions on the packet.

Batterie de Cuisine. Pots, pans and utensils employed in the kitchen.

Bayleaf (Feuille de laurier). Fresh or diced leaf of the bay tree, has a distinctive aroma, used in stews, sauces and milk puddings.

Bind (Lié). The use of an ingredient to blend, secure or hold other ingredients together without separating. Egg is the most employed binding agent.

Black Jack. Kitchen slang for gravy browning. Caramelized sugar usually 'bought in', but can be kitchen made.

Blanc. For cooking calves head, tripe, trotters and other fare. A sliced onion and a whole one stuck with cloves are placed in a pot with lemon juice, salt, peppercorns and a bouquet garni. The pot is then filled with water and brought to the boil. Flour is then sieved in slowly and allowed to cook. Used as required. For cooking tripe, it is usual to add a whole nutmeg to the preparation. It is also usual to cook fare in a blanc wrapped in a cloth to prevent the contents coming into contact with the air.

Blanch. To scald food by plunging it into boiling water, or other liquid, for a brief period. Food is blanched to seal the pores or retain colour. Also used to skin tomatoes and peaches.

Bouquet Garni. Used in the preparation of sauces, stews and braises for flavouring. Parsley stalks, sprig of thyme and a bayleaf tied in a piece of celery with cotton. Made in various sizes. After use may be dried and kept for further employment. English name, faggot.

Braising. Culinary operation consisting of half roasting and half stewing or boiling. The preparation is started in fat and then moistened with water, stock or other liquid. Combination of dry and wet cookery.

Breaded. Means breadcrumbing.

Brigade. Term given to a catering group of staff, i.e. Kitchen Brigade, Waiting Brigade, Breakfast or Luncheon Brigade, all employed in the kitchen or in the 'room'.

Broil. Old English cookery term for grilling.

Brunoise. Denotes finely chopped vegetables, i.e. carrot. turnips, celery. Brunoise des légumes.

Buckwheat (Sarrazin). A grain which grows on the less fertile soils of Central Europe and the Americas. The flour is darker than wheat and has certain culinary uses in Russian, American and other cookery.

Buttercream. Work 250g (8 oz) butter carefully to a pomade, add

360g (12 oz) icing sugar and beat thoroughly till a light and creamy texture. Add required flavour and colour to taste.

Capers (Câpres). Buds of the caper tree, sold dried, and in brine. Used for decorating. Main ingredient of caper sauce.

Caraway Seed (Cumin des prés). Dried elongated seeds whose oil content releases a pungent and aromatical aroma. Used in bakery and in certain liqueurs. Much used in Eastern European cookery.

Cardamon (Cardamore). Bitter sweet Indian spice.

Carrageen. A moss found in Ireland from which a blancmange is made. It is washed, simmered in milk with sugar, lemon rind, vanilla or spice, strained and poured into a mould to set.

Cassoulet. Speciality of the Languedoc in France. Consists of an estouffade of haricot beans, mutton, fresh or salt pork, potted goose or duck, aromates, seasoning and crackling. The principal ingredients are cooked separately and then assembled in a cassole, a special earthenware dish, topped with breadcrumbs and finished in the oven till the topping is crisp and brown.

Cayenne. Hottest of all peppers, bright red, prepared from ground dried chillies. Indispensable in the kitchen. Should always be used sparingly and with care.

Celery Seed. Seeds of celery plant, used in soups, sauces and for flavouring celery salt.

Celestine. Garnish for soup. Savoury pancake flecked with fines herbes, shredded into julienne or stamped out in rondels or stars.

Chanterelle. Small yellow coloured member of the mushroom family, also known as girolle.

Chapelure. French for browned, dried breadcrumbs.

Chemiser. French, to mould, a moulded jelly or blancmange in a chemise.

Chilles. Small pods of a West Indian pepper plant which turns red when ripe. Employed in pickles. Ground and dried pod gives cayenne pepper.

Chive (Ciboulette). Herb member of onion family. Used in salad dressings, cold sauces, garnish to vichyssoise soup and other employments.

Cinnamon (Cannelle). Eastern spice from the bark of a tree. Sold ground or as the dried bark. Very useful spice with particular medicinal properties. Cinnamon water is an ancient remedy for colds and influenza. A powerful antiseptic.

Ciseler. To incise food with a knife in a spaced pattern, i.e. whole mushroom, fish.

Cloves (Clous de girofle). Useful culinary spice from East Africa and the East Indies. Sold in the clove, or ground. Indispensable when cooking apples.

Cocks Combs (Crêtes de Coq). Normally used as a garniture, i.e. financière. To prepare, the raw combs are punctured, well washed to clear them of blood and then plumped in cold water for a period. Next they are blanched and skinned and cooked in white stock or consommé or stewed in butter. Where combs are indicated as a garnish they are generally accompanied by cocks kidneys, i.e. rognons de coq. The combs are sometimes skinned, once blanched, by shaking them in a cloth with bay salt. Combs are also prepared en brochette or as a risotto dish with rice.

Cocks Kidneys (Rognons de Coq). Normally used as a garniture. To prepare, the raw kidneys are washed, blanched, skinned and cooked in water, butter, lemon juice and seasoning for 10 minutes. Where cocks kidneys are indicated as a garnish they are generally accompanied by cocks combs.

Coffee, Speciality. Popular after-dinner feature. Coffee, laced with a spirit or liqueur, topped with cream and served in a stem glass. Place a measure of base spirit or liqueur in glass, sweeten well with brown sugar, stir, leave spoon in glass, fill with hot coffee and top with a thick layer of double cream poured over the back of the spoon.

Irish coffee with Irish whiskey was the original speciality coffee, known as Gaelic coffee; now featured with Scotch whisky. Others include Russian with vodka; Caribbean with rum; Calypso with tia maria; Italian with strega; French with cognac, cointreau, bénédictine and grand marnier.

Collop. Escalope, a slice or a fillet of food, i.e. collop of veal.

Colouring. Natural and chemical colouring agents used in correcting food for appearance. There are some 100 different colours and hues. Most used in the kitchen are carmine, green, blue, yellow, chocolate and strawberry.

Cooking Processes. Food is cooked by one of two basic methods: by dry heat or by moist/wet heat. Dry heat is the direct application of heat to food without the aid of a liquid or steam. Moist or wet heat is the cooking of food in liquids or in steam.

The dry heat methods are roasting, baking, dry frying, griddling, sauté-ing, grilling and deep frying. The moist/wet heat methods are boiling, poaching, steaming, braising, stewing and poêling.

Coriander (Coriandre). Eastern spice in curries and picklings.

Cornflour. Rich, starchy flour from ground maize, used for thickening soups and sauces, for blancmange and in commercial custards and instant sweet sauces and sweets.

Correct. To check a preparation for seasoning, texture, colour and consistency. Correcting for eye and palate appeal. One of the most important procedures in cookery.

Court Bouillon. Preparation of aromates and seasonings in which food is poached. Sliced onion and carrot, parsley stalks, pieces of celery, salt, peppercorns and lemon juice in a pan, covered with water, brought to boil, simmered for 30 minutes and used as required.

Cover (Couvert). A serving, one portion, or a place setting.

Croûtons. There are various kinds and sizes of croûtons. There are the large pieces and socles of shaped deep fried bread for presenting cold work. Then there are the smaller types of round croûtons for tournedos, heart shapes for salmis dishes, squares, rounds and oblongs for large game birds, and croûtons of French bread for smaller birds.

Cuillère (Biscuits à la). Light type of biscuit made with egg whites, yolks, sugar and flour, dessert spooned out, dropped on a tray and baked.

Cuisson. Cooking liquor.

Culotte. French for rump, i.e. Culotte de Boeuf.

Cumin. Seeds of a plant which gives off an aromatic oil. Used in Eastern European cookery and in certain liqueurs. Has digestive properties.

Curry. Originates from Far East and from India where curries are served all through the day. In our northern climes curry has been popularly considered as cold weather fare.

As a culinary term, curry is the name given to an unspecified blend of spices, herbs, roots and seeds. It can be made up with as few as 8 to as many as 20 component ingredients. Blends range from mild, medium to very hot. Whatever the blend there are generally 2 basic ingredients present: turmeric, giving the preparation its green-yellow colour, and cayenne pepper, which supplies the heat. Other ingredients are allspice, cardamon, cumin, caraway, celery, coriander, mustard and poppy seeds; cinnamon; clove; coconut; garlic; ginger; fenugreek seed and leaf; mace; nutmeg; black pepper; and saffron. Eastern cookery does not prescribe a curry powder as such but for each recipe indicates the various individual ingredients required. We usually resort to a ready-made powder or one made up to specification. The right curry is said to be the one which brings beads of perspiration to the forehead.

There are also canned sauces and curry mixes. Most fish, meat and poultry can be curried as well as eggs, pasta, rice, vegetables and divers made-up preparations. Curry dishes appear in the text of this book under their appropriate headings.

Escorts for curries. Rice and mango chutney are the standard escorts, so is chicken, a macédoine of vegetables. The rice is boiled and sometimes flecked with plumped currants, raisins or sultanas.

Other escorts include Bombay duck, a type of dried bummaloe fish from the Indian Ocean; poppadums, a dried biscuit or pancake. Bombay duck is sold in tins of 20 fish and poppadums in tins of 25 biscuits. These are flashed under a grill prior to service and are flaked over the curry at table. A number of side dishes are also placed on the table including sweet and sharp pickles; crispy grilled bacon strips; salted almonds and peanuts, whole and chopped; toasted shredded coconut; pickled walnuts; seedless raisins; preserved ginger; sliced banana sauced with lemon juice; chopped hard-boiled egg; slivers of green peppers; quince preserve; mint and redcurrant jelly.

Dariole. Small, i.e. individual, cylinder shaped mould.

Darne. A steak, i.e. Darne of Salmon, cut across the bone.

Daube (en). A veal or beef ragout, stew or braise, to which red wine is added.

Deep Frying. Frying in deep fat, au friture. Food rarely needs a temperature over 194°C. (380°F.). Usual frying temperatures are 184°C. (360°F.) maximum and 150°C. (300°F.) minimum. Frying should normally be performed between these 2 temperatures. The food may be deep fried as it is, such as pommes frites, or previous to the deep frying operation some food may be breadcrumbed, passed in frying batter, or just in milk and flour, according to the prescribed method or recognized procedure concerned. In 'Fish & Chip' shops, all fish is usually passed in batter and then deep fried.

Déglacer. To swill out a roasting or sauté pan with water, stock or wine to collect coagulating juices which adhere to the receptacle when making a sauce or gravy.

Diablotins. Accompaniment to consommés. Rondels of flute bread or bâton roll, coated with a reduced béchamel and gratiné. Diablotins à la Glace de Viande: meat glaze added to the béchamel and gratiné.

Dill (Aneth). Herb with attractive aroma, used in pickles and pickled cucumber or agourcis. Much employed in Russian cookery.

Dressing. Another term for stuffings or fillings. The following dressings are mentioned in the text.

American Dressing (for poultry). Mince 2 onions and an equal amount of celery and apple and melt in clarified suet. Add the bird's chopped liver and make up bulk with breadcrumbs soaked in milk. Season with salt, cayenne, nutmeg, lemon juice and a good pinch of sage. Bind with an egg and knead.

Chestnut Dressing. 5 or 6 whole chestnuts, consommé, 1 or 2 onions, 50g (2 oz) suet, offal, 500g (1 lb) forcemeat, stock, salt, pepper, mixed spice, lemon juice and 50g (2 oz) breadcrumbs.

Shell and skin the chestnuts and poach whole in consommé. Bake onions whole in their skins. Melt suet and add rough chopped liver and heart of the bird. Peel and chop onions, add to preparation and stew. Add forcemeat, moisten with sufficient stock and mix. Season with salt, pepper, dash of mixed spice and lemon juice. Add chestnuts, mix, cover with greaseproof paper and bake in slow oven for about 30 minutes. Remove from heat, stir in breadcrumbs and use as required. Care is taken to leave the chestnuts whole.

Pork forcemeat, similar to sausage filling, is purchased ready-made.

Derby Dressing. Scale of ingredients 500g (1 lb) rice to 1 litre (2 pints) stock and 1 onion.

Mince onion and stew in butter. Add rice, season, add stock and cook in covered pan in oven until rice has absorbed liquor. Moisten with more stock if required and load with rough chopped chicken or turkey livers stiffened in butter. Add cubes of truffled foie gras. Check seasoning and use as required.

Herb and Onion Stuffing. Set chopped onion and apple to stew in butter or suet. Add shredded suet and sufficient breadcrumbs, pre-soaked in milk, to make up the bulk. Knead, add pinch mixed herbs, and season with salt, cayenne, nutmeg and lemon juice. Bind with egg, one per 500g (1 lb) of stuffing, and knead well. If for poultry, the sauté and seasoned chopped liver and heart of the bird may be added.

Herb and Shallot Stuffing. As for herb and onion, using shallot in place of onion.

Sage and Onion Dressing for Duck. Bake 3 onions whole, peel, chop and melt in clarified suet. Add the chopped offal of the bird, season with salt, pepper, a touch of nutmeg and lemon juice. Make up the bulk with breadcrumbs soaked in milk. Mix well and flavour with rubbed sage. Bind with egg if required.

Duchesse Border. The piping of a dish in a fancy pattern with duchesse potato using a forcing bag and suitable piping tube.

Émincer. To slice, e.g. sliced cooked chicken, Émincé de Volaille.

Épigramme. Small fillets of lamb or mutton, pané and sauté. Term is also applied to fillets of poultry and game.

Escalope. A collop, a slice of lean meat or poultry for cooking. Slice in escalopes or collops.

Essences. Strong concentrated compounds made from natural ingredients and from chemical sources used as flavouring agents in food. There are some 200 flavouring essences; almost every known flavour is reproduced including fruits, spices, liqueurs, as well as savoury preparations.

Étaminer. To strain through a cloth, an étamine or tammy cloth or muslin.

Eviscerated. Term given to drawn emptied poultry and feathered game. Also to cleaned fish. Another term for drawn poultry would be oven-ready.

Extracts. Best known meat extracts are Bovril and Oxo, famous and long-established proprietary products. There is also Marmite, a valuable yeast product. Have extensive uses in the kitchen as flavouring and colouring agents.

Façon du Chef. Menu term to denote the chef's own special way in the preparation and presentation of a particular dish: the chef's speciality, the chef's creation. Also 'à ma façon', my way.

Faggot. English term for bouquet garni.

Farce. French for stuffing or dressing; to stuff or dress food with prepared stuffing, filling or dressing.

Fecula (Fécule). Potato flour, fine white powder, useful for thickening soups, sauces and stews.

Fenugreek (Foin-grec). Eastern herbal spice whose leaves and seeds are used in curries.

Fines Herbes. Chopped parsley, tarragon and chervil in equal quantities.

Flash. To insert a dish in a hot oven or under a grill for a brief period to brown or glaze it.

Fleurons. Half moons of puff pastry used to garnish certain fish-sauced entrées.

Flower Water. Two best known are rose and orange, used in confectionary and certain culinary operations.

Flûtes. Garnish to soups; rondels of fluted French bread, or bâton roll dried in the oven—Flûte à Potage.

Force. Old English cookery term meaning to stuff, e.g. Forced Carpe. Forcemeat, meaning a meat stuffing, usually pork, is a derivative term.

Frangipane. Name for one of 3 preparations: a cake filling similar to that used in bakewell tarts and other preparations; a custard with added flour, butter, ground almonds or crushed macaroons; basic panada of flour, butter, milk, yolks, salt, pepper and grated nutmeg.

Frangipane fillings. Cream 250g (8 oz) butter and 250g (8 oz) sugar lightly together. Beat in 4 eggs, one at a time. Mix in 250g (8 oz) ground almonds and 15g ($\frac{1}{2}$ oz) flour. Add the zest of half a lemon.

French Fried. A bastardization of recent origin of the term 'au friture' (deep fried). In popular catering establishments deep fried fare is often listed on the menu as French Fried. This, in a strict culinary sense, could be misleading. Food for deep frying is pané à l'anglaise (breadcrumbed), passed through frying batter, or frits à la française (as in the case of certain fish and other fare), when it is passed through milk and flour before frying. The menu term of French fried potatoes (or simply French fries) simply means pommes frites. Therefore, French fried used in the above mentioned ways is more of a marketing phrase than a correct culinary term.

Fricadelles. Meat balls or small rissoles made with minced cooked meat, mixed with mashed potato and chopped parsley, seasoned, bound with egg, breaded or not and shallow fried.

Fricassée. Term given to a ragoût of chicken or veal stewed in white stock with onions and mushrooms, lié in the cooking liquor, corrected into a creamed sauce. As a culinary term, means a sort of shallow braising; the fare is shallow fried, moistened and cooked.

Fumet. An essence, a reduction of natural cooking liquor or juices, a kind of rich and concentrated gravy.

Garlic (Ail). Member of the onion family and the most powerful aromatic known. Must be used very sparingly.

Ghee. Type of clarified butter, used in curry work.

Ginger (Gingembre). Hot spice from the East, root of a plant, one of the most popular of all spices. It is ground, crystallized in syrup, and glacé.

Glace de Viande. Meat glaze. Used to colour or garnish certain sauces. Prepared by slowly reducing estouffade over a low heat and in successive pots until a thick treacle preparation remains. Corrected with browning to a black and shining thick mixture.

Glaze. Term meaning to brown food in butter or a sauce to give it a nice shining gloss. To glaze is similar to gratiné, a preparation masked with mornay sauce, or covered with breadcrumbs or grated cheese and then flashed in a hot oven or under a grill to brown.

Glucose. Half as sweet as cane or beet sugar. Extracted as a syrup substance from potatoes and other roots, sugar cane and fruits. The syrup is treated and the refined glucose is produced as a very fine white powder. Glucose is easily assimilated by the body; it is an energy producer and is used for medicinal purposes. Glucose water is administered to maintain strength in feverish conditions and pre- and post-operative conditions. In the kitchen, glucose is used as a grain-cutter, a substance which prevents the granulation or crystallization of sugar. A syrup is produced by boiling together equal quantities of glucose and water.

Golden Croûtons. Accompaniment to several thick soups. Diced bread tossed to a golden brown in butter or lard, well drained and dusted with salt. May also be sprinkled with chopped parsley.

Parmesan Croûtons. While still hot, the croûtons are dredged and lightly coated with grated parmesan.

Croûtons for Marmites. Sliced bâton or bread roll, salted and toasted on both sides.

Gravy Salt. Instant gravy mixes marketed under branded names. Useful in making or correcting gravy.

Grenadins. Small veal collops usually taken from the noix or cushion, and previously larded.

Griddle. Heated stone slab or metal sheet upon which food is cooked. A griddle plate is now a recognized piece of kitchen equipment in fast food restaurants for shallow and dry frying eggs, flapjacks, pancakes and hamburgers.

Gros Bonnet. Kitchen slang for head chef or maître chef des cuisines.

Hachis. French for minced or chopped.

Honey (Miel). Man's original source of sweetness in the culinary sense. Used long before cane sugar was known and still used to sweeten food and beverages. Marketed as thick or clear. The character of a honey is defined by the flowers visited by the bees, so we have pine, heather, lavender, apple blossom and other varieties.

Horse-radish (Raifort). Root with a pungent flavour, used in sauces, butters and creams. Has powerful digestive properties.

Incise. Similar to ciseler, to make shallow slits in food to facilitate cooking, or for decorative purposes.

Individual Dish. Unit control line, one cover or serving.

Jazey. Kitchen slang for a method of thickening a liquid with flour and water or adding liquid or water to extend a soup, sauce or stew. Not strictly a recognized culinary procedure, more of a short cut.

Julienne. Kitchen term, to cut en julienne, i.e. into thin strips. For consommé julienne, preparation consists of shredded vegetables, e.g. carrot, turnip, lettuce, cabbage, celery (give colour and variety), poached in stock. Other garniture julienne, used individually or collectively, include cooked chicken, turkey, ham, tongue, mushroom, hard-boiled white of egg and truffle.

Juniper (Geniévre). Berry of the juniper tree much prized for its oil which has diuretic and other properties. Used in making gin.

Ketchup or Catsup. A savoury thick cold sauce containing a vinegar base. Tomato ketchup is the best known. Others are mushroom and walnut. Sold bottled under brand labels.

Lactose. Sugar present in milk; used in pharmacy and described as slightly sweet.

Larding. The operation of threading meat or poultry with strips of unsmoked fat bacon with a larding needle to facilitate and aid cooking and to moisten otherwise dry flesh. Special fat bacon is sold for this purpose.

Lardons. Piece of unsmoked bacon fat cut into large julienne. Special cold fat for larding and barding processes. They are stiffened under cold for easy handling and inserted into meat (poultry and game) with the aid of a larding needle. Lardons for meat are usually rolled in chopped parsley. This type of lardon should not be confused with bacon lardons, which are cut from streaky bacon in ½cm (1 in) square batons. They are blanched and sauté in half butter and half olive oil.

Laver. Red purple seaweed found on the rocky coasts of Cornwall and South Wales, from which laver bread is prepared. It is washed and simmered in sea-water with a little vinegar, drained and dried. It is mixed with oatmeal into cakes and fried in bacon fat for breakfast, served as a vegetable, sauced or with butter and gravy from a roast as a kind of bubble and squeak. In Scotland, laver is known as slouk and in Ireland as stoke. There is also a green laver or lettuce laver which is better known and more abundant.

Liaison for Soups. A binding and enriching preparation consisting of beaten egg yolk and cream. Once a liaison is added, the preparation must not be boiled lest the egg and cream content curdles.

Lié. To bind or thicken; lié à la crème, bound, enriched or thickened with cream.

Liver Pâté. Mince shallot, stew in butter, add trimmed livers and sauté together. Remove from heat, work with a palette knife and then add butter to make up a smooth pâté. Season with salt, cayenne and lemon juice. Load with chopped parsley.

The type of liver determines the variety of pâté, i.e. duck, chicken, game and so on. Used for spreading on various canapés.

Mace (Macis). Spice made from the external envelope of the nutmeg. A superior spice, used in potted seafoods, pickles and curries.

Macédoine. A mixture or medley of food; usually vegetables, but also fruit.

Macerate (Macérer). To soak a food in a wine, liqueur or marinade for a certain period of time to enhance the flavour.

Mandoline. Kitchen utensil for slicing potatoes and vegetables in even or fancy patterns.

Marinade. To soak and infuse meat, game and other fare as indicated in a preparation of red wine, brandy, salt, peppercorns and bouquet garni. The marinade is usually used in cooking the marinaded commodity, e.g. beef à la mode.

Marinière. Method of cooking shell and other fish with white wine and fish stock, e.g. moules à la marinière.

Marjoram (Marjolaine). Pungent and well known herb; use sparingly.

Mask. The operation of coating an item of food with a sauce.

Matelot. Term for a fish stew prepared with a court bouillon and white or red wine, and garnished with onion, mushroom and heart-shaped croûtons.

Matignon. Appareil of minced or shredded carrot, onion, celery, chopped ham, thyme and a piece of bayleaf stewed in butter in a closed vessel and then déglacé with madeira. Used in meat and poultry braises and stews.

Médaillon. A fillet or collop, also known as a délice, e.g. médaillon de turbot dugléré, délice de sole waleska.

Menu Terms. Certain names are given to dishes for purposes of identification. These are standard menu terms recognized everywhere. The names are drawn from many sources, people, places and events, but geographical names predominate, thereby often providing a clue to the identification of the food listed on the menu.

Argenteuil, asparagus; Bretonne, haricot beans; Caroline, rice; Clamart, green peas; Condé, red beans; Conti, lentils; Crécy, carrots; Diane, feathered game; Doria, cucumber; Dubarry, cauliflower; Florentine, spinach; Freneuse, turnips; Hongroise, paprika; Indienne, curry; Musard, lima beans; Orly, tomatoes; Palestine, Jerusalem artichokes; Parmentier, potatoes; Rachel, fonds d'artichauts; Reine, chicken; Saint Germain, green peas; Saint Hubert, ground game; Soubise, onions; Vichy, carrots; Washington, sweetcorn.

Meunière. Shallow frying operation, finishing with noisette butter and lemon juice.

Milk. Cow's milk is marketed in several ways.
Homogenized. The caterer's milk. Is heat treated and forced at pressure through a vent which breaks up and distributes the fat globules evenly through the milk. Is economical in usage, especially in hot beverages.
Pasteurized. Standard milk. Is heat treated for a certain period of time at a certain temperature and rapidly cooled.
Sterilized. Heat treated, cooled and sealed in containers. Keeps indefinitely under seal.
T.T. Milk from a tuberculin tested herd. Is left raw, pasteurized, homogenized or sterilized as required.

Milk is canned as evaporated full cream milk or condensed with added sugar. It is also spray dried as an instant powder. Filled milk is a spray dried, processed commodity whereby the animal fat is removed and replaced by vegetable fat. Useful for cooking, it's non-perishable and cheaper than fresh milk. These products sell under branded names.

Mincemeat (Francfortaise). Traditional British Fare preparation 'bought in' ready prepared. Consists of a salpicon of raw apple, suet, almonds, lemon and orange peel, dates, sultanas and currants, macerated in orange and lemon juice with sugar and spices. Used for mince pies, mince slice, as fillings for baked apples and so on. At one time mincemeat included diced cooked mutton and ox tongue.

Mint (Menthe). One of the most attractive and best known of all herbs, cultivated in most gardens. Mint and it's peppermint extracts are powerful digestive agents.

Mirepoix, Mirpoix. Preparation of roasted sliced onion and carrot with lean bacon oddments to strengthen the flavour of brown sauce work.

Miroton. Type of ragoût of beef stewed with onions.

Mis-en-Place. Advance preparation; favourite catering term meaning to make ready. Occurs in food preparation and cookery and in food service.

Mixed Herbs. Indicates combination of sage, thyme, tarragon, parsley and chervil.

Mixed Spice. Commercial pack of mixed spice. Always preferable to mix one's own formula from various permutations of cayenne, clove, cinnamon, ginger, nutmeg, pepper, thyme and bayleaf.

Monosodium Glutamate. MSG, the fourth condiment. In appearance it resembles granulated sugar.

Enhances and intensifies the flavour of foods. Much used in food manufacturing and processing in soups and sauces, made-up dishes and meat products. Marketed under a number of proprietary names.

Mount. The mounting of a sauce with butter, cream or eggs to enrich and increase bulk. The mounting of a mayonnaise.

Mustard (Moutarde). Seed of the mustard plant containing a pungent oil. The seeds are ground, refined and packeted for reconstitution in water or vinegar. English should not be confused with the Continental types from France and Germany, which are ready made, milder and fabricated with herbs and special vinegars. Mustard has a stimulating effect on the gastric juices, thereby aiding digestion.

Napper. French for mask. The coating of food with sauce. To nap with a sauce.

Oils, Aromatic. By this we mean the natural oils pressed from fruits and flower roots, herbs and spices. The crude oil is refined and added to or distilled in alcohol. There is a large range of these oils which are used in all sections of the food and drink industry. The most used in the kitchen are oils of peppermint, almond, ginger, lemon, orange, nutmeg, rose and vanilla.

Onion Piquée. Onion stuck with cloves.

Orégano, Origano. A herb, wild marjoram. Popular in American, Italian, Spanish and Mexican cookery. Ingredient in pizza pie fillings. Also the name of an Italian cheese containing this particular herb.

Paella. Spanish national dish consisting of rice, saffron, seasoning, scampi, shrimps, chicken, veal and other ingredients, the whole being cooked together in a large pan.

Paillettes (Cheese straws). Strips of puff paste combined with and sprinkled with grated parmesan and lightly seasoned with salt and cayenne. Served hot with chicken consommé, and featured at cocktail parties.

Panade. Preparation of breadcrumbs soaked in milk or stock.

Pané. French for breading or breadcrumbing.

Pané, Sauté au Beurre. Popular operation to breadcrumb and shallow fry in butter, i.e. pané, sauté, beurre noisette, the sequence of operations. Kitchen terminology.

Paprika. A mild red pepper associated with Hungarian cookery. Prepared from a mild type of capsicum found in Spain and Italy.

Parsley (Persil). Herb most used in the kitchen; chopped, sprigs and fried bouquets are well known finishings to dishes. Along with chervil and tarragon is one of the 'fines herbes'.

Partie. A department in the kitchen with a Chef de Partie in charge. Known also as a Corner. The Partie or Corner system was introduced and perfected by Auguste Escoffier.

Pâte à Frire. French for batter. Pâte à Choux, choux paste.

Pepper (Poivre). Dried berry of the pepper plant. Two types: white for table use and black for kitchen. Should always be freshly ground and this is why the moulin (hand mill) is indispensable. Chefs like to use equal amounts of white and black peppercorns from the mill.

Pincer. The light colouring of poultry or game carcasses, meat bones or vegetables in the oven before moistening with liquid to prepare a stock or sauce.

Piquer. French for larding.

Pistachio (Pistache). Small green coloured nut. Its colour and flavour is much appreciated in ice cream confections, also in galentines. Requires blanching and peeling.

Pitted. Term to denote removing the centre stone or seed from fruit, e.g. pitted cherries.

Ploughman's Lunch. Popular 'pub meal' consisting of cheese, pickles and bread, hot rolls or French bread, pickled onions or sweet pickle, various types of cheese though usually cheddar.

Pluches, Chervil. Used to float on top of certain soups as a garnish. Small, dainty sprigs of chervil. To conserve colour, the pluches are first scalded in boiling water, immediately removed and thrown into iced water.

Plumping. Term given to reconstituting dried fruits by soaking in water, e.g. plumped prunes.

Poppy Seed. Seed of the poppy plant, contains an aromatic oil. Employed in bakery work, curries and pickles.

Praline. Chopped grilled almonds.

Profiteroles for Soups. Pipe out choux paste in tiny balls with a 4mm ($\frac{1}{8}$ in) bit onto a lightly greased tray. Bake at 204°C. (400°F.).

Protect. The protection of a joint, pie or other fare from the heat of the oven. Protection is offered with greaseproof paper or foil. Cooking without colouring.

Quenelles. Small cooked forcemeat pellets. Prepared from a light purée of raw chicken, veal or other ingredients. The purée is worked over cold in a pan with a wooden spoon. It is seasoned with salt, cayenne and lemon juice, bound with egg white and cream and well beaten. The preparation is piped out with a fine bit into 12mm ($\frac{1}{2}$ in) quenelles in a fancy squiggle on a greased tray. The preparation is covered with hot stock and allowed to poach over a slow heat. Fish quenelles are made identically, but using a soft textured fish like whiting. There are several varieties of quenelles. The preparation may also be spooned out into olive shapes for vol-au-vent fillings and other dishes. The quenelle preparation may be coloured and flavoured with curry, horse-radish, mint, paprika and any herb or spice, and flecked with chopped truffle, ham, chicken or game.

Racines. French term for roots, i.e. root vegetables.

Ragoût. French term for a stew.

Raising Agent. Substance, i.e. yeast, baking powder, to make a dough, paste or mix rise. Preparation is aerated by the carbonic acid gas given off from the agent when heat is applied. Flour is sold as plain or self-raising; chefs usually prefer to add their own raising agents.

Ramequin. Small tartlet of short paste for savoury filling applications.

Ratatouille. A Provençale preparation of aubergine, courgette, tomato, onion and red pepper seasoned and stewed in olive oil with a suspicion of garlic.

Réchauffér. To reheat cooked food from cold. Small roasts are reheated by placing the piece in cold water and bringing it to the boil. It is then removed and placed in a medium oven.

Reduce. The decreasing in volume of a liquid over heat through evaporation to form a more concentrated solution.

Refresh. Refreshing cooked or blanched foods, usually vegetables, under or in cold running water.

Relishes. Term given to savoury, spiced and highly seasoned vinegar products. There are numerous relishes covering a wide field of flavours, e.g. hamburger, hot dog, barbecue and corn. Allied to relishes are types of chutnies, e.g. tamarind, pineapple, tomato and mushroom. There are also seafood cocktail relishes and sauces. Many relishes are of American origin.

Rice Cones. Milled rice ground into a flour, available in 3 types: fine,

311

medium and coarse. Rice cones, unlike wheat flour, is non-absorbent and this is why it is now used for deep frying fish, especially in fish and chip shops and other large scale deep frying operations.

Rissoler. To fry to a golden brown or just to brown.

Rondels. Made from a fish, meat, poultry or game quenelle preparation, usually flecked with chopped fines herbes. Shaped to a 2½cm (1 in) diameter, rolled and tied in greaseproof paper and poached for 15 minutes. Then unwrapped and sliced in rondels. As for quenelles, the rondels may be left plain, coloured and loaded with any chopped ingredient.

Rosemary (Romarin). Well-known herb with an attractive flavour, extensively used in old English cookery. Employed in fish, meat and poultry stuffings, stews and certain veal preparations.

Roux. Flour and fat preparation mixed and cooked together or roasted to desired hue.

Royale. Garnish for soups. Baked savoury custard, standard or coloured and cut or stamped out into patterns. Prepared from an infusion of consommé and chervil into which beaten eggs are joined. Seasoned with salt, cayenne and lemon juice. Double cream is added and the preparation whisked into a mayonnaise consistency. Baked in shallow, oiled mould bain-marie style. When cold, cut as required. Royale may be flecked with fines herbes, chopped ham, chicken, game or other cooked ingredients.

Rye (Seigle). Widely cultivated cereal in Europe and the Americas for bread, distilling into spirit or brewing into beer. Rye flour is dark and is used for 'black bread'.

Saccharin, Saccharine. Sweet substance extracted from coal, reputed 300 times sweeter than cane sugar. Soluble in boiling water and in alcohol. Sells in tablets, as a powder and in liquid form. Numerous proprietary sweetening agents of a similar nature are on the market selling by brand name, some derived from other chemical sources.

Saccharine and other sweetening chemical compounds are valuable for those who are on a sugar-free diet, slimmers, overweights and waistline-watchers. Saccharine and allied lines are only used in the kitchen for dietetic reasons or when sugar is in short supply, such as during wartime rationing and similar emergencies, or in manufacturing and food and beverage processing for economic reasons.

Saffron (Safran). Member of the crocus family. Its yellow colour and unusual flavour is appreciated and employed with rice, for stews and certain bakery goods, i.e. Cornish Saffron Cakes. Should be used sparingly lest its flavour overpowers. Said to have been brought in the bulb into England in the staff of a monk returning from the Crusades and first planted in Saffron Walden. Saffron is used extensively in Italian, Spanish and other national cookery.

Sage (Sauge). Popular stuffing herb. Has a strong and perfumed aroma and should be used with care lest it overpowers other flavours.

Salamander. French term for overhead grill.

Salpicon. Combination of several diced ingredients with one predominating, after which the preparation takes its name. This term applies to crustacea, poultry and game. The supporting ingredients may include mushroom, truffle, tongue and ham. Thus a lobster salpicon would indicate the diced meat and mushrooms.

Salt (Sel). One condiment which is indispensable in the kitchen. The basic seasoner of all seasoning agents. Sodium chloride, the chemical term for salt, is mined or extracted from sea salt. There are 3 types: coarse or bay salt, which the French call gross sel, block, and table which is refined and free flowing. For table use the new vogue is the salt hand mill containing bay salt. There are salt substitutes for those who are on salt free diets.

Sauter, Sauté. To shallow fry, e.g. Sauté au beurre, fry in butter.

Sauteuse. Shallow pan for shallow frying.

Score. To incise or ciseler. Thick skin of pork is scored to facilitate cooking and carving.

Seasoning. To season with salt and pepper. Also old English term for a stuffing or dressing, e.g. Roast Pork with Seasoning.

Shallot (Éshalote). Small sized and most useful member of the onion family. Stronger in flavour than the Spanish onion and nowhere as harsh and pungent as garlic.

Sippets. Diced toasted bread for soups as against croûtons, which are fried.

Smetana. Russian term for sour cream.

Smörrebröd. Buttered bread, term for open sandwich Scandinavian style.

Smörgasbörd. Scandinavian term for appetisers. A cold table from which guests serve themselves. Now a speciality restaurant theme.

Socle. A plinth for mounting and displaying special preparations made of stearine, sugar or other substance. Could also be a large croûton, i.e. a piece of shaped bread deep fried to a golden brown. Socles are usually inedible or not intended to be consumed.

Soy Sauce. Chinese bottled sauce made from soya bean flour, salt and monsodium glutomate. Used extensively in Chinese cookery.

Suet Dough. 360g (12 oz) chopped suet to 500g (1 lb) flour, seasoning and water.

Combine suet and flour, season with salt and pepper, add sufficient water to form stiff and pliable dough. Work until it clears the hands. Roll out on a floured board.

Sugar (Sucre). Synonymous with sweet. Chemically known as sucrose, it derives from 2 main sources: sugar beet and sugar cane. In its refined state both have identical sweetening and dietetic properties. Sugar is marketed in various forms, from the unrefined demerara to the refined lump, castor, granulated, icing and white and coloured crystals. Sugar in the kitchen is seldom defined in exact quantities; the ingredients to which it is joined are sweetened to taste.

Sweat. To cook or heat food in butter (or fat) in a closed receptacle. Sweating chopped onion or sliced mushroom.

Swill (Déglacer). The swilling out of the pan with stock or wine to form a gravy or make a sauce.

Tabasco. Famous hot condiment sauce made by the McIlhenny Company, Avery Island, Louisana, U.S.A. Specially grown red peppers are aged in cask and then macerated and matured in vinegar. Has many uses both in the kitchen and as a table condiment.

The company was founded in 1868 by the McIlhenny family. The peppers were originally grown from seeds handed by a veteran of the Mexican War by the name of Gleason to Edmund McIlhenny upon the soldier's return to the U.S.A. in 1853. McIlhenny planted the seeds and reared the peppers with which he made sauce for his family and thus began an experiment which grew into a large industry.

Tammy. Kitchen slang for étamine straining cloth.

Tarragon (Estragon). Member of the fines herbes with chervil and parsley. Has a perfumed aroma. Used in vinegar, pickles, aspics and for decorating chaudfroids.

Texturized Vegetable Protein. Spun or extruded soya bean. Rice and other vegetable protein may also be used for the process. T.V.P. is employed as a protein filler in manufactured products. When coloured, flavoured and appropriately shaped it is able, so it is claimed, to simulate various meat and other protein foods and products.

Threaded Eggs (Oeufs Filés). Garnish for consommé. Beat eggs, season with salt and pepper, strain through a sieve, place in a fine conical strainer, hold and shake over boiling consommé so that the preparation falls into shreds and cooks. Drain well and handle with care.

Thyme (Serpolet). Popular garden stuffing herb with a scented aroma, similar in type to sage.

Titivate. To correct; the titivating of a sauce to check it for flavour and colour; to titivate a dish for service, to dress it up.

Tombé au Beurre. The cooking of vegetables, usually sliced, in butter, sometimes with the addition of a small amount of water and seasoning.

Tourte. Large, round tart, or flan case made of puff paste for sweet and savoury fillings.

Treacle. Prepared from sugar cane molasses. Sells as black treacle or refined as golden syrup.

Tronçon. Usually applies to flat fish, e.g. Tronçon de Turbot, a fish steak cut across the bone.

Trou Normand, un. A glass of calvados, i.e. apple jack, a spirit distilled from cider, served during a banquet in the manner of a sorbet to stimulate appetite for further dishes to come. It is usual to serve the calvados in a balloon glass.

Truffle, Imitation. When truffle is unobtainable or too expensive to procure, it can be produced synthetically. One is a bought product manufactured from ox blood, resembling a black kind of preserved meat. Another is kitchen-made from dried coffee grounds mixed with gelatine and shaped as truffle. Few of these efforts compare with the richness of colour and fragrance of the real thing.

Turmeric. Dried ground root of an eastern plant, yellow in colour. Its main use is in curry powder.

Turtle Herbs. Basil, sage, marjoram, rosemary, parsley root, thyme, bayleaf and peppercorns.

Vanilla (Vanille). Pod from a species of tropical orchid, the sweetest of all natural sugars. The pods are blanched and dried and are then ready for culinary use. They may be employed many times over providing they are kept dry and in an airtight tin. Vanilla is also available in powder form and as an essence.

Vinegar. Basic commodity upon which the manufacturing of pickles, bottled sauces and relishes of all types are founded. In the kitchen we use malt and wine vinegars. Name of vinegar is derived from vin aigre meaning literally soured wine. There are red and white wine vinegars, fruit and herb-flavoured malt vinegars. Pure malt vinegar is colourless, but for general use it is tinted with caramel.

Visega. The spinal cord of the sturgeon. It is marketed whole and dried and requires a prolonged soaking in fresh, cold water. It is then simmered in consommé for 4 hours till soft and tender. It is used, diced, in consommé as a garnish, in coulibiac and other Russian fare.

Voiler. To mask or veil.

Wet Entrée. Inelegant kitchen slang, to indicate a meat or poultry dish, an entrée in sauce.

Whisk. To beat or whip with a wire whisk.

Yeast (Levure). Tiny spore or fungus, focal point in making raised or fermented goods. It is a live substance so must always be used very fresh. Excessive heat will kill its raising powers. Usual proportions are 25g (1 oz) to 500g (1 lb) flour. When yeast is added to a dough in the form of a ferment, it should always be left to prove in a warm place.

315

Menu Composing

Menu composing is one of the most exacting tasks in catering. This is because it is the production sheet, the blueprint, upon which the entire catering operation is structured. The menu also performs another function: the important one of informing the client as to what is available.

Menus can be classified into 3 categories: the set meal, or table d'hôte, selling at a fixed price; the à la carte, offering a choice of dishes and prices; the combined table d'hôte and à la carte where, as is usual, the price of the main dish determines the price of the meal.

An à la carte is often supported by one or more plats du jour, dishes of the day. A table d'hôte may be augmented by supplement dishes priced additionally. Drawing up a regular menu is difficult enough, even more demanding is composing a menu for a function or banquet. This becomes a real test of creative ingenuity when the client requests something special, novel or different. Fortunately there are certain guidelines to be followed which are applicable to all menus.

Guidelines

Cost is the prime consideration; how much the client is prepared to pay. We may be catering to a price or money could be of secondary importance to the selection of dishes, quality of food and appointments of the service. Menus should be topical, imaginative and weather-wise. Lighter foods and cold fare are given preference in warm weather, and heavier and more substantial dishes when it is cold.

At Christmas, festive fare is featured; on Shrove Tuesday, pancakes; new potatoes, strawberries, lamb, salmon, when in season; and a fish dish on Fridays. Local specialities should also be a menu feature and this is always appreciated. There should be variety and adequacy of choice, i.e. a three-course set meal should offer choice of first course, soup or starter; meat, poultry, fish and a cold dish at the main course: sweet, cheese or savoury at the third course, with the option of sweet and cheese or savoury; and then coffee.

Further considerations are the type of clientele, their tastes, numbers to be catered for and menu balance, without undue repetition of colour, flavour or commodity. In this strain a chicken dish should not follow chicken soup; steak and kidney pudding should not preceed an apple pie; fried fish, fruit fritters; a risotto, a rice pudding, and so forth.

Nutritional values may need to be taken count of as well as the service of wines. Though, at a function, it is more usual to match the wine or wines to the dishes, where a client elects to show a certain wine list, the foods may need to be partnered accordingly. In all these matters,

316

especially with menu choice and balance, some discretion should prevail. The caterer is there not to educate but to provide the type of service the client requires and, of course, at the price the client is prepared to pay. This has a bearing on the development, in the more popular sectors of the industry, for the short or restricted menu.

A menu needs to be evenly distributed throughout the kitchen so it will neither overburden nor monopolize any one partie, or corner, and its equipment.

Practical Considerations

Naturally the menu should be well within the capabilities of the kitchen and the service personnel. This means thought should be given to the actual service of the dishes in the room. Hot food should be served really hot and cold food cold. The food must be adequately seasoned, well presented, properly garnished and accompanied by its correct escorts. Better a simple bill-of-fare well cooked and served than a pretentious menu beyond the ability of the food preparation and service personnel and available equipment.

The menu should read well. It should also be clean and attractively presented. If there is anything worse than a badly composed and mis-spelt menu, it is a soiled one. In accordance with the type of clientele and the policy of the establishment, the menu is written in English or in French. Attempts to translate French standard culinary terms into English, or English (or other national dishes) into French should be avoided.

While menu composing does require a certain flair, proficiency comes with practice. In this connection, it is always instructive to see what others do, by collecting a menu file.

Marketing Aspects

The menu performs a marketing function. The caterer sells his service through the menu. When a client reads the bill of fare, an immediate impression, usually a good one, is formed of the food listed. But it is one thing to compose a menu and something else to produce the food. They are complementary and, therefore, the menu should not disappoint. The actual dishes, when served, must always be as good as the impression that the menu conveys. Therein lies the art of menu composing.

Note: A menu should be a true statement of dishes and should not misinform lest, in Britain, the Trade Descriptions Act 1968, is in anyway contravened.

The Service of Wine

There are red, rosé and white; still and sparkling; table and fortified wines. France is one of the biggest producers and her wines are among the world's finest. The great wine-growing districts of France are located in the provinces of Champagne, Bordeaux and Burgundy and others in Alsace, the Val-du-Loire and Côtes-du-Rhône.

Germany produces Hock and Moselle wines in tall slender bottles from the areas of the Rhineland and the valley of the Moselle river.

There are many good wines from Spain, Portugal and Italy. From Spain and Portugal come sherry and port respectively, 2 well-known fortified wines. The wines are fortified with the addition of brandy; this treatment, besides making the wines fit to travel, greatly appeals to the British palate.

There are wines from Australasia and South Africa and others from the Americas, Central Europe, the Mediterranean, North Africa and the Soviet Union.

André Simon, possibly the greatest of all authorities, defined wine as 'the suitably fermented juice of freshly gathered grapes'. Wine is made wherever the grape is cultivated. It is, therefore, a considerable subject about which one never ceases to acquire knowledge. Our main concern here, however, is the service of wine as a complement to food.

It is very essential that the sommelier (wine waiter) and all who serve wine know their wine list. Furthermore, wine service personnel should have the opportunity of tasting the wines they serve so, when the need arises, they are able to describe and recommend the wines to their clients.

Service Temperatures

There is, or should be, nothing pretentious about wine. It is a fact that certain wine goes with certain food. But people drink the wine they know and like best and this is to be encouraged.

What is far more important than the so-called correct partnership of dishes is the temperature at which wine should be served. The whole enjoyment and appreciation depends on the temperature at which wine is served. The rules are simple: white, sparkling and rosé wines should be served iced; red wine should be served at room temperature 18°–20°C. (65°–70°F.). White and sparkling wines such as champagne and all rosé wines are served 'off the ice' and when poured out should frost the glass. Red table wines are served with the 'chill off' (chambre), at room temperature. This acclimatization should be gradual, i.e. by just leaving the bottle in the room. Never resort to the barbaric practice of plunging the bottle into warm water or placing it in the close proximity of a fire. A warm white wine tastes quite different —flat and uninteresting—compared to one adequately iced. Likewise, one cannot really appreciate a cold red wine. Gentle warmth develops the bouquet and cold suppresses it; but better serve a red too cold than a white wine which is tepid.

Other Points of Service

Apart from the critical factor of correct temperature, the only other rules revolve around a few points and refinements of service.

A good wine deserves a good glass, a thin stem glass of good quality. Hock, Moselle and Alsace wines are served in special tall, tinted hock type glasses. At the table the wine is presented to the client and is then opened. The capsule is cut at just below the lip of the bottle—not torn off—the top of the bottle wiped over with a clean serviette, the cork drawn and a sip of the wine poured into a glass for the approval of the host.

This ritual is no idle fad; the intention is for the client to verify the order and to sample and approve the wine. Is the wine at the correct temperature, is it in good condition or is it corked or otherwise ullaged? If white, sparkling or rosé, does it show the tell-tale frosting of the glass or does it need further cooling? The temperature of red wine is told by sipping. Whether the wine is out of sorts or corked is indicated not so much by the palate as by the nose; the sensitivity of the nose is far more accurate than the taste buds on the tongue. Whether a wine is cold enough is also told by feeling the bottle with the hand. If the wine is corked or out of condition, confirmed by the sommelier, it should be replaced immediately by another bottle and the one 'on ullage' returned to the supplier.

The fine red wines of Bordeaux and Burgundy, also vintage ports, which improve with age, must be handled with care and respect. It is important not to shake the bottle unduly and, therefore, for service the bottle is placed in a wicker basket called a cradle. If the wine has thrown a sediment, it should be decanted. In restaurants the wine is decanted through a paper filter and glass funnel into a decanter. The correct method, however, is to stand the bottle upright to allow the sediment to settle and then to pour the wine very gently direct into a decanter until the sediment is reached.

It is the vogue in most restaurants to serve not only vintage, but all red wine in a cradle which displays the cork drawn from the bottle for the client to see. There is no harm in these rituals; they add a certain ambience to our subject.

The partnership of wine and food can be discussed in a generalized manner. A dry white wine goes well with fish. A delicate or a fuller bodied red with meat, poultry and game. A sweeter white, or a champagne, with the sweet course. Port is the perfect partner to cheese. Liqueurs are served with the coffee. Unless a special gastronomic occasion, the custom is now for one wine throughout the meal; a champagne, hock, moselle or alsace for a lighter luncheon wine, a rosé 'off the ice', very popular now, or a wine—any wine—the client likes the best!

Vintages

Some wines, particularly reds, improve with age under cork, providing the wine has ageing qualities and is properly stored. Every year when the grapes are gathered, a wine is produced in the wine growing districts and this is termed a vintage. If it is a good year, a long dry summer, which produces an exceptionally sound wine, it carries the year on the label and this is known as a vintage wine. A vintage is, as we know, produced each year and the wine is either good, moderate or indifferent. Since the wine trade is a business, the vintage wines are usually those of a known and considered good year. Wines not up to a vintage rating are either sold as non-vintage or used for blending with other wines of the same or of other years. Vintage wines are usually more expensive than non-vintage and the most expensive, hence the best, are bottled on site. The leading example here are the famous château bottled clarets, i.e. mise en bouteille au château. This does not mean to convey non-vintage wines are in any way inferior in quality. Many non-vintage wines, champagne in particular, are excellent. Incidentally, the champagne vintners normally only bring out vintages in exceptional years. Of course, even poor years do sometimes produce red and white vintage wines of character in some areas; this makes our subject rather complex and leads onto the actual purchasing of wines.

The Wine Trade

Recently, in common with all spheres of commerce, the wine trade has become marketing-conscious and highly commercialized. As a result more wine is now being sold than ever before. But the wine trade has always been an honourable one and the best way to purchase wine is to go by the shipper of repute and deal with a reputable merchant.

Wine sells in bottles, halves and quarters. There are larger sizes, usually reserved for champagne, which is bottled in magnums equalling 2 bottles; double magnums or jeroboams equalling 4 bottles; rehoboams, 6; methuselahs 8, and other sizes. Clarets and hocks are also, on occasions, bottled in the magnum size. Bordeaux wines are bottled in square shoulder bottles, burgundies in sloping shoulder bottles, the tall, slender hocks in reddish brown coloured bottles, and moselles in green bottles. The larger the bottle the better the wine. Thus a wine in a bottle size, for example, shows better than the same wine in a quarter bottle.

In restaurants, wine also sells by the glass and the carafe in a choice of 2 measures: large or standard glass, and half or large carafe.

Take champagne again as an example. It sells by branded name and such well known labels as G. H. Mumm, Lanson, Mercier, Moët et Chandon, Veuve Cliquot, Krug, Bollinger; Piper-Heidsieck and others are the cachet of authenticity and quality. The same applies to the names of well-known shippers of table wines and their products. Here we have what we now know as the brand image. Heavily advertised and popular brand wines from France, Germany, Italy, Spain, Portugal and elsewhere maintain a continuity of standards of quality.

Beauty, however, may only be bottle deep. The ultimate test of quality is in the actual sampling of the wine. You get what you pay for. So we come back to the reliable supplier and the sampling of the product by the buyer.

Mention should be made of country wines made from fruit, other than grapes, and of mead, made from honey. These are sometimes known as English wines; they are of good quality and popular.

Storage

While good reds should have a little age, whites, with some exceptions, do not necessarily improve with age and are drunk young. For storage, the bottles should be laid horizontal so the contents come into contact with the cork; wine, being a live substance (with a life span), is said to breathe through the cork. Spirits do not improve in the bottle and they are stored standing up so that the contents do not come into contact with the cork; a spirit would cause the cork to shrink and the bottle to weep.

Brandy and Liqueurs

Brandy matures and mellows only in the wood and ceases to age as soon as it is bottled. There are 3 main types of brandy; the standard (or three star) which is a spirit taken with soda, dry or American ginger ale; and the liqueur which has aged in cask and is served in small quantities in a balloon glass. The glass is held in the palm of the hand and the warmth permeates through to the liqueur so the client may admire the natural bouquet. On no account should brandy glasses be pre-heated. This misguided practice spoils the liqueur by dissipating the bouquet ethers when the brandy comes into sudden contact with a warmed glass.

It will be observed how gentle heat, whether the warmth of a room at 18°C. (65°F.) or the palm of the hand, promotes the nose and palate appreciation of red wines and liqueur brandy. Cold also promotes appreciation, as in the case of white, sparkling and rosé wines. It also enhances the enjoyment of sherry when served as an aperitif and of such liqueurs as kummel, crème de menthe, cointreau and others. This is the theme of the 'on the rocks', the service of whisky with cracked ice, other drinks featured frappé, i.e. with shaved ice, and of course the shaking of cocktails in ice. So we see that the vital matter of temperature takes priority in the service not only of wines but all drinks, alcoholic and non-alcoholic.

Convenience Foods

The term convenience foods is applied to all foodstuffs which are 'bought in' ready or partially prepared for cooking or for service. Convenience foods may be classified as fresh, canned, frozen or dried. The advent of these products, which offer certain advantages in quality control, purchasing, handling, portioning and costing, has been a gradual process. Bread, ice cream and pasta could be considered as the original convenience foods; they were among the first to be purchased ready-made instead of being on-premise prepared.

Advantages

Convenience foods which are wholly or part prepared are virtually 100 per cent usable. There is no undue waste and therefore less heavy and laborious kitchen preparation and usually less storage is required in their handling. Since the initial preparation waste has been removed, convenience foods are more amenable to portioning and costing than bulk unprepared supplies. Most manufacturers recommend a portion size for their products but the final decision must rest with the caterer, depending upon his particular requirement. In order to facilitate accurate costing the net weight from convenience foods is printed on the container by the manufacturer.

Pre-prepared fresh, canned and frozen foods are costed and portioned as applicable by weight or by the count.

With most dried foods, i.e. soup mixes, vegetables and certain sweets, portioning and costing is applied after the reconstitution of the product. Dry weights in this paricular context are not of immediate concern; it is the yield of the finished product which is apportioned.

FRESH FOOD

The partial preparation of fresh foods relieves the caterer of the heavy preparation and handling of certain raw materials with the attendant space required and refuse disposal problems involved. The raw commodity is usually prepared to specification by a specialist supplier. Meat is ready butchered into joints, grilling or stewing cuts, or minced; fish cleaned and filleted; poultry plucked, drawn and oven dressed; vegetables washed and trimmed; and potatoes washed and peeled, left whole or cut for frying. The actual methods of preparation employed follow orthodox culinary procedure. In the case of meat, fish and poultry, the caterer has at his service, on a sub-contracting basis, the craft skills of the butcher, fishmonger and poulterer.

CANNED FOOD

An extensive variety of foods are canned. These include fruits and fruit juices, vegetables, potatoes, soups, meat, fish and poultry products, made-up dishes and snacks, and sweets.

There is a wide range of packs but basically they are known as retail, individual portions and bulk catering packs.

The majority of canned foods are pre-cooked and, as appropriate, just need reheating. Care should be taken not to overcook the product. Delicate fare, such as asparagus and celery, are best heated in the can; the can is opened, placed in a pan of hot water and simmered until the contents are heated right through. With condensed soups and other speciality cannings the manufacturer's instructions should be carefully followed.

All cans of food should be inspected before use. If blown, no attempt should be made to reclaim the contents; they must *not* be eaten. If a can is dented but shows no signs of leakage, the contents should be sound. If the contents of cans smell fresh and appear normal they are fit for consumption.

Storage of Canned Food

Canned goods should be stored in a cool, dry place. High storage temperatures should be avoided because in time they tend to impair the colour and flavour of the contents of the can. Damp storage will cause rusting of the outside of the can which may cause the can to perforate and spoil the contents.

FROZEN FOODS

The first successful consignments of chilled meat were shipped to England in 1880, but it was not until the 1920s that an American scientist, Clarence Birdseye, developed the commercial quick-freezing process which led to the various techniques of today.

With few exceptions, most food may be processed by freezing and the variety is, therefore, extensive. The groups of food available in frozen form include: fruit and fruit juices; uncooked meat and meat products; poultry and poultry products; bakery and confectionary lines; ice cream and iced confections; unbaked pastry; soups and sauces; and pre-cooked meals in bulk, plated, and cook-in-the-bag. There is a wide choice of pack sizes, basically in 2 main types: retail packs and catering packs. Some foods are available individually frozen and others block frozen.

Storage of Frozen Food

Frozen foods should always be held at the controlled temperature of minus 18°C. (zero F.) or below in a freezer or frozen food cabinet. The

323

external wrapping or packeting of frozen foods in storage should not be removed since this is intended to be a protection against spoilage. Frozen foods should not be allowed to thaw in storage and once thawed should be treated as fresh. Frozen food which has been thawed, i.e. defrosted, should *not* be re-frozen. Ice cream and frozen sweets, such as mousse, should be stored at minus 18°C. (zero F.) or below in the case of many specialities.

Properly prepared and stored frozen food will keep in good condition. Nearly all foods can be stored for 3 months, and many for longer. Stocks should always be used in proper rotation. Any food which has to be thawed prior to cooking or service should be thawed out within the wrapping.

A freezer must not be confused with a refrigerator, where the internal temperature is in the region of 5°C. (40°F.). This is meant for holding certain foods at a chilled temperature, i.e. milk, butter, salad materials.

DRIED FOODS

Sun drying is the oldest method of food preservation known to man. This form of dehydration is still practised in many parts of the world. Dehydration by artificial means has been employed for some 200 years but it is only in comparatively recent times that technological progress in this field of food processing has developed methods which produce dehydrated foods of first-class quality.

The principle of dehydration is to remove the water content of foods and thereby control or destroy the micro-organisms which cause deterioration and decay.

A wide range of food is available in dried form, including soups and sauces; vegetables; potatoes; fruit; meals and snack dishes; meat and vegetable dishes; sweets; prepared mixes; catering and bakery mixes; beverages—instant coffee and tea; and instant products for vending machines.

Many dehydrated lines are a mixture of dry ingredients prepared to a carefully balanced formula which, when liquid is added and the product has been reconstituted or cooked, makes up the article of food for which it has been designed. In most of the quick drying processes, dehydrated products will reconstitute during cooking without presoaking.

Bulk packs and controlled 'end result' packs are available. Prepared mixes are packed in boxes, paper sacks and tins.

As a basic rule of procedure, uncooked or partially cooked fried foods are reconstituted by the addition of hot or cold liquid—water, milk, stock—and are then cooked. Certain products do not require cooking and are ready when reconstituted. In all instances the manufacturer's instructions must be closely followed; this is most important because of the variation between products.

Storage of Dried Foods

To ensure a reasonable long life, dried food packs are designed to give adequate protection from air and moisture. High humidity and high temperatures may cause slight deterioration in storage so dried foods must be stored in a cool, dry place. Once a container is opened the contents should be used in a reasonably short space of time. Since most of the water content is removed during processing, there is a shrinkage of the product and a greatly reduced bulk results. The weight is also reduced to about one fifth of the original with the consequent reduced transport and handling costs, as well as giving economy in storage space.

As a general rule, providing storage conditions are correct, dried foods should be consumed within 12 months of being received, with the exception of prepared catering and bakery mixes which should be used within 2 or 3 months.

THE ECONOMICS OF CONVENIENCE FOODS

The comparative costs between bulk unprepared fresh commodities and convenience foods should be appreciated. It is the difference between the 'gross and unprepared' and the 'nett and prepared' weight.

Account must be taken of the wastage in preparation of the 'gross and unprepared' items, together with the labour and general on-premise handling involved. It is, however, reasonable to assume that since the production of convenience foods is geared to factory methods and by reason of the volume of output and the bulk buying of raw materials, the manufacturer's costs can be considered proportionately lower than those of the caterer purchasing his own unprepared commodities and performing his own on-premise preparation. The use of convenience foods makes for a fair degree of price stability and this is a further favourable characteristic of convenience foods.

CONVENIENCE FOODS IN CATERING

The use of convenience foods can be seen in 2 different contexts. One concerns the complete and standardized convenience food product, evolved by following the manufacturers' instructions. The other relates to the utilization of convenience foods as a labour- and time-saving product. Skill and expertise is then applied to create finished products in accordance with the specific requirements of the caterer.

Chefs generally agree that convenience foods cut down on kitchen staff, reduce wastage, speed up production and increase control. They also make the point that convenience foods take the skill out of cookery. This may be quite true, but other skills—more of a handling

325

nature—are required, which are perhaps not as sophisticated as the more conventional.

In contemplating convenience foods, the actual quality of the product must be considered; products with varying qualities are marketed and the caterer must select the commodity best suited to his particular requirements. It is essential to start with a good quality product because an inferior one is not likely to be improved by any craft skills. Convenience foods must be handled with care and efficiency. The 'titivating' or correcting for service, as required, of the finished product, demands the skills required of normal culinary products.

Author's Note.

The term convenience food is often the subject of debate and controversy. Since no suitable alternative name has, as yet, been forthcoming and as it is now generally recognized, the term has remained. It is, however, possible that eventually convenience foods may be redesignated 'advanced prepared foods', which is really what they are.

Food Costing and Portion Control

There is more to catering than just cooking. Food is not purchased and prepared, cooked and served regardless. The entire sequence is controlled. This is because food represents money and should, at all times, be regarded as such. We are dealing here with the economic aspect, the office side of cookery, an inter-related progression of costing, portioning, selling and controlling. This is known as food costing and portion control.

FOOD COSTING

Food is purchased by weight. Some commodities may also sell by the count, case or container. Something like 300 separate commodities are handled in the kitchen. Prices vary and few foodstuffs remain static. Many commodities, e.g. fresh vegetables and fruit, are prone to seasonal and market supply and demand price fluctuations. This means, for example, that in summer, when there is a call on cold foods, the price of salad materials may rise accordingly. Likewise in winter, the price of salads drops and that of other commodities, such as vegetables, may rise.

Food is known as perishable or non-perishable. If wastage is to be minimized, the object of the exercise, the handling of perishables requires greater care than that of non-perishables. Thus the growing tendency to handle the maximum quantity of food which has a long shelf life, in order to cut waste. Food costing implies knowing the price paid for food purchased. This stage is known as the first or gross cost. The next step is to portion the food, which may increase its cost, since in the preparation and cooking processes a certain amount of loss occurs. With meat and poultry, for example, there is a bone loss and a further loss by shrinkage during cooking. The same applies with fresh vegetables; loss in preparation, possibly a further loss in cooking and often a weight loss in storage caused by evaporation.

FOOD PORTIONING

Firstly we must define what is meant by a portion. There are in fact 2 kinds: the portion of *raw* or *uncooked* food, and the plate portion of prepared or cooked food.

To illustrate this, it may take 3 kilo (6 lb) raw potatoes to put 1 kilo (2 lb) cooked potato on the plate, because there has been a weight loss in preparation—washing and peeling—and a shrinkage in cooking.

Portioning has a bearing upon the type of customers catered for. A selective clientele could be more discriminating than hungry travellers. In popular catering, large portions are generally appreciated; white collar employees may have smaller appetites than heavy manual workers.

Portions, therefore, are geared to the catering market, i.e. to whom do we cater. This entails the compilation of a food portions chart which determines the portioning of all food handled. These charts are 'developed', i.e. once devised, the portions may need adjusting, in the light of practical experience, until the correct portioning is assessed item by item with a fair degree of accuracy. But even then the chart should not be left to its own devices; it must be checked over continuously. As the whole catering activity is geared to the Portions Chart, it is essential that all concerned be familiar with the food portioning policy of their establishment.

Portions are worked out, as appropriate, by weight or by the count. The count could be termed the unit control, i.e. a 250g (8 oz) chop or a 175g (6 oz) fillet of fish, and the pre-packeted units of wrapped butter, portioned cheese, biscuits, cake and similar 'bought in' or on-premise portioned lines.

Unit control lines are simple to cost; more complicated to apportion are joints of meat, fresh vegetables and any bulk food, because of the wastage element in preparation and cooking. In the case of made-up dishes, the ingredients stated on the recipe are weighed and priced in order to obtain the cost per portion and then the selling price.

Over and above appetites, portioning has a direct bearing on the type of operation. A popular catering operation, in order to contain costs, may work on tight costings which will mean rigid portioning of food. This does *not* imply small portions but *accurate* portioning. Portion control should never suggest meanness; it simply indicates that once portion sizes are established they must be followed through.

In a top income and exclusive restaurant working on more conventional lines, portioning is far more liberal, to imply ostentatiousness, and is taken care of by the prices charged on the menu.

Portions may vary according to the type of menu featured, i.e. à la carte or table d'hôte. It is a general practice to feature larger portions for an à la carte service and smaller portions for the set table d'hôte meal. The reason for this is that a set meal may consist of 3, 4 or even more courses, whereas the à la carte is often 'restricted' to the appetite and/or pocket of the customers and they may require only one or 2 courses. In actual practice, caterers find an à la carte service more flexible to adjust both portions and mark up price. A set meal is often difficult to alter since the customers are accustomed to the price of the meal, the number of courses and size of the portions. It is in a kind of box from which it is not always easy to break out. There could be, and usually is, resistance to any change affecting anything which seems to be to the disadvantage of the customers. Therefore, the à la carte, offering a choice of prices and dishes, is really far more acceptable all round.

Dishes are priced in accordance with expected profit yield and this important aspect is developed in the next paragraph.

KITCHEN CONTROL

In order to safeguard the financial structure, various controls are placed upon the kitchen. These controls start with the actual purchasing and this entails the checking, by a trained and experienced person, of all goods purchased by weight or by count *and* also for quality standards. At the same time the invoice, or delivery note, will be checked to ensure it conforms with the agreed price at which the goods were purchased. These checks are important since it is possible, through human error, to buy at one price and to be charged another, usually a higher one!

Once the food is received and taken on stock, stock records should be kept. The main control on catering is what is termed kitchen control and there are 2 principal systems: the percentage system, and the selling price system.

Kitchen Percentage System

This system consists of charging all food issued to the kitchen at cost price and then relating this to the business done, i.e. the money taken in return for the food served. The cost of the food is subtracted from the selling price and this will produce the gross profit. A percentage is then struck, either on cost or on profit. The usual profit now rotates between 60–66 per cent gross profit or 40 and a 33 per cent food cost respectively. Some establishments find they need to work to a 75 per cent gross profit which equals a 25 per cent food cost. This pertains to the pricing up of the dishes:

Food Profit		Food Cost
50%	Cost of food multiplied by 2	50%
60%	,, ,, ,, ,, by 2½	40%
66⅔%	,, ,, ,, ,, by 3	33⅓%
75%	,, ,, ,, ,, by 4	25%

To obtain the *gross percentage* of profit
the following formula is applied:

$$\frac{\text{Gross Profit} \times 100}{\text{Takings}} = \% \text{ of profit}$$

To obtain the *food cost* the following formula is applied:

$$\frac{\text{Cost} \times 100}{\text{Takings}} = \% \text{ of cost}$$

Kitchen control should follow hard on the heels of business done. Ideally it should be worked out daily, based upon the previous day's business, or weekly, but certainly not less than fortnightly or, in extreme cases, monthly. The objective of working out the kitchen percentage quickly—the sooner the better—is to check any wastage which may undermine the target.

Selling Price Control System
This system consists of charging the kitchen with food at the selling price and comparing the total with the amount of takings from the business done. This means the kitchen account is debited with the price the food fetches when it is sold to the customer. The results should always come out over—never under—the original amount charged to the kitchen. Here we have a simple and effective control system, especially applicable to the popular catering field.

There are divers variations to this system, such as charging out the protein content of the meal only (meat, fish, poultry) and the hot beverages (coffee, tea) at the price the customer pays and letting the other and less expensive commodities—the carbohydrates content (vegetables, sweets, bread, rolls)—take care of themselves. This is a looser system but it suits certain quick service operations.

Comparative issues between the two systems
The caterer selects the type of kitchen control to suit the requirements of the particular operation. The simpler the operation (steak house, fish and chip restaurant, omelette bar, refreshment room) the easier it is to devise a control system.

The growth of the popular catering market and the trend in restricted and set menus could mean a wide application of the selling price control system. But this system has to be devised with care and attention to detail since it is very closely related to selling prices and it must be kept in accord with all changes in prices as and when they occur.

In some popular speciality operations the menu could be considered as 'subordinate' to the control system and would, in the main, only include items susceptible to a strict portion control to which the selling price system could be applied without any complicated accountancy work in the office.

The kitchen percentage control provides a flexible system where an operation features a selection of dishes at various prices at different times and for different meals. For a complex operation, such as this, the selling price control system would be impractical. This kitchen percentage, therefore, is more suitable to a varied catering policy and also to a higher priced operation than to a popular catering one working on a restricted menu. Here the selling price system is best and generally practised. The percentage system is readily understood and comparatively easy to work out. It is also a very sensitive system, especially when worked out to 2 points of decimals. Yet it is sufficiently elastic and works to the principle of the 'swings and round-abouts'; the selling price control, on the other hand, is very tightly integrated.

The situation could therefore be summed up as follows: the selling price system is applicable only to a simple and straightforward catering operation, and the kitchen percentage control to all other operations, i.e. those which work to a more conventional catering policy.

OTHER ASPECTS OF KITCHEN CONTROL

With both systems of kitchen control, account should be paid to opening and closing food stocks. This is handled through the passing of debits and credits. A debit is passed for stock on hand at the opening and a credit is passed at the end of the control period. If, however, the opening and closing stocks compensate each other, as is frequently the case, the debits and credits can be ignored. In this case they are only checked if any queries arise out of the control of business done. In actual practice the kitchen percentage system is usually sufficiently flexible to absorb opening and closing stocks, but with the selling price control, which is a tighter system, they must be taken into account.

Feeding staff on duty is a condition of service and as such it is a payroll cost and should be treated accordingly. This means a credit should be passed to the kitchen for staff feeding. Where numbers of staff are comparatively few, the chef may be requested to feed the staff within his kitchen percentage. But with the selling price control system, proper credits for staff feeding must be passed, otherwise this will disturb the system by providing a false figure.

LOW KITCHEN RETURNS

If the kitchen percentage or the selling price system results fall below the expected target, the position requires immediate investigation. The cause, or causes, of the discrepancy should be found and the situation adjusted without delay.

Several considerations affect the gross profit margins in the kitchen; one of the most common is over-advanced food preparation—too much is prepared in advance and this leads to wastage. This particular fault is easy to identify and is also remedied by frequent inspections of the dustbins. Wastage equally occurs through poor workmanship in the kitchen, food spoilt by indifferent cooking, or by not conforming to the portions chart and serving too large portions. Here we may have a training need.

Or the actual purchasing side of the operation may need looking over; there may be uneconomic buying or inefficient goods-receiving procedures, or insufficient checking of goods by weight, count, quality or price upon delivery. Wastage could occur from circumstances beyond normal control, such as a sudden drop in business due to bad weather or industrial unrest, but these hazards, or business risks, may sometimes be anticipated and are usually of short duration.

When normal fault analysis procedures fail to reveal the cause of a low kitchen return the caterer may have to delve deeper. Could it be due to some form of malpractice such as petty pilfering, or even to defalcation? Such hidden leaks are not altogether unknown and they may require stern disciplinary measures. All factors which may undermine the business highlight the importance of control and the advisability of putting in a system which will safeguard the turnover, prevent wastage and reveal immediately anything unusual.

So far we have written of results falling below expectations. It is sometimes as bad to have results way above the target. This also needs investigation, because it could mean the customers are not getting value for money; somewhere they are either skimped on portions or are being overcharged.

It is essential that the chef is kept fully informed of the results of his kitchen. When queries arise he should have full access to all the facts.

OTHER CONTROLS

A further system is known as commodity utilization control. This entails dividing the number of covers served into the weight of food consumed to give a per capita consumption. The figures produced are then compared with the portions chart and any discrepancies investigated.

The per capita theme may be applied to areas such as fuel consumption, food costs, payroll costs, or the per capita spending power per customer. The per capita is a useful independent tool—a double check—on any area in catering. Managers and supervisors may always reinforce office control by visual checks. This means the inspection of foodstuffs with spot checks on any particular commodity for weight, count and especially quality. One of the most effective of all physical checks is the random inspection of the garbage bins. A lot of money could find its way into the swill bin by such things as over-advanced kitchen preparation, food spoilt by careless cooking, too large portions served to customers and even to articles of equipment dumped in error.

OTHER COSTS IN RELATION TO FOOD COSTING AND PORTION CONTROL

In setting the gross profit yield on food it may be asked by what yardstick is this arrived at. It must be recognized that in a catering operation there are other operating costs over and above that of the food. This point needs stressing as it is not always appreciated.

Though this chapter deals primarily with food costing and portion control, a knowledge of the other costs is essential in order to comprehend the whole of the economic picture. There are 2 other sets of costs: the payroll and the overheads. The payroll embodies wages, social security payments, protective clothing, welfare, recruitment, training, administrative and other staff costs and taxes where applicable. Overheads include fuel and power, maintenance, equipment, replacements, depreciation, rents and rates, laundry, printing, stationery and sundry disbursements.

So we have 3 main sets of costs: food, payroll and overheads. The gross profit yield on food is calculated in relation to the other 2 sets of costs. The payroll may account for anything between 20–30 per cent of takings; the overheads for 15–25 per cent, depending upon the type of operation.

Formula to calculate costs to revenue:
$$\frac{\text{Cost}^* \times 100}{\text{Revenue}} = \quad \%$$

*Payroll or overheads (also food and beverages)

In a commercial operation (the profit sector) the food is priced for selling with the objective of defraying the costs of the food, payroll and overheads and at the same time to provide an acceptable margin of nett profit—or return on capital invested.

In the non-commercial field (the welfare or non-profit sector) policies differ accordingly. One example is for the revenue to break even with the combined food and payroll costs, the operation being subsidized to the extent of the overheads. Another example is a cash per capita daily or weekly food allowance based upon the numbers to be fed with other arrangements being made for the payroll and overheads. In yet another, no charges are made and the whole operation is subsidized, the caterer working to within a pre-budgeted financial arrangement.

ADDITIONAL NOTE

The practice we now know as food costing and portion control, together with its related activities, was originally pioneered in the thirties by Harold R. Taylor, then Controller of the Savoy Hotel Group. His book *Hotel Operation and Control*, published in 1949 by Practical Press, is still by far one of the best of its kind.

Taylor, the Father of modern hotel and catering control administration, later set up his own consultancy. He was a dynamic personality and constantly urged managements to become more control minded; it's certainly worth all involved with professional catering heeding this advice.

Portions Chart

This chart is a guide to purchasing, menu compilation and menu costing. The pricing up of the menu is performed by consulting the chart for quantities in order to calculate the cost per serving, and then setting a selling price to yield the required gross profit.

The caterer, when placing orders for supplies, refers to the chart regarding quantities required. The chef, in planning his kitchen production, does so with the aid of the chart. As the chef is required to maintain a certain return on his kitchen, he makes sure that his assistants are reasonably portion-control conscious. The same applies with those responsible for food service.

Portion control begins with efficient purchasing, since the commodities must be of a prescribed standard of quality and 100 per cent sound.

Commodity	Portions and Notes	Metric Portions
Bacon	8 to 1 lb straight	8 to 500g or
	16 to 1 lb composite dish	16 to 1 kilo
	BACON is cut at 18 back or 24 streaky to the 1 lb (500g)	16 to 500g or 32 to 1 kilo
	GAMMON STEAK (raw weight) 5 oz or 6 oz units	150g or 175g
	GAMMON (bone in) joints at 2 to 1 lb uncooked and 4 to 1 lb cooked	2 to 500g or 4–5 to 1 kilo and 4–5 to 500g or 8–10 to 1 kilo
Biscuits	Loose, sweet or dry allow 3 to the portion or 1 unit pack per portion	
	Average portions of loose biscuits, 14 to 1 lb	14 to 500g or 28 to 1 kilo
Bread	Sandwich quartern loaf: 44 slices thin for bread and butter or 22 slices thick for toast	
	Sandwich half quartern loaf: 24 slices thin for bread and butter or 12 slices thick for toast	

Commodity	Portions and Notes	Metric Portions
	One portion bread and butter: 2 full rounds	
	One portion toast: 2 full rounds	—
Butter	64 portions to 1 lb, i.e. $64 \times \frac{1}{4}$ oz pats	70×7g to 500g or 140×7g to 1 kilo
	Wrapped individual units $\frac{2}{3}$ oz and $\frac{1}{2}$ oz	10g and 15g
Cake	Slab cake 8 to 1 lb for 2 oz portions or 1 individual unit pack to portion	8 to 500g or 16 to 1 kilo
Cereals	1 individual unit pack ($\frac{3}{4}$ oz) to portion	20 to 25g portion
	Bulk pack calculate at 1 oz to the portion — weight is given on the packet	25 to 30g portion
Cheese	Basic calculate at 2 oz per portion or 8 to the lb bulk	50g portion or 8 to 500g and 16 to 1 kilo
	Individual unit packs, one wrapped 'square' or 'wedge' to portion	
	Grated parmesan cheese, 4 portions to the oz, 64 per lb	70 portions to 500g and 140 to 1 kilo
Chocolate (Drinking)	1 lb = 1 gallon or 20×8 fl oz cups	500g = $4\frac{1}{2}$ litres and 20 cups (227ml)
	$\frac{3}{4}$ oz to 8 fl oz cup	20g to portion (227ml cup)
Coffee	Ground coffee pure blend: 12 oz to 1 gal	360g to $4\frac{1}{2}$ litres
	Ground coffee with 'extender': 8 oz to 1 gal	250g to $4\frac{1}{2}$ litres

Commodity	Portions and Notes	Metric Portions
	Instant coffee: 2 oz to 1 gal 7 fl oz cup: 6 fl oz content= 4½ fl oz coffee and 1½ fl oz milk	60g to 4½ litres 200ml=170= 115 and 45ml
	8 fl oz cup=7 fl oz content= 5 fl oz coffee and 2 fl oz milk	227ml=200= 142 and 60ml
	3 parts coffee and 1 part milk, cups are filled to ¼ in to top	6mm to the top
	In making up coffee and milk in bulk calculate at 1 gal coffee and ½ gal milk	4½ litres and 2¼ litres
	Hold coffee at 165°F. and milk at 160°–170°F.	75°C. and 70°–76°C.
	An establishment is judged by the quality of the coffee and tea served	
Cream	(Dairy cream single and double) 1 fl oz to the portion 10 fl oz pack=10 portions	25ml 10 to ¼, 20 to ½ and 40 to 1 litre
	1 pint pack =20 portions	½ litre pack = 20 portions
Eggs (shell)	1 per portion	
	Omelettes and scrambled eggs per portion: 6 fl oz ladle. Garnish: 1–2 oz	200ml, 30–60g
Fish	Fresh fish fillet raw weight 2 to 1 lb basic; this should equal 1 large or two small fillets	2 to 500g or 4 to 1 kilo
	DOVER SOLE: 10, 12 to 14 oz graded (raw) Dover Sole for filleting: 1½ lb raw weight minimum	300, 360 to 420g 750g
	TROUT: 8 oz graded (raw)	250g
	SALMON, TURBOT, HALIBUT: 2 to 1 lb (raw) 8 oz steak bone in or 6 oz fillet	2 to 500g 250g or 175g

337

Commodity	Portions and Notes	Metric Portions
	COD: 2 to 3 to 1 lb (raw) or 6 oz steak	2 to 3 to 500g or 175g
	Cod Fillet: also 3½ oz and 4½ oz	100g and 130g
	PLAICE FILLET: 5–6 oz quarter cut or 4–5 oz cross cut (raw)	150g–175g or 125g–150g
	HADDOCK: fresh 6 oz (raw) smoked: 2 to 1 lb (uncooked); calculate 2 portions per haddock or ½ haddock per portion	175g 2 to 500g
	SKATE: 8 oz (raw)	250g
	WHOLE SALMON: 8 to 10 lb headed and gutted fish minimum weight	4 to 5 kilo
	Salmon for mayonnaise: 3 to 1 lb uncooked for a 4 oz cooked portion	3 to 500g and 120g
	SMOKED SALMON: 12 to 1 lb for plate service, 18 to 1 lb for sandwiches (brown bread)	12 to 500g 18 to 500g
	KIPPERS: 1 large or 2 small (a pair) per portion	
	SCAMPI: 35–48 count to 1 lb, 6 to 7 pieces per portion (3½–5 oz portion) depending on size; 4 to 6 portions to 1 lb (raw weight, unbreaded or battered)	35–48 to 500g (100–150g) 4 to 6 per 500g
	PRAWNS for cocktail: 2 to 3 oz portion	50 to 75g
	POTTED SHRIMPS: one individual 2 oz tub	50 to 60g
	CAVIAR: 1 oz to the portion, 16 to 1 lb	30g portion, 16 to ½ kilo
	OYSTERS: sold in 6 and 12 to portion	
	Note: Gross wastage on fish in bone loss and in cooking 50 per cent	
Fruit	FRESH FRUIT: average at 3 portions to 1 lb unprepared	3 to ½ kilo
	CANNED FRUIT: average at 4 oz per portion and 4 to 1 lb	120g and 4 to ½ kilo

Commodity	*Portions and Notes*	*Metric Portions*
	Canned in A2½ cans (1¾ lb): calculate at 7 portions	—
	Canned in A10 cans (6¾ lb): calculate at 25 portions	—
	FRUIT SALAD: 4 oz	120g
	FRUIT COCKTAIL: 4 oz	120g
	FRUIT FOR CONDÉS AND MELBAS (and allied composite dishes); 3 oz fruit per portion	75g
	GRAPEFRUIT segments A2 can= 4 portions A2½ can=7 portions (4 oz portion) Fresh grapefruit 2 to portion	120g
	AVOCADO PEAR (according to size) 1 or 2 portions per pear	
	Note: With canned fruit it is the drained weight in which the caterer is concerned rather than the gross weight inclusive of canning liquid	
Fruit Juice	Canned A2 (20 fl oz)= 5 portions (4 fl oz) Canned A2½ (28 fl oz)= 7 portions (4 fl oz)	125ml portion
	Individual unit pack, 4 fl oz 'baby' size bottle or 5 fl oz canned	125ml and 150ml
	Bulk juices: 5 to 1 pint for 4 fl oz portion	4–5 to ½ litre
Ice Cream	Bulk gallon calculate at 50 portions basic	50 portions to 4½ litre
	Catering brick: 16 portions	
	Family brick: 8 portions	
	Pre-cut 'individual' unit portions and shapes	
	Ice cream gâteaux=12 and 18 portions per cake according to size	

Commodity	Portions and Notes	Metric Portions
	*Ice cream scoops (twin-grip servers) are marketed in various sizes:	
	Size *Target per gallon* Per 4½ litre	
	12 38	
	*16 50	
	†20 64	
	24 76	
	30 96	
	* Usual catering size for straight and à la mode service	
	† Usual size for coupes, parfaits and glories	
Jelly	Crystals 3¾ oz, 7½ oz and 1 lb 14 oz to the pint, quart and gallon respectively	100g, 213g and 850g to 0.57 litre, 1.14 litre and 4.55 litre
	1 pint tablet slabs	½ litre
	32 × 5 fl oz portions to the gallon from crystals	32 × 142ml to to 4½ litres
Meat	Roasting joints raw weight 2½ portions to 1 lb, all meats	2½–500g. or 5 to 1 kilo
	BEEF	
	Strip sirloin of beef: 3–4 portions to 1 lb raw trimmed	3–4 to 500g
	Sirloin (entrecôte) rump and fillet steak: 2 to 1 lb to give 8 oz trimmed, raw portions	2 to 500g= 250g
	Sirloin: minute steak 4 oz, entrecôte steak 8 oz, double entrecôte steak 16 oz, (raw trimmed standard cuts)	120g 250g 500g
	Sirloin (entrecôte) and rump steaks: raw, pre-cuts at 5, 6 and 8 oz portions	150g, 175g and 250g
	Mini-steak: raw pre-cut 4 oz	120g
	'T' bone steak: raw pre-cut 12 oz	350g
	Steak for grill dishes; raw trimmed 5 oz	150g
	Stewing steak for pies; raw trimmed 4 oz	120g

Commodity	Portions and Notes	Metric Portions
	Braised steak for entrées: raw trimmed 6 oz	175g
	Minced beef: raw trimmed 4 oz	120g
	Hamburger type steak: 2–4 oz	60–120g
	LAMB/MUTTON Chop: graded raw trimmed 6 and 8 oz	175 and 250g
	Cutlet: raw trimmed 4 oz	125g
	French trimmed 2½–3 oz	75–100g
	Two cutlets go to the portion	
	Roast leg: calculate at 2½ to 1 lb raw trimmed	2½ to 500g or 5 to 1 kilo
	Roast best end, saddle and shoulder: calculate raw trimmed at 2 to 1 lb minimum (because of bone loss)	2 to 500g or 5 to 1 kilo
	Lamb and mutton should be roasted at 350°F. to minimise shrinkage	177°C.
	PORK Chop: graded raw trimmed 6 and 8 oz	175–250g
	OFFAL Liver: raw 4 oz straight and 2 oz composite dish	120g and 50g
	Kidneys 2 (pairs) for straight and 1 composite dish	
	VEAL Stewing meat: raw and trimmed 4 oz	120g
	Escalope: raw and trimmed 4 and 6 oz	120–175g
	COOKED MEATS Ham, tongue and other cold cuts of meat: Main dish: 4 to1 lb basic	4 to 500g
	Sandwiches and composite dish: 8 to 1 lb	8 to 500g
	Ham, brisket and ox tongue plate portion: 3 and 4 oz	100g and 120g

Commodity	Portions and Notes	Metric Portions
	Ham and tongue (dish); 3 oz tongue and 3 oz ham	100g and 100g
	Turkey and ham (dish): 3 oz turkey and 3 oz ham	100g and 100g
	Roast beef and tongue (dish): 3 oz roast beef and 3 oz tongue	100g and 100g
MELON	Cantaloupe and honeydew types: 6 and 8 portions fruit as specified 6 portion preferred 2 portion fruit of charentais type	
Milk	Calculate fresh milk (homogenized) on following basis: Tea: 1 fl oz=20 to pint for cups and 10 to pint for pots per person	25ml=20 to ½ litre for cups and 10 to ½ litre for pots
	Coffee: 1½ fl oz=13–14 to pint for 7 oz cups	42ml and 12 to ½ litre
	Filled or 'instant milk' powder 2 oz (4½ heaped tablespoons) to 1 pint water	50g to ½ litre
	Milk is heated to 160°–170°F.; no higher and *never* boiled	70°–76°C.
	Glass of milk 10 fl oz or 2 to pint, 10 oz glass filled to ¼ in to top	300ml or 2 to ½ litre, 300ml and 6mm
	Milk for cold service is held at 36°F.	4°C.
Mushrooms	Calculate at 8 to 1 lb raw	8 to 500g
	Canned: 12 to 1 lb as a garnish and 6 to 1 lb as a savoury	12 to 500g and 6 to 500g
	A2½ can: 2 lb go into the can and yield 1½ lb drained weight	1 kilo 750g
Pasta	Spaghetti, macaroni, noodles: 3 oz dry pasta for straight dish 2 oz dry pasta for composite dish 8 oz cooked pasta to the portion	75–100g 50g 250g

Commodity	Portions and Notes	Metric Portions
Pâté Maison	2–4 oz plate portion	50–120g

Commodity	Portions and Notes	Metric Portions
Pies	SAVOURY	
	Hot meat pies: 6 oz plate portion	175g
	Steak and kidney pie: 6 oz plate portion	175g
	'Bought in' meat pie: 4 oz and 4½ oz pie	120g and 150g
	Steak and kidney pie (individual): 6½ oz	200g
	Meat pie for cold; 4 oz portion	120g
	Veal and ham, and other gala-type pies: 3 to 1 lb for 5 or 6 oz portions	3 to ½ kilo=150–175g portion
	Hamburger, 3 oz	100g
	SWEET	
	Fruit pies: 4 oz and 6 oz plate portion (also individual)	120–175g
	Fruit pie (one crust): 4 oz	120g
	Fruit pie (two crusts): 4–5 oz	120–150g
	* Best handled in 6 and 8 portion pies (fruit and other fillings)	
	* i.e. 9 in flan to yield 8 portion cuts	230mm
	VOL-AU-VENT CASES:	
	Large entrée: size 3½ in	88mm
	Medium size 2½ in	65mm
	Cocktail: size 1¾ in	42mm

Commodity	Portions and Notes	Metric Portions
Potatoes	Basic issue of raw potatoes unpeeled 2 to 1 lb	2 to 500g
	Frozen blanched 'chipped' potatoes 10 to 2 lb pack (3 oz basic portion)	10–12 to kilo pack 100g basic portion
	Instant potato mix: 1 oz rehydrates to 5 oz portion	25g=150g
	Backed and boiled potatoes: 4 oz plate portion	120g
	Mashed potatoes from twin grip servers: 3, 4 and 6 oz portions, average portion is 4 oz (2 × size 20 server=4 oz)	75, 125 and 175g 120g average
	Chipped potatoes: use 4 oz scoop	120g

343

Commodity	Portions and Notes	Metric Portions
Poultry	CHICKEN (raw weight) 2–4 lb eviscerated (no giblets) bird=4 portions	1–2 kilo=4 portions
	2 portion (broilers) 20–24 oz graded eviscerated (no giblets) bird	600–700g
	Capon 4–5 lb bird eviscerated (no giblets)=8 portions	2–2½ kilo =8 portions
	Portioned chicken raw weight per portion=12 oz	360g
	Plump fowls for boiling and sandwich-making: 6 to 1 lb	6 to 500g
	Cooked chicken off the bone: allow 4 oz per portion	120g
	Chicken looses 25 per cent in drawing and 50 per cent bone loss and all wastage in roasting Boiling loss 30 per cent	
	Chicken roll: 3 oz to portion or 5 to 1 lb	100g =5 to 500g average
	DUCK Oven-ready (eviscerated) 4 to 5 lb bird=4 portions or 3 lb bird=2 portions	2–2½ kilo=4 portions or 1½ kilo=2 portions
	TURKEY (Oven ready) 2 to 1 lb raw Calculate at 2–4 oz plate portions to each 1 lb of uncooked bird	2 to 500g 2×120g
	An 8, 12, 16 and 20 lb bird will yield 16, 24, 32 and 40×4 oz cooked portions	4, 6, 8 and 10 kilo=16, 24, 32 and 40×115– 120g cooked portions
	There is a 50 per cent bone loss and shrinkage in cooking	
	Each 2 lb raw turkey will give 1 lb cooked or 4×4 oz portions	1 kilo=500g= 4×120g

Commodity	*Portions and Notes*	*Metric Portions*
	A 16 lb bird takes 4½ hours slow roasting at 350°F.	8 kilo and 177°C.
	Boneless turkey: 4 oz to portion or 4 to 1 lb	120g=4 to 500g average
Preserves	Jam, marmalade and honey: 1 miniature pot per person (approx. 1½ oz)	40–45g
	Bulk basic issue 16 portions to 1 lb	16 to ½ and 32 to kilo
	1 lb pack=16 portions, 7 lb pack=112 portions	500g=16; 3½ kilo=112 portions
Puddings	MEAT PUDDINGS: 6 oz plate portion	175g
	Steak and kidney pudding: individual 8 and 10 oz portions	250g and 300g
	COTTAGE PIE/SHEPHERDS PIE: 8 to 10 oz portions	250g and 300g
	SWEET PUDDING served with sauce: 4 oz plate portions	120g
	This includes all steamed puddings and rolls	
Rice	½ oz dry rice per basic portion	15g
	1 lb dry rice=3 lb cooked rice	500g and 1½ kilo
	1 lb dry parboiled rice=4 lb cooked rice	500g and 2 kilo
	Rice puddings: 4 oz plate portion	120g
Sauces	HOT THICK SAVOURY SAUCES: calculate at 2 fl oz to portion or 10 to 1 pint	50ml to portion or 10 to ½ litre
	COLD SAVOURY SAUCES, MAYONNAISE, TARTARE, KETCHUP AND RELISHES: calculate at 1½ fl oz or 14 to pint	50ml to portion 10 to ½ litre
	Savoury sauces also marketed in unit miniatures	
	GRAVY (thin): 1 fl oz or 20 to 1 pint	25ml or 20 to ½ litre

Commodity	Portions and Notes	Metric Portions
	GRAVY (thick): 2 fl oz or 10 to 1 pint	50ml or 10 to ½ litre
	SALAD DRESSINGS: 1 fl oz to portion or 20 to 1 pint	25ml or 20 to ½ litre
	SWEET SAUCES: calculate at 2½ fl oz to portion or 8 to 1 pint	70ml or 7–8 to ½ and 14–16 to litre
	CUSTARD: 8 to 10 portions to the pint	8 to 10 portions to ½ litre
	In dispensing sauces, use 1 oz and 2 oz ladles	25ml and 50ml
Sausages	PORK SAUSAGES: 2 links per portion straight or 1 link for composite dish (8 or 16 to 1 lb)	8 or 16 to 500g
	FRANKFURTERS: 1 link per portion	
	DELICATESSEN SLICING SAUSAGES: 2 oz portions and 8 to 1 lb	50g and 10 to ½ kilo
Savouries	WELSH RAREBIT: 2½ oz mix	75g
	SARDINES ON TOAST: 3 sardines	
	MUSHROOMS ON TOAST: 4 mushrooms (average weight raw 2–2½ oz)	50–75g
	ANCHOVIES ON TOAST: 6 anchovy fillets	
Soup	THICK SOUP: 6 fl oz per portion	170ml
	CLEAR SOUP GARNISHED: 5 fl oz per portion	142ml
	CLEAR SOUP: 4 fl oz per portion This indicates 26 (6 fl oz), 32 (5 fl oz) and 40 (4 fl oz) portions to the gallon	114ml 26, 32 and 40 to 4½ litre
	CANNED SOUP (standard): A10 can=3 portions 1 tall can=4 portions A2½ can= 7 portions A 10 can=20 portions	

Commodity	Portions and Notes	Metric Portions
	Or individual unit can For condensed soup double the above mentioned portions; contents of can are doubled with water (or stock) Soup should be served at 190°–200°F.	87°–93°C.
Stuffings	Calculate 2 oz dry stuffing per 1 lb meat or poultry	50g to ½ kilo
Sugar	Wrapped 'Fairie' cubes: calculate 1 wrap (2 cubes) per cup basic 100 wraps (Tate & Lyle) to the lb=200 cubes As a guide to lump sugar calculate 1 lb to 1 lb coffee 2 lb to 1 lb of tea for hot beverage service	500g to 500g and 1 kilo to 500g
Sweets (various)	TRIFLES: 4 oz plate portion	120g
	RICE CONDÉ (various fruits): 3 oz fruit and 3 oz creamed rice	100g and 100g
	MOUSSE: 2 oz portion	50–75g
	BREAD AND BUTTER PUDDING: 4 oz plate portion	120g
	FLANS (sponge flan case) filled with 8 to 10 oz fruit and 'gel' masked=6 portions per flan	250–300g
	PEAR HÉLÉNE, PEAR CARDINAL: 3 oz fruit, 2½ oz chocolate or preserve sauce and ice cream	100g and 74 g
Tea	Best handled in 'pot for one' tea bags	
	LOSE TEA: 100 pots or 220 cups to 1 lb basic	500g
	There are 120 heaped teaspoons to the average 1 lb	500g
	Pot for 1=3½ drams Pot for 2=6 drams 1 gal=1½ oz 5 gal=7½ oz	5g 10½g 45g 225g

Commodity	Portions and Notes	Metric Portions
	(16 drams to the oz avoirdupois) Tea is made with *fresh boiling water*	
Tomatoes	1 per portion 8–12 to 1 lb (Pink and White) is the recommended count for salads and cold service	8–12 to ½ kilo, 16–24 per kilo
Vegetables	FRESH Green vegetables: 4 to 1 lb basic raw Root vegetables: 6 to 1 lb basic raw	4 to ½ kilo 8 to 1 kilo 6 to ½ kilo, 12 to 1 kilo
	CANNED 6–8 to 1 lb basic Peas: 10 to A2½ and 48 to A10 Beans in sauce: 36 to A10	6–8 to ½ kilo, 12–16 to 1 kilo —
	FROZEN Peas: 8 to 1 lb	8 to ½ kilo, 16 to 1 kilo
	Broccoli: 4 to 1 lb	4 to ½ kilo, 8 to 1 kilo
	French beans: 6 to 1 lb	6 to ½ kilo, 12 to 1 kilo
	DRIED According to reconstituted yield	
	COOKED VEGETABLES – PORTIONS: Beans in sauce (baked): 3 oz Cabbage: 3 oz Carrots: 2 oz Cauliflower: 3 oz French beans: 3 oz Peas: 2 oz Spinach: 3 oz Sprouts: 3 oz	100g 100g 75g 100g 100g 75g 100g 100g
	WASTAGE IN FRESH VEGETABLES: Broad beans 75 per cent; French beans 7–10 per cent; cabbage 15 per cent; peas 60 per cent; cauliflower 55 per cent; sprouts 40 per cent	

Note: With canned vegetables it is
the drained weight in which the
caterer is concerned rather than
the gross weight inclusive of
canning liquid

Additional Note: To minimize loss in cooking, all poultry and fish
(i.e. salmon) for cold should be allowed to cool in its cooking liquor.

Author's Note: For practical reasons the portioning of food in this
chart is based on imperial weights and measures, upon which the metric
conversions are related with appropriate adjustments as necessary.

Personalities

Listed under this title are notable people who have contributed in some way to gastronomy. These personalities are predominantly chefs, but also hoteliers, entrepreneurs, writers and others whose creative talents have enriched our heritage. What, it is often asked, is the definition of a great chef? Obviously a master of the culinary art. But a chef becomes famous when he has contributed to culinary literature and to the culinary répertoire through the creation of dishes to which he is, or should be, attributed. Some of the biographies are of well-known personalities, others, possibly because of the passing of time, are now not so well-known. All have in their own way pioneered the traditions of service of a great industry. Since from the past we should seek inspiration for the future, the names and the work of those whose dedication and vision contributed so much should be recorded as a source of inspiration to future generations of chefs and restauranteurs, hoteliers and caterers.

Acton, Eliza (1799–1859)
Early Victorian cook and authoress of *Modern Cookery*, the forerunner of the contemporary cook book. A lady of considerable talent as cook and culinary writer.

Beeton, Isabella (1837–1865)
Almost legendary early Victorian housewife and cookery writer. Her first book, *Book of Household Management*, took three years to write and was published in 1859. Her second, *Dictionary of Household Management*, was never completed because Mrs Beeton died in 1865 at the early age of twenty-eight. But her name and her work have lived on right into the twentieth century, for books up-dated and rewritten by noted, if incognito, authors continue to be published long after her premature death, one of the most recent being *Mrs Beeton's Cookery in Colour* (Ward Lock) 1971.

Boulestin, Xavier Marcel (1878–1943)
Culinary author and restaurateur of the thirties, a Frenchman who made his home in England. The restaurant he founded in London and which bears his name still exists at the time of writing. Boulestin was the first television chef and, to date, is still considered the best. It was as a writer on food he shone the brightest; a man of letters, all his writings are real literary gems. He died in France during the Second World War.

Brillat-Savarin (1755–1826)
Celebrated French statesman, magistrate and gastronome, author of
La Physiologie du Goût which earned him immortal fame as the Father
of Gastronomy.

Baron Brisse
Non de plume of Ildefonse-Léon Brisse, noted French gastronome and
culinary author who died in 1876.

Cambacérès, Jean Jacques (1753–1824)
Councillor at the Court of Napoleon Bonaparte, noted gourmet to
whom chaudfroid is accredited. Legend goes that his chef had prepared
his master's favourite dish, Fricassé de Volaille à l'Ancienne (a sauté
of chicken with button mushrooms and onions in a white velouté),
but unfortunately, Cambacérès arrived home late and the preparation
had become cold. Since he was famished, he ate it and pronounced
the dish excellent. Next time he called on Napoleon, he ordered his
chef to prepare the 'chaud-froid' just in case he would again be de-
layed. By this he meant his favourite preparation could be eaten hot or
cold with equal enjoyment. The story goes that Napoleon heard about
the incident, was much amused and poked gentle fun at his minister's
gourmandise.

The Emperor was no gastronome and ate when he felt hungry, at
any time of the day or night. He liked roast chicken and grilled cutlets,
expected them always to be on call, which meant the fare had to be
cooked in relays round the clock. Before a battle, however, Napoleon
would request Poulet Sauté à la Marengo to bring him luck. On the
eve of Waterloo, he noticed the crayfish were missing and was informed they were unobtainable. He took this as an ill omen. When
Napoleon was exiled, his chef, the faithful Chandelier, accompanied
his master to Saint Helena and often, under extreme difficulties,
continued to cook for him until the end.

Carême, Antonin (1783–1833)
'L'astre de la cuisine française', born in Paris in dire poverty, the
sixteenth child of a stonemason. Rose to become one of the greatest
chefs of all time. Was in the service of Talleyrand, the Prince Regent
(later George IV), Czar Alexander I of Russia and other notable
personages. Worked in Paris, London, Vienna and St Petersburg. Spent
8 months at the Court of the Prince Regent in London and at the
Royal Pavillion, Brighton, for the reputed salary of £1000 a year.
His full name was Marie Antoine Carême, but he liked to be known
as Antonin Carême. He lived only for his work and never took a
holiday. He died in Paris exhausted from his labours, after a long
illness.

Author of: *Le Maître d'Hôtel Français; Le Pâtissier Royal
Parisien; L'Art de la Cuisine au 17ème Siècle; Le Pâtissier Pittoresque.*

Diat, Louis
French born chef who worked at the Ritz Hotel, Paris, with César Ritz and then at the Ritz Hotel, London, under Henri Malet. He then went to the Ritz-Carlton Hotel, New York, where he was chef-des-cuisines for many years. Created numerous dishes, including the celebrated crème vichyssoise. This preparation, named after the town near his birthplace, was originally featured in 1917 at a banquet in New York. He died in America in 1957.

Author of *Cooking à la Ritz*.

Dubois, Urbain
Nineteenth century French chef and culinary author who wrote numerous books on his art, including *La Cuisine Classique* and *La Cuisine de Tous les Pays*.

Dutrey, Marius
Well-known French chef of modern times, formerly of the Savoy Hotel, the Langham Hotel, and the Westbury Hotel, London. Author of *Calendrier Gastronomique*.

Escoffier, Auguste (1847–1935)
'The King of Chefs and the Chef of Kings' was born at Villeneuve Loubet, Alpes Maritimes, France, where there is a statue of him. Escoffier saw service in the Franco-Prussian war of 1870 and was at the siege of Metz on the staff of General Bazaine.

He worked in a number of hotels and restaurants in France and in 1890 was brought to London as chef-des-cuisines at the Savoy Hotel, by Cesar Ritz. From there he went to the Carlton Hotel where he remained until 1922, retiring, loaded with honours, at the age of 74. He went to live in France but still retained an interest in his art and often came to London. He died at the great age of 88 after 62 years as a chef.

Escoffier was without doubt the most famous chef of all time. He created innumerable dishes, wrote several books, his last, *Ma Cuisine,* in retirement. But his greatest of all contributions to culinary literature is the classic *Guide to Modern Cookery*.

Francatelli, Charles Elmé (1805–76)
An Englishman of Italian extraction, noted Victorian chef who became chef to Queen Victoria at Windsor. Author of *The Modern Cook, The Cook's Guide, The Royal English & French Confectioner*. Credited with a number of dishes including Potage à la Windsor. Claimed to have known Antonin Carême.

Gilbert, Philéas
French chef and gifted author, friend, contemporary and collaborator

of Auguste Escoffier. His works include *Cuisine de Tous les Mois* and *La Cuisine.*

Gordon, Frederick (1835–1904)

A solicitor from Herefordshire, he came to London to practise in the City. There, through a client, he became interested in hotels and catering. After initial ventures in pubs and city eating houses, he opened the Holborn Restaurant and later purchased Frascati's Restaurant. Frederick Gordon eventually became chairman of both the Gordon Hotels and the Frederick Hotels, two vast companies which he promoted with hotel interests in London, Brighton, Folkstone, Dover, Margate, Isle of Wight, Eastbourne, Harrogate, Bexhill, as well as in France at Cannes, Dieppe, Monte Carlo and Antwerp in Belgium. The London Hotels included the Grand, Metropole, Victoria, Grosvenor, Great Central, Russell and First Avenue. Apart from his financial acumen, he was said to be a man of considerable charm with great powers of persuasion.

Gouffé, Jules (1807–77)

Carême's principal pupil, chef and author of *Le Livre de Cuisine, Le Livre des Soupes et Potages* and other works. Gouffé was born in Paris where he had his own restaurant and later became chef-des-cuisines at the Jockey Club.

His brother Alphonse was chef pâtissier to Queen Victoria.

Grimod de la Reynière (1758–1838)

French gastronome and man of letters, author of *L'Almanachs des Gourmets* and *Le Manuel des Amphityrons.*

Herbodeau, Eugène

Many lay claim to have known and been pupils of Escoffier. Very few, in actual fact, had that rare distinction and privilege. One of the few was Eugène Herbodeau.

Born in 1888 at Rosnay in the Indre, France. After experience in his native country, Escoffier engaged him in 1913 as a commis fish cook at the Carlton Hotel, London, until the outbreak of the First World War, when he was called up by the French Army. After the war, he returned to the Carlton as chef saucier (by this time, Escoffier had been succeeded by Henri Malet). He then went as chef-des-cuisines first to the Metropole, Brighton, then to the Ritz Hotel, London, and finally returned in 1928 to the Carlton as maître chef. When the Carlton closed, he opened his own restaurant, the 'Écu de France', in Jermyn Street, which he sold on his retirement when he returned to France.

Herbodeau, who has contributed to culinary literature and is possibly one of the last of the great name chefs of recent times, was

353

truly a pupil of Escoffier. He was also one of his literary executors. In 1955 Herbodeau combined with Paul Thalamas, another pupil and literary executor of the great master, to write *Georges Auguste Escoffier* (Practical Press), an appreciation of the man under whose orders both had served. Thalamas had been engaged by Escoffier at the Savoy Hotel, London, and was later to be associated with César Ritz in a number of European hotels as chef-des-cuisines. He practised his art up to the outbreak of the Second World War, when he retired and devoted himself to the literature of the profession.

The actual authorship of Escoffier's *Guide to Modern Cookery*, first published in 1902 as *Le Guide Culinaire*, had often been something of a controversy. Obviously so complex and masterly a book must have been the work of several, under the overall direction of Escoffier. Herbodeau pointed out that 2 other French chefs and culinary writers, Philéas Gilbert and Emile Fétu, were principal collaborators; others consulted included Urbain Dubois and Alfred Suzanne. All, however, acknowledged the right of authorship to Escoffier, since when *Guide to Modern Cookery* has been translated into many languages. *Author's note:* I once had the honour of being introduced to Herbodeau at l'Écu de France. The manager at l'Écu, Paul Lehrian, who had come from the Carlton with Herbodeau, became a friend of mine. Later he took up an appointment with British Transport Hotels and for a number of years, prior to his retirement, was manager of the Charing Cross Hotel.

L'Écu de France, which Herbodeau opened, is still one of London's leading restaurants.

Hilton, Conrad N.

Distinguished American hotelier. 'The Man who Bought the Waldorf', was born in San Antonio, New Mexico. Destined for a banking career, but after several successful ventures, he bought the Mobley Hotel, Cisco, in Texas. Thus began a series of phenomenal hotel promotions throughout America and elsewhere. There are Hilton Hotels in most of the world's capitals, including the fabulous London Hilton.

Conrad Hilton will best be remembered by hoteliers for his introduction of industrialization to hotel-keeping and catering, the forerunner of scientific management and the advent of the influence of the social sciences.

Jones, Henry Albert (1907–66)

Yorkshire-born hotelier and colourful personality. Managing director of Grosvenor House, London, an hotel he created. Noted for his instigation of hotel and catering education and training, personnel management, and tourism. A.J., as he was affectionately known, was a man of considerable drive who possessed that rare quality of management, and the greatest of human virtues, courage.

Languipière
Little is known of this cuisinier except he was Carême's principal tutor.
Was chef to Napoleon's Marshall Murat and perished, with a large
number of other chefs, in the snows at Vilna in 1812 during the retreat
from Moscow, which caused Carême profound grief.

Latry, François
Born at Gex in the Ain Department of France. Served apprenticeship
at Voisin's in Paris, came to London in 1912 to the Savoy and
Claridges Hotels. Appointed maître chef-des-cuisines, Savoy Restaurant,
in 1918. Awarded Chevalier de la Légion d'Honneur. Retired in 1942
and died in France, aged 77, in 1966. Created many dishes at the
Savoy. Latry was an indefatigable worker, a great organizer and a
formidable personality.

Montagné, Prosper (1865–1948)
Born at Carcassone in France. Noted chef, culinary reformer and contemporary of Escoffier. Made a study of military cookery and reorganized field and garrison cookery for the French army. Best known
as the author of the original edition of *Larousse Gastronomique*.

Ranhofer, Charles (1836–99)
French chef, born at St Denis, Paris. Came from a family of cooks.
Chef to Napoleon III in 1860. Went to U.S.A. and for 30 years was
chef-des-cuisines at Delmonico's, New York, where he established a
great reputation. Author of *The Epicurean*, the bible of American
chefs.

Reeves-Smith, Sir George (1855–1941)
Scarborough-born hotelier. As managing director, he created the
Savoy, Berkeley and Claridges Hotel Group, London, which he
directed for over 40 years. Noted connoisseur of wines and gastronome,
leader of British hoteldom. Rose to fame as manager of the Victoria
Hotel, Northumberland Avenue, later moved to the Berkeley as
managing director; Rupert D'Oyly Carte had to buy the Berkeley in
order to secure the services of Reeves-Smith for the Savoy Hotel.
Sir George was living at Claridges when he died in 1941, aged 86, still
in harness.

Richard D'Oyly Carte, who succeeded Rupert, his father, as chairman, then appointed Mr Hugh Wontner as the managing director.
Later, as Sir Hugh Wontner, he became chairman of the Savoy Group
of hotels.

Ritz, César (1850–1915)
The hotelier destined to become 'Host to the World' was born in
Niederwald, Switzerland. His parents were farmers, but he decided to

go into the hotel business. His first job was as a waiter at the Hotel des Trois Couronnes et Poste at Brieg, where he was fired by the owner for being no good. Young Ritz went to Paris and after several jobs as a valet and a waiter entered the service of Voisin's Restaurant, where he laid the foundations of his career.

After Voisin's, his rise to fame was meteoric; he blazed a trail of luxury hotels of his creation in Biaritz, Cairo, Frankfurt, Monte Carlo, Madrid, Menton, Paris, Rome, Salsomaggiore, Trouville, Weisbaden, New York and London, where he was associated with the Savoy, Claridges, Carlton, Ritz and Hyde Park hotels. Relentless work and ceaseless travelling brought ill health at an early age, compelled him to retire in 1903, and he died in Switzerland 12 years later.

Ritz discovered Escoffier, installing him first at the Savoy and later at the Carlton in London.

Mention must be made of Madame Marie Ritz, a remarkable lady who came from Strasbourg, Alsace. Upon her husband's premature retirement, she continued to direct his interests in the Ritz Development Company. She lived at the Ritz Hotel, Paris. Marie Ritz came to London in 1953 for the Coronation of Queen Elizabeth II and revisited the Savoy Hotel after an absence of well over 50 years. There she renewed acquaintance with a few employees who were originally engaged by César Ritz. Marie Ritz died in Paris in 1961 at the great age of 94. She is survived by a son, Charles Ritz, also associated with the Ritz in Paris.

Senn, C. Herman

Swiss born chef, caterer and prolific culinary writer. Founder of the Cookery and Food Association. Author of *The Menu Book*, *The Art of the Table*, *The Century Cookery Book*, and many others. He contributed to hospital catering and to Army cookery. Awarded M.B.E.

Simon, André Louis (1877–1970)

Famous French gastronome, gastronomic author, founder of the Wine & Food Society and world's foremost authority on wine, originally in the wine trade. He made his home in England. A.L.S. wrote over 100 books on wine and food. On food he wrote well, on wine he was without equal.

Soyer, Alexis Benoit (1809–58)

Born at Meaux-en-Brie, near Paris, the son of a shopkeeper. Came to London in private service and then as chef-des-cuisines at the Reform Club. Went to the Crimea with the British Army, advised on field cookery, reorganized the catering at Scutari, base-hospital for Florence Nightingale. Back in London, he became involved for the Government, advising on army, hospital and other institutional activities. Author of several books, inventor of the Soyer stove, creator of countless dishes.

Soyer was a great showman and flamboyant personality who cooked for rich and poor alike with the same enthusiasm and zeal. On one occasion, he conducted a distinguished peer around the kitchens of the Reform Club, and he commented on the good looks of the kitchen maids. 'I am in favour of plain cooking, but not of plain cooks,' replied Soyer.

Soyer, Nicholas

Grandson of Alexis Soyer, chef-des-cuisines at Brook's Club, London, author of *Soyer's Standard Cookery* (Andrew Melrose, London, 1912) and instigator of paper bag cookery. This, a derivative of 'en papillote', consisted of cooking food or finishing off dishes in a greased bag to 'seal in the flavour'. It could be claimed these methods inspired the contemporary 'boil in the bag' or 'boil in the pouch' water-heated food idiom.

Author's note: In my capacity of catering superintendent of the former Pullman Car Company, I once engaged a lady clerk by the name of Dorothy Soyer whose husband was a descendant of the great Alexis. It was with real pride I had a Soyer on my staff, and she proved an excellent employee, thereby following in the famous à la Soyer tradition.

Towle, Sir William

Farmer's son who ran away from home in 1865, went to London to become a page boy in a Spiers & Pond hotel, became hall porter at the Midland Hotel in the railway town of Derby. There he caught the attention of the directors of the Midland Railway Company. They offered to make him manager of the hotel on condition he married the girl in the front office. At that time, the Midland Railway decided to take over and operate their own hotels, refreshment rooms and dining cars from their contractors as the agreements lapsed. William Towle was made manager of the department. Eventually Sir William, assisted by Lady Towle, took up residence and established his H.Q. at the Midland Grand Hotel, St Pancras Station, London.

The Towles had two sons, both destined to become as famous as their parents. Arthur Towle studied the hotel business in New York and with César Ritz at the Grand Hotel, Rome, then owned by the Savoy Hotel, London. He joined the Midland Railway in 1897, eventually to succeed his father. After the railway amalgamation of 1923, Arthur Towle became Controller, L.M.S. Hotel Services, retiring in 1944. He was succeeded by his personal assistant. Frank G. Hole, O.B.E. who, upon the nationalization of British Railways in 1948, became managing director of British Transport Hotels Limited. It is of interest that this vast organization of hotels, rooms and cars is still directed from the former Midland Grand now renamed St Pancras Chambers.

357

Sir Francis Towle became managing director of the Gordon Hotels Ltd and was the first president of the Hotel & Catering Institute.

Spiers & Pond Ltd, who originally employed Sir William Towle, was founded by 2 Englishmen who had met in Australia where they were catering contractors, Felix Spiers and Christopher Pond. Returning to England they obtained the catering contract to the Metropolitan Railway, London, and set up refreshment rooms at all the principal stations. To this they added various main line railway contracts, the Criterion Restaurant, Piccadilly Circus, London, several public houses and a chain of hotels. The contracts on the Southern Railway passed to Frederick Hotels and eventually to British Transport Hotels. The name Spiers & Pond is no longer, and their assets are now owned by a variety of multiples.

Virlogeux, Jean Baptist (1885–1958)

Celebrated cuisinier, born and apprenticed at Nevers, France. Served at the Ritz Hotel, Paris, Grand Hotel, Moscow in 1906, and Les Ambassadeurs, Monte Carlo. Came to London and was at Claridges for the Coronation of King Edward VII. Chef-des-cuisines Savoy Grill for 17 years and at the Dorchester Hotel for nine. Died in retirement in London.

Author's note: I had the honour of serving under his orders at the Savoy Grill in the early thirties.

Index

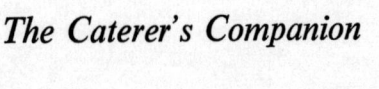

The Caterer's Companion